D1248704

THE REAL McGRAW

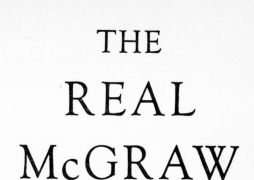

THE
REAL
McGRAW

By Mrs. John J. McGraw

EDITED BY
ARTHUR MANN

Illustrated

New York
DAVID McKAY COMPANY, INC.

MANUFACTURED IN THE UNITED STATES OF AMERICA

VAN REES PRESS • NEW YORK

To the boy and a baseball

ACKNOWLEDGMENT

A printed record such as this is not possible without under-standing and co-operation from many sources. We would like to express our thanks in this meager way to the many individuals whose memories and efforts helped augment the facts herein. To the Baltimore *Sun*, the Elias Baseball Bureau, and the New York Public Library we extend our special thanks.

BLANCHE S. MCGRAW
ARTHUR MANN

ILLUSTRATIONS

THE REAL McGRAW

1

HIS TANNED FACE seemed to stand out suddenly from the young group circling the piano, which my older sister, Jeannette, played with flourishing fingers at our Sunday evening gatherings. His face was conspicuous chiefly because he wasn't helping sing "Silver Threads among the Gold," and also because he was staring with dark brown, penetrating eyes. His hair was black, parted a little on the left and brushed down over a portion of his rather pale forehead in the fishhook effect so popular in the fall of 1900.

Of course, I couldn't have noticed all this had I not been staring too, or at least letting my eyes wander from the words and music on the piano, which everyone knew by heart. His thin lips parted finally in a smile, and his teeth were white and even. He left his place in the circle and came over to where I stood. He was slight and, I suppose, small, but he was taller than I. He wore a dark blue suit and a high starched collar. Below the knot in the four-in-hand tie was a small, gem-studded fleur-de-lis.

"Why aren't you singing?" he asked.

His voice was light and pitched rather high, but it was hatpin sharp, and it easily pierced the volume of piano and song. I shrugged and said, "I can't sing."

"Neither can Hughie," he said, nodding across the circle toward a freckled, reddish face. "But look at him."

For a person who couldn't sing, Hughie was struggling mightily to achieve a reasonable facsimile. Sheer physical effort deepened

I

the natural flush of his pained expression. His generous mouth would open wide, pushing up high cheekbones, whereupon his eyes, blue as two buckets of sea water, would disappear behind the squinting lids.

And so we had a little fun at Hughie's expense, which gave us an excuse to wander from the piano. The vocal circle continued on with the usual repertoire—"Break the News to Mother," "Daisy Bell," "Mama's Boy," "The Old Flag Will Never Touch the Ground," and the prettiest of all, "Blue Bell." Meanwhile, I was trying to remember whether his name was McGaw, like the man who ran the big grocery store on North Charles and the famous Rennert Hotel, at Saratoga and Liberty, or McGraw. And I couldn't recall that his first name had been mentioned when Charlie Schryver introduced him.

"Hughie gives it all he's got," he said, "whether it's a song or a ball game."

"Oh, is he a baseball player?"

"Sure, that's Hughie Jennings. He used to play here with me. I went to St. Louis, and he went to Brooklyn. He's an old friend."

"If he's your friend, why do you make fun of him?"

"I'm not making fun of Hughie," he protested. "He always sings that way, and I like to watch him. He makes a big thing of it—rolls up his sleeves and really gets into the spirit of the song."

"Are you playing baseball games here now?"

He struggled to conceal a deep reaction of pain and pity. He didn't quite succeed, but he was patient and surprisingly calm in the presence of abysmal ignorance. I didn't know Baltimore had been without league baseball in 1900.

"No, the season is over," he explained. "We returned here to see friends . . . and on business. We always do that, Hughie and I, sort of run together like hounds in a pack."

This was one of the countless things I didn't know, but I set about reducing the appalling total immediately. I learned that his name was not McGaw, but McGraw, that his first name was John, and that he was a professional baseball player.

"What position do you play?" I asked with quickening interest. "I'll bet you're one of the batters."

Batter was one position I was fairly sure of, for I had heard my three younger brothers, Howard, Leo, and Frank, arguing in our back yard near the carriage shed over who was to play batter first, or something. But even then he didn't laugh or frown at me. As I look back upon that evening and recall my glib comments and my feeble efforts to keep the conversation somewhere near his scope of interest, I marvel at his self-control. Particularly since, over the years that followed, I heard him storm at home and berate even his favorite players for having the lowest possible I.Q., accelerating idiocy, cabbageheadedness, or anything else that would, at the moment, account for the brief lapse of judgment that had figured in the defeat of his team a few hours before.

But I talked on blithely and fearlessly, gleaning bits of information about him during odds and ends of conversation and laughter. Most of it came after the girls had begun serving refreshments.

Like our fun, the refreshments were simple. That night we had creamed chipped beef with or without buttered toast pieces, old-fashioned potato salad (made with boiled vinegar, sugar, and butter), and all the cottage cheese we could consume. Thirst was quenched most often with homemade root beer. Given a few days' notice, our cook could do wonders with a bottle of root-beer extract, a yeast cake, and plain water. Served chilled, it would sparkle and tingle just as if carbonated. When there wasn't root beer, we would have lemonade, a fruit punch, or plain water.

And it was the same elsewhere in our modest circle of youth and fun—at the home of the Hedricks, the Hindes, the Boggs, Brownells, Goldmans, and many others in suburban Waverly, Guilford, Hampden, and Roland Park. Most fun, I guess, came on the straw rides, and they were ever popular with us teen-agers.

Early arrival and departure was a vigorous domestic issue for young people in those days. Curfew reared its ugly head the very night that Charlie Schryver, my more-or-less regular caller, brought around the baseball players. My father was a conscientious builder and contractor who had risen early all his life. He failed to see why everybody couldn't keep reasonable hours of retirement. Naturally, and foolishly, we supposed he would regard this evening as a special occasion. Poor Charlie Schryver never dreamed Father would use his annoying sign. But there it was, as always, hung upon the hall tree where nobody could miss it:

3

No young man of that day would think of disregarding Father's subtle sign, and Charlie obeyed, but he was the picture of shame and chagrin. He had met the baseball players through his father, James M. Schryver, General Passenger Agent for the Baltimore & Ohio Railroad. The baseball teams used this line mostly, though we had fifteen railroads and forty steamship lines out of Baltimore at the time. Thinking their distinguished company would be novel, as well as heighten his own prestige, Charlie prevailed upon my sister to let him invite the famous players.

Now they were bowing and shaking hands and expressing thanks for an evening of fun. None of them seemed upset over the "early" departure, and Father invited them all to call again "as soon as you get over the shock of this first meeting." And there went Hughie Jennings, despondent Charlie Schryver, the other girls and boys, and black-haired John McGraw. But I knew he'd be back.

Mother was completely out of patience. The idea, Scott Sindall, she stormed, cutting off the girls' fun as though with an ax. She called Father Scott, an old family name, instead of James.

"You know my motto," Father reminded. "Come early and go early!"

"At least you could've forgotten that sign just once," she exclaimed. "What on earth will those new young men think?"

"Yes," I chimed in, "one of them was John McGraw!"

"Who did you say, Puss?" Father asked.

"I said one was John McGraw."

"Well, who is John McGraw?" he demanded bluntly.

I couldn't tell him exactly, nor could Jeannette. It is quite possible that my father actually didn't know who John McGraw was. That seems improbable, in view of John's fame as a player and Baltimore hero at the time. Father may have meant, "Who is John McGraw to stay later than the others?" And yet, I have always believed he knew little or nothing of the sporting world because of his intense preoccupation with his work, along with complete devotion to his beloved wife, Mary Blanche, and his five energetic children, who adored him.

Father had started out in the stove business with his brother

Joshua. Besides being a good installation man, he was a carpenter and a planner, but my mother, a Smick before her marriage, also had imagination. Sensing Father's restlessness and impatience in the stove supply field, she urged him to "get out now" and do the thing he wanted to do: build those endless lines of brick houses with pretty, wood trim and the steps of gleaming white marble. Together at the dining-room table, she told me, they designed floor plans, and she emphasized the need of closet space, an item that men designers always manage to overlook, even today.

Somewhat like the man who found a periscope and decided to build submarines, Father had two close friends as backers. Lewis N. Mullen was a skilled and successful woodworker, and Lawrence Molloy was in the marble business. The company of Clough and Molloy turned out millions of those white marble steps for which Baltimore is rather celebrated. They also fashioned hand-chiseled fireplaces, mantels, bureau tops, and the best of monumental work in both marble and granite.

And so Father, thanks to wifely urging and the co-operation of friends who believed in him, became a builder and contractor, but Mother found that the new career had its periodic drawbacks. Father would build a row of fine houses of yellow-face brick and marble steps, and she would move into the last or best one, usually on the corner. As the family grew in number, each move became more of a burden. When the row of houses was finished on York Road, years before the electric-car lines were built, Mother took over the biggest and best on the corner at 1353. It had large bedrooms, a cavernous serving pantry, and a hand-carved marble fireplace in the parlor. Then Mother said with foot-down firmness:

"Scott, this is the last. Here we stay."

With plenty of grounds, a stable for one horse, and a shed for two carriages, there was never a reason to move. The memorable York Road house still stands at this writing, silent testimony to Father's care and skill. Sometime in the 1930's it was made into four apartments for as many families. But there I knew happiness, security, and good things. It is the Baltimore home I best remember, and the one I'll never forget.

During the fall of 1900 I was a student at Mount Saint Agnes College for Young Women, established in 1890 and located on winding Smith Avenue in the Mount Washington section, just inside the north city line. The Sisters of Mercy operated the school. The massive buildings—especially one of octagon shape—and heavily wooded grounds gave the whole place the appearance of a well-guarded fortress. It was a strong fortress, indeed, of the mind and spirit, though I could scarcely appreciate the fact during my daily trips, with interest in books and assignments rapidly diminishing.

The reason, of course, was John Joseph McGraw, whose visits to our York Road home became more frequent and of longer duration. I had to formalize Charlie Schryver's calls, so that he wouldn't simply "drop by" at the wrong time. Father even stopped using the 11:00 P.M. closing sign, partly because it wasn't needed, but chiefly because my mother put her foot down.

Then came our first crisis. It was in December. Christmas was approaching. John wanted to give me a present of some kind. I thought it flattering and quite all right, though I didn't know whether a set of pins would be permissible. I'd have to ask.

"Absolutely not!" Mother exclaimed, as her foot came down again. "A modest gift? Well, I suppose that's all right, though you haven't known him long. But mind you, Blanche, you cannot accept anything elaborate!"

After New Year's Day of 1901, the new century, John became a regular caller and was always good company. He did not smoke, and, despite part ownership of a café downtown on North Howard, he did not drink. He showed good and conservative taste in clothes, which had to be hand-tailored because of his short arms. He had his shoes and shirts made in Havana, the shirts because he had found a particularly good shirtmaker, and shoes because of interest in Cuba's economic growth as a new nation.

His conversation at our house was such that we never realized his importance in the field of sports. He talked of baseball plans, and the new team he was leading, but there were few details. None of us knew any baseball background. Father didn't know a backstop from a shortstop, and I only knew that if John was associated with anything, it was good. He gave you that impression, for he was always considerate and soft-spoken. I think my brothers got more baseball out of him than we older people.

Then came Lincoln's Birthday and the big turnout of people

at York Road and Twenty-ninth Street. It was a biting cold day, but that failed to hold the crowd down. Newspapers the next day carried four-column pictures of the crowd, which numbered more than a thousand. There in the center was John, wearing a soft beaver hat, a fur-collared greatcoat, and standing next to Dr. John B. Schwatka, Sheriff of Baltimore, who represented Governor Smith of Maryland. Dr. Schwatka was holding the silver spade and breaking ground for Baltimore's new American League baseball park!

This was exciting indeed, and gave us a wholly new conception of professional baseball and its civic importance. Father said that the ball-park site was an excellent selection. It was only four blocks north of the old Union Park, right on York Road, where it would be served by the electric cars. It was across Twenty-ninth Street from the landscaped grounds of the Whiteley and Brady mansions, square colonial structures that dated back to 1740.

Before we could get any details, or fit what we had together for understanding, John McGraw was ready to leave for Hot Springs, Arkansas. There he planned to boil out, he explained, which seemed to be necessary in order to play baseball well. He asked if he could write, and when I said yes, he explained that he wasn't much of a letter writer. But somehow it didn't seem to make much difference. A quiet mutual understanding seemed to be developing, and I couldn't feel worried about anything except my class work at Mount Saint Agnes.

After John left to start training in the Midwest, we saw nothing of him and heard little from him until the opening of the 1901 baseball season. By then my brothers had succeeded in explaining the game to me, but I still didn't understand it.

All of the papers devoted a surprising amount of space to the new baseball park and the opening day, April 24. John had called and given us a sketchy account of matters. More important, he brought out enough tickets for a large box party, and we took advantage of the opportunity. It would be our first baseball game —Mother, Father, all five children, Charlie Schryver, and a friend or two of his. We planned a picnic lunch, had the carriages polished, and hired a second horse.

Then it rained and the grand opening was postponed twice.

The delay failed to dampen our enthusiasm, and we arose finally to face enough warmth and sunshine for two days. We were part of an overflow crowd that filled the five thousand grandstand seats and bleachers and spilled along the perimeter of the outfield. Our seats were directly behind first base. John played third. (He also played batter!) As I recall, the park was built so that the catcher looked almost south, with the afternoon sun shining in a right-handed batter's eyes. But that was necessary to have the grandstand entrance at the more accessible southwest corner of York Road and Twenty-ninth Street.

A band played, and the stands were decked out in colorful bunting. There were many, many flowers. Municipal dignitaries were there in abundance, and the game was exciting. I couldn't keep track of the score, but Charlie Schryver told me that John made two base hits, stole one base, and played well. I watched him throughout the game, and he fielded all the batted balls that came his way without a mistake.

He didn't look at us once during the game. He played and walked around and ran just as if the stands were empty. We even waved to him, but he paid no attention to us.

But it was fun. The picnic lunch was good, and the enormous crowd was exciting. Baltimore won, and the new American League season had got off to a great start. Charlie Schryver came home with us, and his entire conversation was baseball. He talked so rapidly about names, and runs, and hits, and probabilities, as we sat on the porch, that I couldn't keep up with him or understand him. It was during one of these complicated explanations that the wagon drove up. York Avenue was still unpaved, and we didn't know that the horse and vehicle had approached until the driver yelled:

"Blanche Sindall live here?"

I nodded, and Charlie shouted, "Yes!"

"Well, here's some flowers for you," the driver called, and thumbed over his shoulder at a big load. "Johnny McGraw sent 'em over!"

The wagon was overflowing with bouquets, sprays, enormous wreaths, horseshoes, and a number of "Success" and "Good Luck, Johnny" ribbons streaming from the high bank of color. I never saw so many flowers before in my life. Poor Charlie Schryver took one long look, and, as he prepared to race down the steps, he said:

"This is my exit!"

2

YOU CAN'T appreciate the beauty of Baltimore from a speeding car or taxicab, streetcar or bus. You can see only a small portion of it, and very few of its many monuments and parks, on foot. The best way to see Baltimore, and really appreciate it, is from the seat of a horse-drawn carriage with an attentive and humorous young man of the world at your side.

I did the driving, perhaps because Fannie was our mare and a smart one. We borrowed the horse and buggy, just as children usurp the family automobile today, when they're persistent and lucky. On our evenings for a drive, Corcian, our colored coachman, would have the best carriage spotless and shining, with Fannie hitched and waiting. He would warn her solemnly about behaving and doing a good job, but she always knew who had the reins. With the stable scarcely out of sight, Fannie would take over, and John McGraw would begin clucking in dismay.

"Can't you keep her on the bed of the road?" he would tease. "You're becoming the best gutter driver in all Baltimore."

John never took the reins, though he could certainly handle horses. Years later in Los Angeles he saved me and a friend from New York, Mrs. B. K. Weller, from serious injury and perhaps death by jumping from the carriage to stop our runaway team. A Spring Street car collided with the rig, throwing our driver, Frank Dean, out of the front seat and into the street. The reins went with him. The maddened horses reared angrily, twisted, and dashed off in a wild gallop. We were tossed like a salad in the light carriage, but John crawled over the dashboard, leaped, and grabbed the loose reins as he slid over one horse's back and down into the street.

How he managed to hold on, I'll never know, because the galloping horses dragged him and us from one side of the street to the other. He not only held on but pulled himself hand over hand along the reins to shorten the hold. Of course, both Mrs. Weller and I screamed and drew all kinds of attention. Bystanders yelled and pointed helplessly to John being hauled like a rag doll through the dirt and mud, but he kept a tight grip on the reins and sawed his arms back and forth to pinch the bits. Within a few blocks he succeeded in bringing the frightened animals to a halt.

Our favorite drive in Baltimore was along Thirty-third Street from York Road, through the Johns Hopkins University grounds, and then into heavily wooded Druid Hill Park, which I think is the most beautiful city park in America. It is nearly as large as New York's Central Park, about eight hundred acres of stately trees and a sizable lake, but with many rolling hills that create rushing streams into Jones Falls. That was our usual goal for a drive, and Fannie sort of headed that way out of habit, though John would sometimes arrive in his own hired horse and rig.

Despite his reputation and publicized actions on the baseball field, John McGraw was essentially a quiet man who could respond to surroundings. He didn't convey the impression of being a particularly happy or joyous person, yet he could laugh easily, and he could react to the ridiculous aspect of a situation (his favorite humor) as quickly as anyone I ever knew. From the start I saw him as a young man of indestructible confidence, even of visible optimism and hope, but not of the Pollyanna variety.

He was always kind, considerate, and affectionate, but never demonstrative. He never used pet names or nicknames as a substitute for Blanche. His was a serious devotion, deep and mostly hidden from others. It was the same with his countless friendships all over the world. No one ever knew the full extent of his affection for old friends except the friend himself. He was tight-lipped and firm and secretive about this all his life.

He had attended college, but he wasn't the bookish type, and he said almost nothing about his education unless some unfortunate heel overstepped the bounds of good manners to take a few pot-shots at baseball people as a group of low-lifers. Then John defended all baseball and everybody in it, teammate or rival, educated or not, and he was never above swinging his fists as part of the defense.

Between such excursions or expressions, he clung to simple

pleasures and fun, and he welcomed the carriage drives, or the hours on our porch, or an occasional dinner in the Northampton Hotel at Charles and West North. Mr. and Mrs. James L. Filon set an excellent table as part of the hotel's operation, which made it popular with Oriole baseball players.

I viewed John's liking for quiet relaxation and the comfort of our York Road home as a sort of gnawing hunger. Sometimes he would just sit with us in the parlor, speak only when spoken to, and watch my father and mother for minutes at a time. He admired the family warmth and the air of peace, though I didn't realize the deeply hidden reason at the time.

Baltimore evenings in spring and summer were always warm, and, except on Sundays, John would still be fuming silently over the day's baseball game. The drive would help smooth out his ruffled nerves and temper. He talked little of baseball, and then only to say something about the score of the game, or another player, or the "lobster of an umpire," usually Jack Sheridan or young Tommy Connolly. Though my trips to the baseball park increased, I still couldn't ask many questions, and I had learned not to volunteer comment at all.

My three brothers more than made up for it. They never failed to usurp the first part of his visits with questions that I couldn't understand. That was when he laughed the most heartily, but with the boys, rather than at them. My mother would try to shoo them upstairs or out into the yard, but he held on to them and invited more questions. Nothing they could ask, however senseless, was too much for his patience.

My lack of baseball knowledge or appreciation could have set up a barrier, but it never did. We were always good companions, and there was a tender solace in mere proximity. We had fun and we laughed. I knew very little of the world, if anything, and I made no attempt to conceal it. He seemed to know almost everything and everybody. The extent of his reputation and importance was the first cause of concern for him when my attention was called to a four-column story in the *Herald* one day late in July, 1901. The paper said that Ban Johnson, president of the newly formed American League, charged John J. McGraw, a player-manager in Johnson's own league, with "startling crimes," which included dickering with the rival National League. I asked him about it as we drove.

"Did you read the whole story?" he asked.

I said that I had.

"Did you read that I called the charges wholly groundless, and challenged Mr. Johnson to produce proof of any kind?"

Yes, I'd read that too.

"What I said was the truth, Blanche," he assured me. "You'll read many things like that, one way or another. You can't get too upset about them, because sometimes they're said deliberately and published for a reason. I'm in a highly competitive business."

Fannie paused at a fork in the wooded road. I pulled the left rein and she ambled on.

"A lot of men in baseball are tugging in different directions," he said. "Some of them will win. Others will lose out."

"Who will lose out?" I asked anxiously.

"Those who haven't played baseball, or those who forget it's a game first, then a business," he replied with a heavy sigh. "The game itself and the entertainment, the competition, and the fight—all that comes first. Without it, there's no game, and certainly no business to battle over."

It mattered only that Mr. Johnson's charges were untrue. John had said so, and that was enough for me. The various principals in whatever fighting was going on didn't interest me, and I hadn't the slightest idea of what the issues were about.

Every drive through Druid Hill Park was a pleasant and unforgettable memory. Even Fannie was happy, though not for the same reason. She knew the turns well, and when we steered her back from the promontory overlooking the twinkling gas lights of Woodberry and Hampden below, her hopes and speed rose. I had to rein her from breaking into a gallop back to the stable.

Leaving the park by way of the Pennsylvania Avenue Road, we would drive along West North and then to Fouch's Drug Store at North Charles. They had the best ice cream sodas in all Maryland, or so they seemed. We always talked of having two apiece, but never after the first one.

After we unhitched Fannie from one of the posts in front of Fouch's, no amount of reining could keep her from a brisk trot to the stable, where Corcian would be waiting to bed her down for the night.

There were no motion pictures, but John and I attended the theaters downtown. He preferred light productions, musicals, and especially vaudeville, to dramatic plays, claiming that he had enough problems during the day without trying to solve the actors' stage woes at night. He insisted that the theater was for relaxing entertainment, and he always patronized it as such.

We had many fine theaters in Baltimore at the time—Academy of Music, Lyceum, Holliday, Music Hall, Monumental, and, of course, Ford's, which was managed by Charlie Ford, son of the founder. Ford's was always talked about excitedly, and it was surprising how many visitors asked if that was the Ford's where President Lincoln was shot. The shooting in Ford's at Washington had almost ruined John T., but he managed to build the new opera house in Baltimore at West Fayette and Eutaw for an opening in 1871. My father often talked about the theater because of its construction. Across the high backstage area were four supporting beams of western Douglas fir, 110 feet long and 12 inches square. They had been brought across the country on two special cars. And in the deep basement, which extended under the whole area of the theater to cool it in summer and retain heat in winter, was a little railroad line, with switches and sidings. The small cars were used to carry anything—even people, but mostly coal. The theater was lighted, we were told, by the first dynamo for an individual electric system in the country.

Happily, this was one of the landmarks spared in the terrible fire two years later when most of the downtown business district was burned out. I had left Baltimore, but I returned to stare in horror and actually weep at the sight of nearly three thousand buildings within an area of seventy blocks reduced to smoking ruins. The loss was put at fifty million dollars. Many of Father's friends were burned out, and he couldn't help them much. Illness had caught up with him, and he slowed down toward retirement.

I have tried to show how our lives and our companionship were slow paced and simple. There were few expectations and fewer demands. We were thankful for whatever happened, and an evening's drive, a matinee, a vaudeville performance, the circus, or a visit to the baseball game were precious things. John joined us

13

for mass at St. Ann's, on York Road at Twenty-second Street, every Sunday when he was in town, and with him always came a bunch of Parma violets for me. When he was away with the Orioles, the violets arrived anyway.

As you may well imagine, by the time John first mentioned marriage, there wasn't any doubt about it, though the proposal was wonderful to hear. More important was my father, because I was still in school and registered at Mount Saint Agnes for the fall term. There was no question about my feelings in the matter, but I observed feminine decorum in accordance with standards of 1901. John simply had to ask my father.

Well, he tried to bring himself to pop the question and failed three times. Then he left on a western trip with the Orioles, and he couldn't ask by mail. He returned to Baltimore with his right leg in a cast, for he had pulled some tendons in the knee. Up until that time, mid-August, the Orioles had done quite well, thanks to his management and his playing. His batting average was .352, and the team was in third place a few games behind Chicago and Boston. A month later both Detroit and Philadelphia had pushed by, and Baltimore was in the second division. During the final weeks the Orioles won only thirteen games while losing twenty. The team finished fifth, and John finished on crutches with his leg still in a cast.

We spent many evenings on the porch, talking of the future and obtaining Father's permission. Of course, John had troubles, but this seemed more a matter of courage than troubles. What about the fearless John McGraw I had heard my baseball-minded brothers discussing? They boasted of how daring he was on the field, challenging opponents, running the bases, and defying the most savage umpire. I asked if this were really true.

"Not exactly," he explained. "Of course, I argue and—well, Blanche, in baseball you have to fight all the time for survival. And if your father was an umpire for one minute, I'd have it all over in half a minute. But he's not an umpire, and this is different."

"How?"

The stiffened leg seemed to make him uncomfortable. He shifted uneasily and turned to look into the parlor where Father was reading. He rose, sighed, and said:

"I guess I'll make it this time. He's by himself."

The engagement was announced on October 24, and my ring was enough to make any girl's eyes sparkle. It consisted of three beautiful diamonds set in a row along the curve of the ring. The two outside stones were of three carats each, and the center one almost four carats. My sister Jeannette and I used to stare at that brilliant ring for minutes at a time. Over the years I've lost it and found it, left it several places—once on a Boston boat—but I still stare at it for minutes at a time.

A family's first marriage in Baltimore at the turn of the century was no casual matter. Tradition and custom governed all procedure. My mother felt that January 8 was almost too soon, not so much for propriety as the sake of Miss Maude. Could her flying fingers complete a trousseau in so brief a time?

Miss Maude was our seamstress who came to live with us twice a year. She remained to measure and cut and fit and baste and sew until everybody had clothes. Miss Maude declared that she could manage the trousseau without difficulty, but Mother took no chances. She assigned some of the dresswork to Lottie Barton. Maggie Dorsey was given the honor of making my wedding dress.

Then Mother really broke a tradition. In view of the heavy sewing schedule, I could have my first ready-made coat, a beautiful broadcloth of rather brilliant red, costing $25.00. We bought it at O'Neill's, where we did almost all of our shopping for dry goods. I remember two unforgettables about O'Neill's. One was going to the store so many times and waiting long intervals for Miss Maggie Murphy to become disengaged from the customer she was serving when we arrived. It was tradition to be served by Miss Maggie, though I never knew why.

The other memory about the store was the billing system. We bought and bought, always charging, and received a bill, no matter how large, only twice a year. It seems incredible in these days, but such was Baltimore then, and even at this writing, I believe O'Neill's has one or two of those "old settlers" who pay only twice a year.

Throughout the final weeks of 1901 in our house the scissors snipped, and the needles flew, and the end result was all that any girl could possibly want. My trousseau was generously complete, but Maggie Dorsey had exceeded all expectations with a labor of love that is still breath-takingly beautiful to me, fifty years later.

Jeannette, my bridesmaid, wasn't too unhappy with a beautiful gown of white crepe de Chine trimmed with handmade Irish lace. She wore a picture hat of lace with white plumes and carried American beauty roses. My veil was tulle and of storybook length, caught at the crown with orange blossoms. I carried a spray of lilies of the valley. And I wore a dazzling diamond crescent, John's wedding present to me.

St. Ann's Church was overflowing with people and flowers long before Father and I reached the altar at 6:00 P.M., for John J. McGraw could draw a crowd anywhere in Baltimore in baseball uniform or evening dress. Fans and just curious numbering many hundreds waited in the street, hoping not only to see John and me, but Wilbert Robinson, Willie Keeler, Joe Kelley, Steve Brodie, Hugh Jennings, and other historic Orioles, who always seemed to migrate back in a flock when something of importance occurred in Baltimore.

Father Cornelius Thomas, pastor of St. Ann's, performed the ceremony with the assistance of Father Boland and Father Kenny. An enthusiastic baseball follower, Father Thomas sent us on our way with what I believe is the most unusual admonition ever uttered to a wedding couple.

"You have come to this altar," he began, "to ask the blessing of God and His Church on the love of your hearts; to utter before Him your vows of fidelity; and to receive from Him assurance of His paternal regard and loving affection.

"Let selfishness be no barrier to your happiness, but understand that each must often give up much, renounce himself, that both may enjoy delightful fruit. For you know that it is the sacrifice hit that adds to the number of runs and wins the game."

3

SAVANNAH, GEORGIA, contained a few more than fifty thousand people in 1902, though you'd never know it from the quiet, palm-lined streets and slow approach to living. It was my first glimpse of the green and glistening live oaks and the beardlike Spanish moss—in fact, of anything southern that couldn't be seen in Baltimore. But I wasn't so thrilled over the Pulaski Hotel. It contrasted sharply in every way to the rather sumptuous Raleigh in Washington, D.C. We had spent the first twenty hours of our trip there after the beautiful wedding reception at home.

Before I could say anything about the Savannah hotel, or how much less attractive it was than a couple of others, John volunteered an explanation.

"You know we're coming back here to train in about six weeks. It's not the best place, but the club can't afford to splurge. The hotel is making an attractive rate for the whole party with several important concessions. Well, I can't very well accept their generosity for the team, and then take my personal business elsewhere. It wouldn't be fair."

It was quite all right with me. In fact, everything was perfect as we continued south and into Florida. We lived at the celebrated Breakers Hotel in Palm Beach, and we laughed at the mere thought of trying to bring a baseball team to such a social place. Little did we dream that players of the future would turn up their noses at a rambling, wooden structure like the Breakers with its polished brass bedsteads, coiled ropes at the window for fire escape, and complete lack of air-conditioning!

There were scarcely half a million people in all Florida at the time. John had been through some of the villages twelve years before on his trip back from Cuba. But Miami was mostly swamp and sand bars and shacks. St. Petersburg, a sandy peninsula, had only a few thousand people. Tampa and Jacksonville were the cities.

After a few days at the Ponce de Leon Hotel in St. Augustine, we continued on directly to Baltimore. Mr. and Mrs. Filon had prepared fine quarters for us at the Northampton Hotel. And Fouch's ice-cream sodas were just across the street. But we hadn't been back from the south long before John began the first of many secret trips, sometimes to Philadelphia, and sometimes to New York. And they were more than secret.

"It concerns New York baseball," he confided, "but we can't even talk about it out loud. If anyone asks, you can't even say where I've gone, or when I'm coming back. Something may come of it, and maybe not. I've just got to visit and meet people and listen and wait."

As a bride of a few weeks, I learned that John's business was indeed highly competitive. I also learned not to talk about him or what he did or said. Trusting him was a part of my love, and I was certain that whatever he was doing or would do was the right thing. It was not in my province or my mind to ask for facts or explanations. He needed understanding and silence, and obedience to his needs was a sacred mission in itself.

We left for another visit to Savannah again at the end of February. The party was small indeed by modern standards, comprising Mr. and Mrs. John J. Mahon, Mr. and Mrs. Wilbert Robinson, Mr. and Mrs. Joe Kelley, John McGraw and I, seventeen baseball players, a trainer, and one sports writer, John J. "Andy" Anderson, of the Baltimore *Herald*.

Compare this with a half-century later when the total complement on the spring safari of big-league baseball consisted of playing personnel numbering upward of fifty veterans and rookies, and a dozen or more baseball writers, half of whom brought their children; club secretaries, publicity directors, and executives.

Ours was not a particularly happy camp at Savannah for many reasons, all of which involved the complicated and shaky structure of "organized" baseball at the time. John had "lost" several important players to the National League—thin Jack Dunn and stocky Steve Brodie. But he had lured a few from them, too. The loss he regretted most, however, was the young and harum-scarum Mike Donlin. John had brought him from St. Louis a few years before as a boy of great promise.

"He was born on Decoration Day, and he's been parading ever since," John would mutter about Donlin. Then he'd add, "But he can really field and hit and play anywhere."

From what little I could gather at the time, John wasn't too sure of his own future. He had invested money in the Orioles, and there was no promise of returns. The American League was new, and the eight teams were fought hard by the older National League, especially in Boston, Philadelphia, St. Louis, and Chicago, where two rival clubs operated. Moreover, the New York situation had failed to materialize to his satisfaction. He was in the position of putting the best possible team on the field for Baltimore while thinking in terms of greener National League pastures.

Yet, the Orioles gathered at the Savannah park each day to run and sweat and bat and catch. John drove them in the best Oriole tradition. They worked on new strategies, and I heard him assure club president Mahon repeatedly at dinner, "We'll field a good team, John. No fear of that."

It wasn't a difficult prophecy with a pitching staff headed by a smiling young man named Joe McGinnity, of Indian Territory. He had won eighty victories in the three previous seasons. Besides him John had Tom Hughes and Harry Howell. For the infield Donlin had been replaced by Dan McGann at first with a good young hitter named Jimmy Williams at second and John himself at third. Bill Keister, the hard-hitting shortstop, had gone to Washington, and John tried everybody there, including Howell, the pitcher. He finally got Billy Gilbert from Milwaukee before the shift of that franchise to St. Louis. His outfield mainstay was a veteran, Cy Seymour. The president's son-in-law, Joe Kelley, another veteran, hit well and played the outfield and infield. The catching was the best in all baseball, Wilbert Robinson and an Irish-born young man of twenty-one, Roger Bresnahan, who could play anywhere and proved it that year. It was the nucleus of a strong and hard-hitting team.

Before the season opened, however, John confided, "We may be in New York before long."

There were no details. The secret trips to meet the emissary of the New York club continued, and upon his return to me at the Northampton Hotel, he would whisper another development or two in the negotiations. There was no question about a firm agreement of some kind. That was a fact. An endless number of influencing details held up the final papers. But he definitely would be playing manager of the New York Giants. It sounded exciting. New York was only three hours by train from home—practically a suburb of Baltimore!

The Orioles had barely played twenty games when the Detroit club came to Baltimore for the first series on May 24, 1902. It was a Saturday and nearly four thousand people, including me, had turned out. I sat behind third base, and the whole thing happened only a few feet away.

Dick Harley, an outfielder, hit a clean single off Tom Hughes in the first inning. Another outfielder, Dick Barrett, also singled, sending Harley to second. Both were speedy runners. They were young, and it was spring, and they were playing the "old Orioles." At least one was on third. Harley and Barrett decided to put on the double steal.

Roger Bresnahan saw their sign or read their minds. They had scarcely broken when he whipped the ball down to John with the speed of a bullet. John stood there waiting for Harley to come in. The Detroit outfielder was out by fully twenty feet, and yet he slid with his spikes flashing and slashing in the dust. John didn't flinch. He made the tag, and Harley got him in the left leg, just below the kneecap. The orange and black stocking immediately was soaked with red, but John paid no attention. Silk O'Loughlin, the umpire, had called the runner out. John tossed the ball to Hughes and made for Harley.

It was the first outburst of his rage that I had seen, and it wasn't easy to watch. But neither was the leg, which had turned a solid red. Other Orioles rushed over to pull John away. Harley scampered for cover. John was held down on the ground. Hughes took one look and yelled for somebody to get an ambulance. I prayed and sat there, unable to move or cry.

Back at the Northampton Hotel they called Dr. Standish McCleary, the club physician, whose office was nearby. He removed the tourniquet and examined not one cut, but three!

"They're not deep, Mrs. McGraw," he comforted. "Don't worry. It'll be all right. You just keep quiet, John."

John obeyed, for it was a shock, especially with so much at stake in New York. He was supposed to be playing manager. While Dr. McCleary wanted first to reassure us, there was a chance that complications would set in. John had seen them in lighter injuries.

"It's usually the outfielders," John said finally. "They're always the bravest with the spikes. That's because they don't have to stay on the bases and take it from the ones they cut."

"John, please," I warned. "You're to be quiet."

"Call the ball park and see how the game's going."

I called. It wasn't quite over. We were winning, and Detroit hadn't scored. Robinson was catching, and Bresnahan was playing third base. In less than twenty minutes Harry Goldman telephoned the news. Tom Hughes had allowed only two more hits and had pitched a 6–0 thriller over Win Mercer.

"Good!" John laughed. "My leg feels better already."

That was for my benefit. On Monday he was apologizing for his bad temper, which wasn't a temper at all. The leg was throbbing, and the pain had to be deadened by sedation. I kept a steady vigil to make sure he didn't rip off the dressing in a rage. The Memorial Day holiday was approaching, and that meant doubleheader. Every game he missed was certain to cost the club heavily in gate receipts or victory or something, he stormed.

June came and he could hardly bend the leg. The stitches were still in. I had changed the dressing, and it was ghastly. Dr. McCleary said it wasn't awful, but good. The healing on the outside was coming along fine. The inside? He wouldn't know until the area had been rested and tested. He could do both at the same time, first by walking without bending the knee.

Meanwhile the New York situation hung in the balance, even though the deal was "set." The Orioles went west without John, and that made him more impatient than ever. He made a secret trip to New York, walking stiff-legged, but carefully, and returned next day to report that things looked good again. Then he tackled the telephone, running up needless bills to learn about scores and hits and the condition of his Orioles.

Two weeks passed before he could bend the leg naturally, but Dr. McCleary's prophecy was right. The area had healed inside and out, and there was no question about John's playing. Then the New York situation percolated, and both of us felt better.

After trying out the leg for ten days, John appeared in a game for the first time on June 25, a month and a day after the slashing. He batted for Billy Gilbert in the ninth inning and grounded out. Three days later, exactly five weeks from the time of the injury, he started a game at third base, and it was one to be remembered.

It was memorable chiefly because he could use the leg well. In his first time at bat he tripled to right center and ran as fast as ever. Then he scored the Orioles' first run. In the seventh inning he bunted to the third-base side and beat Manager Jimmy Collins' snap throw to Buck Freeman at first. He raced around to third base on an error. With the end of the game in sight, his leg felt fine, but the Orioles were losing by a score of 9–4.

What appeared to be a last-ditch rally found Dan McGann on third base in the home half of the ninth. When Seymour's bounder went to Long, McGann was caught in a run-down. As Long and Lou Criger, the Boston catcher, ran down McGann, Seymour raced around to and beyond third, but he retreated as McGann edged back to the bag. With both runners on the base, Seymour was forced off, whereupon he started back for second.

At this point Tommy Connolly, the plate umpire, called Seymour out. John was off the bench quickly. He approached the umpire and asked for a reason. Connolly said that Seymour, in running back, failed to touch third. John said, with surprising calmness, that Seymour *had* touched the bag, and he wanted Jim Johnstone, the base umpire, to rule. Connolly then ordered John off the field and into the clubhouse. John refused to go. Without further delay, Connolly forfeited the game to Boston by a score of 9–0.

And Ban Johnson suspended John indefinitely!

The sparks and smoke of the battle between John McGraw and the umpires continued for two weeks. Meanwhile the New York situation crystallized officially. All details were ironed out and reduced to concrete terms. On July 1, 1902, John McGraw became playing manager of the New York Giants in fact.

In six months of marriage I had discovered many things about John McGraw, his character and personality. Somewhat smugly I had gauged the extent of his fame, popularity, and importance to baseball. But the splash of accusations, vilification, and insinuation in the headlines made me wonder if I knew anything at all.

When does a wife really know her husband? When, if ever, does the public know or even understand a controversial figure when knowledge depends upon hearsay and the reading of limited or partisan delineation by the press? I have asked myself those questions many times over the years without being able to supply specific answers.

As we prepared to leave for New York City I knew that "men in baseball were tugging in different directions," but it was still John's business and none of mine. My job was faith. We were young, and New York was a fine city. He would succeed, because of his unquenchable fire and desire to succeed.

In the pages that follow I have set down what the years have given me in knowledge and insight concerning John and his world.

4

FIVE YEARS AFTER the Civil War ended, Truxton, New York, consisted of Main Street and some rutted roads. In addition to the luxury of wooden sidewalks, its few hundred people supported Peckham's one-chair barbershop, Jerry O'Connor's general store, Mary Goddard's two-story frame "hotel" called the Truxton House, a smaller inn, a bank, and three churches of as many denominations, Catholic, Methodist, and Baptist. There was a Union Free School and several of the one-room variety located at the foot of roads leading up into valleys, or hollows, for the convenience of people who hard-scrabbled subsistence from the patches of cleared land in the wooded hills.

The village was southeast of the Finger Lakes and about fifteen miles due south of Syracuse, almost at the beginning of the New York–Pennsylvania watershed. It was surrounded by gravelly soil that yielded farm crops with a reluctance equaled only in northern New England. Though high above sea level, it was in a valley, and, thanks to the east branch of the Tioughnioga River, it was a trap for early frost. Winter was felt soon and long.

It was into this perpetual challenge to survival that an Irish-born Civil War veteran in his thirties, John McGraw, came in 1871 with a tiny, motherless baby named Anna. He wasn't sure that the place offered opportunity, but his older brother, Michael, had found work teaching school in the area. Both had left Ireland in the 1850's with high hopes of putting their fine parochial-school education to good use in the land of opportunity. In his aimless wanderings before the war, John had taught some classes, but he had lost touch, what with the fighting and the postwar reconstruction period. Now he was a widower with an infant daughter. He was in dire need of proper care for the child and any kind of work for quick cash. The E. C. & N. (Elmira, Cortland & Northern) Railroad ran through the valley. The roadbed and tracks always needed attention.

John McGraw was a short man, but powerfully put together. More important to the section boss, his dark eyes burned with desperation under the shaggy, black hair. He looked like a workman who would work. He was sober and a devout churchgoer. He became a member of the maintenance crew. Trackworkers were more than mere dollar-a-day unskilled laborers. John received nine dollars for a sixty-hour week and was glad to get it.

Within a short while his Irish eye had picked a pretty stepmother for his baby and a wife for himself. She was Ellen Comerfort, from one of the town's oldest and most respected Catholic families. She was very young, quiet, gentle, and soft-spoken. Certain of domestic peace and comfort at last, John rented a small frame house on West Hill, almost two miles out the road from O'Connor's general store on Main Street.

April of 1873 brought a strong hint of spring and sunshine. April 7 brought a new life, and they named their first baby John for the father and Joseph for the learned grandfather still in Ireland. Dr. Nelson, a veteran Civil War surgeon, studied the baby's gleaming, dark eyes that resembled two pieces of embedded licorice, and the shock of his father's black hair, and said that it was a strong and healthy child. Having brought most of the township's babies into the world, he spoke with reassuring authority.

There is no recorded evidence to show how or where little John McGraw got his first baseball. He was understandably reticent in later years about much of his youth, and he scoffed at such questions as unimportant. From time to time over the years I plied the oldest residents of Truxton with questions about him, and everyone who knew him only slightly was happy to contribute some favorite recollection. Everyone liked him. Many had such fondness for him that my questions not only produced memories but sympathetic tears.

Almost everybody agreed that he was first seen with a baseball when he was about seven, and one recalled John most vividly:

"He looked like a person afflicted with permanent tumor of the buttock, which was not strange for a boy on the street or in school, but he was the only one who 'wore his tumor' at the church altar!"

From that I assume John was never without his baseball, not even when he served at mass for the itinerant priests who drove eleven miles from Cortland winter and summer to hold services and hear confession. You could identify John on the altar not only by the incongruous lump at the rear just below his white blouse, but by the red stockings that his mother had knitted for the weekly service as an altar boy.

He may have earned the money to buy the baseball, for he was on a sharp lookout for sources of income as soon as he was able to walk into town. But in 1880, ten years before Spalding's famed "Nickel Rocket," a good Peck & Snyder "professional dead ball" with a center of molded red rubber cost $1.50, postpaid from New York City. A. G. Spalding and brother Walter, operating out of Chicago from a small factory on Madison Street, had been in business only five years. They were selling an "amateur dead ball" for one dollar, postage extra. John had no worry about gloves, for only the catcher wore one, a sort of skintight kid glove with the finger tips off. Since masks were also in the future, the catcher wore a rubber mouthpiece and tooth protector, like that used by boxers today.

Where or how John managed to get his baseball, I don't know. Certainly his father didn't buy it, because there were three more babies besides Anna and John—Margaret, Mary, and James Michael. At least one more was expected. Unfortunately, Mike was too young for baseball, and pint-sized John traveled regularly to the village to meet boys and play catch, one o'cat, or bat flies and, if nobody turned up, to bat stones or throw at a target.

There is no explaining this phenomenon, and it is a phenomenon, of a boy and a baseball in America for the past century. It has long been one of the mysteries about our country that Russia cannot solve. Having no comparable game, the Soviets are amazed by the fact that you can assemble eighteen boys from as many sections of the United States, give them a baseball, a bat, and a catcher's mitt, and, without a written word, they will play and enjoy two hours of vigorous but friendly competition.

No psychologist at this writing has been able to explain why a boy named Edward Grant Barrow, born in a covered wagon on the way west, would spend every spare minute of his early teens playing and organizing and managing teams in far-off Des Moines,

Iowa, during the 1880's. But he did, and he built the New York Yankees into the greatest of baseball empires.

No one can explain why a bowlegged, barefoot boy named Honus Wagner, homely and ungainly son of German immigrant parents, would walk fourteen miles from Mansfield, Pennsylvania, to Allegheny City, climb to "his" limb in a tree outside Exposition Park, and for two hours watch his hero, Cap Anson, play first base for visiting Chicago. Honus made this twenty-eight-mile round trip not once, but countless times, and became a player who had no equal in his day.

Nor can they explain why little Johnny McGraw, also bare-footed, trudged down from West Hill day after day to hunt for baseball players of any age or size, and he was always little. The boys gathered on the school green for the game... to play... and play... and play. Eventually one would wander away—an errand that should have been done hours before. Another would sigh and leave—early supper, and it was probably cold. John would continue running and batting and throwing, even without a full team. That was the beauty of one o'cat. You could play it with many or few.

"But I'm tired, Jack—"

"No you're not. Look, I won't call high or low. Throw me what you want."

"I can't lift my arm!"

"Then I'll stroke 'em to you."

"I can't stoop over any more."

"All right. So long... think I'll throw a few...."

"It's gettin' dark, Jack."

"It's still light enough. So long."

"See you tomorrow."

"Be here early."

Played into near exhaustion, the stragglers would shuffle away. And that was when John would get out his chalk and draw a circle on the carriage shed behind the Methodist church in "right field." It was never a big circle, because his right arm was star-tlingly accurate. From the regulation pitching distance of forty-five feet, he would take careful aim, skip across the box, and whip an underhand sizzler right into the circle. He would retrieve, and throw underhand again, with the hand *never* coming above the line of the shoulder, into the circle ... and retrieve ... and throw ... and retrieve ... and throw ... thump ... thump ... thump ... until dusk ... until sunset ... until the target was part of the darkness.

Truxton people who happened to pass didn't even look over. They recognized and understood the thumping noise. It was Jack McGraw from West Hill ... a boy and a baseball in 1880 ... in 1881 ... in 1882 ... in 1883. ...

You could earn a few cents by driving milking cows to and from pasture when farmers were busy with calving season. John O'Connor often hired him to drive them. Later farmer John trusted him to herd the culls clear over to the market at Cortland. He carried crops to the sales in September. Sometimes Jerry O'Connor had a basket of groceries to be delivered, as did the other stores that mushroomed to care for the growing population —Hoffmann's, Harry Kenney's, Frank Wescott's. Later Bert Kenney ran the smaller hotel. Bert liked baseball, too.

John took most of these occasional earnings home, except when he bought a little something for the youngest baby. It was mostly little, though he did buy a bonnet once in a while, and twice he brought home tiny baby shoes. He loved the children, because they never had anything.

His big financial goal, though, was to deliver the Cortland edition of the Elmira *Telegram*, Truxton's only contact with the outside world. He walked over to Cortland to see about getting the route. It was eleven miles, one more than his years, and they said he was too young, or too small. The Truxton agent had to be older and reliable, strong, too, on account of the weather. The paper, like the mail, had to go through. Sorry, some other time, when you've got a little growth.

On the way home he stopped at the Carrs' in East Homer. Ellen O'Brien Carr was his mother's niece and she always prevailed on him to stay overnight. He could have walked the remaining five miles, but it was warm and cosy at the Carrs'. It was easy to eat food that didn't belong to babies or to an overburdened mother. And cousin Ellen could patch pants. She could make pants from an old coat, or an old pair of pants. While he slept, she would sew up a new blouse, complete with drawstrings, from a man's castoff shirt. Or she could have something cut and sewed for him the next trip. With a family that was soon to number nine young children, including thirteen-year-old Anna, John always needed something. Everybody was in need, and the harassed father was still a section hand on the E. C. & N.

It is not an unusual story for America. The John McGraws had no monopoly on poverty or privation or shoeless travel or hunger or cold on windswept West Hill. They had a peculiar and meager happiness and an indefinable comfort that only a large family can give. They had it until the winter of 1884–85, when Ellen bore her last baby, a little girl. She was barely "up and around" when her throat felt the first stab of diphtheria, and two days later she was dying.

The half-crazed husband raced down the hill while nine children sat frozen with fear and almost frozen from cold. But there wasn't even a priest to say the last rites. Within a week the youngest boy followed Ellen—diphtheria. Black diphtheria, they called it. Now the cry went over the valley. Others had it. The Union Free School was closed. Doors were locked, and all churches suspended services. Poor Dr. Nelson was blamed as a carrier. He had treated two diphtheria patients "in the hills" just before ushering in Ellen's last baby, Nellie, who miraculously survived.

Anna, tight-lipped and frightened, was feeding and washing and cooking over a wood stove, and consoling a mystified and motherless brood, but she came down, and diphtheria took her within a week of the baby's death.

A sister was stricken, cried through the night, choked, and died. There were pine-box burials. Money for anything else simply didn't exist. There were prayers and tears and nights of horror and fright, for still another child was to go. Its life was flickering to a feeble glow like the neglected kerosene lamps.

At age twelve John McGraw lost his mother who was still in her thirties, his stepsister of thirteen, his sister of eight, a curly-haired, lisping brother of four, and a baby brother—all within a period of a few weeks. Half of a family swept from his life and into the unthawed earth of Truxton by a plague that no one could understand or cope with.

Weeping neighbors rushed up the hill as soon as quarantine or conscience would permit. They worked and spelled each other. They fumigated. They cleaned. They bathed and cooked and washed. But it was simply too much and too far from their own homes. The decimated family would have to be moved. The benumbed father nodded—anything, if he could only keep them together "for Ellen's sake."

And so he and little Jack and littler Mike packed the few belongings into a borrowed farm wagon and moved from tragic West Hill into a small frame house on Main Street, right across from Mrs. Goddard's hotel.

John's father, unable to understand the appeal of baseball, couldn't tolerate it as a pastime or future occupation. And yet John, Jr., never condemned his father as a boy or in later life.

"It was hard not to, but he wasn't to blame," John told me many years later. "After all, I was the same way about his favorite sport, Irish hurling. I used to hear him and Uncle Mike wishing for the days in the old country, and wishing they could see one more clash. There was a game, they said. And what was it? A gang of men with shillelaghs, racing up and down a big field, whacking each other over the head when they couldn't hit the ball. They had a few rules, but no organization or measured competition like baseball. Still, he and Uncle Mike thought it the greatest sport ever devised."

John McGraw, Sr., saw baseball only as an invitation to a misspent life. As the warmer days came and passed, baseball playing increased. Until June it was before and after school. Vacation meant only more baseball, and more trouble.

Twice the boy was caught on the E. C. & N.'s tracks, and it had to stop, or the worst flogging of anybody's life would take place. To John, Jr., it was like this: baseball bats cost money and you used them only in good games. For mere practice, you couldn't afford to use either ball or bat. The best substitute was a discarded whiffletree or singletree, usually a little rotted at either end. When scraped and shaved and molded into proper shape, the hickory was hard enough for batting good-sized stones.

The best stones were down on the railroad bed, cracked to the right size and all you could strike in a day. Fine, but a boy with his insatiable desire to hit a flying object could have removed a whole section of bed-dressing from the railroad. And that was the cause of one more paternal outburst. The boy was down there day after day whacking perfectly good and costly stones that had been "stolen" from a newly banked railroad bed.

"You could throw a stick into the air for Jack," another old Truxtonite told me, "and he could hit it in mid-air with a stone. He could actually hit a tree, or stump, or skunk, or woodchuck with a single sidearm swipe of a stone at an incredible distance away. He couldn't pass a one- or two-inch stone in the road or field without bending down and throwing it somewhere, usually at something."

But there were fist fights and black eyes, too, and that disturbed the already harassed father, who was fighting his own losing battle against further disruption of his family. The two older children were not quite eleven and ten. There were two younger tots. The house needed everything, and he couldn't afford help. A boy nearly thirteen with some sense could be of use around a house, at least till the girls grew. People were talking about the neglect, and exaggerating, because the children weren't neglected. They went to confession and to mass, shabby or not. The lateness at service wasn't his fault. He had to hunt for Jack on Sundays.

Now the fights. Jack explained that they were bound to come in a game when you have no umpire. You get punched, and you have to punch back.

"And they don't know the rules," he cried.

"And you know *all* the rules, I suppose!"

Yes, he did know the rules. He had read them over and over. How? From the books. What books? The books they put out. Who puts out? The baseball rules change from year to year, something's different each year, so you get a book and learn the changes. Jack McGraw got the books. He knew when the pitcher's box was changed from seven feet to six, what the fielders could do or could not do. There was an angry promise that the books wouldn't last long "if I get my hands on them!"

And then Ellen's folks began to suggest that maybe it would be best for the little ones to live out a while. How could a father hold a family together and work ten hours a day on the section gang? His temper would shorten between struggles as he tried desperately to figure out some magical method of keeping the children from slipping out of his callused hands.

One rainy late-summer night when things seemed particularly

black, a neighbor came around for another fifteen cents. Another window pane! How many was it now? The boy had paid for some, but this was too much. The kids had run away, because none of them had any money. Jack McGraw had hit the ball. Pay the fifteen cents.

It was paid, and the father lost all sense of sanity and went for his boy, yelled at him, called him names, and ran through the Main Street house trying to catch him. The children sobbed in fear and cried for help. In a blind rage, destructive rage, the father grabbed for the agile Jack and spilled him into a corner. Before he could get away, the father had him, holding and cuffing blindly. You couldn't reason with this boy, and words wouldn't come for the purpose. But he could feel, and the father cuffed savagely as the cries went out from the house.

Jack took several hard blows before he could squirm loose. He raced upstairs, grabbed some things, hid as his father charged after him, and then raced down after he had passed. He ran out of the house, into the rain and across muddy Main Street. He raced down the side alley of the Truxton House and to the back pantry door, which he whacked with his wet fist, and cried:

"Mrs. Goddard! Mrs. Goddard!"

He pounded and called hysterically for nearly two minutes before a startled, bosomy widow appeared to open the door.

"Jack!" she exclaimed. "What on earth's wrong?"

"Can I come in?" he pleaded. "It's Pop . . . he's . . . he's all upset again—"

"Look at your face—your eye! Come in out of the rain!"

John wiped his feet mechanically and stepped into the pantry and then into the warm kitchen. Mrs. Goddard gasped again and clutched him close. She murmured sympathy, not only for him but for that poor man with those children.

"Can I stay here tonight, Mrs. Goddard?"

She said that he could sleep on the top floor. Maybe in the morning she could talk to the father. It was late now.

"You'd better get up to bed, Jack," she said. "What have you got there?"

"Some . . . books," he said, clutching a small sack.

"Schoolbooks?"

"Books I . . . I have to study," he murmured.

"Well, I'll take you upstairs," she said, picking up a kerosene lamp. Will and Frank Goddard stood by in wide-eyed silence. She held her hand in front of the chimney top and led the way up two flights. The corner garret room had no window, but it was warm and dry. She put the lamp on a washstand and pulled down the blanket of a small cot.

"Just forget everything till tomorrow," she said. She hugged him again and kissed his rain-soaked forehead. "Good night. Be careful when you blow out the lamp."

"Yes, ma'am," he promised.

The sack under his arm was damp, but it had been only a short dash across the street. They couldn't be damaged. He pulled out five small, brown-covered, paper volumes and spread them upon the cot. Each precious volume had cost ten cents. The "library" consisted of:

> *De Witt's Base Ball Guide for 1875*
> *De Witt's Base Ball Guide for 1876*
> *Spalding's Constitution and Playing Rules for 1877*
> *Beadle's Dime Base-Ball Player for 1877*
> *Our Boys' Base Ball Rules for 1877*

All except the last were well thumbed, but unmarked. A paragraph on page eleven of the *Our Boys'* book had been heavily circled with a graphite pencil. It was under Rule III and had impressed him more than anything else:

> Sec. 2. Any player who shall conspire with any person whatever against the interests of his club, or by any conduct manifest a disposition to obstruct the management of his club may be expelled from his club.

After inspecting each for damage, he piled them neatly on the washstand, "blew out the lamp carefully," and crawled in between the clean linen.

5

FOR THREE NIGHTS after work John McGraw walked the streets and roads of Truxton and vicinity and searched the playing fields in vain for his son. He called at a few homes that harbored known baseball-minded boys and asked casually for Jack, saying nothing, of course, about the two nights of absence. No one had seen little Jack. Then he must be at Ellen Carr's, five miles down the Cortland road. Before starting there, he went over to ask Mrs. Goddard if she would look in on the children while he was gone. To his great relief, there was the boy he had chastised so severely, safe, but still hiding.

Mrs. Goddard was a woman of deep compassion. She led the harassed and weary father to her small living room at the back of the hotel and there asked if Jack could stay on with her.

"It's a terrible thing, John," she said, "but with conditions as they are, it might be for the best."

The father couldn't see it that way.

"Jack's a wild boy," he sighed, "and getting worse. Maybe he's not really bad, but anybody will be who disregards all rule and order and time, that's sure. He's godless—"

"No, he's not."

"He's straying from the church. That I will not have."

"But he can attend church."

"He won't," the father despaired. "He'd rather play games and waste his time than eat or go to church. I won't have it that way, Mrs. Goddard. He's got to go to church!"

"He *will* go to church, John," she assured him.

"How can you promise?" he argued wearily. "Sunday after Sunday I have to hunt for him. Where do I find him? On the green or trespassing on somebody's field with that wild and screaming pack, blaspheming the holy day with baseball. Mrs. Goddard, I have to drag him by force from the game he plays. I've been so ashamed, hauling him like a prisoner to the bar, and late for the mass, too."

"Don't worry, John, he'll go to church," Mrs. Goddard promised. "He'll go, if I have to take him there myself. Or, you can stop by and take him. Why don't you do that? I'll have him clean and ready. And he'll be kept track of here, John, and safe. He can do enough to earn his board and keep and clothes. He'll be company for my Will and Frank. He'll go to school, too, and your mind will be rested."

John McGraw stared at the neat braided pattern of the rag rug. Ellen had started one years before, to cover the bare floor, and never had finished it. Slowly he surrendered to the inevitable. This was the first. They'd take the oldest from him. Then the Carrs or his own relatives would take Margaret... and Mike... and baby Nellie....

"It's not as though he was going away, John. He'll be right across the street from you."

The head of black hair nodded finally in assent. There was no defense, no argument against a good, warm home, a clean bed, sturdy boots and clothes, and regular meals, with a motherly woman like Mrs. Goddard to kiss the bruises and dry the tears.

He rose and offered no further protest. He murmured his thanks and crossed Main Street to the house that the rest of his brood would soon be leaving, one by one, to be scattered among understanding relatives and sympathetic friends; back, gradually, to the "single blessedness," the loneliness and emptiness after daily labors on the railroad track, to pray and have faith and try not to wonder what on earth had happened, to say nothing of why.

Young John was grateful for Mrs. Goddard's motherly intervention and lost no time proving it. He was twelve and a half in the fall of 1885 when he began living at the Truxton House, but he became older overnight, and looked upon his chores as a serious responsibility. He rose early each day and took care of the horses. He drew and carried water for the animals and filled the hotel tank. He attended Union Free School five days a week, and after classes he reported back to see if there were satchels to be carried to or from the railroad station. Mrs. Goddard bought him a new stout pair of leather boots, for he ran errands, too.

The Truxton House was a rambling, two-story landmark of clapboard and slate roof. It was white and neat with green shutters on all of its many four-pane windows. A small sign stuck out from the roof of the square-pillared porch that extended halfway across the wooden sidewalk. The sign was lighted at night by a

34

single street lamp, and it was John's job to see that kerosene was always in the lamp.

The hotel was big inside, or so it seemed to John, who was almost tiny for his age, but he liked its winter warmth, even if he did have to help Will Goddard with the fire-lighting in the morning. The place was comfortable, and as he watched his brothers and sisters moved from the house across the street into foster homes, he knew that they were warm, too.

As soon as the roads were fit to use in the spring, John got over to Cortland and talked about the job of delivering the Cortland edition of the Elmira *Telegram* in Truxton. He explained that his "home" wasn't far from the station, and he promised that every farmer in the area would get his newspaper, rain or shine, snow or sleet. They surveyed his woolen shirt, long woolen pants of stout weave, grown-man's suspenders shortened to fit his narrow shoulders, the muddy boots, the slicked-down black hair, the pork-pie felt hat in hand, and made him their Truxton agent.

Money was always needed, but especially in the spring when the baseball playing season neared. It wasn't only for new baseballs; rule books had to be bought. Luckily John got his 1886 *Reach Guide* early. He was one of the first in Truxton to know that the pitcher's box was lengthened to seven feet, placed fifty feet from home base instead of forty-five, and that the pitcher could now raise his arm *above* his shoulder and throw overhand!

This was important news. The batter still called for the pitch he wanted, and if he didn't get it, there was no penalty of a strike. But the pitcher now could wind up, take a skip-step, and really throw. To John, the longer box was like an open pasture.

Of course, Albert Kenney, who had opened Kenney's hotel, knew the rule changes. He was way ahead of everybody in baseball, but among the school kids, John knew the regulations by heart, and his well-thumbed guides of that period, still among my treasured possessions, indicate as much.

A year later the books brought even greater changes. The size of the pitcher's box was shortened to five feet six inches, and the pitcher could no longer lift his rear foot or take more than one step. But the batter had to strike at a "fair" pitch over the home base and between his knees and shoulders. If he refused four times, the umpire called him out. Seven "unfair" pitches, outside the strike area, gave the batter first base.

It was here that the umpire and his judgment of fair or unfair pitches became all-important. The umpire himself became king.

The year 1887 brought John another unforgettable in the formation of the Truxton brass band. They started a year ahead so as to be in good shape and harmony for the Benjamin Harrison presidential campaign. The backbone of the band was the Roche brothers—M. T., who whacked the bass drum; D. M., who blew the trumpet; and W. J., who tootled the peck-horn, or low alto. Will and Frank Goddard both played cornets. Jack O'Neil played the snare drum, and Charlie O'Grady the fife. John didn't play any musical instrument, but he followed them around as though he was a member, and he helped carry the bass drum in all the parades.

The bass-drumming Roche later became president of the New York State League in baseball, and then went into the hotel business with his brother D. M. in the operation of the Empire Hotel on Portwatson Street in Cortland. W. J. Roche ran the historical David Harum Hotel in Homer, which was made famous by Edward Noyes Westcott's novel of that name.

The Truxton band was available, or perhaps couldn't be silenced, at the drop of a provocation. Holidays and picnics and anything requiring music in the vicinity found the Roche and Goddard brothers, O'Neill, and O'Grady, with their weapons poised. And John McGraw seldom missed a concert. They usually preceded the baseball game, which he *never* missed.

He tried for every team, not only in Truxton, but for twenty-five miles around. His success on the school team won him a post on the Truxton Grays, a town nine spurred by the irrepressible Bert Kenney, and it was on this team that John's playing was first noticed. Once a stranger offered him a dollar to pitch a game at Fabius about fifteen miles from Truxton. He grabbed the offer without thinking, particularly about transportation.

He could have walked to Fabius, but getting back in time for his chores at Mrs. Goddard's was another matter. He was obliged to bargain at great length in order to salvage fifty cents from his fee, but he did get a horse and buggy for a half-dollar to make the thirty-mile round trip.

Meanwhile, he continued his paper route with a diligence that prompted high tribute from the Elmira *Telegram* twenty-three years later when the newspaper recalled:

John McGraw was an enterprising newsboy who sold the *Telegram* in Truxton with great success. We are proud to say that he would walk a mile or two miles in the country, as the case might be, about Truxton through blustery snow storms in mid-winter to deliver the *Telegram* to farmers. The secret of John McGraw's wonderful success in life began there, in doing thorough and well, that which came to him to do. He is an example in that respect that should be followed by all other boys, particularly *Telegram* boys everywhere.

John located another source of income on the E. C. & N. "accommodation" train that was conveniently scheduled between his morning and evening chores. He got a job as butcher boy, or "butch," as the vendors were called in those days. He walked through the swaying wooden cars with a basket containing bananas, magazines, "O.K." gum, loose candy, small candies in glass pistols, and many of the tempting articles sold by Union News butchers today. The basket was almost as big as he and often weighed a third as much, for his weight when he was sixteen totaled only 105 pounds.

He caught the accommodation train on its southbound trip in the morning, and sold his wares between Cortland and Elmira, which he reached before noon. With about three hours of layover time on his hands in Elmira, he found his way to some baseball competition, and played hard until just before time to leave on the northbound journey at 3:00 P.M.

Once a fierce clash of mercantile interests occurred as the train puffed to a halt at little Freeville, about five miles northeast of Ithaca. It was a hazard that John had dealt with once before, but only with a sharp warning. Now here it was again, the same Orrie George, a bold poacher with candies and cookies standing in the path *outside*, selling his wares through the train windows.

With a cry of rage to be found only in a boy of John's competitive nature, he put aside his own large basket, dashed to the end of the car, and jumped to the cindery ground.

"Luckily I heard him shout," Orrie George recalled with a sigh of painful recollection back through his seventy-eight years. "That gave me time to light out, basket in hand, and dash up the steep embankment. It was a hard climb, but I simply had to make it. I was running for my life, and so was Jack. He'd have killed me sure. We were both handicapped, me by my basket, which I had to throw away. And him by using up valuable breath calling me names and yelling what he would do when he caught me.

"I never ran so hard before or since. My flying feet kicked the dirt into his red and sweaty face and I reached the top of the sandy hill with just a little to spare. Then I quickly put plenty of distance between us while he struggled the rest of the way. Jack had picked up my basket and he gave it a long heave in my direction, spilling everything. Then he stood there shouting threats after me till two quick train whistles called him back. No, sir, I never sold anything through the train window at Freeville again!"

He kept his supplies in the smoking car, reserved for men and their eternal discussions about the greatest, the strongest, the best at this or that. I suppose gossiping women have their counterpart, but I have never been able to fathom the exact reason why men love to argue so—and occasionally fight—over comparative values that cannot be proved. I don't know enough about the innate appetite for war and destruction in man, whether it is a masculine parallel of the feminine maternal, or whether it exists at all. But I do know that men, particularly the sports-minded breed, can and will find a difference of opinion where none actually exists. I have seen it thousands of times. I have seen a stranger come up to John McGraw, tap his shoulder, and hurl some insult over the finest delineation of baseball strategy with which he disagreed and always after the celebrated second guess. Had I not been present on these occasions, the list of John's arguments and altercations would have trebled. And so I can well understand and appreciate the celebrated "curve-ball" episode that took place when John was barely sixteen.

The art of making a baseball curve was credited to Arthur "Candy" Cummings before 1870. That he could curve the ball and control the curve from an underhand delivery makes his pio-

neering feat all the more remarkable. The smoking-car argumenta-
tors finally got around to the curve ball, and a passenger declared
that it was impossible.

"What are you talking about?" said a man well acquainted with
the work of the Truxton Grays. He pointed at the boy with the
big basket. "There's a little fellow who can pitch a curve."

"Bet you ten dollars he can't," the other replied. "At least, he
can't prove it to me."

John often laughed in recollection of the heated argument that
followed and how the temperature rose when he asked for a
dollar's worth of the bet that he couldn't make a baseball curve.
Then the train conductor came along and joined the discussion.

"I'll put up three stakes, twenty feet apart," John said. "I'll
stand at one end of the row and the catcher at the other. I'll bet
I can make the ball go on the right-hand side of the middle stake
and the catcher will catch it on the left-hand side of the end one.
That would be a curve, wouldn't it?"

"Yes, that would prove it all right," the disbeliever said, "and
I'm betting ten dollars you can't do it."

As you may well suppose, John had a baseball and a fingerless
glove right among his supplies. Since it was an "accommodation"
train, the conductor held up the trip at the next stop, where the
party hastened to a vacant lot near the station. They were followed by all the passengers. The station agent removed three
signal flags from their staffs and drove them into the ground at
the desired spots as markers. A man from the train put on John's
glove to catch the throw.

"It was easy with an overhand motion," John explained years
later. "I threw a real outcurve that went to the right of the middle
stake and hooked back to pass on the left side of the third stake.
That was at forty feet, and the curve broke only about four or
five inches. From the modern distance of sixty feet I could have
made it break a full foot."

The backer collected the ten dollars and gave John his dollar.
The doubter admitted that a ball could be curved. Some sixty
years later a photographer on the staff of a pictorial magazine
tried to demonstrate with camera shots that a ball didn't really
curve, and that the effect was an "optical illusion." His "proof"
impressed everybody except baseball players.

Three victories for the Truxton Grays within as many weeks served to widen John's reputation as a pitcher. One of his victims was East Homer, and they offered him two dollars to pitch a game. He accepted and walked to the scene of action, and happily, too, because he could see Cousin Ellen and his sister. He pitched and won the game.

"I want you to pitch again Saturday," the manager said.

"All right," John agreed, "but it will cost you five dollars. And what's more, you've got to send a hack to bring me here and take me back to Truxton."

The manager flatly refused, and John became a holdout at the age of sixteen. A sharp argument followed, but John had learned his lesson in transportation from the trip to Fabius that had netted him fifty cents. The East Homer "magnate" finally agreed to the five-dollar fee, with John supplying his own hack.

"Oh, no," John replied quickly. "The livery man would find out what you're paying and hold me up for most of it. Five dollars and travel to and from Truxton."

"I'll pay your transportation one way!" the manager exclaimed.

"Both ways, or I pitch for Truxton on Saturday!"

John received his price and hack service both ways, and over a route he had covered on bootless feet most of his life.

I might point out here that John's value was not confined to his pitching skill. Changes in the rules were constant as administrative pioneers struggled to solve ever rising problems and clarify the regulations in the annual guide. Since there were two leagues, the National, founded in 1876, and the American Association, organized in 1882, there were two official guides.

Very few boys had the rule books, but John was never without his copy. Hardly a situation on the playing field could arise without his being able to solve it. If he couldn't shout the solution immediately, he would produce the book from its wrapping and read the rule. The umpires of those sand-lot or cow-pasture days were merely baseball-minded businessmen, or farm workers, or anybody who didn't insist upon playing, and they were stumped when a new problem arose.

"Look it up!" was the cry of both sides.

If John couldn't remember, he was already "looking it up." If the situation wasn't covered by an explanation in the book, they would let it go, and make a rule to cover that point the next time it arose.

He learned place hitting on the school green. Swinging left-handed, he could hit a ball quite a distance with a full arc, known as "pull hitting." A sharp deterrent to this practice was the school-house in right field, and the Methodist church in right center-field. Both buildings contained windows, and each pane of glass, as he had learned that tragic night, cost fifteen cents.

Instead of pulling the ball with a full swing, he learned to shorten his swing, and to bring the heavy end of the bat around in a drag, and to swing late with a shortened grip. He learned to place his hits and, more important, to avoid smashing windows in right field. While only sixteen he had practiced the all-important art of bat-end control, the secret of place hitting, and a skill that I heard him bemoan as lost many times after the arrival of the "wagon-tongue" boys, and home-run behemoths in the early 1920's.

Because of an insatiable desire to express himself through this fascinating game, he had become valuable on the offense as a hitter, on the defense as a pitcher, and on the side of justice as an arbiter of ever changing rules. He was good to have on your side, because he knew how to take advantage within the rules. He could think up situations and strategies not yet in the book.

Team managers could always pay his fee by the simple process of betting more on their chances of winning. Gate receipts in those days were nonexistent. "Passing the hat" was still in the future at Truxton. Teams had backers, and when none was available, players put up individual stakes, pooled the money, and backed themselves. John might have got ten dollars from the East Homer manager. If so, that worthy would have been obliged simply to bet that much more on his players.

Teams were classified in accordance with how much money was needed to play them. A manager or organizer would hire players at a dollar or two dollars per man, with an extra five for the pitcher or a skilled hitter. This would total close to twenty dollars. Baseballs and umpire would bring the game cost to twenty-five, and such a team would be known as a "thirty-to-fifty-dollar game." There would be side bets among spectators and friends, and some of this money would be handed to the manager or organizer in gratitude. This is a practice even today.

The year of 1889 was one of peak excitement for John McGraw. The rule changes were drastic. Substitutions were permitted at any time. Padded mitts and masks for the catcher were permitted so that the receiver could stand closer to the batter and reduce the plague of stolen bases on muffed pitches. The four-strike rule was reduced to three, and seven balls to four. The flat bat for bunting was ruled out after five years. Fielders were permitted the use of gloves, padded for catching and fingerless for the throwing hand.

Most exciting of all for John McGraw was the story of the big-league Brotherhood revolt, and the list of published salaries in the baseball guide. His head began to swim as soon as he saw the fantastic sums paid to the giants of the game. Three, four, five thousand dollars for six months of doing what he had sacrificed everything to do because he loved it.

As a professional he could afford to wear the leather playing shoes, instead of the dollar-and-a-half "amateur" shoes of canvas sewed to leather strips. With new shoe plates screwed securely to the soles, he could really fly around the bases, no matter where the catcher was squatting.

It was a cold winter as usual in Truxton, but never were John's dreams more exciting. Never was he hungrier for a chance to play with a really professional team. He had done everything and gone everywhere to play. He had walked and sweated and hurried through chores and worked overtime to make up for game delays.

Then spring came and with it Bert Kenney's news. Bert was organizing the team that would represent Olean in the New York and Pennsylvania League. His brother Harry would remain in Truxton to run the hotel. John couldn't stand it. He simply had to go, and he said so. He pleaded for a chance. Bert wasn't sure. John was good, very good on local teams, but out in the organized competition—well, other kids all over America had worked just as hard, and played and sacrificed and driven their parents to distraction. And Bert couldn't play favorites, though he wanted to, you know.

John knew, for nobody had encouraged or helped him more

in baseball than Bert. Suppose there was a contract, and he failed to make good, Bert suggested.

"I'll return the money," John said. "I'll earn it, and return every cent."

Bert had a better idea. "I'll give you a contract, and if you don't make good, I'll loan you enough to go on."

And so John McGraw became a professional player in the spring of 1890.

6

MISS KATIE RUSSELL has made hats for me in Baltimore for more years than either of us will admit. All have been fashioned with care and love and taste peculiar to Miss Katie, and I wouldn't think of visiting Baltimore without stopping at her shop for my new creation. They have given me pleasure, comfort, peace, and joy, as any woman will understand. But none of them provided the thrill that was John McGraw's when he put on his first *real* baseball uniform at Olean, New York, in the spring of 1890.

Here was realized a fantastic dream, a veritable nightmare that had tortured his sleep, that had plagued his waking and walking and working hours for as long as he could remember. He had taunted himself with an almost unhealthy yearning, a fierce childish fixation that few outside of baseball can understand. He had poured all of his hopes and wishes into this one distant goal, and here it was, a delicious reality.

Only through searching retrospect can we evaluate or even appreciate the true depth of a boy's longing. Before me is John's first concrete link to the magical baseball world, his precious ten-cent booklet, *Our Boys' Base Ball Rules for 1877*, published by Norman L. Munro & Co., New York City.

With red and blue water paint, the first colors that appeal to a child, he colored the many baseball caps in the Peck and Snyder advertising as he imagined them to be. Some were solid red, others of red, white, and blue sections, others solid blue, or striped. One of the four stockings was striped red and white, a second solid blue, the third blue and white, and the fourth checkered blue and white. With great care he had striped or checkered the fascinating worsted web belts, one of which had "Captain" woven in the front.

The cap of his Olean uniform was cream white with two wide encircling stripes of bright red. It was pillbox shape with a hard peak. The shirt had long sleeves with buttoned cuffs, a soft, wide-front collar, and it was buttoned down the front. On one side of the break was O-L, and on the other E-A-N in large block lettering. The pants were cream-white knickerbockers. The belt and stockings were bright red.

The first official act of a uniformed team in those days consisted of rushing to a studio for a photographic exposure. Led by mustachioed Bert Kenney, the team posed with arms folded, but with OLEAN in plain view—Doyle, Fee, Judson, Ansell, Beggy, Shea, Egan, Heine, Wetzel, and seventeen-year-old John J. McGraw. Eleven in all.

John, of course, needed a personal photograph to send back home as proof of his new career. His father had doubted the wisdom of the precarious move. Mrs. Goddard was reluctantly willing, but worried. He promised many things, however—fame and money, good behavior, care of himself, and attendance to his religious duties.

The rush to the photograph studio was premature, because stark failure greeted John's first few games in league baseball. Bert Kenney had a pitcher and played John at third base. He hit fairly well, but he blamed the newness of the position for his wild throws across the diamond to first base. It was undoubtedly due to stress and strain and the nervous struggle to make good for his home-town sponsor. The team lost its first six games, and with only eleven on the team, John was benched!

There was no choice but to try elsewhere. Again, or rather, still, money was a problem. The team had failed to impress anybody. Attendance was almost nonexistent in a town that numbered more than five thousand at the time. And yet, Bert Kenney made good his pledge. He loaned John seventy dollars as a stake.

"Watch every penny of it, Jack," Kenney warned. "Make it last till you hook on somewheres. It may be a long time."

John promised and left Olean. Thirty-two miles to the east was the village of Wellsville, with a team and a ball park and a franchise in what was called the Western New York League. John hooked on. As Kenney's road in Olean grew rougher, more players were cut adrift to follow John. Judson, the second baseman, was first to arrive and then came Ansell, the pitcher. By mid-August Heine, the catcher, Shea, and Kenney himself were playing on the Wellsville team.

Despite the six black defeats at Olean, John had profited greatly from the brief engagement. Kenney was kind and understanding, but John never forgot that he had let down his Truxton benefactor. And he had established warm friendships among the Franciscan fathers who operated little St. Bonaventure's Seminary, founded in 1856 and which now proclaimed itself a college. The seminary was about three miles west of Olean on the Allegany road. Father James quickly saw the need for help and guidance and was one of the first to reach out and touch John just when a spiritual lift was needed most. Nothing else could alleviate the shock of nine errors in one Olean game, John's lifetime record.

But over the years I have learned that, no matter how brief or tragic a ballplayer's tenure in one place may be, it is never without its light moments. In greeting each other, old ballplayers lose no time at all recalling "that game when . . ." I have heard it so often, and I have seen John's stern look melt into laughter as he harked back to the quip, the joke, the embarrassment, the predicament. Yet most of the time while he was laughing in recollection, John was studying the old player's frayed cuffs, the soiled linen, the nervous hands, the general look of hard luck, and he would be reaching into his pocket and folding a bill for his old friend even as he guffawed.

The big laugh at Olean that spring came when a little dog ran out from the crowd in the home half of the ninth inning to grab a bounding baseball in left field. The dog avoided the fielder long enough for the batter to score a home run and win for Olean. What made it worse, the manager of the losing team, Al Smathers, had bet six dollars on the outcome.

Wellsville was different. John played at third base again, but not permanently. No player remained in one position long, on account of the limited roster. Pitchers played the outfield, and outfielders played anywhere. One game against Bradford, just across the Pennsylvania border, ended in a runaway score of 22–4. John pitched the nine innings and held the "Browns" to six hits. A hint of the competition may be gleaned from the fact that nine players played twenty-two positions. Two Bradford players, Daniels and Mooney, played four positions each!

Pitching against Bath, New York, John held that team scoreless and to four hits while Wellsville piled up twenty-nine runs on twenty-two hits. John himself, batting fifth, made three runs on as many hits in six times at bat. Wellsville's bitter rival then was Hornell, New York, as it still is today in the Class D Pony League. Bradford and Olean are still fighting in the same league sixty-odd years later as part of organized baseball. But against the bitter rival on August 26, 1890, John caught the opposition asleep.

The score was 8–8 at the end of nine innings. Wellsville failed to score in the tenth, and the "largest crowd of the season" cheered enthusiastically in the home half of the inning when shortstop Burrell reached third base with two out. A hit would win the game. Centerfielder Cameron was at bat. The pitcher was to follow as lead-off batter. The faded clipping tells it better than I can:

> Cameron hit a foul. McGraw with his eye alert as usual for "points" (rule violations) noticed that Burrell failed to return to his base and at once posted (warned) Ansell, the pitcher, and Umpire Byrnes. Ansell purposely threw a wide ball (a fair pitch would have nullified the necessity of the runner returning to the bag after the foul). Burrell ran home amidst wild enthusiasm on the part of the Hornell men, but McGraw got the ball, touched third and Burrell was declared out. Hornell refused to continue play and at the expiration of five minutes the game was declared forfeited to Wellsville by a score of nine to nothing.

John's batting skill was second only to that of outfielder Kellogg. John's figures for his first year in baseball were:

Team	Games	At Bat	Runs	Hits	Sacfcs.	Avg.
Wellsville	24	107	40	39	12	.365

Significant to the baseball student is the fact that John scored more runs than his total of hits.

One of the new players on Wellsville late in the season was Al Lawson, a fellow with high versatility and imagination. He had pitched a tryout game for Boston and two for Pittsburgh in the National League. That he won none and lost two failed to dim his luster in John's eyes. Here was a country boy's first glimpse of an actual big-league player. What was it like? Did he really *see* the great Dan Brouthers and Mike "King" Kelly with Boston?

No, they'd hooked up with the rival Players' League.

What about Pittsburgh? Did he see Billy Sunday?

Fast as a deer.

And the new manager, Hanlon, what was he like?

Great manager, great outfielder, great fellow. Wonderful man to work for.

Lawson practiced what is now called "name dropping" like an expert. He called off descriptions of imposing personalities that John had known for several years but only through the cold black letters and impersonal figures in his record books.

Lawson took a fancy to the idolizing little infielder, especially after the publicized forfeit-game victory over Hornell. When he invited John to make an "international baseball trip, all expenses paid, to foreign countries that would include Cuba," the offer was accepted without further thought, especially of money.

John returned to the Truxton House at the end of the Wellsville season and picked up where he had left off in the spring, working for his board and keep. He wasn't a great baseball success, but he hadn't failed. Lacking the money that went with high conquest of any kind, he couldn't exaggerate his status. Besides, Bert Kenney knew. Bert had extended the $70 loan again, because John needed all he had to safeguard his trip with Al Lawson's American All Stars. He visited with his father and was able to buy his brothers and sisters Christmas presents. After the New Year, he reported to Mobile, where he boarded the good ship *Mascotte* for his first and roughest sea voyage.

From the time he sailed through the narrow entrance to beautiful Havana harbor, John was always fascinated by Cuba. Cubans were the first foreign people he had ever seen, and he was amazed to find they had developed an enthusiasm for baseball that was almost matched by their skill at playing it.

47

As a result of the leadership of sports-minded Carlos Ayala, Havana had a ball park and grandstand that were the equal of most big-league grounds in the United States. Ayala was known as "the Nick Young of Cuba," a tribute to the perennial president and secretary of the pioneering National League in American baseball. Ayala had already founded a Cuban baseball league. He had organized the "Fe" (Faith) Club, the most popular organization on the "Ever Faithful Isle," which was under Spanish rule.

CARLOS AYALA

Ayala was a handsome man, John said, greatly resembling the pictures of A. G. Spalding in his prime. He had established and edited the first sporting paper in Cuba. He was official host to the All Stars, took them sight-seeing among the vast sugar mills and plantations, and explained that Cuba even then was turning out nearly two million tons of sugar a year. He showed them over Havana, which had a population of nearly a half-million people, almost all pitifully poor and restless in their shacks and hovels. He was sporting editor of two daily papers and three weeklies. His zeal in pioneering Cuban-American relationships greatly aided international understanding when his dominated people needed help seven years later to throw off the chafing yoke of despotic rule by absentee royalty.

"We laughed ourselves out of a couple of ball games," John told me later. "The Cubans hadn't heard about the pitching rules —keeping the right foot stationary, as we do on the rubber today. Either that or they didn't care. But most of the pitchers would wheel around with their backs to us, as though on a swivel, spin back, and take a good illegal run before winging the ball at us."

The invading party, besides John and Lawson, included Eddie Mars, of Syracuse; John "Pat" Luby, of Chicago; and Jake Wells, of St. Louis, all big-leaguers. Lawson had a truly pioneering spirit, as he proved later by starting baseball teams and leagues in all parts of the world. He dressed his team for the Cuban trip in brilliant yellow uniforms, and within two days little John McGraw was hailed by Havana fans as *"El Mono Amarillo,"* the Yellow Monkey. He made many trips to Havana in later years, and his arrival never failed to produce the headline, *"El Mono Amarillo está aquí!"* The Yellow Monkey is here!

The players were called other things, too. One of the pitchers, Harter, was sent home after starting and losing a single game. A Cuban writer wrote: "This man could do better sawing logs than playing ball."

While playing the first game, Lawson suffered a badly sprained finger, which put the pitching burden on Mars and Luby. But the promoter bandaged the injury, played errorless ball in the outfield through the ten games, of which his team won five. Average attendance was 220 fans a game, and the admission price ranged from 25¢ to $150 in inflated Spanish money.

Of John one Cuban sports writer said:

"Young McGraw is putting up a fine game at short. Here is a player who would add great strength to some good minor league team, being an A No. 1 fielder, batter, and base-runner. He played at Olean, New York, last season."

The touring party stopped off at Key West on the way back to the mainland. There the resourceful Lawson split his squad, looked up a few more players, and put on four exhibition games. This was a necessary expedient to finance transportation of his troupe by boat to Tampa and then to the north-central part of the state, where he hoped to play any of the big-league teams that traveled within hailing distance.

The Cuban trip was far from the bonanza that Lawson had

promised. Expenses had eaten up everything, but it was an unforgettable experience for seventeen-year-old John in other ways. It was a trip to a new world, for he had never seen or felt green in winter—only boot-high drifts of snow, steamy breath, and biting wind. Here were endless stands of marblelike royal palms, and fruit, melting sunshine and midsummer warmth that made the arms and legs feel good. It was the ideal temperature for training. Cuban ground was real loam, not tropic sand, and it sustained plenty of natural grass. And he had seen enough of the desperately poor to make his own youthful travail seem like luxury. John's high admiration for the courageous Cuban people never waned.

The sheer intrepidity, or unmitigated gall, of the nomadic Al Lawson can be gauged by the fact that he located the remains of his barnstorming team in Gainesville, fourteen years before the University of Florida was opened there. It was only seven years after the millionaire oil man, Henry M. Flagler, had "discovered" the state, to begin developments at St. Augustine. It was four years before Flagler's Florida East Coast Railway had been extended to Palm Beach, and five years before he opened the Royal Palms Hotel in what was to be Miami.

Some of Lawson's barnstorming players quit in disgust, which brought about one of John's earliest baseball "contracts," if not the first one. Lawson signed up at least five players with a blanket arrangement as follows:

OCALA, FLORIDA
February 14, 1891

Directors of the
Ocala Baseball Assn.
GENTLEMEN:
We, the undersigned baseball players, and members of the Ocala Giants, agree to play with the Ocala Club until further notified for board, shaving and washing expenses; also a cigar once a week.

(Signed) JOHN J. McGRAW
C. F. THORP
J. CONNER
ED MARS
FRANK STRATTON

I can't say what John did with the cigar, unless he sold it for pocket money. He never smoked in his life. But I don't think the contract was entirely binding. Only Stratton played with the Ocala team. Thorp, Conner, and John played with Lawson as part of the Gainesville team. John said he remained partly because he had no other club to go to, but chiefly because he liked Lawson and his adventuring spirit. Besides, they had found a kindred baseball spirit in twenty-five-year-old "Lou" Burkhim, who backed, managed, and befriended the intrepid and penniless baseball pilgrims.

The quarters at Gainesville were bare, and the food was skimpy. The field was sandy and treacherous, a makeshift affair on which John and Lawson worked daily to improve it. A few rows of open bleachers made of boards sawed from local slash pine were called the "grandstand." With some freed-slave labor, they managed to erect a small portion of fence. Then with his split squad and a few fill-ins, Lawson announced a five-game series "for the baseball championship of Florida"!

Pitching for Gainesville, Lawson allowed Ocala two hits in winning each of the first two games. John covered himself with a degree of glory in the field and at the plate. Drawing from three to four hundred customers every few days, Lawson's troupe went on to win the state baseball honors. The telegraphed results attracted considerable attention in the several big-league training sites to the north.

John's reward for youthful loyalty to Lawson came when Pat Tebeau, a great player-manager of the day, brought his Cleveland Indians, including the great Cy Young, from Jacksonville for a widely publicized exhibition game. The visiting line-up reeked of well-known players. Tebeau started Eddie McKean, John "Dirty" Doyle, Charlie "Chief" Zimmer, Clarence Algernon "Cupid" Childs, George Davis of later New York Giant fame, and a rookie first baseman named Jake Virtue. John was properly impressed, but not outwardly. He badgered the big names on Cleveland and heckled them at every opportunity, like a terrier that barks to avoid or scare off trouble, rather than to create it. The local excitement mounted, and 650 spectators paid to see the game on March 26, 1891, a pivotal day in John's life.

Opposed by the veteran Leon Viau, Lawson pitched as never

before. He held the strong Cleveland batting order to five hits, but six of his players committed eleven errors, and the champions of Florida lost by a score of 9–6.

As so often happened in his life, John's competitive spirit rose to meet the big challenge. He made great stops and throws on the field and played errorless ball. He swung fearlessly at Viau's deliveries, hit three two-baggers in five times at bat, and scored half of his team's six runs.

Several clubs had expressed interest in hiring him, and seemed to lose it when he asked $125 a month with $75 advance money. After the Cleveland game, the offers flooded him. The total finally reached twenty-eight, including one from his old friend, Bert Kenney, who was putting another team in Olean.

"Look out for the interests of John McGraw," Al Lawson advised. "Nobody else will. Make sure you get the best offer, and don't take any nonsense."

John then telegraphed the same terms to several clubs. Rockford, of the Illinois-Iowa League, wired that the money was being expressed. John went to the express office on March 30, and found an order for $35 from the Davenport manager, Hugh Nicol, of Ramsay, Scotland. John returned the money. He accepted a remittance of the full $75 telegraphed from "James Plumb, manager, Cedar Rapids, Iowa."

Within a couple of weeks John had his first bad press. His services were claimed by Guy Hecker, manager of Fort Wayne in the Michigan-Indiana League, and by Davenport and Rockford of the Illinois-Iowa League. Rockford announced the hiring of a lawyer "to stop his coquettish antics, and teach him a needed lesson. At best he is but an experiment and is altogether too gay for a young blood who has had but one season out."

John's selection of Cedar Rapids proved a good one. The league was strong, comprising six cities with population of better than 20,000: Rockford, Joliet, Quincy, and Aurora, Illinois; and Cedar Rapids and Davenport, Iowa; Ottawa, Illinois, and Ottumwa, Iowa, were about 5,000 each with great baseball interest.

The city's big day came on April 16, two weeks before the opening of the regular season. Cap Anson and his famed Chicago White Stockings arrived in town for an exhibition game. They were en route to Chicago from Denver, where they had trained.

In 1891 Anson was starting his twenty-first year in professional baseball, and he brought a dazzling line-up of luminaries "right out of the baseball guide." He had Jim Cooney, Elmer Foster, Bad Bill Dahlen, playing the first of twenty-one big-league seasons; Jim Ryan, a Chicago star for seventeen years; Cliff Carroll, Walter Wilmot, and Malachi Kittredge to do his catching. He brought two pitchers, Wild Bill Hutchinson, of Yale, winner of a record 122 National League victories in 1890-91-92; and Dandelion Fred Pfeffer, who served as umpire.

The big-leaguers were greeted with city-wide enthusiasm all day, and a heavy downpour of rain early in the afternoon. Hundreds of fans had buggied in from the outlands and huddled dispiritedly in the drenching downpour. The skies brightened at 3:30, and Manager Plumb rushed to the park to find more than six hundred paid admissions in the covered grandstand. That really brightened things up. The groundkeeper was put to work with a pail and sponge.

John's biggest disappointment was in being unable to wear his new Cedar Rapids uniform of black stockings, black knickers and cap, with a white blouse and coat. But Manager Plumb said they had cost too much to be ruined in the mud.

At 4:45 P.M., April 16, 1891, John J. McGraw, rookie shortstop, stood on the same baseball field with Adrian Constantine Anson, greatest baseball player in the world. He was a giant of a man, six feet three inches tall, 215 pounds, yellow hair, and large eyes of bright blue. Both of them stood in the same mud in the same game of baseball, little Jack McGraw of Truxton, New York, and legendary Cap Anson, born only thirty-two miles to the west in Marshalltown, Iowa. Jack was eighteen on April 7. Anson was forty on the eleventh.

The big man stood at the plate to open the second half of the second inning (the home team had batted first) and swung hard in missing two pitches. He batted right-handed. Jack edged to his left. Anson swung hard again and hit the next pitch with great power. Jack raced to his left and leaped to spear the line drive with his gloved hand. It was by far the finest play of the game, but he tossed the ball to Cutler, his pitcher, and returned to his position with a newly acquired nonchalance. Anson stood at the plate studying little John with great interest.

53

Chicago was leading 1–0 when Henry Fabian, Cedar Rapids center fielder and lead-off batter, started the sixth inning with a base hit off Hutchinson. John sliced the next pitch into left for a clean hit, sending Fabian to second. Yelling at Anson to get out of the way, he rounded first base, and returned quickly. He looked up into the big man's face and growled:

"Say, old timer, so that's what you call big-league pitching! We'll murder that fellow."

But the laugh was on John an instant later. Both Cooney and Foster were thrown out at first, and after the second out, Anson looked over to see Henry Fabian actually stuck in the mud ten feet from third base. Expecting a force-out at third, Henry decided to slide for speed. He hit the goo too soon, lost his momentum, and then settled in what seemed like quicksand. The whole ball park began to laugh as Henry thrashed around in the slick mud, trying to regain his feet. Anson was laughing, too, but threw the ball quickly across the diamond to Bill Dahlen, who sloshed out carefully to tag the struggling Henry for the third out.

Chicago won, as everybody expected, but only by 2–0. John had another field day at shortstop, making seven assists and three put-outs without once slipping in the mud. After the game Anson complimented him and asked how he would like to play for Chicago someday. John never remembered what he replied, but insisted that it was nothing fresh, because the game was over.

The I-I League season began on schedule with a burst of enthusiasm on the part of newspapers and fans. John attracted attention everywhere with his speed, his sure hands, and his growing aggressiveness. He developed a confidence that mushroomed into a conviction that he was better than anyone in the league. He couldn't prove it by his batting average of .275, but his hits were timely, and he always hit first or second in the line-up. And he scored 68 runs in 85 games.

By mid-August he had played in 85 games for Cedar Rapids, but he felt uneasy about the league. Attendance was miserable. Aurora was reorganizing. Players on other teams complained about "back pay." Cedar Rapids was solvent, but the league wasn't. A third of the games wouldn't be played. John had received a flattering offer from the four-club California League. He was actually considering it when Bill Gleason, of Rockford, approached him.

54

"I have a letter from Billy Barnie, manager of the Baltimore Orioles," he said. "Wants to know how good you are."

John's shoe-button eyes blinked. Gleason could be fooling, but he didn't look it. He was a veteran and a famous shortstop for the St. Louis Browns when Charles Comiskey was manager.

"I scout a little," Gleason confessed. "Tip off my old friends about promising young players. They appreciate it—sometimes."

"Well, you can tell Barnie I'm just about as good as they come," John said.

A few days later Gleason met John again and advised him to join Baltimore "as soon as you get the train ticket from Barnie." John received the ticket, said good-by to several of the players, and headed for Baltimore.

This was not contract jumping, for there were no written contracts. And even if contracts had existed in the league, they wouldn't have contained a so-called reserve clause at the time. In this case, John acted to protect his future, because only one minor circuit, the California League, finished the season of 1891.

A few days after he had left Cedar Rapids John stood before an unbelieving Bill Barnie. The Baltimore manager, a former player, was nearly forty, and the first sight of John seemed to age him ten years.

"You don't mean to say that this is the ballplayer I've been writing to Billy Gleason about!" he gasped. "Why, you're just a kid—can you play ball?"

"If you don't think so," John replied with growing indignation, "get me out there and watch my smoke. I'm bigger than I look."

John weighed exactly 121 pounds, and had to wear the uniform of Sam Wise, a stocky six-footer who had gone to Washington.

Barnie got him out at Union Park against the Columbus Senators with Phil Knell, a twenty-seven-game winner in the American Association that year, pitching. John played second base and kicked his first chance for an error. Batting for the first time as an Oriole, he struck out with the bases full.

But before the game ended he had hit safely, scored a run, made a sacrifice hit, and fielded five chances without an error to help Baltimore win by 6–5. He was a big-league ballplayer at last.

7

IN ORDER TO evaluate fully and fairly John McGraw's eleven pivotal years in Baltimore, which began when he was only eighteen, it is necessary to understand the simple principles of organized baseball. It is important to remember that, as both business and sport, the game is made up wholly of human beings. As a result, it reflects human qualities, or lack of them, in administration as well as on the field.

The many men, great and small, who form these two sides are as night and day. The player is not the administrator. The administrator who has never played professionally stands quite apart from the player he employs or directs. They are separated by an intangible gulf. It is the difference, for instance, between banker and inventor, producer and actor, publisher and storyteller.

And yet, like force and resistance, one cannot exist without the other. Baseball could not survive as we know it, enjoy it, and even live comfortably because of it, without the efficient administrator. And there could be no administration without the player—the boy with the ball—whose dreams and struggles and practice have given him unique appeal to those who pay to see him demonstrate his skill in organized competition.

Between these two dynamic forces there have been many differences over a period of more than eighty years since 1870, when the athletes began to play for money as well as fun. Differences have ranged from laughably minor disputes to irreconcilable cleavages. And they run the gamut of human motives from avarice to zeal. Organized baseball, frequently disorganized, has produced as by-products of its splendid growth, honor and disgrace, wealth and poverty, profits and bankruptcy, lasting friendships and undying hatreds, joyous marriages and tearful divorces, evangelists and drunkards, personal happiness and ghastly suicides.

But as a sport or business, the game no more justifies a single cry of shame or censure than does civilized society in its desperate struggle for survival with dignity. My sole reason for going so deeply into this aspect at all is to portray my husband accurately.

He was a controversial but very human personality and an integral part of baseball's development as both player and administrator.

I wish with all my heart that I could make this story of John McGraw one long series of light and happy recollections, a chronicle of harmless baseball characters, screwballs, and patsies. I could fill a volume with these tales from John's smiling lips and twinkling eyes. I could fill another book with stories of his so-called feuds and fist fights, most of which he lost. All this is part of him, I know, but it is only part of him. I want to tell the whole story of how he became the most hated, admired, envied, feared, and respected player of all time; of how he became the game's greatest manager; of how he permitted his skill, reputation, integrity, and aggressive personality to be used as a foundation stone when the so-called front office of baseball was in a state of bankruptcy, and the playing field a disgraceful shambles.

And so, for the Baltimore part of my story I must go back again, this time to the early 1880's where, with the help of vital notes, John's vast collection of clippings, key correspondence, records, and tireless editorial checking, I find that baseball received new impetus in Baltimore from a good-natured bewhiskered brewer who saw the game as an ideal method of selling beer.

As I said, players started playing for money as well as fun in 1870 with the formation of the National Professional Association. The secretary of the Washington club, thirty-year-old Nicholas E. Young, became its president. Member teams lost no time proselyting star players from one another. Four of the greatest, including the game's outstanding pitcher, A. G. Spalding, were induced to switch from the four-time championship Boston team to Chicago. The head of the latter team then went east to spearhead the formation of a sounder and better league with proselyting outlawed, and the National League was born on February 2, 1876. Young was appointed secretary.

This is the same organization that operates today, though its path of survival was a rough one indeed. During the first twenty-five years it had teams from thirty-one member cities. Some were expelled. Some resigned and re-entered. Of the eight charter members, only Chicago remains today.

The league pioneered for six seasons on a noble platform of equal and prearranged schedules, fifty-cent admissions, no Sunday games, no gambling or pool selling, and no alcoholic beverages to be sold on the premises. It was not always a strong league. In 1881 it lacked membership in five of the biggest cities, New York, Philadelphia, Brooklyn (then a city), St. Louis, and Baltimore.

The situation invited opposition, and it came from the sports department of the Cincinnati *Commercial-Gazette*, a name to be remembered. The baseball editor, O. P. Caylor, enlisted the administrative help of James P. Williams, who had founded the first so-called minor league, and the backing of several capitalists. One of these was the legendary Christ Von der Ahe, a St. Louis brewer. The attraction to investors was a twenty-five-cent admission for "the working man" and the sale of beer on the premises. The new league had lined up only four members at the first meeting in the fall of 1881 at Cincinnati.

Harry Von Der Horst, in association with his brother Herman, operated the Von Der Horst Brewing Company in Baltimore at 10 Belair Road, just off West North. It was one of the forty-odd wholesale beer sources in the city at the time, and competition to slake Baltimore's thirst was understandably keen. Harry's only retail outlet was Von Der Horst's Hall at 9 South Street near the wharves in which he also maintained downtown business offices. Herman and his wife Christina, did a little language interpreting from their Carrollton Avenue home.

Through channels of trade during the winter, Harry learned of Von der Ahe's move in St. Louis. He attended the spring meeting in Philadelphia, March 13, and returned with an Association franchise for Baltimore. The Athletics of Philadelphia made the sixth team. Harry then leased a large lot at Huntingdon Avenue (now Twenty-fifth Street) near Greenmount Avenue, and erected historic Union Park. He built a fine grandstand to seat six thousand people, and even double-decked it. He also put in a roomy restaurant with tables in an end section for convivial people who might come out by buggy or horsecar merely for beer. Watching baseball was never compulsory.

Though the ball-park beer garden was novel, the general idea was not. Baltimore had a substantial "Alleman," or German and middle-European population, and the term, "Let's have a *gemüt-lichkeit*," (good feeling, in this case from beer) was common and popular. The farsighted brewer of the period gratuitously provided pavilions in shaded gardens, tables for picnics, band music for singing and dancing, and even fields and cinder paths for athletic meets. He went to great length and expense to provide reasons for happy congregation, and happier consumption of his product.

Von Der Horst hired Henry Myers, of Providence, to organize and manage his first Baltimore team, which won only nineteen games in an abbreviated season and finished last. During the winter he signed Billie Barnie, one of the Association organizers, and Barnie brought in his Brooklyn Atlantics, who had played in the Eastern Association with the New York Metropolitans. The Mets, and also the Columbus, Ohio, Senators joined up to make it a strong, eight-club group and force recognition and co-operation from the rival National League. They agreed not to raid each other's stars or hire outlaw players.

The outstanding developments in Baltimore baseball of 1883 were several. The skill of the personnel was completely undistinguished, but the team for the first time was called Orioles, among other things. They won only 28 victories, against 68 defeats. Von Der Horst, however, made a profit of $30,000 in the second season of his Union Park operation.

As long as the fans jammed the horsecars out Greenmount Avenue, Von Der Horst seldom worried about the club's artistic success. On October 4, 1884, he staged baseball's first doubleheader, two games for the one twenty-five-cent admission!

After that came turnstiles, and annual rule changes. There were two years of strong competition from the efforts of disgruntled players to manage their own financial and playing destinies through co-operative leagues, 1884 and 1890. To get needed revenue all owners worked the exhibition-game angle to death. Half of the patrons didn't know whether the big-league teams were playing official games or exhibitions. Von der Ahe's team of St. Louis champions under the popular Charles Comiskey played 96 exhibition games in 1886.

Von Der Horst soon was swamped by administrative problems, and all he had wanted was extra beer sales. Too late he learned that Von der Ahe had not only bested everybody in players, receipts, and four straight pennants, but had outmaneuvered Baltimore in league councils. The St. Louis and Pittsburgh owners dominated the Association at all points. Rather than buck the new Players' League, as well as the rival National, Von Der Horst quit the American Association in 1890 and put his team in the weaker Atlantic Association. When Brooklyn's desertion in August left an opening, he applied for readmission and played Brooklyn's remaining thirty-four scheduled games.

The distraught brewer started the 1891 season with Billie Barnie, but fired him in September. He was undecided about the next year, and he knew little of what went on behind the scenes.

Von Der Horst's eight years of baseball and beer-selling had impressed substantial citizens in Baltimore. They noted the growing interest among the fans and the increased horsecar travel on the Greenmount line. After the league-wide financial distress in 1890 and 1891, Von Der Horst made no secret of the fact that he was disgusted with western shenanigans in the Association, and that he might use Union Park for carnivals instead of baseball.

The situation drew the attention of one William H. Herzog in late summer. He learned that the National League was secretly moving to coax four strong Association teams into forming a twelve-city league. The four culls would be scrapped or bought off, and Washington was favored over lukewarm Baltimore for retention. Herzog found quick response in forming a syndicate to salvage the Orioles. The idea was backed by Robert C. Crain, of the Baltimore Traction Company; proprietors Stokes and Kelly, of the popular Eutaw House and Kelly's Hotel; and the cigar-manufacturing Mencken brothers, August and Henry. They were father and uncle of twelve-year-old H. L. Mencken, whose first jibe on morals and manners, or lack of both, had not yet been published. The syndicate pooled $35,000 for the project, which included a new baseball park.

Crain anticipated early electrification of the transit lines and negotiated successfully for the Brooks estate near the Druid Hill Avenue powerhouse. The owners agreed to lease the grounds free of charge on condition that the lot be put in good shape.

During the third week of September, Herzog wrote to Nicholas Young, then in his seventh year as National League president, revealing the syndicate's plan to save Baltimore baseball by purchasing a franchise. Young replied on October 3, 1891, stating that no vacancy existed and that sale of a franchise couldn't be considered until the November meeting.

Instead of keeping the matter confidential, as Herzog had asked, Young spread the information freely. Presently newspaper columns teamed with discussion of the Baltimore group's plans and possibilities. Von Der Horst offered his holdings to the syndicate for cash. Herzog refused because of several undesirable leases and features in the proposed contract, which included use of Union Park and no interruption of the brewer's beer sales.

Von Der Horst then appealed to Young for a National League franchise. The request was taken under advisement with a suggestion to clear it through the despised Von der Ahe. Though long ridiculed as a bulb-nosed, German dialect comedian, Chris had somehow emerged from a sleazy situation of baseball politics in St. Louis as a power in council chambers.

The National League began a secret four-day conference in St. Louis on December 3. Another was staged in Indianapolis, John T. Brush's headquarters, on December 15. From this latter meeting came the new twelve-club National League. Rival teams in Philadelphia and Boston were bought off. Milwaukee, which had replaced Cincinnati, was scrapped as was Columbus. Four Association cities were admitted: Louisville, Washington, St. Louis, and Baltimore. Von Der Horst got the franchise, and Herzog's civic-minded syndicate was dissolved.

"After my first Baltimore game," John McGraw once said, and laughed at the painful recollection, "I never knew what happened or what might happen. I remember only one important thing about our September road trip. It was a little man with a bright red coat and cap in Columbus, Ohio. He went through the small grandstand yelling in a booming voice how it was impossible to tell which player was which unless you bought one of his hand-printed score sheets for a nickel, with or without a pencil. He also sold his own roasted peanuts. All through the games he waved his cap at fans and even at the players. He was a happy and friendly fellow supporting a wife and five kids in Niles, Ohio, on a simple idea. I met him—you couldn't avoid it—and joked and talked with him and learned that he was an English iron molder named Harry M. Stevens.

"But the rest of the trip, and for six months or more, it was like being tossed around inside a big, rolling barrel. I had no contract, no promises, no money. But within a space of eight months, I had four Baltimore managers, and one of them was a beer salesman!"

Such was "organized baseball" in late 1891 and early 1892. Many pioneers were struggling in their own way to prevent a great ideal from falling into chaos. Each believed sincerely that he had the correct answer and acted accordingly. The Baltimore Oriole situation didn't begin to straighten out until after a guiding genius named Edward Hugh Hanlon arrived from Pittsburgh in late May.

"Ned had a wonderful faculty of organization," John recalled. "It was a trait he never had a chance to develop until he reached Baltimore. His policy was always one of construction. People hailed him as a developer of inside baseball, which was right, but he was a greater organizer and field builder than a field general.

"Another thing: he was a great outfielder and could really go get 'em."

If pressed, John would admit that he never saw Hanlon really play. They had been in different leagues, and Hanlon wrenched his knee badly just before taking over the Orioles. He appeared in only eight games, and his leg was unequal to the strain.

John's proof that Hanlon was a great player came from a yellowed clipping of a game played at Denver, Colorado, on October 28, 1888, between the American All Stars and Cap Anson's Chicago Nationals. The teams were on their way around the world with A. G. Spalding, and Hanlon was an outfielder on the All Stars. The well-thumbed clipping reads:

Almost out of sight and into the blue sailed the ball, and away across the field sped Hanlon at a rate of speed that a professional would have been proud of. Marty Sullivan, who had hit the ball, in the meantime made the dust fly around the runaway; just once Hanlon turned to look above, and then ran on again faster, if possible, than before. Suddenly, however, he stopped, turned his face to the crowd, ran backward for 15 or 20 feet, then threw his hands up above his head; at the same time his heel struck a hillock of sand and pitched him headlong through the air upon his back. As he fell, however, his right hand was held above him and as he sprung to his feet the crowd saw that he had the ball. For probably five seconds the big assemblage held its breath, and then as the famous outfielder started in for the diamond such a cheer went up as one rarely hears on the ball field. For baseball enthusiasts and lovers of the game, it was, indeed, a scene for an artist, and Hanlon was cheered and cheered until he paused to raise his cap in front of the grandstand.

"And that was in an exhibition game, too," John would sigh. "With *bare* hands!"

After playing 31 games for the Orioles in 1891 and batting .245, John returned to Truxton and Mrs. Goddard's hotel for a few months. He declined another chance to barnstorm in Cuba, and spent the winter among old friends and older haunts. He enjoyed the holidays as never before when they brought news that Baltimore would be in the National League after all.

On his nineteenth birthday, John McGraw stood in the damp and chill clubhouse at Union Park wondering about two things: whether the weather and grounds would be dry enough for opening day with Brooklyn the following Tuesday, and if he would ever have enough nerve or hair enough to join the seven mustachers on the Orioles. Half of the team had lip decorations that ranged from the gigantic soup-strainer carried by Captain George Van Haltren to the dainty fishhook effect of pitcher John Healy.

George Cobb, Lou Whistler, Jack Pickett, Curt Welch, and the big catcher, "Yank" Robinson, had no such trouble with low visibility. The only trouble Wilbert Robinson had was with his weight. After taking off at least twenty-five pounds, he still looked fat. Yet he was fast and shifty. Like most well-weighted men, he was good-humored, and John liked him. Yank was nine years older and always talked about "Ma and the kids" in Philadelphia.

"If this situation holds its own," Robinson confided, "I'll move Ma and the kids over."

"How many kids do you have?" John asked.

"Four—all devils. Their mother's Irish."

"What's her name?"

"Mary, but I've always called her Ma."

And so did most baseball players for the next forty years.

Because of the uncertainty of things, particularly financial, the

Orioles took no spring training trip. "Van" Van Haltren was captain, but Von Der Horst had relieved him of team management pending the outcome of his deal with last-place Pittsburgh for Ned Hanlon, a $4,000-a-year player-manager. The Oriole's manager pro tem was John W. Waltz, Von Der Horst's best beer salesman.

The players had trained on calisthenics for nearly a month in the Baltimore Athletic Club gymnasium at Eager and Charles Street under the direction of Professor John C. Doyle. He had special Indian club exercises for pitchers, dumbbell exercises for catchers, rowing-machine activities for outfielders, and rope-skipping for infielders. In fact, Professor Doyle had devised an "ideal" training course for baseball players. At the price, considerably less than the cost of a trip south, John W. Waltz bought it as a bargain. Seven months later the beer salesman still insisted Professor Doyle's course had nothing to do with the last-place finish.

"He was wrong," John always said with a chuckle. "If it hadn't been for Professor Doyle we wouldn't have finished that high!"

John's biggest day of the year by far in that first full season with the Orioles came on June 6 and brought him face to face once again with the great Cap Anson and his Chicago Colts at Union Park. Hanlon, having taken over a last-place club, was trying to get acquainted with all the players. John was only a substitute, and starting him at all was more experiment than judgment.

John remembered the Chicago pitcher well. He was Jack Luby, who had worked half the games for them on Al Lawson's Cuban trip. The Orioles had all possible information on Luby before he faced them for "first licks" in the last of a three-game series on June 6. The home team elected to bat first, and were hot enough to set fire to the grounds. Billy Shindle opened with a double. Jocko Halligan singled. The great Anson made the first of his four errors on a throw, and Shock was safe. Welch walked. Whistler doubled. McGraw singled. Anson made another error. On and on it went. The inning wasn't over until the Orioles had scored seven runs, one of which was a home run by the pitcher, George Washington Cobb. Thanks to eleven Chicago errors, Luby's seven bases on balls and twenty-one hits, the Orioles humbled the great Anson by a score of 23 to 1.

The work of the infield was magnificent and surprised everybody [the account of the game reads]. McGraw was the bright particular star. His work at second base was as fine as anything ever shown by the masters of the profession and drove the crowd wild. McGraw supplemented his beautiful play in the field with a great display at bat. He cracked out two singles and a three-bagger and ran the bases like a deer. Just at present the little second baseman stands very solid with the baseball public.

He also stood very high with Cap Anson, who remembered him from Cedar Rapids the previous year, for he offered Hanlon one of his best outfielders, Jimmy Ryan, for John. It was the talk of the clubhouse as the sweating players paraded to the basins and tubs with buckets of water for their sponge baths.

Four days later it was Chris Von der Ahe's turn to be burned by the Oriole's fire. The prosperous St. Louis beer merchant and property holder had become more than a colorful character in baseball; he was now a manager who broke a record amount of English daily in the coacher's box. His great player-manager, Comiskey, joined the Players' League movement for 1890. Von der Ahe got him back for 1891, only to lose him to another merchant, John T. Brush, who had become a power in baseball by financing Cincinnati in the new twelve-club National League.

But after ten years of watching, Chris was certain that he knew enough to manage. Besides, he was popular all over the league. He didn't care whether he was laughed with or at, as long as people were in the park. At the slightest provocation he called the umpire a crook and the opposing players murderers and thieves. Red-faced, sporting a long handle-bar mustache, and with his hair brushed in a low loop over a naturally meager forehead, he was indeed a source of humor in every way.

"But after a while," John once revealed in a tone of regret, "he was more pathetic than funny, even to us players. Of course, we'd roast him to a turn and poke fun, but he didn't know field strategy or opposing weaknesses. He led his team into the second division and remained there. During the mid-nineties he had twelve managers in three seasons—four each year!"

The unforgettable June 10 game was the first of a double-header and came the day after a 6–6 tie with St. Louis. The Orioles should have won it before darkness, and the players were smarting. They took it out on three of Chris's pitchers, Charles "Pretzel" Getzein, J. P. Young, and Theodore Breitenstein, scoring twenty-five runs in the first six innings. With the help of ten St. Louis errors, the final score was 25–4 and an easy victory for Sadie McMahon. Even more memorable to John was his first glimpse of Wilbert Robinson as a truly outstanding ballplayer. Hanlon was trying out young catchers, and Robbie usually got last call. The newspapers referred to him as "Yank" because of his Massachusetts origin, but he confessed to John that he disliked the name.

"I don't want to be mistaken for the real Yank Robinson," he said. "Five years ago that bird made seven errors in seven chances at second base."

Robinson did just the opposite in the big-score game against St. Louis. He went to bat seven times, hit three singles, then a double, and three more singles. He also stole a base. John went to bat six times, made three hits and three runs, but Robbie's seven hits for seven times at bat put down everybody. It has stood as a major-league single-game record ever since. Many players have made six for six, but none could get the seventh.

Von der Ahe's woe was complete in the second game. The Oriole hitting continued against Getzein, who started for St. Louis. In winning 9–3, they totaled nineteen hits for twenty-two bases—forty-four Baltimore base hits in eighteen innings. John and Robinson got only one apiece in the second game.

"We were all playing our heads off to show the new manager, Hanlon, how good we were," John explained. "That and some luck accounted for our going wild during those first two weeks in June. We all knew that Hanlon would clean house. We had some pretty strong drinkers on the team, but they played hard, too. Four days after that double-header against Von der Ahe we lambasted Louisville for eighteen runs on seventeen hits. I remember that one best of all, because I didn't get any of the hits. I didn't mind so much failing against Alex Jones but when that Leon Viau stopped me, I wanted to hit him with the bat. He was easy to hit for three doubles in Gainesville the year before!"

But John really exploded a few days later when Hanlon spoke to him about going out "for experience." For instance, if he

66

played a summer at Mobile, Alabama, he'd be a better player. "And a smaller player, too!" John stormed. "I know about Mobile. Sometimes it's like a furnace. It's in the tropics. I'd sweat right down to nothing. If you send me there, I'll run away."

John was getting a salary of $200 a month. At that price he felt he'd be welcome anywhere—Chicago, for instance—if Hanlon released him. Hanlon kept him, but on the bench, because he made a deal with St. Louis for a thirty-three-year-old infielder, John "Cub" Stricker, and John concluded bitterly that the beer salesman, Waltz, was a pretty good manager after all.

8

ALLEGANY COLLEGE was a small school in the fall of 1892. As St. Bonaventure's today, it is quite large. When John enrolled immediately after the close of the Orioles' season on October 15, it was just a group of small, stove-heated buildings huddled in the wooded Cattaraugus Hills on the road from Olean to Allegany, New York. About 125 miles southwest, at Meadville, Pennsylvania, there was another Allegheny College, spelled differently, and accounts of John's early days erroneously placed him there.

It was Allegany College when he entered, and St. Bonaventure's Seminary and College when he left a few years later. The friars ended the two-Allegheny confusion by honoring the great Franciscan scholar and philosopher, John of Fidanza, who was canonized St. Bonaventure in 1482 by Pope Sixtus IV. Of all the profound theological and philosophical writings that won him the name of *Doctor Seraphicus*, St. Bonaventure's best were those that touched the heart and the imagination. And the good Franciscan monks at Allegany emulated their patron saint in influencing the life of at least one humble spirit, John J. McGraw.

During those dismal days at Olean in the spring of 1890, John had promised Father James he would return as soon as possible to resume his interrupted schooling. It wasn't an easy decision. It was a strange one for professional baseball in those days. Too many players spent their winters in the corner saloon telling of their great deeds and exploits, or cooking up alibis for why there were none to tell.

After paying his Baltimore bills—tailoring, clothes, what was due at the Eutaw House, and the $70 owed to Bert Kenney, John had little enough. Even so, he managed to start a savings account in Baltimore and have enough for his board and room at Allegany College. He paid for his tuition by setting up a plan to start a baseball team and an athletic program after the first of the year.

Father James was deeply impressed with the way John could recite the contents of the ever changing baseball rule book. The elderly friar believed that anyone able to understand the *Spalding Guide* for 1891 would have little trouble making up Latin and reading the classics. And so John, in his twentieth year, joined classes made up of boys five and six years his junior. But he was still small, and he worked hard, and there wasn't time for worry about the difference in ages.

Besides, he was a big-league baseball player. His name was in the record books. He had played against the greatest in the game. He had clippings to prove it!

Against Philadelphia:

> Both nines fielded well. McGraw's brilliant work at second clearly earned many rounds of applause for the little second baseman. The run-getting began in the first when Baltimore scored on Shindle's single, McGraw's sacrifice and Stovey's double. . . . In their half of the sixth Baltimore started again on singles by Vickery, and Shindle, and McGraw's sacrifice. . . . In the ninth they scored three more on singles by Cross, Robinson and Shindle and McGraw's double.

Against Brooklyn:

> There was a trio of fine two-base hits, no less than five three-baggers, clean ones, too, and, to crown all, a nicely placed home run which should completely establish young McGraw's reputation as an excellent and promising player.

And on the final day, also against Brooklyn:

> In the first game the visitors bunched their hits and the Baltimores their errors in the first and fifth innings. The errors of McGraw and Stovey, two apiece, were very costly.

He had played in 76 games, about half the schedule. He batted 288 times, made 77 safe hits, stole 14 bases, and scored 41 runs. His batting average was .267, a 22-point improvement over his first year. He fielded .901.

> McGraw is one of the youngest and most promising youngsters in the business [said a writer in the Baltimore *Sun* during the winter] and undoubtedly has a brilliant baseball future before him. He is as lively as a cricket, plays an admirable game both in the infield and the outfield and has a good eye for the ball. He hits hard and often and, under the experienced hand of Manager Hanlon should show great improvement this year. He is quiet and industrious and has made a host of friends.
>
> Last year McGraw was not assigned to a regular position on the team, but his work when he was on the field was almost above criticism. This year he will probably be played regularly at second base unless "Cub" Stricker makes up his mind to sign and the management makes up its mind to sign him. If a vote of the bleachers were taken however, on the question of whether McGraw or Stricker should be given the bag, the little fellow would win by a large majority.

Long before the snow showed any sign of disappearing, or even letting up, John was starting his baseball program at Allegany. They began in the cellar of the largest building—now Alumnus Hall. They cleared out one corner and erected a batting cage of old lumber and chicken wire. "They" were students, principally Shehan, Clune, Purcell, Murtaugh, Smith, Clyne—all candidates for the team. Miles Sweeney became team manager and assistant to John. From this humble beginning, in a cramped corner of a cellar lighted by kerosene lanterns, the college got its start in a regulated baseball program. John showed them how to practice as much of baseball as the limited quarters would permit. Sweeney took on the responsibility of leading the calisthenics and directing the actual baseball movements. By mid-March, when John had to leave for training with the Orioles, the team had a written program, detailed instructions, and a full set of rules for "inside" baseball, or what passed for it at the time.

The Orioles gathered at Charleston, South Carolina, on Monday, March 20, and there John received what I believe is the deepest impression of his life. Hanlon had been one of baseball's higher-paid stars, particularly after joining the outlaw Players' League of 1890. Records showed his earnings as totaling $25,000 in ten years. More important he had enough to buy controlling interest in the Orioles from Van Der Horst. Hanlon was now president of the club. The brewer was treasurer and Waltz, the salesman, was vice-president. Hanlon was complete boss.

His authority was reflected in many ways, but chiefly by the signing of new players and the release or trade of the old. From an old outfielding friend, Danny Long, a native of California, Hanlon had received some good tips from an untapped source, the Pacific Coast. He signed Billy Clarke, a catcher; Henry Reitz, an infielder; George Treadway, an outfielder; and Edgar McNabb, a pitcher. George Van Haltren, who had been traded to Pittsburgh for twenty-year-old Joe Kelley late in 1892, offered to bet Reitz $50 that Treadway would lead the Orioles in hitting.

The new power to hire, fire, trade, sell, or release players ended the bickering between players and management of 1892. Hanlon was supreme boss, and those who violated any rule of conduct on or off the field could be, and were, punished severely. There was no more running to Von Der Horst for sympathy or trouble-making. The good-natured brewer emphasized the change in management by wearing a lapel button that read, "Ask Hanlon." The buttons were so popular that he put in a supply and handed them out at Union Park after the season opened.

"Nobody on the team seemed to be set in one spot," John recalled in explaining the Hanlon methods that impressed him so. "He had us all worrying, not only about where we would play, but *if* we would play. Billy Shindle had a business and refused to report till he got it in good hands. We thought Hanlon would fire Sadie McMahon, but he didn't. Hanlon wouldn't let go of a player he thought could help him. But he was sensible about it. Tim O'Rourke could knock over a wall with his base hits, but he insisted upon knocking over the glasses, too, and even Tim's high batting average couldn't keep me from taking his shortstop job."

Judging from the way John could remember every move Hanlon made, I imagine he must have studied the manager by the hour all spring. He couldn't get over the way players hustled and listened to the voice of authority. Young Joe Kelley seemed to take charge in the outfield. When Shindle reported, Hanlon put him at third with John at shortstop. Reitz took over second base.

The season opened in Washington on April 27 with a two-game series, and the Orioles dropped both. They defeated the Senators in the Oriole opening at Union Park, but late May found them in tenth place and Hanlon made another great move. He gave Billie Barnie, manager at Louisville, two infielders, Tim O'Rourke and Bill Brown, for Hugh Jennings and Harry Taylor.

"He was a loud but likable fellow," John said in describing his earliest impression of Jennings. "He had the reddest hair, a reddish, freckled face that looked blotchy because of the sunburn, and a mouth that was usually open. At first I thought he was noisy to cover up shortcomings, because I had never seen him hit much. But Hanlon had watched him two years before. Not only could he hit, he could play at either shortstop or first base.

"I think one play in Lousiville convinced Hanlon that he ought to get Hughie Jennings. It was in the first week of June, a few days after we had lost a fourteen-inning heartbreaker at Philadelphia in front of a big crowd. I was on first base in this Louisville game, and running when Robbie smashed a beauty over second base. This red-head Jennings leaped through the air, knocked down the ball, and fell on it. He didn't have time to get up and catch me, so while he was still rolling on the ground, he threw to Dandelion Pfeffer and forced me at second by a whisker. Only a great player could have made that recovery and throw."

Hanlon continued to experiment with line-ups through the first half of the 1893 season. His greatest satisfaction came from the hard work and victories of the popular Sadie McMahon. Not only was the pitcher's deportment and disposition above reproach; he refused to be hampered by the lengthening of the pitcher's distance from the plate to 60 feet 6 inches. The old-fashioned box was replaced by a pitcher's plate, 12 by 4 inches. Instead of a step or advantage of any kind, the pitcher was obliged to keep his rear foot on the plate during his windup and delivery. It was a decided advantage to the batters, and all averages rose, but Sadie worked in 49 games and won 23 while losing only 16.

John's favorite pitcher of that year was Charlie "Crazy" Schmidt, a left-handed rookie, and he always recalled him with a smile.

"Everybody liked Charlie. Win or lose, he was good-natured. But he almost drove us crazy with his little dope book. He kept a written record of what pitch was best to throw at each hitter. It was the first I'd ever seen.

"Crazy would stop right in the middle of pitching to check a batter's weakness. He would turn to a page, nod in agreement, return the book to his shirt pocket, and throw the ball. We tried like mad to get Crazy's book, but he always hid it. Then one day he dropped his shirt carelessly after a game and left the locker room. That was my chance. All I wanted to know was what he had down for Cap Anson's weakness. So, I rushed over, sneaked the book out, opened to the A's, and what do you think he had written down for Anson? *Base on balls!*"

John and Hughie Jennings struck up a laughing acquaintance early in 1893 and decided that the world would be a happier place if they roomed together. Hanlon, when asked, said it would be all right "if you keep out of trouble." Little did he know—or maybe he did—that this was one of the smartest decisions he ever made. There began one of the game's great friendships that outlived both by a generation or more. On my way to New York City from a recent visit to Truxton, I stopped off at Scranton, Pennsylvania, to visit Grace McWilliams, Hughie's only child, and now a grandmother of four. She had suffered an accident, and her spirits were low. So, I brought her home with me, and the visit to New York, with shopping, dinners, and theater, did us both a lot of good.

John and Hughie were truly kindred spirits. Kindled would be a better word, because they set each other afire. Behind the laughing freckled façade, John found one of the finest minds he had ever encountered at his own level. I hasten to add that first baseman Harry Taylor's was an excellent mind, which he proved by leaving baseball at the end of the year to study law. Ten years later Governor Higgins, of New York, an Olean boy, appointed him to a judgeship in Erie County, and he remained on the bench through several elections.

But Taylor was nearly thirty and more mature. Jennings seemed younger than twenty-four, and John seemed older than twenty. Since Hughie was born a day ahead of John, they always celebrated their birthdays together, April 6 or 7, whichever was more convenient.

John had finally caught up with "another boy and a baseball," for Jennings confessed that he had gone through the torture of making the game his meat and drink as a hungry boy in a poor coal-mining family. He was born in Pittston, Pennsylvania, a coal town between Scranton and Wilkes-Barre, and made his home in nearby Moosic. Already he was a hero in Moosic. He could be mayor or constable or even have a county job because of his big-league baseball playing.

"No two people ever talked more baseball than Hughie and I," John has said. "No two people ever had so much unexpressed baseball packed away in their craws, so many experiments and un-tried ideas. We had dreamed and schemed for so long we couldn't wait till one was finished with a new play before the other had a new one to tell. Often we'd find ourselves talking like a streak at the same time, not even knowing the other couldn't hear. We would talk all night. We could forget sleep entirely, there was so much baseball to talk. I never thought I'd ever meet anyone so baseball-minded as Hughie. And I never thought I'd ever meet anyone so gentle and patient and understanding."

The Oriole fledglings began their flight in midsummer of 1893, and, without any reflection on the rest of the team, this was the genesis of the "Old Orioles." It was essentially a spiritual thing that permeated the team, one player at a time. It was not a sudden conflagration, but rather a gradual awakening to the fact that games could be won in many new ways, and that two or three or four baseball demons with one-track minds were working at it twenty-four hours a day.

At the base of it all, of course, was their implicit faith in Ned Hanlon as a great baseball mind and manager. Players will give

McGraw and Jennings leaving the clubhouse

beyond their utmost when they believe deeply in their manager.
And they are like lost souls when they do not believe in him and
lack leadership. They try just as hard, but the results are never
the same. They are a half-step slower on an infield hit, a few
feet short on the long drive, a few put-outs shy of a great nine-
inning pitching job.

Its counterpart can be found in many fields of endeavor where faith in somebody or something is a vertebra, if not the entire backbone, of achievement. Among the Orioles of 1893 it asserted itself in a late-season burst of cohesive play that heralded the end of Hanlon's experimentation. They finished only eighth in the twelve-club race, but they won ten out of twelve from sixth-place Brooklyn, and eight out of twelve from second-place Cleveland. Frank Selee's Boston team of speed and imagination had won all the games from the 1892 Orioles. In 1893 they lost two of the twelve. It was a beginning.

John had appeared in 127 games, missing only 3. He batted 475 times, made 156 safe hits, led the Orioles in stolen bases wth 40, made 25 sacrifice hits, and scored 123 runs. His batting average, .328, was the best of his career to that time.

Wilbert Robinson, the portly catcher, also had his best of eight big-league years. His average, .328, was his first over .300, and he had caught nearly 100 games. So pleased was he with the new Oriole management and policy of hustle, that he moved "Ma" and the kids over from Philadelphia.

"It looks good here," he told John. "I'm going to find myself a business and get settled."

"What kind, especially?" John asked.

"Oh, a hash house, I guess—some kind of beanery. People always have to eat."

"We had a good attendance all year. We'll all get raises."

"It won't be enough. I want a house of my own, a good one and a big one for the kids, not too far from the park here. So, I'll open a beanery somewhere. That'll do it."

John hoped so, and left for upstate New York, but with company. He prevailed upon Hughie Jennings to start school again, and Hugh persuaded easily. I'm afraid the lure of higher education was less of an attraction than the chance to talk baseball all winter and play it while the snow was still on the ground. It makes no difference. More important is the knowledge that their love of baseball was responsible for two poor boys returning to the classes and books they had left so many years before. John had written Father James about his new-found lode of baseball enthusiasm. The friar welcomed Jennings and made certain that their room was comfortable and big enough "to swing a bat in."

The baseball fever was contagious, and Jennings proved more

than an asset when the squad gathered in the cellar for opening practice. Six holdovers from the 1893 team were joined by twenty-five hopeful candidates. The energetic Miles Sweeney had sent challenging letters to many eastern colleges, particularly Seton Hall, Fordham, and Manhattan. John divided the squad and turned over half of them to Hughie for fundamentals and the "new inside stuff" they had attempted at Baltimore.

And when the squad was otherwise occupied, John took Hughie into the cellar and put him in the improvised cage. While his fielding was superb, Hughie's right-handed batting had impressed nobody but John, and he was determined to do something about it.

"You pull away from all the curves," John said, "and most of the close pitches. You never get back in close enough, and they get you on the outside pitches. Now, if we put the plate here—"

He shifted the square (it was not a pentagon until nearly ten years later) so that Hughie would have to stand with his back against the chicken wire.

"You can't pull away!"

John began the first of many hours of pitching baseballs to the inside of the plate. Hughie scraped his back and his elbows and tore his sleeve, but he soon got into the habit of striding forward with his front foot instead of "into the bucket." John said it made all the difference in his timing and the way he met the ball. How they managed this and the team training and the studying, I don't know, but they got passing marks in everything, Hughie corrected his hitting, and their classmates regarded them as the finest of fellows.

"Not until a week before we left for training," Hughie once revealed, "did we learn that the whole class had chipped in to buy us a couple of gold-headed canes. We tried to stop it, but the hard-earned money had been sent away for the canes. I shrugged it off, but not Mac. He surprised me by taking it seriously, and I saw a new side of him that I'll away's remember.

"Mac memorized a long acceptance speech and made me his audience. I'll never forget how solemnly he stood at the head of the bed. I sat at the foot. Daniel Webster, in his famous oration at Bunker Hill, had nothing on my little roommate, and if I got a million, I couldn't keep my face straight.

" 'I'm not half as funny as you'll be when you get up to talk,' he said, 'if you don't frame up a speech.'

"True enough, when my time came, I fell back on the old stuff, that I was too full for utterance. While I wasn't nervous, I couldn't think. After I sat down I remembered many things that I might have said, but Mac's acceptance rolled off his tongue like water off a duck's back. Three times or more he stalled, as if seeking the right word, although he had learned it by heart. The stalling was intentional, to make believe it was impromptu.

"But that was Mac all the time, all our years. What was worth doing, was worth doing well. That was the secret of his preparation. That's been the secret of his success."

Two major developments occurred during the winter of 1893–94, and both contributed heavily to the popularity and success of the Baltimore Orioles. One was the electrification of the streetcar lines out York Road. Transit from the downtown business center became rapid, especially by way of the Blue Line, a direct route. Two other lines poked along, despite the new power, for pickups and departures. The Blue Line was always packed for the 3:30 ride to Union Park.

The second development was a trade of players by Ned Hanlon and Charles Byrne, real-estate operator and owner of the Brooklyn Bridegrooms.

"It was not only Hanlon's greatest trade," John insisted, "I consider it the greatest and shrewdest trade in all baseball history. Later events made a gift of Shindle and Treadway for Willie Keeler and Dan Brouthers look good, but when the deal was set, everything was in Byrne's favor. Both Treadway and Shindle had turned in good years. In fact, they had better years in ninety-four with Brooklyn. Brouthers was a large, overweighted veteran of thirty-six. Keeler was not only an untried rookie infielder; he was the smallest fellow you ever saw. He claimed five feet four and a half, but wouldn't let anybody measure him.

"The greatness of the trade was in Hanlon's being able to see in those two extremes exactly what he needed. He gave away known value for the biggest man in the game who was just about through, and the tiniest rookie in baseball, only twenty-two, who wasn't much of an infielder. Hanlon got one more great year out of Brouthers, and put Keeler in the outfield where he became a star in his very first year."

Hanlon had figured on John to replace Shindle at third base, and on Brouthers' known power to make up for Jennings' weak hitting at shortstop. He got the surprise of his life the first time Hughie took batting practice at the Macon, Georgia, training camp. Hughie waded into the pitch, stepping straight ahead, and blasted it to the outfield. He hit several more cleanly, meeting the ball and placing it. Gone was his "bucket foot," thanks to the winter at college.

It is sheer heresy in many quarters to suggest that the Old Orioles didn't invent everything worth while in scientific baseball. They could be credited, and often were, with originating just about everything associated with inside baseball. And with outside baseball, too, for John was the first, according to his own claim, to hook his finger into the belt of a runner at third, from the back, and yank him off stride when he started home after a sacrifice fly. He was also the first to wind up with the belt in his hand. The intended victim, Pete Browning, simply unbuckled his belt when he detected the trick and raced to the plate holding up his pants.

The Orioles were the first, I believe, to be caught with an extra baseball hidden in the high outfield grass "for emergencies." It might have remained a secret, had not Steve Brodie failed to see that Joe Kelley had already thrown the real ball in and that it wasn't necessary to throw in the emergency baseball. Brodie's blunder, I'm happy to report, cost the Orioles a game by forfeit.

They may have been the first team to use beefsteak as an inner sole in baseball shoes. I'm not sure. I do know they actually bought a thickness of steak and placed it between their stockinged feet and the bottom of the shoe. It sounds strange, but, with the shoe laced tightly, their flying feet had no blisters from friction. The layer of steak acted as a "solid lubricant." It would be a fairly expensive practice today, even with the cheaper cuts.

Whether first or not, they thought of everything, and there is glory enough for all the pioneering and dreaming players of early days. I have heard John say many times that Frank Selee, who led Boston to National League championships in 1891–92–93 and again in 1897–98, ranked fairly close to Ned Hanlon as a smart and constructive manager. Let's assume that his great hitters and speed boys, such as Hugh Duffy, Herman Long, Bobby Lowe, Billy Nash, and their counterparts on other teams, were also "boys with a baseball" and tried many things in the gay nineties.

I know that countless daytime field experiments followed the nocturnal discussions of John and Hugh after they had become roommates in midsummer of 1893. They did such things as measuring each other's running speed from first to second against Robinson's throw to second. One would stand on second base and shout when he caught the throw. The other would mark the farthest progress. In that way they measured leads off first, the slides, and the speed from first to third.

They tested running speed from home to first against different speeds of rolling balls down the third-base line.

They practiced hitting to spots vacated when either shortstop or second baseman ran to cover second on an attempted steal.

John and Hugh hit thousands of fungoes to each other before practice, and even after a hard ball game, to correct fielding mistakes, or covering an area. And of the infielders, only the first baseman wore a padded glove.

Signs from batter to runner or vice versa had been used for several years to warn of impending sacrifices and stolen bases.

John and Hugh were working on the hit-and-run principle in 1893. John was a fast runner, and so were Jennings, Reitz, Brodie, and young Joe Kelley. The longer pitching distance invited more attempts at base stealing. It was natural for any alert player to see that an infielder, rushing to cover second base on an attempted steal, would leave a wide and inviting gap to the hitter. All a base stealer needed, then, was a batter who could hit the ball through a given or vacated spot.

The very best arrived at Macon, Georgia, in late March of 1894, and his name was William Henry Keeler, of Brooklyn, New York. He batted left-handed, and he held his bat with a wide-apart grip that enabled him to control the heavy end and push a ball in any direction. He had dark, beady, twinkling eyes that had no equal for accuracy.

"We tested it in many exhibition games," John recalled. "When I reached first as lead-off batter, I'd make a false dash for second. Keeler would note which infielder was covering. Then I'd sign that I was going on the next pitch. Invariably he would hit the ball through the vacated spot. With a running start, I'd keep on going and, to the amazement of the opposition, I'd wind up on third base. If the outfielder made an error, I'd try to score.

"By the time we completed our exhibition games, we had that play down so every runner on first, including big Robbie, could sign for the hit-and-run play. But that wasn't all. We discovered it was impossible for anybody to field a well-placed bunt down either foul line in time to throw out a runner at the plate who had started from third base with the pitch. We timed it over and over and it worked even with short bunts. That was the origin of what is now called the squeeze play."

Speed was the answer, and Hanlon had gathered a bunch of super-speedsters, hitters, and young men who loved to run and play baseball. Here is the fabulous and somewhat historic Baltimore Oriole line-up of 1894: John McGraw, 3b, aged 21; Willie Keeler, rf, 22; Steve Brodie, cf, 26; Dan Brouthers, 1b, 36; Joe Kelley, lf, 22; Heinie Reitz, 2b, 26; Hugh Jennings, ss, 25; Wilbert Robinson, c, 29; Sadie McMahon, p, 26.

Few teams in baseball have started a season with greater city-wide support than the Orioles had for their opening on April 19, 1894. An overflow crowd of 15,000 jammed the double-decked Union Park and stood many deep behind ropes around the perimeter of the field.

And no group of fans were better rewarded, for Hanlon's team was afire. They completely outclassed John Montgomery Ward's New York Giants. Many home rooters accompanied the Giants, one of whom was a 350-pound loud speaker named "Judge Collum." Also in the party were twelve New York newspapermen who dismissed Hanlon's "training" in Georgia with a shrug. The Giants had merely played a few exhibition games.

It was a different story when Willie Keeler turned his back at the crack of Mike Tiernan's bat in the second inning, yelled to the crowd to open up, hurdled the restraining rope, and caught the fly ball!

It was different when Ward, George Davis, and Van Haltren, all speedy runners, were thrown out by Robbie as they tried to steal second base. On the other hand, Jennings, Brodie, John, and even big Brouthers stole second on the high-priced and poorly conditioned catcher, Duke Farrell.

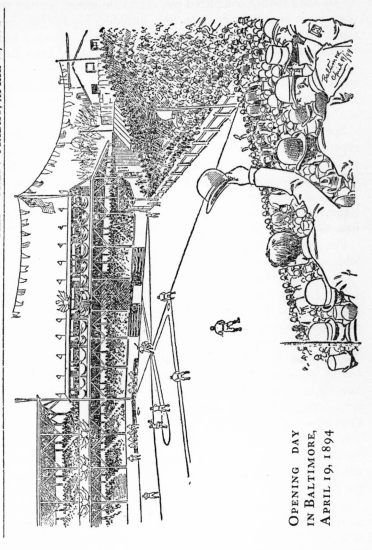

Opening day
in Baltimore,
April 19, 1894

"The biggest difference was the perfected hit-and-run trick," John insisted. "The experiment of the year before became an important weapon of attack. We worked it three times in that opening game to win easily, eight to three. McMahon's outpitching Amos Rusie helped, but John Ward didn't realize our attack was prearranged. We used it twice in the second game on a damp field and won, twelve to six. The score of the third game was four to three, and we scored the winning run on the hit-and-run. We took the four-game series from a hand-picked team that was supposed to murder us. We made *thirteen* hit-and-run plays in the series!"

The correspondent of the New York *Recorder* wrote:

> The Baltimores under Manager Hanlon's clever guidance were in perfect trim and they "played the game of their lives." One thing was demonstrated: Every club in the league will hustle to take a trip south next spring.

Boston followed the Giants into Union Park for a three-game series starting April 24, a schedule of seven games with the two most powerful clubs in the league. Boston had the Orioles beaten, 3–1, after eight innings of the first game. Then Charlie "Kid" Nichols was victimized by the biggest ninth-inning rally on record. It seems especially unusual now, but home-team managers of those days, when only one ball was used, liked to get in first licks on the lively and unscuffed ball. When they finished with Nichols and his successor, Jack Stivetts, fourteen runs had been scored, and the Orioles won, 15–3.

But Boston got even in the morning game of the Bunker Hill Day double-header. It was observed on June 18, a Monday, because of the Sunday rule against baseball. Hanlon was short on pitchers, and he let Tony Mullane pitch to twenty-two batters in the one inning. He gave up eleven hits, seven passes and hit a batter, Lowe. At the end of the inning, Boston had sixteen runs, and Wilbert Robinson retired so he would be in shape for the afternoon game. Mullane wasn't relieved until the seventh, and the final score was 24–7. But it didn't discourage the Orioles. They went out and took the afternoon game, 9–7.

They went to New York to open the Giants' season at the Polo

CHEERING THE TEAMS AS THEY MARCHED UPON THE FIELD.

Grounds before 18,000. It had rained heavily. The ground was soft and muddy. McMahon's pitching was spotty, while Rusie held John, Keeler, and Brodie hitless to win by 9–6.

But they bounced back and ran again when the footing got dry, and John said half the season went by before the rest of the league realized the true meaning of the apparently "wild" base running. Newspaper accounts repeatedly lauded the effect of the new hit-and-run attack. An early-season report of a 9–2 victory over Washington is an example. It reads:

> McGraw and Keeler got in some of their fine teamwork at bat for which they are becoming noted. They commenced the scoring in the first inning. McGraw took first on balls. Keeler hit safely behind him and Mac went to third easily on George Tebeau's bad throw-in.
>
> In the sixth inning McGraw was on first again with Keeler at the bat. At the signal, Mac started to steal second, and Keeler picking out an open spot, placed the ball past third for two bags, bringing home Mac. Keeler is the finest place hitter on the team.

But John always insisted that the peak of Oriole hitting perfection came with the Decoration Day series with Pittsburgh, or Allegheny City, as the north side of the town was called.

"We gave the prettiest exhibition of place hitting that I ever hope to see. It was like a contest among us. The left-handers poked the ball into left field, and the right-handers poked it into right, time and time again. The Pirates were completely confused and their catcher-manager, Connie Mack, was even more so. The fans at Exposition Park had never seen anything like it—and neither had we.

"It almost silenced the little score-card fellow with the red cap from Columbus, Harry Stevens. He didn't yell quite so loud about his score card and peanuts, but he sold just as many—more, in fact, because he had a lot of kids working for him through the holiday crowd. He sure was a hustler.

"We silenced those Pirates again when they appeared in Baltimore right after Fourth of July. They had a nine-run lead on us at the end of four innings. Then eight of our nine began to hit—

eight, because Steve Brodie had hit from the start. We knocked out Frank Killen and continued with a kid named Tom Colcolough, and we won fourteen to ten. Brodie finished the game with three singles, two doubles, and a triple, six for six, the best day of his life."

Many have the mistaken idea that the Baltimore Orioles of 1894 were invincible. They were far from it. In late season they had to break the league record for consecutive victories in order to win. They were undoubtedly the fastest, headiest, and most daring of their era, and the best-hitting team of all pennant winners with a grand average of .348. All averages were helped from 1893 on when the sacrifice was not counted as a time at bat.

But Hanlon had pitching problems throughout the season. Sadie McMahon was the only steady winner with twenty-five. In contrast, the Giants had two pitchers, Rusie and Meekin, who totaled seventy-two of the Giants' eighty-eight victories. Fortunately Hanlon had no financial worries, and other clubs did. He took some of his fantastic profits and bought pitchers—Duke Esper from Washington, George Hemming from Louisville, and Kid Gleason from Chris Von der Ahe, who was rapidly going bankrupt in St. Louis.

"The money was wisely spent," John said. "We started our final western trip only a half-game in the lead. When we clinched the flag in Cleveland on September twenty-fifth, we were four games ahead. To do that we had to win eighteen straight games and twenty-four of the last twenty-five. We might've won all of them, if Robbie hadn't slipped in the mud trying to make a play."

The final averages of the eight regulars were: Kelley, .391; Brodie, .369; Keeler, .367; Robinson, .348; Brouthers, .344; McGraw, .340; Jennings, .332; and Reitz, .306. Hugh Duffy, Boston outfielder, set the all-time individual high that year of .438, but no team record in baseball equals the Orioles' of 1894.

Some cities are rather famed for their outbursts of fervor when their team wins a pennant. Washington in 1924 was a moving thing. St. Louis in 1926 was fairly raucous. Brooklyn in both 1941 and 1947 was far over on the frenzied side. But nothing in the annals of the game matches the sheer municipal delirium that greeted the Baltimore Orioles' first National League championship.

The tributes were countless. The crush of hysterical fans at

NING 🛡 HERALD

6148.   BALTIMORE, WEDNESDAY, OCTOBER 3, 1894.

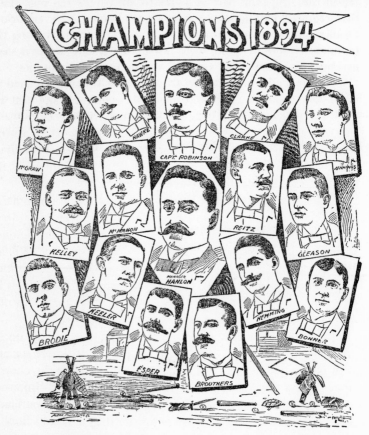

THE BALTIMORE BASE BALL CLUB.

Camden Station for the evening arrival has never been equaled in the history of the city. The entire police force was alerted, and most of it was used to prevent unbridled demonstration and physical harm.

A gigantic parade formed at the station, and everybody got into the act. Anyone caught with his mouth closed was threatened with arrest. Nearly two hundred floats, representing every industry in the city, took part in a free-for-all parade ten miles long that required two hours to pass a given point. The victorious Orioles, already weary from many stops for receptions along the homeward route by train, were distributed among a dozen sleek carriages complete with political or mercantile dignitaries.

The evening parade, lighted with Chinese lanterns, wended its noisy way from the station through a circuitous route that included Holliday Street, Lexington, Charles, Saratoga, Howard, and terminated at the Fifth Regiment Armory, where a formal reception awaited. Mayor Latrobe greeted the players individually. The National Guard, with fixed bayonets, held back the unruly crowd struggling to gain entrance.

After many speeches, and letters of regret from league officials and executives of rival clubs, the Orioles in full evening dress, were transported to the Hotel Rennert for a full-scale banquet. Chairman of the Dinner Committee was ex-Postmaster William W. Johnson, then in a prosperous towing and lighterage business and soon to be police commissioner. The secretary was Ernest H. Wardwell, editor of the *Commercial Nugget;* and the treasurer Alfred E. Booth, the oyster king.

The menu of that memorable October 2 banquet, which finally got under way at 10:30 P.M., was standard for Baltimore society, with plenty of Booth's oysters, fish, and lobster. But the cherry-stone oysters were washed down with plenty of dry Sauternes. The soup à la Julienne was followed by delicious Amontillado. The chicken sauté à la Marengo was joined by a steady flow of Mumm's Extra Dry. Every Oriole was regarded as a king and treated like one with gifts of cash and jewels and unprecedented adulation in dozens of private parties that followed the banquet. The entire city held open house!

And two days later, after they had lost the first game of the

87

postseason series for the new Temple Cup to the despised Giants, John announced publicly that he would play no more.

"It is shocking and a disgrace to baseball," he said, fighting against tears and the sting of a 4–1 defeat. "I have kept myself in trim for these games, notwithstanding the temptations that have beset me every hour since our return to Baltimore. The great reception we received here was too much for some of the boys, and they have rested but little and practiced less. The New Yorks were in the pink of condition, and are under supplemental contract to Mr. Ward. We are under no sort of contract now, and are really without a head, and therefore without everything that goes to make a winner of a baseball team. The team is not in fit condition to play, and we should forfeit the Temple Cup to the Giants. I was induced against my will to play the first game, but I will go no further."

9

A FEW OF THE more sober Orioles joined the threat to abandon the 1894 play-offs for the Temple Cup, but John was at Union Park next day to lead them on the field for the second game. Though a "disgrace," it was baseball and, in his youthful code, had to be held above personal opinion and pride. However, his frank and public stand in behalf of the game itself won him a host of sympathizers and friends, especially among the newspaper people.

All player contracts, or Articles of Agreement, as the standard contract was called, had expired. They were six-month documents starting on April 1 and ending on September 30. Paragraph six specifically cited penalties of $25, $50, $100, and suspension without pay for successive jousts with "malt and spiritous liquors during the said term of his employment." The contract contained permission to release players for any reason with ten days of pay, and for an advance of $30 against salary if the player needed it to buy new baseball shoes (uniforms were supplied). But it contained no clause reserving services. The only holdover agreement was a stipulation binding the player to honor the club's "option or right to renew this contract with all its terms, provisions and conditions for another period of six months beginning April...."

Neither John nor any of the Orioles was employed. The owners were to split the play-off gate receipts 60–40, but there was no clear-cut division for the players. Actually, they received very little, but this did not disturb John, because the Baltimore fans had made up generous purses for each player through donations and theater benefits at both Ford's Opera House and Harris' Music Hall. He recognized only one factor: a moral obligation to play the games, and as well and as skillfully as possible, regardless of the written word. Virtually running his head off in 1894, he had made 175 hits and scored 155 runs in 123 games, thanks to 77 stolen bases, his all-time high. He knew only one way of playing the game—to win.

Duke Esper had pitched and lost the first game. Kid Gleason was beaten in the second, 9–6. The teams left for New York where George Hemming lost the third for the Orioles, 4–1. After a day of idleness, Bill Hawke started the fourth game on October 8. He had pitched the first no-hit game from the new 60-foot distance the year before, but a joyous Polo Grounds crowd saw Baltimore routed in a great Giant "victory," 16–3. Manager Ward had alternated his 72-game winners, the great Amos Rusie and Jouett Meekin.

John returned to Baltimore only long enough to pack his things and hurry to the cleaner air of upper New York state. He was concerned over more than the Orioles' dissipation and loss of the Temple Cup. The sporting papers had denounced the desperate steps that league officials had taken to keep the New York club in the championship race, for certain games lost by the Giants during the season had been ordered replayed on a "technicality." One writer wrote:

> Baltimore's has been clean winning, too. There have been no duplicating of chances and playing over again those once lost. There have been no legislative or administrative wire-pulling—no political economy nor anything of that sort, but the manager and the boys have simply played ball and won it out straight from the shoulder. And it has won it, too, in

the face of acknowledged manipulations in favor of New York, by the baseball economists who conscientiously but mistakenly believed they were doing the best for the business of baseball when they were conniving to give New York more chances to win than any other club. What an exceedingly dangerous thing to do. The baseball public is a mercurial one and quick to take alarm. Fortunately, it knows the pennant was won fairly on the merits of the team, but how would it have been had New York just barely pulled through after the acknowledged gerrymandering in that club's favor.

It is a great deal more dangerous than monkeying with a buzz saw. The sooner the League suppresses such maneuverings as those of Mr. John T. Brush the better it will be. The danger of one man with an abortive sporting spirit holding large financial interests in more than one club of the League and playing both ends and the middle to accomplish an object for the purpose of personal financial gain in the main end at the sacrifice of true sporting result has now been shown to be more than a mere danger—an absolute fact.

The New York Giants situation in 1894 was one of several club problems involving near-insolvency that plagued National League officials. John B. Day, a baseball pioneer in Manhattan since 1881, had defeated competition from the old American Association, but not the Players' League, who built their park on the lot adjoining his Manhattan Field grounds. The high cost was loss of corporate control of the Giants in 1892. In order to remain in business during lean years, Day had exchanged blocks of stock for help from A. G. Spalding, the baseball manufacturer and co-owner of the Chicago club, and from Walter Spalding, Alfred's partner in the sporting-goods business; from Arthur H. Soden, owner of the Boston club; from John T. Brush, owner of Cincinnati, who, by "selling" him minor-league Indianapolis in 1890, had contributed the great Amos Rusie; from Andrew Freedman, New York real-estate operator and Day's close friend in Tammany politics; from Edward Talcott, Brotherhood backer. Centralized authority, such as Ned Hanlon exercised in Baltimore, was impossible in New York because of the diversified and absentee ownership.

More important, as the one writer had pointed out, none of the League officials seemed disturbed by the fact that owners of at least three competing clubs controlled the finances, policies, and fate of a fourth. This was known as syndicate baseball, and all participants appeared quite satisfied to continue with it.

The Giants might have gone on indefinitely as a league-controlled operation but for a thoroughly unexpected coup by John B. Day's friend and Tammany ally. Andrew Freedman, New York born and graduate of City College, achieved the impossible by first picking up small blocks of Giant stock, which had little individual value. He then purported to act as "agent" for James A. Bailey, of Barnum and Bailey circus fame, in buying A. G. Spalding's large holdings in the New York club. With more than half the outstanding shares in his pocket, Freedman revealed that he had bought strictly for Freedman and emerged in incontestable control of the Giants. As was the custom, he elected himself president immediately. Soden in Boston and Brush, the Indianapolis clothing merchant who owned Cincinnati, were left with nothing to say in the operation of a club into which they had poured many thousands of dollars to sustain it over a period of years, including the Indianapolis franchise.

There is only one type of fury more furious than a woman scorned. That is the unbridled temper of a minority stockholder in control who suddenly finds himself shorn of control. Freedman's Giant coup after the 1894 season overturned the whole National League applecart. As an object of reprisal and vilification through the next eight years, Freedman completely altered the course and destiny of organized baseball.

An "agreement" for the coming season reached John at college early in March. It was on the blue-lined stationery of The Baltimore Base Ball & Exhibition Company, Inc., E. E. Hanlon, President; H. H. Von Der Horst, Secretary; J. W. Waltz, vice-president, and read as follows:

John McGraw Esq.

St. Bonaventure's College

Allegany, N. Y.

DEAR SIR:

   Enclosed find contract calling for $2100.00. We leave here on the 11th. Should you not make the trip and report later, you will do it at a reduction of salary.

                                        Yours etc.

                                        ED HANLON

                                        #2403 N. Calvert St.

John signed the contract and explained to Hanlon that he simply had to finish getting the Bonas in shape to start their base-ball season. He added that both he and Hugh were in excellent condition and would reach Macon, Georgia, in far better shape than some of the early arrivals.

   The Orioles of 1895 emerged, you might say, from their fresh-man state, except that they were far more advanced than sopho-mores. Matured isn't the right word, either. A competitive flame, burning within each player, gave them a defiant swagger and individual personalities. They knew that the entire league was waiting to extinguish their flame, and they developed high con-tempt for every other player by simply working at it as a project.

   Behind their rapidly expanding ego, however, were the best hitters, the most daring and original play makers, and the greatest collection of base stealers ever assembled on one team. Just look at the outfielders' batting averages for the four play-off years:

Name	1894	1895	1896	1897
Kelly, lf	.391	.370	.370	.389
Brodie, cf	.369	.365	.294	—
Keeler, rf	.367	.394	.392	.432
Stenzel, cf	—	—	—	.351

Now add to this the four-year record of two infielders:

Jennings, ss	.332	.386	.397	.353
McGraw, 3b	.340	.374	.356	.326

Certain conditions admittedly were different from today, but the Orioles weren't playing today. They operated in the nineties when eleven other clubs had the same opportunities. Their stolen-base record is beyond comparison with any team record in all baseball, for they totaled between 350 and 400 stolen bases a season. Yet they never had a base-stealing champion. Billy Hamilton was the perennial king. This was in the days of the "lively feet."

They considered themselves team champions in every department of the game, and their only fear was that the opposition wouldn't know about it. To meet this hazard, they entered the field of applied psychology, applying it with great effect.

THE ORIOLE CLUBHOUSE

On the wall in back of a bench at Union Park, just outside the visiting club's dressing room, they kept a row of files. As the players came out, one or two Orioles would be sitting on the bench filing the spikes of his baseball shoes with great flourish and vigor. Then the sharpener would look up and growl:

"Better get out of our way today, if you don't want your legs cut off."

With the sacrifice not counting as a time at bat, which helped raise averages, all the Orioles became expert bunters. The special flat-sided bat had been outlawed, but John saw other ways to help the home cause. He enlisted the aid of Thomas J. Murphy, the blue-eyed grounds keeper. Tom had the largest mustache on the grounds since Van Haltren, with Duke Esper's a close second.

"Keeler, Jennings, Kelley, and I combined good bunting with very fast running," John once recalled, "and we made it our main form of attack, especially against the beer-bloated pitchers. We got Murphy to mix the soil of the infield with a form of clay which, when wet and rolled, was almost as hard as concrete and gave us a 'fast track' to work on. We went even further in having Tom build up the third-base line from the outside so the bunt wouldn't roll foul. And I do believe Tom had the first-base line on a slight downgrade from home plate to help our running speed. I know it wasn't uphill.

"Another favorite trick was to have Tom soap the soil around the pitcher's box, so that when the visiting pitcher picked up some dirt to dry his perspiring hands, his palm and fingers were so slippery he was unable to control the ball. Of course, our own pitchers knew where the unadulterated earth was, or carried some private stock in their hip pockets.

"Was it fair?" John would always echo the inevitable question. "We thought so, because the other fellow had a chance to do the same or worse to us, and they often did. Players in the old days never complained much about being victimized, so long as they could square it the same way, or improve upon a trick. We prided ourselves on being able to think up things like the hit and run, the 'run and bunt' from third base, the hidden ball tricks. . . .

"In the case of that spare outfield ball Brodie threw, I might say that grounds keepers kept grass high purposely in certain areas for their own hitters. They even let infield grass grow ridiculously high to stop our bunting. That didn't make the double-ball system right, but it was the best idea at the time.

"We never thought up such advantages on the basis of sportsmanship or lack of it. I had trained myself from the earliest days to think up little and big things that might be anticipated by the rule changers next year. With us, only the written rules counted, and if you could come up with something not covered by the rules, you were ahead of the slower-thinking opposition by at least a full season.

"Connie Mack, a great and smart catcher, caused a rule change with his clever stunt of making both umpire and batter believe he had caught a foul tip. In those days the batter was out on any caught foul tip, regardless of the strike count. Connie would snap his finger against his leather mitt to create a double-click sound that was simply perfect. He drove us crazy with it, until 1895, when they stopped him by ruling that the batter was out on a caught foul tip *only* if the ball went over the batter's head. And that's the rule today.

"My specialty that brought a rule change was fouling off pitches down the third-base line. As lead-off batter, it was my job to get on base so Keeler and I could work the hit-and-run play. Fouls didn't count as strikes, which helped averages, of course, so I kept fouling off until I got my base on balls. In a single time at bat against Jimmy Callahan, of Chicago, I fouled off twenty-four consecutive pitches. To prevent this, they passed the rule making each of the first two fouls a strike and a foul bunt on the third strike an out. That fixed my wagon, and upset a few other carts, but we sure had fun while it lasted."

Even with high batting averages and running speed, the Orioles did not run away from the opposition in 1895. Manager Hanlon sacrificed the slow and aging Dan Brouthers by turning him over to Louisville, but this was more to help that financially stricken club than anything else. Hanlon figured that George Carey, a .345 hitter in the Western League, would make up for Brouthers. He fielded well, but he was slow afoot and hit only .271.

Other changes, however, bore the mark of Hanlon's genius. When Heinie Reitz was hurt the first time, Kid Gleason, the little pitcher, played second base and remained there, hitting .323. Hanlon also picked up a young right-handed pitcher named Bill Hoffer from Buffalo. He was no stranger to John, because they had been teammates at Cedar Rapids three years before. He was a complete surprise, though, when he turned in twenty-nine victories for the season. He helped make up for Sadie McMahon's miserable showing. The popular right-hander had only four defeats to show for his efforts until midseason when he reeled off ten victories in a row just when Cleveland was pressing close.

The Orioles' reputation for hardiness of body as well as spirit was made in 1895. The old sayings, "They used to stick broken fingers in the dirt to heal them," or "He played for two weeks with one eye hanging out on his cheek," are reflected somewhat by the following sports-page excerpt:

> The Baltimore Orioles are perhaps the gamest team in the League. They have retained their position at the head of the list despite the fact that Reitz, their second baseman, is laid up with a broken collar bone. They have had innumerable other misfortunes to contend with. McGraw, probably the best third baseman on the diamond, has been laid up twice, once with sickness and again with a broken finger. He is playing now with a hand so sore that only pluck and love of the contest keeps him in. Captain Robinson has a sprained ankle. Carey hurt his ankle, as did Reitz early in the season. Jennings' arm is sore. Hawke is out for the balance of the season. Hemming has been sick most of the time and Esper has stomach trouble. That is a hospital list big enough to discourage any team, but the Orioles do not seem to mind it.

For the second straight year, the Orioles had a difficult time coming through, and they finished the season at the Polo Grounds, in New York, needing two victories of the final five. They lost the first game, and faced the "speediest pitcher of the day," Jouett Meekin, in the second. But they won the second and the third, clinching their second straight flag. Cleveland, led by the batting champion, Jess Burkett (.423), finished second by three games.

The Giants slipped to ninth under three managers, and joined the three other "trouble spots" of the league: St. Louis, which had four managers; financially embarrassed Washington; and desperate Louisville, which had borrowed $4,000 from the league in order to finish last with only 35 victories in 131 games played.

More important than the pennant victory, or the play-off for the Temple Cup, was John's physical condition in the latter part of the season. He developed what today would probably be called influenza. To him, it was just a cold or the sniffles, and he fought it as though it was some personal enemy out to see that the Orioles didn't win. He stole sixty-nine bases before leaving the line-up. The effect of his absence from more than thirty games was summarized by one writer two weeks from the end of the season as follows:

A gentleman and club owner prominent in league company, while in this city a few days ago, was discussing the remarkable achievements of the Baltimore team during the last two years. Said he, "Do you know who is directly responsible for the fastness of that team?"

He waved off the wrong answers, and went on to say that McGraw inspired the other members of the team for fast work. When McGraw became a member of the team he at once displayed an activity on the field that astonished some of his associates, and eventually they commenced to acquire his rapid style of playing. Following his example, Kelley, Keeler, Jennings, Reitz, Clarke, Gleason and the rest of the team, who were not considered fast before they went to Baltimore, took to handling the ball quickly in practice, and finally they developed that remarkable form which made them famous throughout the baseball world.

The story of the Temple Cup play-offs of 1895 can be told in two words—Cy Young. That remarkable right-hander, who led all pitchers at the end of his 22-year career with 511 victories, won 35 of them that year. The limping Orioles fought him tooth and nail through the opening game on October 2 at Cleveland before 8,000 happy fans. Their enthusiasm moved one fan to jump from the bleachers in an effort to stop Joe Kelley from catching a fly ball. Hundreds of others threw potatoes at the Orioles, antedating the vegetable shower of Joe Medwick in Detroit by forty years.

But it was good and exciting baseball all the way. With the score tied 4–4, Zimmer singled off McMahon for the winning run in the ninth, to take the first game for Cy Young. "Nig" Cuppy, a 25-game winner, bested young Hoffer in the second game, 5–2. After a day of rest, Young returned to outpitch McMahon again, 7–1. The teams then journeyed to Baltimore, where Duke Esper scored a 5–0 shutout over Cuppy. But it was Cy Young again over Hoffer, giving Cleveland a 5–2 victory and the Cup.

But John went to bed and under a doctor's care for the rest of the year. At first his affliction was called nervousness, a sort of breakdown, and then it was diagnosed as malaria. He was weak, had recurring fever and regular headaches. He had rooms on Twenty-fourth Street near Charles, only a few blocks from Union Park, and within easy walking distance of his many friends in the neighborhood.

It was a long and discouraging battle, for his low weight went lower, and just when he seemed better and ready to pack up for college, his strength would disappear. There could be no college, the doctor said, if he expected to have enough strength for baseball training in the spring. Jennings called and said good-by and promised that the Bonas would be as good as ever.

John's biggest release from the tension of convalescence came in following the baseball news of the winter.

The speedy Billy Hamilton was traded to Boston for third baseman Billy Nash, who would manage Philadelphia.

Hanlon traded the popular Kid Gleason to the Giants for the hard-hitting first baseman, Jack Doyle, unpopularly known as "Dirty" Doyle.

This deal produced a row among officials at the November meeting of the National League in New York. John T. Brush accused Andrew Freedman of conspiring to help Hanlon, who had long sought a good-hitting first baseman since the departure of Brouthers.

Freedman replied with an accusation that the schedule-makers had deliberately plotted to make it hard for the Giants and easy for Charlie Byrne's Brooklyn team.

Brush replied by having Byrne elected to the league's all-important executive board by eleven to one and Freedman elected to none. He also had T. Hunt Stucky, of the impoverished Louisville Club, put on the board as a "Western representative."

Byrne introduced a resolution, aimed at the supposedly conspiring Soden of Boston, Freedman of New York, Rogers of Philadelphia, and W. W. Kerr of Pittsburgh—all pledged to oppose Sunday baseball—calling for expulsion of "anyone conspiring to reduce the league membership from twelve clubs."

Freedman announced that New York would never see Sunday baseball as long as he was connected with the game.

Brush then moved in reprisal for Freedman's "secret" purchase of A. G. Spalding's Giant stock that gave him Giant control a year before. Brush's western ally, Frank DeHaas Robison, of Cleveland, moved that the exclusive contract for National League baseballs be awarded to the Overman Wheel Company, of Chicopee Falls, Massachusetts, makers of the "Victor" baseball. Brush seconded the motion. Action on the move was postponed until the spring meeting. Eventually Spalding was obliged to buy out the Chicopee Falls plant to protect the contract, and Spalding baseballs are still made there today.

They struggled at each other's throat in council, John reflected with understandable remorse, giving little thought to the harum-scarum players running themselves into a physical decline on the ball field. Duke Esper was on a special diet for his stomach, and they suspected cancer. Could the beginnings of consumption account for Hemming's steady loss of weight and fever during the season? Bill Hawke had quit with it a year before. What would happen to John McGraw, weight 136 pounds?

Considerable happened before he played baseball again. He got up and around and outside. He expressed a hope that Hanlon would train at New Orleans, but it was Macon again, and John managed to get there. He worked out carefully in the warmer weather and felt good, but he was soon down again, tired and listless. Hughie Jennings brought a good report of baseball progress at St. Bonaventure's, but the news was overshadowed on "their" birthday when John learned that he'd be out of baseball uniform for many weeks.

Typhoid fever!

He had to leave training before the team, and then begin another long and lonesome convalescence in Baltimore. The battle was against more than fever. He had to fight impatience and self-torture, for it seemed as if he never would play another game of baseball. Even his doctor couldn't convince him that many players recovered from typhoid and rejoined their teams.

10

IT WAS August 25, 1896, and the second game of a Tuesday double-header with Cleveland, before John was able to rejoin the Orioles. An overflow crowd of 11,505 at Union Park paid him high tribute, and he repaid them with a display of his old speed and aggressiveness. It was more than welcome, because Willie Hoffer was hit for five runs in the first inning of the opening game. A twenty-year-old rookie, Joe Corbett, brother of the heavyweight boxing champion, gave up seven more runs in the next eight innings. Cy Young was the winner by 12–2.

John started in the lead-off position for the second game, and even though darkness ended the game with the score at 4–4, the newspapers treated it as a Baltimore victory. The *Herald* said:

> There is only one McGraw, and he is a revelation. It does the other members of the team no injustice to say that but for McGraw they would not have been in it. His work at bat was simply wonderful. He was up five times and made three clean hits and further than that, did more to rattle Cuppy than the whole team combined. He gave the phlegmatic Cleveland twirler a merry chase, and made him pitch ball after ball which Mac would foul off, until Cuppy began to show signs of weariness and anxiety. In the last inning, when a run was needed, Mac did his part. He hit a clean single and put Clarke on third and would have scored a faster runner.
>
> By all means let McGraw play third base, if he feels that he is strong enough, and this is no reflection on that sterling substitute, Jimmy Donnelly.

On the morning after John's return, the league standing showed the Orioles in the lead by one and a half games over Cincinnati. Twenty-six games later Baltimore completed the schedule with a lead of ten games over second-place Cleveland by winning twenty of the twenty-six. John played in eighteen of the games, scored eighteen runs, and stole thirteen bases. His batting average was .356. Though he appeared only briefly, writers called his contribution the difference between a close finish and a runaway.

Von Der Horst, Hanlon, and a few newspapermen were struggling to whip up city interest in the start of the Temple Cup series, when they learned that the entire team of Cleveland Spiders was either killed or maimed in a railroad wreck near Rockford, Pennsylvania. Then came word that they weren't quite killed, and would arrive four days late. They reached Baltimore in good health on Thursday, October 1, and the series began a day late.

Union Park was decorated with colorful bunting. The pennants of 1894 and 1895 were hung at either end of the grandstand, and the new 1896 championship flag floated from the centerfield flagpole. But scarcely four thousand fans journeyed out York Road for the game. Many insisted that diminishing attendance, which had commanded more newspaper space than Oriole victories through the season, was due to the election year, McKinley against Bryan. Others claimed that Baltimore was tired of a winner. The more indignant insisted that the high admission price kept them away. Why charge a dollar for a game usually half that? Hadn't they seen Baltimore and Cleveland *twice* for fifty cents a month before? The series opened with little fanfare.

John scored one of Baltimore's two runs in the third inning off Cy Young, and then left the game to rest. Keeler and Jennings kept up the barrage against Young, and the Orioles gave an easy 7–1 victory to Bill Hoffer, who allowed only five hits.

But even this triumph failed to whet enthusiasm for the series. The second-day crowd was announced at 3,100, and on a Saturday, too. The Orioles opened up on Bobby Wallace in the very first inning to drive in four runs. They scored another pair in the third, one in the fifth, and ended with two in the ninth that were canceled on account of darkness. Meanwhile Corbett pitched masterfully and would have had a shutout, but for three Oriole errors that helped Cleveland make two runs.

"We used that game to roast Bobby Wallace for years," John used to say and laugh in recollection. "Five of us walloped him for nine of the ten hits, and Kelley got three. We chased him right out of the pitching business, because he played third base the next year. After two seasons there, he moved over to shortstop and became one of the greatest. He didn't quit until he was forty-four and had played twenty-five years in the big leagues."

After a Sunday of idleness, Van Der Horst decided to cut the prices in half, to the same rate as for regular games. Even then fewer than three thousand fans appeared at the gate to see the Orioles, outhit by Cleveland ten to eight, take the third game by a score of 6–2. Hoffer bested Cuppy, who worked with a sore hand. The outfielders of both teams put on the greatest display of the year, but Baltimore remained quite calm.

Cleveland fans were even more so three days later when only 1,200 of them paid to root for the Spiders. Joe Corbett pitched the best game of the four, to defeat Cuppy again, this time with a four-hit shutout. The Orioles made five runs on eleven hits, with Keeler and Corbett getting three apiece.

It is interesting to compare the Temple Cup financial bonanza with that of modern times when each player's share in a World Series runs from $5,000 to $7,000. Here are the old per-player figures of long ago:

	1894	1895	1896
Winner	$768.10	$528.33	$200
Loser	360.00	352.22	117

The Oriole shares for 1896 were actually $194.88 apiece, but another $80 each was realized from a few exhibition games and two theater benefits in Baltimore.

The year-long combat with illness had given John much time for serious thought. Despite the visits from friends, there were many lonesome hours in his rooms on Twenty-fourth Street. Hanlon had paid his salary, $200 twice a month, during the 1896 illness, and he had saved carefully. But he had thought a great deal about his economic future, of being alone, and of his kid brother, Mike, now finishing high school in New York state.

As a result, he took several important steps during the winter. First was the old dream of Wilbert Robinson to start a "hash house or beanery." They planned well and opened instead a substantial and high-class place. They leased three floors of a large building at 519 North Howard Street, across from the popular Academy of Music, now the Stanley Theater. The building had 40 feet of frontage and a depth of 150 feet.

On the right just inside the door was a bar "tastefully arranged," and on the left were dining tables, far from the "bean-ery" type. They put in a good kitchen, but not a big one. Both were interested in bowling. The Brunswick-Balke-Collender people installed bowling alleys in the rear of the first floor. The front of the second floor was laid out as a reading room and gathering place. The walls were completely covered with photographs and lithos of famous baseball players, boxers, and even the victorious American athletes in the first modern Olympiad in Greece the previous year. Baltimore's Bob Garrett, son of the banker, was a winner in both shot-put and javelin throw.

On the second floor rear the bowling alley people set up pool and billiard tables, which also fascinated John. He became skilled at both balk-line and three-cushion billiards. On the third floor were club rooms for meetings of small social clubs and societies, of which Baltimore had many. The building is still standing at this writing, but as a record and radio shop. Understandably, they called their place the "Diamond."

Robinson and McGraw's was popular and successful from the start as a gathering and lingering place for fans of indoor and outdoor sports. It was a center of conviviality, good feeling from both beer and liquor, arguments, laughter, and wagering. Would Corbett beat Fitzsimmons on St. Patrick's Day? Could Gallatin beat Simpleton in the Herring Run feature? It was also a place for bowlers and billiard players.

The popularity of bowling may be gauged by an incident that occurred in the Diamond just before the turn of the century. Robinson had dragged John off on a duck-hunting trip, which Robbie loved and John disliked. While they were in the nearby marshes, Frank Vansant, manager of the café, noticed that the maple pins were checked and splintered from the steady beating. He took them to a wood turner, John Dittmar, on East Falls Avenue, for a planing.

Trying to tool them down all even on the lathe, Dittmar soon had a problem, for all were of different size. Vansant told him to keep at it. When the pins were obviously undersized, the manager had them made all the same size as the smallest, brought them back in a burlap bag, and dumped them at the end of the alley. He was setting them up when the hunters returned. Robbie roared at the sight of the maples. "What the hell happened to the pins?"

He rolled an eight-inch ball down the alley and the under-sized pins flew wildly.

John roared with laughter. "Robbie," he said, "they look like the little ducks we've been chasing down the bay."

ROBBIE TAKES A SPONGE BATH

A newspaperman, Bill Clarke, of the *American*, on hand to pick up some news, joined the laughter. Vansant then brought out a couple of six-inch balls, used for the summer games, cocked-hat, five back, and Newport. They had no finger holes and seemed ideal for the smaller pins.

Clarke raced back to his office and wrote a story about the little "duck pins" at the Diamond Café. He urged everybody to go down before the new and regulation-sized set replaced them. But they never were replaced. Curiosity and then competition made it the most popular alley in the city. You couldn't knock down as many pins as with the sixteen-pound ball, but it wasn't such hard work.

That was the origin of duckpin bowling in America. Baltimore became and remained the center of the "new sport." Five years later several leagues were formed as the game, most popular in the summer, spread through the East. Northern New England and New York City refused to take duckpins seriously, but by 1910 the first duckpin tournament had been held in Washington. The "championships" were still limited to Baltimore and Washington thirty years after the origin, but the growth of converts brought a really national tournament in 1928. Today there flourishes a National Duckpin Congress annually with alleys, pins, and balls standardized by rigid regulation.

John's second big step after the opening of the Diamond was a quiet marriage at St. Vincent's Church to the daughter of one of his newspaper friends, Michael H. Doyle, the printer.

At spring training that year Hugh and John learned that Father James had become quite ill, and so they telegraphed to Olean and had a large bouquet of flowers sent over to the Seminary. But on their return, they received a letter that John has prized more than any other all his life. Written in a beautiful script, it read:

St. Bonaventure's Seminary and College
Allegany, New York
April 15, 1897

Messrs. J. McGraw & H. Jennings
My very dear Friends:

Please to accept my heartfelt thanks for your beautiful floral tribute which was duly received and also for your kind sympathy and grateful remembrance to us in our present affliction.

Poor Father James was taken away rather suddenly from our midst after a few days' illness. Only the day previous to his death as symptoms became alarming and himself conscious and aware that his time was almost come he expressed a wish to have us all come into his presence. He then requested a remembrance in our prayers and gave us a last farewell after which he said remember me to all my friends and especially to McGraw and Jennings.

Oh, my dearly beloved friends, you were in reality among those for whom Fr. James entertained the deepest sentiments of respect, sincere admiration, and affection.

How often did I hear him relate your great exploits on the "Diamond," and he was never done extolling your noble and manly principles.

The faculty and students here are deeply afflicted over his unexpected departure, and, I can say, in truth, that not one among them feel it more than I do; however, we must accept it as coming from the hand of God.

Thanking you again my dear friends for your extreme kindness and the deep interest you have taken in the progress of our institution and with heartfelt feelings of gratitude and praying that God may bless you,

I am very gratefully yours,

JOSEPH BUTLER, O.S.F.

"I wish I'd seen him again," John said after reading the letter.

"Maybe it's better you didn't," Hughie confided. "He lost a lot of health during the winter."

"If it wasn't for him, I wouldn't have gone to college at all."

"And because of him," Hugh said, "I'm going to keep on. I promised him I would."

The little white-haired Franciscan friar had exacted another promise from a baseball player. As a result, Jennings kept up his school studies even though he was nearly thirty.

A low spot of the spring training that year was the absence of young Joe Corbett. "Gentleman Jim," the heavyweight champion, had used his husky kid brother as one of his sparring partners, after promising Hanlon to ship him east in good shape. Then on St. Patrick's Day Corbett had lost his title to Bob Fitzsimmons by a knockout in the fourteenth round at Carson City, Nevada. Joe worshiped his distinguished brother and had remained with Bill Lange, the Chicago outfielder, to see the fight. Joe appeared late for training in lower spirits than Jim.

"I shouldn't have allowed it," Hanlon moaned. "He may never pitch again."

Robinson tried him out, and added to the pessimism. "He'll never make it," the catcher declared. "Oh, it's not his arm. He's got good speed, but I think he's been punched around too much by his brother. That's why he acts so dopey. John L. Sullivan wasn't much good either after Jim finished with him."

The 1897 season opened with a number of surprises, best of which was city-wide enthusiasm. A parade of the two teams, the Orioles and the visiting "Beaneaters" from Boston, was well received, and another overflow crowd of 13,000 flocked to Union Park, even though it was a Thursday afternoon. After appearing at bat once, John suffered a badly bruised heel and had to retire. Hoffer was shaky at the start, but the Orioles came from behind to win easily, 10–5. They scored 24 runs off Boston's three best pitchers to take the first three games.

More important was the announcement from League President Young's office that John B. Day, former owner of the Giants, had been appointed "Chief of Umpires and Inspector of Players." This was the very move that John had suggested in a newspaper interview the year before. Whether Day, then fifty years old, was strong enough or capable, only time could tell, but it seemed a step in the right direction.

The steps, however, were few, and the year 1897 was one of the worst on record for umpires. Reporters of the day openly accused umpires of deliberate favoritism as part of their news stories on the game. Baltimore's "day of iniquity" came on Friday, August 7, at the old Walpole Street grounds in Boston. Before the game the teams were at the top of the league, tied in defeats with 27 each, and the 8,500 fans rattled the historic park with noisy anticipation.

Under the subtle heading, "HELD UP IN BOSTON, Champions Sandbagged by Umpire Tom Lynch," the Baltimore *Herald's* two-column dispatch read:

> The work of Lynch today, coupled with the work of other umpires whom Baltimore has met, would lead one to believe that a conspiracy is on foot to down the Champs. Yesterday Lynch's work was bad enough. Today it was awful.

He gave Boston two runs outright, one in the sixth and one in the seventh. And then, to add to his bad decisions, he robbed the Orioles of the tieing run and a chance to win out in the ninth after they had once held a five-run lead.

The only reason suggested for Lynch's alleged partisanship was his New England nativity. The disputed calls in the home team's favor involved certain "put-outs" of Boston runners who were called safe. Baltimore's tying run was scored by Joe Quinn, a former Boston star running for John, who had sprained his ankle sliding into second. Quinn was on the plate long before catcher Bergen caught Duffy's high throw and tagged him, the story said.

John "Dirty" Doyle, the Oriole first baseman, was born in Killorglin, Ireland. Naturally he led the Baltimore bench in a verbal assault on Lynch's ears. Taking his fielding position in the eighth, he passed Lynch and said,

"Old man, just wait till you get to Baltimore!"

Lynch promptly thumbed Doyle from the game, whereupon the Oriole said more of the same. The *Herald* reporter wired:

Lynch, without a moment's warning, shot out his right and caught Doyle over the eye and Jack retaliated with a right hook that closed Lynch's left optic and will probably put him out of the game for a couple of days. Then the two men clinched and without another blow being struck they swung and twisted around in front of the plate for half a minute.

The players of both teams now interfered and dragged the contestants apart. Kelley and Corbett had hold of Lynch, who in his anger, resented their interference and started to hit at them, but was restrained. By this time the mob of gentlemanly Bostonians on the bleachers had overrun the field, and with threatening countenances and belligerent intentions tried to get at the Orioles. But the police interfered and finally drove them back. Doyle was escorted to the bench by Corbett and there remained despite the shouts of the peaceful-minded spectators that he should be arrested. Then the game went on.

Shortly after the fight Joe Kelley was hit by a couple of

bottles thrown from the bleachers, and, despite the fact that a hundred of his Cambridgeport friends, ready to take his part, were in the immediate neighborhood, and urged him to retaliate, he let the incident go by unnoticed.

On the way back to the hotel rocks were thrown at the Baltimore players by gentlemanly and cultured Bostonians, but good sense restrained them from resenting the assault.

Lynch's eyes, closed by Doyle's blow, will hardly be in fit shape to allow him to umpire the final game of the series here tomorrow. It is said that as a result of today's affair he will resign. Bad umpiring is Baltimore's lot, it seems, but it will take more than that to keep them out of the pennant.

For the record, umpire Lynch worked the next day's game with only one good eye, and without incident. No substitute was available from President Young's small staff, as umpire Jack Sheridan was under suspension for drunkenness.

Another outburst of player temper took place in a bar at Louisville when Oliver Tebeau, Jimmy McAleer, Ed McKean, and Jess Burkett, all Cleveland stars, assaulted a league umpire. They hurried from town, but were hauled into court on their next appearance in Louisville. Manager Tebeau and his utility player, Jack "Rowdy" O'Connor, also teamed up in handing a beating to a Cleveland reporter, Elmer Pasco, for his severely critical story about Tebeau and McAleer.

Nor were the outbursts confined to players. Andrew Freedman, owner of the Giants, lashed out with his cane on the person of Ed Hurst, baseball writer for the New York *World* and scorer at the Polo Grounds. Hurst preferred charges of assault and battery. Freedman's defense was that he had become infuriated by a completely bogus interview published by Hurst with intent to injure him, and furthermore that Hurst refused to return money he had borrowed.

Hurst replied that he had earned every borrowed cent. The magistrate held the club owner guilty of technical assault but felt obliged to suspend sentence because of "extenuating circumstances so obviously in the defendant's favor."

The Orioles, apparently heading for their fourth straight National League championship, were making a joke of the rival owners' attempts to build strength against them by pooling of players and financial interests. They were running the legs off the eleven other clubs, and outhitting them by many points. The peak of Oriole power came at Union Park on Friday of the Labor Day week end. Last-place St. Louis, with owner Chris Von der Ahe the fourth manager of the year, offered Red Donahue and Percy Coleman as "pitchers." Jack Doyle hit for four singles and two doubles, while Willie Keeler hit five singles and a triple—six hits apiece by two players in a single game for the first and only time in baseball history.

Keeler's hitting was the storybook variety from start to finish of the season. He led all the hitters with an average of .432, second highest in baseball history. He set a record of 243 safe hits, of which 199 were singles. It has never been broken, because he played in only 128 games (154 games were first scheduled in 1898). Cobb's 248 hits in 1911, Sisler's 257 in 1920, and Hornsby's 250 in 1922 were made in 145 or more games. Little Willie began his batting rampage on opening day, April 22, and hit safely in every game through June 18—44 consecutive games. This remained a record for exactly 44 years and until Joe DiMaggio hit through a string of 56 games in 1941.

After recovering from his heel bruise at the start of the season John played in 105 games and hit for an average of .326. He wasn't a Willie Keeler, but he had lots of company, for no one else was, either.

Five Orioles hit better than .350 and scored more than 500 runs. Five of them, not including John, totaled 312 stolen bases. For some unaccountable reason, Henry "Father" Chadwick, venerable editor of the *Baseball Guide*, failed to list John's 42 stolen bases, though he included 22 stolen by a rookie named Honus Wagner, who had been sold to Louisville in midseason for $2,200.

John has said that latter-day base stealers often suffered by unfair comparison with the famous runners of the Oriole period. While the players of his speedy day might have been faster or more aggressive, they were helped considerably by the rule that prevented them from losing a stolen base because of "wild throw or muff by a fielder." Today a fielder's muff or a bad throw usually is scored an error, rather than a steal, if the stealer could have been retired by clean fielding.

Boston and Baltimore seesawed down the stretch, alternating for the league lead. The key was in sound pitching by Corbett, Hoffer, Jerry Nops, a left-hander; and Arlie Pond, who later became an outstanding surgeon. But Boston finished the final month with nineteen victories while losing only five. The Orioles won as many, but lost two more and missed their fourth straight pennant by a single defeat! They took an extra setback, 19–10, from Boston after the pennant had been decided. A joyous throng of 25,000 saw this meaningless game in Boston.

Another answer to the Orioles' fine showing was a trade of outfielders during the previous winter. Hanlon sent Steve Brodie and cash to Pittsburgh for Jake Stenzel. Brodie hit under .300 for the second straight season, while thirty-year-old Stenzel had one more great year. The rest of the Oriole line-up was the same. It was this type of deal, always in Hanlon's favor it seemed, that confounded all baseball, and no club owner had a method of stopping him.

In contrast to the record crowd of a week before, only 9,600 Boston fans went to the Walpole Street Park on October 4, and few took the first Temple Cup game seriously. It was by far the largest turnout of the five games, and they were repaid with a poorly played free-for-all. The Orioles outhit Boston 20 to 12. John, Keeler, Kelley, and Doyle made 11 of the hits, and Jennings made 5. They lost, 13–12, and each side had four errors.

Officials tried to perk up waning interest with a parade through the business section of Boston, followed by a pennant party at the Tremont Theater. Mayor Quincy supervised the ballyhoo, and the actress, May Irwin, presented Frank Selee with the 1897 flag. Both teams joined the cheering. The Orioles then won four straight games from the so-called champions.

"We never felt that they had beaten us during the season," John explained, "because of the bad umpiring breaks, which we exaggerated in our minds. We won eight of every ten games played at Union Park and wiped the field with Boston in the first three games. We had the best hitters and base runners and fielders. They had one truly great pitcher, Kid Nichols, and Corbett could beat him. No matter how many runs they scored, we were always sure of getting more."

This thinking affected playing and converted the 1897 Temple

Cup games into the wildest and woolliest "championship" series on record. The 5 games showed Baltimore with a total of 54 runs, 73 hits, and 13 errors. Boston totaled 41 runs, 69 hits, and 15 errors. In addition, the teams played exhibitions at Worcester and Springfield on successive days after the third game in Boston. The Orioles took both of these fill-ins, 11–10 and 8–6. Finally, fewer than 1,600 Baltimoreans paid to see each of the last two games at Union Park, and most of those were twenty-five-cent bleacherites. Indifference had reached an alarming peak. The once enthusiastic newspapers ignored the games almost entirely and the cash return to the players was negligible.

"I could never blame the Baltimore fans," John said. "The Temple Cup was a beautiful thing, presented by a real sportsman. But the fans refused to get excited about two teams who had been playing each other all year. No matter who won the series, nothing new was ever decided. So, at the annual meeting in Baltimore that fall, the league packed up the big cup and returned it to Mr. Temple with thanks."

But life went on, as it always does. Joe Kelley and Hugh Jennings rushed their girls to the altar, and several of the Orioles joined a barnstorming tour to the Pacific Coast. Jennings took the team captaincy, and also his bride, on a wedding trip. The net result was $341 to each player above expenses, and an unforgettable fist fight in the west between two real battlers, Jack Doyle and Joe Corbett. It was so rough that Gentleman Jim prevailed upon his brother not to play baseball any more, and Hanlon traded Doyle to Washington with Heinie Reitz. Doyle became a manager.

John and Wilbert Robinson remained in Baltimore to oversee their prosperous café business, which was netting them three times their baseball income. Here, at last, was a degree of security, a bit of relief from worry over the uncertainty of baseball as a business. Things looked so bright that the partners invested in real estate. Robbie made good his threat to get a big home for Ma and the kids. He bought a fine, three-story stone house with bay windows at 2740 St. Paul Street. It had nine rooms, a patch of lawn, shade trees at the curb, and a long back yard. Here Wilbert, Jr., Mary, Howard, and little Hannah, Robbie's pride and joy, took up residence in well-earned comfort.

John bought the house just like it next door at 2738 and moved in with his bride, the former Minnie Doyle. He also brought his brother Mike down from Truxton and put him into business school to specialize in bookkeeping and clerical work. It had been a long, long struggle. John and Robbie had used up most of their savings to start the café and buy the adjoining houses, but this much they owned, and only three blocks from Union Park.

The 1898 playing season was almost a duplicate of the year before. The Orioles finished second again to Boston, slipping far behind in the closing weeks. But Keeler was the batting champion again. Kelley, Jennings, and John turned in good seasons. John hit ten points better than the year before and stole the same number of bases, 42. Once again Hanlon's midwinter deal, Doyle and Reitz, plus a pitcher, for rookie first baseman Dan McGann and infielder DeMontreville, cemented his line-up. McGann was a great fielder and hit .298. "DeMont" was a fine replacement for Reitz and hit .325 to Heinie's .302. Doyle rowed with his Washington employers and in midseason was traded to New York.

But long before the season started, the clouds of war cast a shadow over the whole baseball scene. John and Wilbert Robinson were sweating it out as tutors in the gymnasium of Johns Hopkins University on the day the battleship *Maine* was blown up in Havana harbor. Several Orioles followed the "St. Bonaventure plan" by coaching college teams. Jennings was teaching the University of Georgia teams between his own classes. Joe Kelley was supervising at Georgetown. Clarke was at Princeton.

The Brooklyn team began a four-game series with the Orioles at Union Park on April 25. Before the game ended, word came from Washington that President McKinley had asked for a declaration of war on Spain. Would the States be invaded from the island strongholds, Puerto Rico and nearer Cuba? Eyes and thoughts wandered from the play of the game, and then the fans began to wander from the ball park.

The war continued, overshadowing baseball interest. Important events were reduced almost to insignificance. Jim Hughes, who, with Dr. Jim McJames, was Hanlon's new pitching ace, shut out Boston with no hits at Union Park, on the same day in April that Ted Breitenstein pitched one in Cincinnati against

Pittsburgh. But they seemed unimportant, as did two other no-hit shutouts by pitchers in Philadelphia and Chicago that year.

The decline of interest was reflected by the wholesale decline of attendance as the Spanish-American War continued throughout the baseball season and beyond. Parks were virtually empty in the final six weeks, on account of a runaway race by the Orioles and Boston.

"It was worst in Cleveland," John recalled with a sigh. "Things had been getting terrible there, but we never expected to play before seventy-five paid admissions, which happened."

The have-nots of the league, those perennial second-division clubs, grew increasingly desperate. Young Henry Clay Pulliam, of Louisville, first a secretary to Zach Phelps and then president for several backers, was obliged to sell control in the Colonels for fresh money. The buyer was a former German immigrant, Barney Dreyfuss, who had reached America penniless less than twenty years before. He had married a lady of wealth and increased the fortune in the liquor business. She was Florence Wolf, youngest of thirteen children.

Louisville would survive, but the fabulous story of Chris Von der Ahe was rapidly reaching a tragic climax in St. Louis. He had parlayed his small saloon and baseball club into valuable real-estate developments after building Sportsman's Park, and then into great wealth. But he had dissipated, or perhaps he was swindled out of, more than $500,000. During his abject desperation he was spirited out of Missouri and into a Pittsburgh jail by outraged debtors. The league had to take over his pioneering franchise. Soon his ball park would be sold on the courthouse steps in St. Louis to a creditor, E. C. Becker, who would turn it over to John T. Brush's friend, Frank DeHaas Robison, owner of the Cleveland team. While Frank was in St. Louis, his brother, Matthew Stanley Robison, would operate in Cleveland for one dismal year.

But the most unusual situation developed in Brooklyn. This was once a defiant city across from New York but, after January 1, 1898, a borough of Greater New York through consolidation. When Charles H. Byrne, president of the Brooklyn Bridegrooms, died in late 1897, young Charles H. Ebbets, office boy, ticket taker, schedule maker, and small stockholder was elected president. In his first year at the helm, the team had lost money, ground, and managers. Ebbets wound up managing the club in a brand-new empty ball park. But he had an idea.

The Robisons were interested in two teams. The Spalding brothers were interested, directly and indirectly, in two clubs, Chicago and New York. Arthur H. Soden, owner of Boston, had a $30,000 interest in New York. John T. Brush, Cincinnati owner, still held stock in New York.

Why couldn't Brooklyn and Baltimore combine forces, capital, and players, and perhaps drive the unpopular Andrew Freedman out of baseball? Being majority owner of the Orioles, Hanlon could transfer the choice players to Brooklyn and take over with a free hand.

And who would manage the leftovers?

Why not the popular John J. McGraw?

11

THE ONLY difference between the Brooklyn-Baltimore baseball syndicate of 1899 and other interlocking ownerships in the National League was lack of secrecy. The owners in control of Brooklyn were young Ebbets and bewhiskered Ferdinand A. Abell, who had long financed the club with an income from operating the profitable society gambling concession at Narragansett Pier, Rhode Island. Acting openly, they purchased a minority holding in the Orioles from Hanlon and Von Der Horst, who used the money to buy substantial Brooklyn shares from the estate of the late Charles Byrne and the holdings of one George Chauncey, pioneer in Brooklyn real estate and baseball.

The directors of both corporations were the same. Hanlon had full charge of field operations at Brooklyn's new Washington Park. He assured John a free hand in managing the Orioles. However, a comparison of players exchanged is proof positive that Baltimore was considerably less than a stepchild:

Player, position	1898 Record	Player, position	1898 Record
Keeler, of.	.379	Sheckard, of.	.290
Kelley, of.	.328	Jack Ryan, c.	.298
Jennings, ss.	.325	Magoon, ss.	.227
McGann, 1b	.298	LaChance, 1b	.243
Hughes, p.	21–17	Howell, p.	2–0
McJames, p.	27–14	McKenna, p.	1–7
Maul, p.	20–7	* McGinnity, p.	10–3

* Played in Peoria; drafted by Brooklyn.

"I had no cause for complaint," John once explained. "The main reason for the deal was to make Brooklyn a dominating power in New York City baseball, and we sure did. Hanlon and I understood that thoroughly. He made certain promises to me and kept every one. I made promises, too—that I'd beat him in every ball game, if possible, and take the pennant, too. It was the only way I could play or manage. I would fight every minute to win, even if it meant ruining the whole Brooklyn situation. Hanlon laughed, half in amusement. He wished me luck everywhere but against Brooklyn.

"I never forgot that he gave me the chance to be as big as he was, to do the things I'd seen him do in field management, transferring old and new players, testing them in different positions on the field, and directing the team in play. Hanlon could have sold my contract for a lot of money—ten thousand dollars or more—but he knew that Robbie and I didn't want to leave Baltimore because of our homes and thriving business there. Sure, he got the good players, but I got the good opportunity. I considered myself better off than he was."

But the apparent ease with which Ned Hanlon won pennants as both field manager and president lulled many club owners into a belief that managing a team was a simple matter. The growth of this front-office delusion, which bordered on contempt, was more dangerous than ridiculous, for many club presidents tried to manage. In most instances, it was a late-season economy move, but too many actually believed managing a simple matter, harder than checkers, perhaps, but much easier than chess.

The sum and substance of this thinking mushroomed into an alarming neglect of baseball on the field. As an example: John T. Brush spent most of the 1897–98 winter developing his infamous "Brush Resolution" intended to "clean up the game." It was termed infamous by players and press, because it was unenforceable. If it was carried out to the letter, no sharp-tongued player, John McGraw included, could have survived four innings of a close ball game. By his own admission, John was often a difficult problem, because he was an expert "needler." He did it deliberately to destroy concentration, without which a player cannot bat, field, or pitch his best. His victims had every right to retaliate, and never failed to.

The greatest period of needling or jockeying, as it is also called, lasted for several years after the terrible 1894 play-off games for the Temple Cup. Before the liquefied celebrations in Baltimore, several of the New York and Oriole players agreed to divide their shares equally, win or lose. That deepened John's disgust at the time, though he said nothing. When New York had won four easy victories, some of the New York players ignored the pool agreement.

Not much money was involved, but as long as the New York welshers remained in baseball, the "hedging" Orioles never let them forget the fact. The bitter taunting began as soon as the players took the field in New York or Baltimore, and lasted the full nine innings.

"Robbie was of immense service in soft-soaping the umpires behind the plate," John said in discussing his vocal technique. "He had a disarming way of jollying and making them like him. But for his diplomacy and salve, we would have suffered even worse from umpires. I was constantly picking at them from third, and it took the combined efforts of Robbie and Hanlon to keep me from being put out of games. Robbie was the sugar and I was the vinegar—a good combination."

After presenting his purity resolution, John T. Brush was openly accused of drawing attention to his self-made halo, which was wrong, because his intentions were sincere. He was a hard-working proponent of Sunday baseball. As such he was denounced in several eastern cities that opposed the west's clamor for the Sunday games. He lost valuable ground in April, 1897, when

New York State passed the Raines Law, not only forbidding baseball, but all public amusements, liquor and beer sales, and allied pursuits of happiness. Private clubs were exempt. Brush's resolution was designed to paint the Sunday-baseball group as good-influencers.

Mr. Brush eventually pushed his resolution through the spring meeting of 1898, but not until his original draft was peeled of its impractical punishment terms. They included quick expulsion for minor offenses and life banishment from the game for chronic users of foul or indecent language, habitual belligerents, and wearers of flying spikes.

And while office executives were busy with this and other methods of making the game "respectable," while they were maneuvering in council for control of different franchise areas, the game itself cried in vain for technical improvement. A soft but most authoritative voice was that of Henry Chadwick, sports writer on the Brooklyn *Daily Eagle* and editor of the annual *Baseball Guide*. He pleaded repeatedly for more and better umpires and dismissal of the incompetents. He asked for strict enforcement of the balk rule, to stop pitchers from taking illegal advantage of the great base stealers. He recommended that the visiting team bat first, to shorten playing time. Since the home team won more often, only half of the ninth inning would be played, and fewer games would be called by darkness.

Chadwick suggested a reduction of fielding practice to permit an equal period of time for batting workout. Many teams regarded batting skill as a fixed quantity and didn't practice at all. He recommended subordinating the individual batsman to further over-all batting as a team. He pleaded for all teams to follow the scientific "hitting and running" pioneered by the Orioles in 1893–94. He had made many other constructive suggestions that went unheeded for too many years. Eventually they were all adopted. The bewhiskered Chadwick was called "Father of Baseball" and enshrined in the Baseball Hall of Fame at Cooperstown, New York.

I have pointed out again how the values of administrative and playing factors differ in baseball to help explain John McGraw's astonishing results in his first opportunity to manage. The reason lay in his knowledge and understanding of problems on the field.

He knew how to creep close to his players without cajoling or babying, how to share the suffering, the inexplicable agony of an undeserved defeat. He knew how to keep up spirits even by being cruel. Through that close, almost spiritual proximity, a manager learns to interpret far more than the mechanical skill of his player. It lies behind the success of all the great pioneering managers, Comiskey, Hanlon, Clarke, Chance, Mack, Huggins, and many others, including John McGraw.

When a manager loses that touch, he loses his players, then the close games, and finally the pennants.

There were many high spots in the Orioles' training trip, which began on March 21, with a boat ride to Savannah. The peak arrived with the "birthday" on April 6, in Augusta, where the Orioles went to play Ned Hanlon's "Superbas." Brooklyn had been called "Bridegrooms" because of mass marriage among the players years before. Then came the nickname "Trolley Dodgers" or "Dodgers," as pedestrian hazards developed with Brooklyn's rapid transit. A somewhat dazzling vaudeville act named "Superbas," owned by another Hanlon, no relation to Ned, was responsible for the last nickname of Brooklyn's all-star line-up.

The big problem in the game was a husky, blond, and blue-eyed right-handed pitcher of twenty-eight, Joseph Jerome McGinnity. He spent his winters bending iron in a shop at McAlester, Indian Territory. At Savannah he had bent curves in such manner as to alarm Captain Wilbert Robinson.

"Take it easy, kid," Robbie said when he saw the succession of wide curves. "Don't that hurt your arm?"

"No," McGinnity replied. "I can throw that way all day. I pitched a twenty-one inning game that took four hours one day at Peoria last year. Before that in pickup games around Fort Smith and Springfield, Missouri. Amateurs couldn't foul it."

"Well, throw the little curves, but not that big one too much," Robbie cautioned. Then he confided to John, "Mac, this fellow will cause trouble from now till opening of the season. Hanlon'll never let us keep him. Everybody backs away from his roundhouse curve like Jennings used to."

Hanlon's agreement was not to take any Oriole players after April 15. That was why McGinnity received such a scolding as he turned back the Superbas in the Augusta game.

"Mac, he did it again!" Robbie shouted. "He's showin' off!"

This was the signal for John to call for time, run over, and tear into the rookie.

"How many times do I have to tell you to stop that swell-headed throwing?" John asked loudly. "Want to ruin your arm?"

"No, sir," McGinnity said solemnly, joining the little act.

"Want to throw your arm out here and go back to Peoria?"

"No, sir, I'll be careful."

"Then stop throwing that Nickel-Rocket curve ball!"

With that, John would return to third, shaking his head in mock despair. The scene was repeated each time McGinnity put over a particularly wide bender, which he did to fool everybody but Bad Bill Dahlen, who got three of Brooklyn's seven hits. Willie Keeler got only one hit and scored the run. The Orioles hit Hanlon's two pitchers, Kennedy and Yeager, freely and scored five runs.

"Maybe we didn't fool Hanlon all the way," John recalled and always with delight, "but those Brooklyn players sure thought McGinnity was all luck and no brains. He looked it, too, because he wasn't fast and anybody could throw a wide, sidearm curve. What they didn't know was that Joe could throw several different curves—and all day.

"Besides, we knew Hanlon needed a pitcher. Doc McJames was still in medical school. Jim Hughes hadn't even started from California. We wanted Hanlon to take Dan McFarlan. He had more experience than rookie McGinnity. He'd been up with Louisville three years before. Hanlon saw no more of McGinnity and finally took McFarlan."

It was a perfect evening for the Jennings-McGraw birthday reunion that began with dinner at the hotel. But Hughie's deep concern soon broke through his freckled smile.

"It's no use, Mac," he confided. "I can't throw."

"Nonsense," John scoffed. "Everybody gets that in the spring."

The flame-red head shook from side to side. "No, it's gone," he whispered. "You saw me out there today."

"I saw you step into McGinnity's curve and get hit," John exclaimed. "If you pull that cheap trick on me during the season—"

"I couldn't hit him, so I let him hit me," Hughie laughed.

Nearly 700 batters were hit by pitchers in 1898, and Hughie

was 35 of them. A pitcher facing the old Orioles really had troubles, what with John's intentional fouls and bases on balls and Hughie's skill at getting hit "accidentally."

"But I'll never be able to wing that ball across to first base any more," Hughie said with a sigh.

"What does Hanlon say?"

"He thinks I can play first base."

"You can play anywhere," John said indignantly, "but playing first base now would be like going to a bone yard. You'd soon believe you were through forever, and you're not by a long shot. I'll get you back here, and you'll play second base, or I'll run you out of baseball. Don't worry, your arm'll come back."

But much of the old birthday cheer had slipped away. They were grown men now—twenty-six and thirty—with grown-up homes, responsibilities, and the troubles that cling to advancing years like barnacles. Once they had defied fatigue by laughing and scheming baseball maneuvers through the long night. Now the day's game had been a strain on both. They parted early to sleep and worry about each other.

The training season was a great artistic success. John got over his message of speed and alertness to the players. Robinson was a revelation as a coach of the pitchers. Dan McFarlan, never a success, was outspoken in his reluctance to leave the Orioles and Robinson to join the Superbas, who had little or no catching.

But it wasn't all work. John was never one to pass up a ribbing opportunity. He and Robinson found an ideal victim to relieve the strain of team-building. It was Frank Caughey, the amateur umpire. He had packed to leave Savannah for Baltimore ahead of the team, after making the trip as a sort of expense-paid vacation. But some kind of complication arose. He couldn't get his trunk aboard. He canceled passage and tried the railroads. Nothing doing. An official bobbed up at each point to block Caughey's departure on pretexts that differed, apparently, but they always contained some clouded and sinister charge involving the trunk.

"It was very funny," John said, "especially after a hard day of training, to see a fellow roaming the hotel lobby explaining to the players why he hadn't gone home after he had said good-by that morning. He was afraid to say he was being detained, and he told a lot of different stories, proving that even amateur umpires were careless about the truth. Of course, nobody would've believed the truth anyway."

The prank was arranged through Si Bash, head of the Savannah detective bureau, whom John and Robinson had known for years from their training days at Macon. Caughey was contemplating an appeal to the Governor of Georgia for a pardon when "clearance" for his trunk arrived.

While the Orioles hustled all spring, John knew that the team was far short by first-division standards. The known quantities were Steve Brodie, who had returned to the Orioles the year before; Ducky Holmes, another 1898 outfielder; Jerry Nops, the left-handed pitcher, and Robinson. Jimmy Sheckard, the outfielder, had only one full season of play behind him. George La-Chance had a six-year record of indifference and temperament at first base in Brooklyn, though he was a wonderful fielder. All else, including young McGinnity, were question marks, willing to hustle, but who still had to come through under fire.

John had been swamped by appeals for jobs from good and bad, old and young. It was hard to pass up Sadie McMahon, washed up at twenty-eight, and begging a chance to "come back" at thirty-two. Dad Clarke, a pitcher who had petered out at Louisville the year before, asked for "one more chance." John wrote them and other veterans to show up at Union Park in good shape for the chance. The single condition, "in good shape," eliminated most of the old-timers.

He tried out a number of amateurs in his quest for undiscovered skill in youth. He even signed a few only to discover that his judgment wasn't infallible after all. One of his biggest hopes was Charles Harris, captain and second baseman of the Mercer College team at Macon, Georgia. Remembering that Harris had hit Oriole pitching hard in 1897 and 1898, John signed him. He looked so well in training that Hanlon wanted him, but the boy played in only 21 games and hit .283.

However, there was Billie Keister, a Baltimore boy, who had played with the Orioles in 1896 and quit, only to appear in a few games with Boston two years later. John took him as a throw-in with the sale of Bill Clarke, the catcher, in March to Boston for $2,000. Keister looked like another Heinie Reitz at second base, and almost a Jennings at short.

And so it went, trial and failure, hope and despair, and the opening of the season. A total of 25,000 fans saw three mighty victories over the New York Giants, now managed by the "Supervisor of Umpires" for 1898, John B. Day. But this short-lived triumph was followed by a somewhat disastrous road trip and another embittering experience with umpires. The two-umpire system had been adopted in 1898 by the addition of an "assistant umpire." For the details, I must again turn to the printed accounts. Once more the headline was, "ROBBED BY UMPIRE, Orioles Run Up Against Gaffney and Andrews." The story continued:

New York, April 20—"Robbed by the umpire" is an old cry, but no other words will justly tell the tale of the Orioles' defeat today. Baltimore was simply held up, sandbagged and left helpless on the highway by that pair of nonpareils, Gaffney and Andrews. This may seem like harsh language, but it is entirely warranted by the facts.

No such exhibition of umpiring was ever seen on the ball field, and the Baltimore public will need no other proof of this than the mere statement of the fact that Captain Robbie was fined $5 and put out of the game for remarks he felt compelled to make against the outrageous decisions.

Good, easy-going Robbie, the peace-maker and jollier, fined and put out of a game! "I have played ball," said Robbie tonight, "15 years and this is the first time I ever was fined a cent or put out of a game."

That tells the tale better than anything. It was not one bad decision, but a series of the most glaring and outrageous mistakes that the Birds were ever compelled to face. Andrews and Gaffney are not fit men to umpire and were proven so last year. Andrews is constitutionally unfit for the position and his work last season provoked a storm of complaints all over the league. He is kept in position through the notorious favoritism of Uncle Nick Young, who spends his winters at Andrews' Florida orange grove. As a sort of compensation therefor he gives a plainly unfit man a position on his staff of umpires.

Gaffney is a man whose habits have caused his retirement from the staff a number of times, and with his whiskey-soaked and shattered nerves, is clearly no man to fill a position calling for clear eye and quick perception.

In the fourth inning Gleason hit up a pop-fly to short center. Magoon and O'Brien both ran for it, and, just as O'Brien caught it, Magoon collided with him, knocking him down. O'Brien held on to the ball, and Brodie ran up and took it out of his hand. To everybody's amazement Andrews decided Gleason was safe, saying he did not see O'Brien catch the ball.

In the fifth inning, Kitson hit a two-base hit. McGraw then bunted in front of the plate and Grady, getting the ball, threw to Hartman to head off Kitson at third. The runner was safe by a block, but was declared out, costing Baltimore a run.

With one run needed to tie in the ninth, McGraw was on first and Sheckard at the bat. He smote the ball a mighty crack into the right field over the ropes. It was a home run and Mac and Sheckard ran around the bases, throwing up their caps in glee. The whole Baltimore team ran out into the field and executed a war dance. Suddenly, after consultation with Grady, the Giants' catcher, Gaffney ruled foul ball.

At least fifty people stood up in the right field bleachers and yelled that the ball was fair.

The decision that aroused Robbie's wrath came in the eighth inning. George Davis was on second when Gleason hit to center. Brodie got the ball and made the most beautiful throw directly into Robbie's hands. Davis was turning third. Coach Doyle saw that he'd be caught and ordered him back. In turning, Davis ran into McGraw, whereupon Andrews waved Davis in to score, claiming that McGraw had interfered. Robbie then boiled over.

A week later John received notice of his first fine as a manager from President Young. It was dated April 29 and called for five dollars, which he paid.

Umpires, of course, had their troubles enforcing the strict obscene-language rule of the Brush resolution (oaths excepted), and the "no-kicking" regulation of the umpire's rules. Exercising the order of prompt dismissal endangered the strength of clubs. Players sulked when their heavy hitter or aggressor was banished.

Umpire Tom Burns put out three key players in a New York–Brooklyn game for gesturing against his strike calls, whereupon the catcher, Parke Wilson, stepped aside and let one of Cy Seymour's fast pitches plunk Burns in his unprotected stomach. He forfeited the game, but Charles Ebbets wrote to President Young demanding the umpire's dismissal.

Jack Hunt was obliged to forfeit a late-season Baltimore game to Brooklyn. Jimmy Sheckard assaulted him after being called out on an attempted steal and refused to leave the field.

For the record, neither Andrews nor Gaffney was rehired the next year. Burns and Hunt were also through. To help keep peace, President Young assigned Hank O'Day to sixty-eight games in Baltimore and fifty-three in St. Louis. And there was no peace.

Six weeks of the 1899 season passed before John got his team into winning stride. Experimenting with pitching was one drawback, and cost him many games, but Joe McGinnity would always come up with the needed victory just when things looked worst. Then the left-hander, Jerry Nops, broke training, missed trains, and lost games that he could have won by attending to business. John even took on the reformed "Still" Hill, who was not nicknamed for his silence. Still pitched hard and earnestly and remained sober, but he had lost most of his speed and effectiveness.

Desperate for hitting, John obtained Dave Fultz from Philadelphia in July, and the team began to roll upward. The fight and speed and hustle quickly became the talk, not only of the league, but the nation. The pupil was showing up the Svengali. The castoff players were running all opposition into the ground, led by John himself.

After his own poor start, he was hitting better than ever before in his life. He was running faster and more often, setting the standard for the team and the league. In one stretch of thirty-four games, he failed to hit in only two. During a June double-header at Union Park against Brooklyn, he reached first base nine successive times on five hits and four bases on balls. He stole two bases in each game. The Orioles won the first, and threw the second away with Sheckard's three errors from the outfield. But the Orioles outplayed Hanlon's team with all the Brooklyn officials looking on.

The parent club began to worry, because Brooklyn wasn't

pulling away. They weren't pulling crowds, either. Baltimore, with a smaller pay roll, was outdrawing Brooklyn with a larger ball park. On the road, John's team was the best attraction in baseball. They took the headlines and commanded praise.

John was deeply impressed, but the job was scarcely half finished. He could win this thing, take it right out of Hanlon's grasp with just a little help. Where was it? He tried to get Kid Gleason from New York, Frank Foreman from Kansas City, anybody from anywhere. Secretly he dealt Topsy Magoon to Chicago for Gene DeMontreville, both infielders. The scorers had shortened the latter's name to Demont, and John sent a $100 money order for transportation to that name in Chicago.

The telegraph office refused DeMontreville the money and it was several days before the misunderstanding was straightened out with a new money order.

Manager Hanlon was furious over the trade. He announced to the Brooklyn press that Hugh Jennings would be traded to the Orioles for Demont and Jerry Nops. Both Ebbets and Von Der Horst backed up Hanlon. John got Von Der Horst in a corner and won by asking him to reconsider on the basis of fairness.

The Orioles simply surged into August with Demont providing spark and base hits, for he had played with the Orioles a few seasons before. John continued his .400 hitting. He taunted Jimmy Sheckard, an impetuous but great base runner, into fighting him for the base-stealing championship. They had stolen nearly seventy apiece. McGinnity, winner of twenty victories by mid-August, was asking to pitch two and three days in a row, relief or start. It was a crusade for victory. And it was best expressed by Pat Donovan, one of the great outfielders of the day and finally manager of Pittsburgh. He said in late August:

"The Orioles are winning games with strategy at bat. It is the point that McGraw works on all pitchers, great and small. The maneuvers of the Orioles at the bat show the brains, pluck and skill of the two leaders. They'll try anything and outgamble you. For instance, with first and second base occupied and two out, Ducky Holmes came to bat against us and bunted and beat Tannehill's throw to first. This brazen, plucky order of McGraw's not only fooled us, but dumfounded us. He pulled a trick that sent our infield up in the air.

126

"I have seen the Orioles hit away with first and second occupied and none out and a run needed to tie. You would naturally look for a sacrifice, but they fooled us again and again with a guerrilla type of baseball warfare that McGraw and Robbie employ, but it wins and that's why the public likes to see them.

"All the world loves a winner and all is fair in the baseball arena if you win. The achievement of McGraw and Robbie in pulling that Baltimore combination up the line to challenge for the big money is one of the most brilliant in the annals of the game."

Friday, August 25, was an off day in Louisville, but a pleasant one. The whole country was talking about the third-place Orioles. But on Saturday there was a telegram saying that Minnie would be moved from their St. Paul Street home to Maryland General Hospital. Her appendix was badly inflamed. The second telegram to hurry home came after the first game of the Sunday doubleheader. John rushed to the railroad station and waited hours for a train that took an eternity to arrive and another to reach Baltimore.

The wordless greeting of Doctors Bolgiano and Russell told him the worst. Dr. Bolgiano had operated Sunday night on the ruptured appendix and the result was far from good. John tiptoed through the corridor and into the room to see a still, waxen figure, barely conscious. Three days later her hand and life slipped quietly from his.

Telegrams from every club in the league ... friends ... rivals ... fans ... flowers ... whispered words ... his hands and arms gripped in silence by Von Der Horst ... Hanlon ... Kelley ... Hughie ... Robbie ... and four tear-stained Robinson children ... and Ma, who had been so helpful during his absences ... absences that seemed so meaningless now....

Across the threshold of the St. Paul Street house of hope and dreams that youth will always build ... and to the cemetery on a quiet Sunday ... and back to a vacant house that seems to mock even your heavy sighs with an empty echo....

I would have given my life to have been there for one minute to help him, to comfort him, but wives and husbands must weep alone ... for only they can understand.

12

BY THE TIME John returned to the Oriole line-up at Union Park, September 23, 1899, much of the baseball picture had changed. In the matter of base hits and runs, though, it had not changed and never will. John's double and single and a run enabled Baltimore to win out in eleven innings, 5–4. It was a hollow victory over a hapless Cleveland team that won only 20 games of 154 played.

Instead of base hits and victories, the Orioles were anxiously discussing prospects of a job for next year. The National League would almost surely be reduced to eight clubs in 1900. The Robison brothers, having siphoned the best players from Cleveland to St. Louis, would abandon the Lake city. The Wagner brothers, having sold $150,000 of Washington players over a period of five years, were ready to accept anything for the eleventh-place franchise. The Louisville baseball park had burned in September, forcing a transfer of games, but it was well-insured. Barney Dreyfuss was negotiating for the purchase of Pittsburgh. He planned a consolidation of the two teams, with himself as president and young Harry Pulliam as secretary.

But there was no news of Baltimore's future. This troubled John deeply through the remainder of the schedule, and he played only when needed. Sheckard ran on to the base-stealing championship of the league, finally totaling 78 to John's 73. This was remarkable, John always said, because Jimmy batted only .298 to John's .390, and reached first base far less frequently.

Wilbert Robinson, playing the best game of his long career at the age of 35, caught more than 100 games and batted for an average of .288. He alone was largely responsible for the amazing record of rookie Joe McGinnity. The iron worker had pitched 380 innings in 49 games, winning 28 victories against 17 defeats, a first-year record that remained unequaled for twelve years.

The team had attracted 123,416 patrons to Union Park, 901 more than Hanlon's all-star line-up drew in Brooklyn. The colorful and aggressive Orioles had drawn 235,080 paid admissions into the eleven other parks as the best attraction in the league. Hanlon's road attendance was 46,417 under this figure. Herman Bormann, manager of Von Der Horst's brewery and secretary of the ball club, reported a profit of $15,000 from admissions at Union Park, and considerably more from the sale of beer and Ross Klosterman's score cards and peanuts.

In spite of all this, the persistent rumor that Baltimore would be dropped snowballed until the season ended. Hanlon won the pennant going away, but the final games with Baltimore were marred in several ways. Outraged at losing a stolen base on Umpire Hunt's decision on October 14, Jimmy Sheckard tore into the official and, of course, was ordered from the game. When the Orioles took the field, Sheckard went to the outfield. Hunt ordered John to remove him. For reasons known best or only to himself, John told Hunt to do his own ejecting.

Hunt appealed to Ned Hanlon, who occupied the unenviable spot of being Oriole president and manager of the Superbas.

"If Sheckard doesn't leave the game," Hunt warned, "I'll forfeit to Brooklyn."

Hanlon shrugged and said, "Whatever you do, I'll back you up."

The Orioles were leading, 1–0. Victory would have assured John of seven from the fourteen scheduled games with his old manager. But Hunt forfeited the contest to Brooklyn, and then ordered the second game started to appease the large Saturday turnout of Brooklyn fans. The enraged Orioles made a farce of the game, which Brooklyn won in five innings.

Hanlon's victory was marred further by the so-called Wrigley case, involving an infielder who had played for Syracuse. With the Eastern League season completed, George Wrigley signed to play with Andrew Freedman's Giants for thirty days beginning September 15. Four days later the Syracuse Club sold Wrigley's contract for a valuable consideration to Brooklyn on the strength of "right of reservation." After playing four games for New York, Hanlon ordered Wrigley over to the Superbas. He obeyed, played fifteen games, and Freedman appealed to the National Board of Arbitration, a league council.

When Hanlon learned that the Board might decide against him, and even throw out all "Wrigley games," he craftily inserted the disputed player into the line-up in the late innings of games that appeared to be lost. Fifteen games were thrown out by the adverse decision, accompanied by a $500 fine, but Brooklyn's percentage remained unchanged, and Hanlon had saved the pennant thereby.

The decision in the Wrigley case bore out John's contention five years earlier that the end of the baseball contract rendered the player free and unemployed, though reserved for service the next year. It read:

> The National Agreement does not give to the reserving Club the right to control the services of a player after his contract has terminated with the said club; and its right to transfer such reservation is not impaired by any action of the player in entering into the services of any other club after the termination of such contract and before the commencement of the next season of the club to which it has been transferred.

The much-discussed reserve clause was clarified a few years later by the Cincinnati Agreement, and became part of the uniform baseball contract. Today it reads:

> (b) The Club's right of reservation of the Player, and renewal of this contract as aforesaid, and the promise of the Player not to play otherwise than with the Club or an assignee thereof, have been taken into consideration in determining the salary specified herein and the undertaking by the Club to pay said salary is the consideration for both said reservation, renewal, option and promise, and the Player's service.

It was a bitter and disillusioned Ned Hanlon that returned from the December meeting of the National League in New York. The ambitious plan of the Brooklyn-Baltimore syndicate to force Andrew Freedman out of baseball had failed miserably. Hanlon and Ebbets won a pennant, yes, but Baltimore received all the publicity and praise. And Freedman, with a tenth-place, disorganized team, was stronger than ever.

"They tried a little game of freeze-out on us," Hanlon said in a long and embittered interview, "but they found it wouldn't work. We were treated very shabbily and unjustly and, worst of all, we were thrown down by men who we supposed were our friends. Six months ago John T. Brush couldn't find words warm enough to express his contempt for Freedman. Now he is Andy's lackey, doing his dirty work and throwing down the friends who have always been loyal to him.

"This whole Freedman business shows the league magnates up before the public. This man is now the dictator of league officers, and has half the gang crawling on their knees while he cracks the whip over them. That is a pretty spectacle, and must give the public an exalted opinion of the caliber of league magnates.

"The unjust fine imposed upon Brooklyn in the Wrigley case was laid simply as a sop to Freedman, and his tools would have gone much further had they not been scared off by public opinion. The question of right and justice never entered into the matter at all. We will never pay a cent of that fine. We have a written opinion from our counsel advising us that our position is right, and we shall resist to the very end."

Asked about Baltimore's fate in the new eight-club league, Hanlon replied:

"It's impossible to say. When the meeting adjourned Saturday, a committee was appointed to devise ways and means of reducing the circuit. Freedman, Soden, Brush, and that clique want an eight-club league, and to get that Baltimore, Cleveland, Washington, and Louisville must be treated with. Last night we held a long consultation in my room at the Bartholdi in New York. Wagner, Pulliam, Von Der Horst, Abell, and Frank Robison were present, and we talked the matter over. Washington wants forty thousand, Cleveland thirty-five thousand, and Louisville fifteen thousand for their franchises.

"We put no price on Baltimore, but we have one man on the team who alone is worth thirty thousand dollars. I mean McGraw. If I had a club like New York or Chicago, I would give thirty thousand for McGraw in a minute. I would get the money back in the first two months of play!"

Had Hanlon read the newspapers more carefully, he might have gained a clearer understanding of the New York picture. John retained a most revealing clipping dated a month before the league meeting. It was headlined, "Peace Ratified, Reconciliation between Freedman and Brush Complete," and continued:

New York, Nov. 14—In the face of threatened opposition of the new American Association of Base Ball Clubs, the magnates of the National League are making an effort to restore harmony in the ranks of that organization in order the better to combat this infantile rival. The first step in this direction has been taken by what is known as the "Brush faction" in the National League. Brush and his associates have been fighting Andrew Freedman, the president and chief owner of the New York club, for two or three years.

They coveted an opportunity to work a "freeze-out" on Freedman, but that person has not lived in vain and knows a trick or two himself. Freedman is a wealthy man and has plenty of nerve. He merely let matters drift, losing money at the rate of $100,000 per annum and let it be understood that he would lose a million dollars before he would knuckle to such men as Brush, and his little circle of acquaintances. Freedman has now been rewarded. Brush has yielded to him, and the National League will have to "see Freedman" for a couple of years before it can do business.

Business at Robinson and McGraw's Diamond Café had boomed during 1899. The proprietors' thrilling results with the Orioles had made it the sports headquarters of the east. John and Robinson journeyed to New York on November 3 to become experts on the heavyweight fight situation. They saw the new heavyweight champion, Jim Jeffries, conqueror of Bob Fitzsimmons, engage Tom Sharkey at Coney Island in one of the greatest fights ever staged. Dressed in evening clothes, the ballplayers were not only visible at the ringside, but identifiable in the motion pictures of the fight shown soon after at Ford's Opera House.

And it was a great conversation piece to the sports fans at the café. Droves came in just to hear the baseball heroes tell of the fight, for now some were saying Sharkey was robbed.

"In his condition," Robbie declared, "you could've stole his teeth and he wouldn't have known it. He got beat good!"

Through the holidays and well into January, 1900, the café became headquarters for baseball intrigue. As Baltimore's chances of remaining in the National League dimmed, whispers about the revived American Association grew louder. John had lost interest in the fate of the National League through its refusal to worry about the game on the field. By the first of the year he was confronted with a chance to operate a team in the new league long before the Orioles were officially out of the National.

The plan was hatched, if not conceived, by Frank Richter, editor of the pioneer sports weekly, *Sporting Life*, founded in Philadelphia in 1883. He was ably abetted by one Al Spink, of the St. Louis *Sporting News*, founded in 1886 by his brother, Charles C. Spink, father of J. G. Taylor Spink. Taylor eventually took over as publisher and built the "Bible of Baseball" to an unchallenged position in the field. The 1900 Association was Al Spink's second offense, for it was he who had interested Chris Von der Ahe as a pioneer in the first American Association in 1881.

The two most glamorous names to the fans and players in 1900 were Cap Anson and John J. McGraw. Anson, who had retired as a baseball player with a modest fortune after 1897, agreed to head an Association team in Chicago. Baltimore capital was easily raised, once John agreed to head a team of Orioles. A franchise was assigned to the Baltimore Base Ball Amusement Company, with Phil Peterson, of the Glosman Ginger Ale Company, as president. Peterson had been captain and outstanding star of the famous Maryland hockey team. John's participation was conditional, however, on an eight-club membership, and not six or even seven. Organizers agreed, and his word was final. John made no secret of his joining the new movement.

The new American Association was actually announced in Philadelphia on January 30, with Harry Quin as president. The various cities and managers disclosed were, Pat Donovan, Detroit; Joe Kelley, Philadelphia; Hugh Jennings, Milwaukee; Bill "Scrappy" Joyce, St. Louis; Billy Murray, Providence; Tom McCarthy, Boston; Cap Anson, Chicago; and John McGraw, Baltimore.

The one drawback was that John's contract for the Baltimore franchise, which he kept, contained only six guarantors. They were, Phil Peterson, of Baltimore; Tom McCarthy, of Boston; George D. Schaefer, of St. Louis; H. D. Quin, of Milwaukee; A. C. Anson, of Chicago; and Thomas J. Navin, of Detroit. There were backers, but no signatures for Providence or Philadelphia.

Peterson pulled a coup in Baltimore by paying $3,500 as a year's rent on Union Park. Hanlon's lease had expired, and through a technicality, Peterson dealt successfully with trustees for the Sadtler estate. Hanlon hurried to Baltimore and got a court injunction, stalling things until the facts could be studied.

John moved quietly and firmly from city to city, talking to the several owners or their representatives, lining up players, and watching for signs of performance bonds. His presence at a pivotal Chicago convention moved the National League to take drastic steps. From Cleveland they announced that the pioneer league had finally been reduced to eight clubs. The four clubs cut loose were purchased by the league and would be paid for by a 10-per-cent levy on gate receipts. New York, last-place club of the eight, would have first pick of the players.

"The Cleveland and Louisville franchises," the league announced, "will be sold to the Western League, or American League, as President Ban Johnson now calls it. In the East the Baltimore and Washington franchises will be purchased by President Pat Powers in behalf of the Eastern League."

But this wasn't enough to stop the Association plans. The National League moved defensively again within a few weeks. They permitted Ban Johnson to bring the St. Paul franchise, headed by Charles Comiskey, into Chicago and play on the South Side, as an American League team. The National League team, owned by Hart and Spalding, held forth then on the West Side.

The Association rolled on, however, and stopped only when John visited Philadelphia in mid-February.

"My visit to Philadelphia," he announced, "was mainly to sign up two star players of the National League there, on whom Anson had an option that expired yesterday. Anson asked me to sign them only if Gilmore [the Philadelphia backer] had put up his forfeit. Last Thursday week, when I finally got Mr. Gilmore into the Association, he promised to send his guarantee money to Chicago by either Mr. Reeger or Mr. Richter, and he failed to. Mr. Gilmore first told me yesterday he had sent the money, and then admitted that he had not, due to the difficulty of finding grounds.

"I told him that this matter must be settled at once so players could be signed. His final telegram said it would take three weeks. That is too long, and I have so informed my Baltimore people.

My own plans now are to attend to my business. I have not heard from Mr. Hanlon, but since we are good personal friends, I'm sure he will advise me on my status as soon as he knows of it himself."

A month later word was first whispered that John and Wilbert would play for Frank Robison in St. Louis.

"I've been working on a good idea," John said, and the crowd edged into a circle around him. "I'm going to take the best amateur talent procurable in the city and coach the players up to a good standard. There are young men here in Baltimore who have made a fine showing on the Lafayette, Atlantic, Woodberry, M.A.C., Walbrook, and other teams.

"Robbie and I would like the pick of these to coach into a cracker-jack nine. Possibly we might get some college players, after the order of the Atlantic City nine. This team of ours would be ready to meet all comers. The next step would be to form the better teams into a league and provide a championship schedule.

"We've already had a talk with Mr. James L. Kernan [proprietor of four large Baltimore theaters at the time], who has offered to put up a grandstand, construct a diamond, and enclose the whole at Riverview Park. With fifteen and twenty-five cents charged for admission, good crowds would likely be attracted. Probably Mr. Fenneman would like to bring Electric Park into the circuit. But I look for lively times for ourselves, a lot livelier than going to St. Louis and coming back here no more than twice a season to see a dying business venture. And we can do a lot more good for Baltimore baseball."

There was no plumbing the depths of John McGraw's sincerity in the matter of Baltimore baseball. He proved it by ignoring a stern legal letter received at the end of March from the Brooklyn Ball Club. Drafted in a neat Spencerian on a lined-paper letterhead, it read:

Brooklyn, N. Y.
March 29, 1900

John J. McGraw Esq.
c/o The Diamond
Baltimore, Md.
DEAR SIR:
I desire to notify you on behalf of the Brooklyn Ball Club, that the contractual obligations entered into between you and

the Baltimore Base Ball Club for your services during the National League Base Ball Season of 1900, were on March 9th transferred as provided in said contract to the Brooklyn Ball Club.

And further to notify you, that on March 10th last the Brooklyn Ball Club transferred to the American Base Ball and Athletic Exhibition Company of St. Louis, Mo., the contractual obligations upon your services as above mentioned and provided for in the aforesaid contract signed by you.

Sincerely yours,
C. H. Ebbets, *Pres.*
The Brooklyn Ball Club

Knowing baseball players, it is hard to imagine any of them holding out all summer. Knowing John McGraw, it was impossible to think of him without a baseball game to be planned and played. A fish out of water doesn't describe it, because fish can't snarl and growl and pace the floor and complain bitterly about nothing at all. That was John when kept from the ball park during the season by illness or emergency. And yet, he always claimed that he had no intention of going to St. Louis, and Robinson had even less.

"But we wouldn't have been away from baseball," he explained. "The amateur teams and the instruction and the building of a practical, self-supporting league would have been harder work and more interesting than managing the Orioles. Both of us were looking forward to it when the Judge came in that night."

"The Judge" was Harry Goldman, a young financier, with a record of baseball enthusiasm ever since he was able to yell. He was one of the youngest sponsors of the 1894 victory banquet. He showed up at the Diamond one evening in April, 1900, with a plan for Baltimore baseball—the next year.

"I've got plenty of backing," he exclaimed. "Fresh money, and good money. Sydney Frank is all for it. So is his brother, Moses. He's on the City Council, Second Branch—used to own part of Hanlon's Orioles."

"What about the park?" Robinson asked. "Got to get a park."

"If we can't get Union, we'll build," Harry said.

"Then you have got money," John laughed.

"You got to have land to build on," Robinson reminded.

The Judge laughed. "We've got our hands on all the land we need—on car lines, too. But you've got to go to St. Louis."

John and Robinson listened to the rest of the plan. They would sign up with St. Louis, hold out, and get more salary, if necessary. Then go out and get in touch with Ban Johnson, head of the American League. Johnson had a strong circuit. Goldman had watched his operation from afar. He never seemed to have trouble. He was a good administrator. Johnson was growing. He had put teams into two big cities. He had a Cleveland millionaire named Somers behind him in Cleveland. Now he was in Chicago and wanted to get into the eastern cities. Well, this was the chance.

John and Robinson would go west, contact Johnson secretly, and line up an American League franchise for Baltimore. Once that was set, Goldman would spend the whole year organizing. John and Robinson would spend the whole year lining up players. It wasn't wrong, because in 1901 the National Agreement was expiring. They'd all be free to sign with any team or league.

And so McGraw and Robinson reported to St. Louis on May 5, 1900.

13

BYRON BANCROFT JOHNSON was a former newspaperman who had come from the same sports department and publication, the Cincinnati *Commercial Gazette*, that had produced Oliver Perry Caylor, co-organizer of the successful American Association in 1881. Through his sports stories Johnson had long criticized the management and policies of Cincinnati owner, John T. Brush. When the Western League became sadly in need of administration, Brush, through a combination of sarcasm, pique, and desperation, recommended Johnson. Brush's Cincinnati manager, the pioneering Charles Comiskey, reached the minor-league meeting ahead of his boss and quickly presented the name of his newspaper friend as coming from the National League power. Reporter Johnson left the 1894 meeting as a league president and began the long and difficult job of building up a minor league at the age of twenty-eight.

At the end of the season, Comiskey left Brush, bought the Sioux City franchise in Johnson's league, and shifted it to St. Paul. Two years later Connie Mack lost out as Pittsburgh manager and joined Johnson by taking over the Milwaukee team as manager and co-owner. Three years later, as I have noted, Johnson developed the Cleveland territory, abandoned by the Robisons, and a few months after that, helped Comiskey move his St. Paul club into South Chicago as the White Stockings or Sox.

When John, Wilbert Robinson, Charles Comiskey, and Ban Johnson held the first of many secret meetings at Chicago in June, 1900, the American League comprised Detroit, Minneapolis, Milwaukee, Buffalo, Kansas City, Indianapolis, Cleveland, and Chicago. Its outstanding pitcher of the previous year was an eccentric named Rube Waddell who had won twenty-six games for Grand Rapids and seven for Louisville after transferring to Louisville late in the season. Waddell, of course, went to Pittsburgh in the consolidation.

"I was deeply impressed by Ban Johnson," John recalled in describing their first meeting in Chicago. "Comiskey brought us together, and Robbie and I did a lot of listening. I think what impressed me most was his businesslike methods and failure to butter us up as the most talked-about baseball stars in the country. He never let us lose sight of the fact that he was a league president.

"He agreed with my expressed views on umpires—that they should be firm and completely in charge. We also agreed that the play on the field, hard, fair, colorful, and aggressive, was the key, the very cornerstone of all baseball, organized or disorganized. The player always had a right to challenge the umpire on a point of rule or interpretation. We also agreed that opinion decisions should be final, since a pitched ball was nothing—could be neither strike nor ball—until an umpire called it, which also applied to base running and everything but the written or unwritten rules.

"Johnson was a big man, and overweight, but he got around very fast for his size. He talked clearly and firmly. He was young and imaginative and fearless, and he sure knew where he was going. He also had sound and fair views that matched mine on the subject of preserving the game of baseball on the field—the contest, the hard playing to avoid losing. While National League owners were fighting each other, Johnson was fighting for baseball as a game first, and for territorial growth after. I liked that.

"Johnson said, 'The National League is being administered to death, and the American League is the only thing that can keep baseball alive.' Robbie and I talked most of the night after that first meeting. For the first time in our lives we were privileged to see a blueprint of sound and sincere administrative baseball. We were stanch American Leaguers after that, but, above all, baseball players."

Much has been written about John's "contract jumping" at the end of the season in St. Louis to join the American League.

"I jumped no contract then or at any other time," John has stated emphatically many times. "The chief delay in our signing with Mr. Robison came from our demand that the reserve condition for the next year be eliminated. Goldman was making big plans in Baltimore. We couldn't afford the charge of contract-jumping at any time. We did a yearly business of hundreds of thousands of dollars on North Howard Street. We had contracts for beer, liquor, food, lights, bowling and billiard equipment, supplies, dishes and glasses, and many other items. To us the baseball contract was as sacred as any legal document."

The four men shook hands in Chicago, and that was their contract. Even the matter of lining up signed players was removed from the "jumping" class. Johnson explained that the so-called National Agreement of 1891, which had governed his minor-league alignment with the big league would expire at the end of the tenth year, 1900. It would not be renewed unless the American League was permitted to enter abandoned territory, like Baltimore and Washington. Players were to be lined up secretly, of course, but Johnson cautioned John and Robbie on pledging or signing players who would not keep their word. Respect for the handshake would have to take precedence over the legal power of the signature.

Over the years, John has implied that he did not give all his attention to St. Louis baseball during 1900, but his playing record doesn't show it. He even recited how he had satisfied his urge to bet on horse races by sending messengers with the money between innings of ball games. Even though the horse track was almost next to Chris Von der Ahe's old park, I doubt that it was regular practice, and I have wondered if the story was told for the sake of "spicing" the account of his career. Not that he wasn't fond of horse racing and the added excitement of betting, for he was. After we had started keeping company in Baltimore, we often drove out to the picturesque Pimlico Race Track, at Pimlico and Belvedere, for an afternoon. I was out there recently, and the grandstand had been altered but little.

The trip to Pimlico was always interesting, and relaxing. It seemed fun to back a winner, and correspondingly disappointing not to. I never heard John complain, except momentarily, over losing a wager. I don't imagine he ever wagered enough to embarrass himself financially.

All this, I realize, does not solve the moral aspects of betting on horse races, or gambling of any kind. But with John McGraw, it was part of his life and times. It was being one of the grown-up group, and matching wits or luck with the bet-holders, each of whom was licensed by law. Betting on horse races, or owning race horses, was never frowned upon openly in baseball until Commissioner Landis arrived as supervisor in 1921. Then it was a necessary expedient to help convince the public that baseball was pure in mind and deed, despite the eight tragically dishonest Chicago White Sox players of 1919. No one, not even John McGraw, suffered from the Landis ruling, and it was good for baseball. With the death of Landis in 1944, the ban was overlooked and then ignored.

The 1900 baseball season was far less than a thrilling one on the field for John and Robinson. The same Oliver Tebeau John had battled in Gainesville, Florida, ten years before, was manager of St. Louis, but he had lost much of his good and bad aggressiveness.

He had a fairly strong team, led by the great Cy Young, Jess Burkett, and Bobby Wallace, all of whom had come over from Cleveland. Long before the end of the season, the following comment appeared in the New York *Sun:*

> It is rumored among baseball players that Oliver Tebeau is soon to be removed from the management of the St. Louis team and that John McGraw is to succeed him. President Frank DeHaas Robison is greatly disappointed over the show-

ing of his high-priced team and has been making an investigation into the causes of the slump. It is said that Tebeau has been too lenient with his players, that some of them have been dissipating, and that there is a faction anxious to have McGraw at the helm. While the St. Louis team was here last week it was apparent that trouble existed among the men and that they were not playing their real game. McGraw was asked if he would assume the management if Tebeau should be removed and his reply was:

"I do not want the place and am not looking for it."

McGraw was a most capable manager at Baltimore last year and several League clubs wanted him in that capacity for this season. But he was sold to St. Louis and has been under Tebeau's orders ever since. He has been captain of the team and as such has exercised his authority, but has not been able to put into effect the methods that made him successful last year. McGraw has been playing excellent ball at all stages, and, like others of his associates, is chagrined at the low standing of the team in the race for the pennant. Tebeau has been with Robison for many years, and is said to be financially interested in the St. Louis Club. If Robison removes him, it will have to be with Tebeau's consent, it is thought, as the latter is not the kind of a man to be thrown down in view of his past relations with his employer. Robison put up nearly $25,000 before the season to provide a winner for St. Louis that would include McGraw and Robinson. The long street car strike, injuries to the players and trouble among the members of the team have made the St. Louis Club a loser, and Robison, in response to public clamor, will be compelled to make a radical move.

For the record, John appeared in 98 games in 1900, made 115 hits in 341 times at bat for a percentage of .337. He stole 28 bases and scored 84 runs. Robinson batted .255, and caught 56 games, during which he committed only six errors. The club finished in a tie for fifth place with Chicago.

The chief reason for the failure of St. Louis and five other clubs lay in consolidation. With the best of the 1899 Orioles transferred to Brooklyn, Ned Hanlon had little trouble winning his second straight pennant. The power of consolidation was further reflected in Pittsburgh, which retained the best of Louisville. Just imagine a team playing better than .500 baseball, as Pittsburgh had in 1899, being augmented by Rube Waddell, Deacon Phillippe, Fred Clarke, and Honus Wagner! Little wonder the Dreyfuss-Pulliam team remained a National League power for ten years. It would have been unbeatable but for subsequent player losses to the American League, like Jess Tannehill and Jack Chesbro, pitchers.

Harry Goldman's results matched his enthusiasm, and the boys returned home after the baseball season to find incorporation papers all drawn for the Baltimore Base Ball and Athletic Company. Capital stock in the amount of $40,000 had been subscribed for 400 shares. Sydney Frank, holder of the biggest block, was president. Goldman was secretary. John and Robinson not only bought stock for cash, but received more for accepting smaller salaries. Robinson's contract called for $3,000. As manager-player, John signed himself for $5,000, about a fourth of what he could have commanded anywhere in baseball at the time. There were several minority holders, and others waited to be called upon.

"What's the latest on Union Park?" John asked anxiously.

Goldman heaved a sigh. "Hanlon still has it tied up."

"What'll he do with it next summer?" Robbie demanded. "Hold Elks' picnics? He'll be lucky to operate in Brooklyn."

"It doesn't make any difference," John said. "He's got it."

"We may still get it," Goldman said optimistically. "But in case not, we had plans drawn. We can build at Electric Park, or two more spots, one near Druid Hill Park, and another on Belair Road. We've got an option on some Johns Hopkins property on York and Twenty-ninth, high, level, and good drainage."

"It don't seem right, not to play at old Union," Robbie muttered. "I'll miss that rickety old two-plank bridge across the drainage ditch to the clubhouse."

"It was only rickety when you went over it," John laughed.

"If you'd grown to any size, Mac, you might've made it shake," Robbie said, and then shook his large self, guffawing at the comparison.

"You'll miss the double-deck grandstand, too, Robbie," Goldman added. "We can't afford to seat more than six thousand under the roof. But we'll have our own ball field!"

Excitement rose to a new high on North Howard Street as the hot-stove league fans gathered and lingered at the Diamond nightly for the latest in baseball intrigue. Where had McGraw been lately and what happened? John was called to a succession of meetings through the fall principally in Philadelphia and New York. It was the same in each city—another plea to reconsider his action in "deserting" the National League.

"I was called twice to see Andrew Freedman," John confided. "But each time he had no solution to baseball's problems. I don't think he knew the real reason for the rapid switch to the American League by many leading players who were not even demanding big salaries. All he could say was that I had a fine future before me in the National League and that I was foolish to quit St. Louis. I reminded him that Robbie and I also had pasts. They should be considered. But he kept on talking future. He wasn't arrogant or threatening at any time, though.

" 'See here, Mr. Freedman,' I said finally, 'you seem to be the whole thing in the league now. Why not talk with Johnson?'

" 'Oh, no, no,' he said, 'I can't have anything to do with Johnson.'

"And when I returned to Baltimore, I sat down and wrote a letter right away to Johnson, reporting the facts of the meeting."

From each of these cities, John made secret side trips to see baseball players in the area. Nothing could be gained by coercion, or promising the moon. He first established a beachhead of personal confidence, and then tried to win belief in the cause. I might say that the famous players, like John, Comiskey, Griffith, Mack, Robinson, and others—and Hanlon, too—could get and hold a player's ear quicker than a wealthy owner who had never played.

Historic Union Park stood in mocking emptiness as half of the new corporation's capital went to Henry S. Rippel, contractor. He trucked thousands of feet of gleaming lumber from his big Pinckney Street yards to York and Twenty-ninth after ground had been broken on Lincoln's Birthday, 1901. Hanlon had every right to tie up the old plant, of course, as a business protection, but it seemed such a financial waste with so much at stake.

Eager to accelerate interest before the ground-breaking ceremonies, which I detailed earlier in the story, John intimated to the press that all might be well in baseball politics in the not-too-distant future. Peace was inevitable. A conference was possible, and he paraphrased the old Yankee saw, "There's only been one storm that never cleared up—and that's this one." How soon? He didn't know. But it might be sooner than people think.

Newspapers and press associations seized upon the intimation and wrote volumes into it for the next few days. The outburst brought an immediate response from the American League president, affording an interesting insight into the spirit of the times:

American League
Professional Base Ball Clubs
1203 Fisher Building
Chicago

February 12, 1901

Mr. John J. McGraw
Baltimore, Md.

DEAR SIR:

I can only guess your motive in giving out the story of a peace conference between the American and National Leagues. Possibly you wanted to crowd the League players in the matter of getting them under contract. At all events it was a good scheme, and put the National League fellows way up in the air. They knew, of course, no peace negotiations were on, and they were at a loss to explain the purpose of that Baltimore story. It put a kink in the American Association contingent, and from this out they will be looking for a "throw down."

The American League teams, with possibly the exception of Boston and Philadelphia, are about completed. The Milwaukee team is made up, and Comiskey has all his players in line with the one exception of Padden. Griffith and Wallace are signed. Comiskey hopes to get Fielder Joes [Jones], of the Brooklyn club. Flick is willing to sign for $2800. but the clubs are afraid to touch him on account of his Philadelphia contract. I will leave for the East tonight. Will be in Cleveland tomorrow and hope to be in Washington by Thursday. With kind regards, I am—

Yours Truly,
B. B. JOHNSON

John's biggest catch of the winter was the Iron Man himself, Joe McGinnity. It must have been a strange and moving sight, the two of them huddled close on a corner bench in the waiting room of Union Station, St. Louis. It was late at night in February, and it was cold. Joe had come up from South McAlester, Indian Territory, to meet John on his way to Hot Springs, Arkansas. Drawn by an affinity that baseball players best understand, the iron worker asked only one question.

"The money good, Mac?"

"Good as gold, Joe," John whispered. "Every penny."

Placing the contract on his knee, and the pen in his rough and grubby hand, the greatest of all curve-ball pitchers signed to play for the Baltimore Orioles of the American League in 1901 for $2,800. He had been offered nearly twice that amount by Ebbets and Hanlon.

They parted with a handshake. McGinnity returned to his "Brass Fittings, Iron Castings, and Mine Pumps," and John continued on to the winter Mecca of the overweighted and sluggish baseball players. Three weeks later a report from the Arkansas spa said:

> It is essentially an American League camp, so much so that a National League agent appearing, even with a flag of truce, would meet the icy glare. The consensus of opinion is that Ban Johnson is the new Moses, who has led the players out of bondage into the land of fat salaries and soft snaps. And with but few exceptions the bunch of players here have all decided to stick by the American.
>
> John McGraw, manager of the Baltimores, came here to recuperate from his arduous labors of the winter, which consisted of counting the receipts of his Baltimore emporium, drawing on Frank DeHaas Robison for back pay and giving his friend, and mentor, Ned Hanlon, the hooks. He is as chipper as the McGraw of old, had a suite of rooms at the swell Eastman and spent his afternoons at the Southern and Arkansas Clubs. The doughtiest magnate of them all—nay not even Andy Freedman, of New York—could cut a wider swath than does the little Pooh Bah of the American League.
>
> McGraw departed yesterday, flushed with the benefits of a

thorough boiling out, a successful coup in the pool rooms and another raid on the National League's stars.

The latter was a broadside fore and aft, for the foxy little schemer gathered in Mike Donlin of the St. Louis Club and Jimmy Williams of the Pittsburghs. The versatile Donlin lent a willing ear to his team mate of last year, for he is sore on the Robisons and sorer on his thirst for St. Louis nectar, which has led him into so many scrapes. Besides, Mike figured that with Burkett, Heidrick and Donovan in the outer garden, there would be little chance for him to play, while McGraw promised him a steady berth.

Understandably there were difficulties, misunderstandings, many unfounded charges, and a few legal violations. Players were striving to help themselves, often in complete ignorance of the law. When necessary or convenient, owners in the rival leagues shifted the responsibility to the player's conscience or lack of it.

The most celebrated of the few contract violations was that of Napoleon Lajoie, one of the all-time great hitters and fielders. The Philadelphia Nationals protected themselves by signing the Frenchman for 1901. But Lajoie signed with Connie Mack, half-owner of the Athletics. His partner was Alfred Reach, equipment manufacturer, who had long been associated with Col. James Rogers in the operation of the Philadelphia National League team. As an inducement to back the Athletics, Ban Johnson contracted to use only Reach baseballs throughout the American League.

The Philadelphia Nationals took the Lajoie contract into civil court and lost. They appealed and won a reversal that acknowledged priority of their contract. By the time they received the good news, however, Lajoie had completed a full and glorious season in the new league. He was the champion batter with an average of .405. After one game of the 1902 season, Lajoie was transferred to Cleveland. He remained beyond jurisdiction of a Pennsylvania injunction by not accompanying the Cleveland team to Philadelphia.

The players' zeal in the matter of self-help is reflected in a lighter vein by the case of troubled Jimmy Sheckard. He was just twenty-two when John and Harry Goldman visited him at his home at Columbus, Pennsylvania, in February, 1901. Jimmy signed an Oriole contract. He asked for and received a $100 check as an advance against salary. Summoned to Brooklyn, he accepted $100 for signing and mailed it to John.

Arriving home, Jimmy found a second Baltimore check, which he had requested, and the Brooklyn check for $100, which John rejected because he had signed with Baltimore first.

"I don't know what to do," Sheckard wailed. "Hanlon and Ebbets have treated me well, and I like Brooklyn. I like McGraw, too, and I want to play under him. He said if the option clause is legal, he'll drop his claim to me. That's the kind of fellow he is."

Like many other hero-worshiping players in both leagues, Jimmy suffered a severe conflict of loyalties. John waited a few weeks and then told Jimmy to play for Hanlon and play hard. Sheckard couldn't play any other way. He batted .353 in 1901 as a Brooklyn outfielder and stole 42 bases.

Perhaps the most graphic first-hand report of the interleague strife came out of the Congressional hearings of 1951 on the study of monopoly power. Particularly impressive was the testimony of Clark Griffith, president of the Washington Senators, and one of the game's great pitchers at the turn of the century. He left Chicago's West Side to join Comiskey on the South Side. Herewith are a few excerpts from Mr. Griffith's testimony as he was questioned by E. Ernest Goldstein, General Counsel for the Celler subcommittee:

MR. GOLDSTEIN: Now, is it not true that when the American League desired to expand eastward, the National League resisted it?

MR. GRIFFITH: That is right.

MR. GOLDSTEIN: And as a matter of fact, this refusal of the National League resulted in the American League's turning outlaw, so to speak?

MR. GRIFFITH: No. We were never outlaw, because we never broke faith. We co-operated with the minor leagues just the same as the National League did. We simply had a fight with the National League for territory they had vacated, you might say. Washington ... Cleveland ... Baltimore had been put out of the National League. We applied to go into those cities, and they said, "No, that belongs to us; that territory belongs to us."

We said, "No, it don't."

So we had an argument, and a fight, over the thing. But we were not an outlaw league at any time, in any sense, because we co-operated with the minor leagues at all times.

Further interrogation developed Mr. Griffith's belief that a reserve factor existed in the re-employment clause. As I have tried to explain before, that "reserve" was merely a promise to sign if and when the new contract was presented. Mr. Goldstein then asked about Mr. Griffith's so-called jumping to the American League.

MR. GRIFFITH: I would have to go back, Mr. Chairman, on the thing. The thing that caused it was this. We had had the Brotherhood; we had had the American Association; and we had had everything, and it had all gone up in thin air. And the National League was the only league in the field, and they were failing. I remember being on the gate in Cleveland at one time. In the old days you pitched today and went on the gate to-morrow. And I counted up in Cleveland that there were 56 people at the ball game.

So we all recognized the fact—we had all been in other leagues in bygone days, Charlie Comiskey and Ban Johnson and all those fellows—we said that we would have to have another league, something, in order to bring baseball back into its own. And we applied, in a nice way, to the National League. We got the idea of the new league and applied to them for the territory that they had vacated, and they would not give it to us. Otherwise there would not have been any fight between the two leagues.

They would not let us have those franchises. They said, "We won't let you go into these towns."

We said, "We are going to go in, anyway."

That was what caused the fight between the two leagues. But the whole idea of the thing was that baseball was on its way down if something did not happen, because there had been a lot of leagues. You can look back in the history of baseball and see three leagues, and then the American Association was

The Stafford

WASHINGTON PLACE
BALTIMORE.

Baltimore, Md
July 16th 1902,

The June deal by clause must be stricken out of this in contract

I agree to play Base Ball for the New York Base Ball Club the balance season 1902 for the the sum of Two Thousand Dollars $2.000. I also agree to sign for season 1903 for Four Thousand Dollars $4.000. Salary above mentioned to be paid in same monthly installments I further agree to live up to all Club rules training discipotion etc.

Joe McGinnity

One of John McGraw's most treasured possessions—his last-minute agreement that brought Iron Man Joe McGinnity to the Giants.

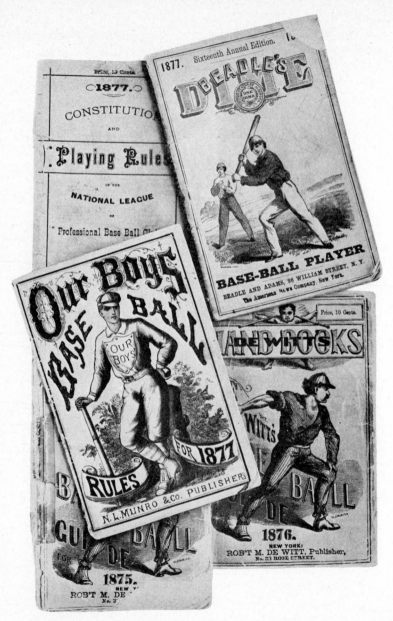

These old and well-thumbed handbooks were the foundation of John McGraw's knowledge of baseball from its early days.

an opponent of the National League for many, many years, the old St. Louis Browns and all the famous teams. But it got to where they were put out of the picture. They could not go on any longer. And they had a twelve-club league, and that was a flop.

Then the National League threw away four of these twelve clubs. And it just got to where baseball was on its way down.

Mr. Goldstein then led into a question that pointed up the importance of signing so many former National League players.

MR. GOLDSTEIN: Now, have you any doubt that the American League would have failed except by taking the direct action that it did by going into the territory of the National League and taking players off the reserve of the National League?

MR. GRIFFITH: I doubt it. We could not have been a big league for quite some time. You know, it takes time to develop ballplayers. You must remember this fact, that the American League was the American League one year before it was a big league. They called it the American League. And when they did start to expand, Connie Mack went from Milwaukee to Philadelphia, and the Kansas City club came to Washington, and so on.

Mr. Griffith's statement is clearly verified by the fact that more than 85 per cent of the American League players of 1901 had played in the National League the season before. It was a ruinous decimation of National League skill and power. John had signed the nucleus of a good team, and most of them were young. For the opening of the 1901 season his line-up was:

Player, position	1900 team
John McGraw, 3b	St. Louis
Mike Donlin, lf	St. Louis
Jimmy Williams, 2b	Pittsburgh
Billy Keister, ss	St. Louis
Cy Seymour, rf	New York (pitcher)
James Jackson, cf	(new)

Frank Foutz, 1b	(new)
Wilbert Robinson, c	St. Louis
Joe McGinnity, p	Brooklyn

The Orioles of 1901 have been called "humpty dumpties" and "worst excuse for a ball club ever" and worse. That simply wasn't true. It was young, fast, hustling, and had six .300 hitters among the regulars. Its main weakness was lack of a strong first baseman, for Donlin was playing there before the season was half over. It also lacked another strong, dependable pitcher to help McGinnity. Joe won 26 victories before his late-season suspension (for using foul language to the umpire), but he also lost 19. Handsome Harry Howell (from Brooklyn) won 14, but lost 21. These two accounted for 60 per cent of the Orioles' victories and also 60 per cent of the defeats.

The American League season opened on April 24 with much fanfare in Chicago, where Griffith's White Sox defeated Jimmy McAleer's Cleveland Indians. Three more games of the schedule were played next day. Baltimore, as I reported earlier, suffered a two-day postponement through rain. But our opening was gala enough, with a big street parade involving forty carriages and loads of flowers. President Ban Johnson attended and threw out the first ball. Some 10,371 fans whipped up lots of enthusiasm, overcrowded the park, and saw John's new team defeat the Boston Red Sox, with the veteran Jimmy Collins as manager, by a score of 10–2. Billy Keister made three hits. John, Donlin, and Jackson made two apiece. Joe Cantillion umpired.

The season was launched. The "war" was on, particularly in Boston, Philadelphia, and Chicago, where the National League had teams. There was no attempt, of course, to avoid conflicting schedules. On the contrary, killing competition was invited as a test of strength.

Much has been written about the supposed differences between John McGraw and President Ban Johnson. For reasons that will soon be obvious, John did nothing to dispel the idea. Basis of the publicized trouble was said to be in Johnson's rules and umpires. But John has always kept President Johnson's first official bulletin. If he failed to understand it when issued, he had thirty years for the task because it never left his private papers:

Chicago, Illinois
May 8, 1901

DEAR SIR:

The clubs will please make their ten percent returns after each series of games. All transportation bills must be paid promptly. For all amounts exceeding one hundred dollars please send a New York draft or Chicago Exchange. The rule requiring the clubs to cut their players to fourteen will not be in force until May 20th. Please notify your official scorer to make his reports after each series of games. I will permit no delay in this matter.

The club Managers are requested to institute such reforms as will shorten the games. In some of the cities of the American League the games have been long drawn out, and there has been much complaint. The catchers hereafter will play up behind the bat throughout the game. This is a standing order.

CLEAN BALL is the MAIN PLANK in the American League platform, and the clubs must stand by it religiously. There must be no profanity on the ball field. The umpires are agents of the League and must be treated with respect. I will suspend any Manager or player who uses profane or vulgar language to an Umpire, and that suspension will remain in force until such time as the offender can learn to bridle his tongue. Rowdyism and profanity have worked untold injury to base ball. To permit it would blight the future of the American League. This bulletin you will please hand to your Manager so that he may impart its contents to the players.

All fines must be paid within five days of the date of mailing notice. In the event of a club failing to pay a fine the player will be suspended until the fine is paid. You will please forward to me at once your contracts with the players so that they may be approved and filed. I am—

Yours truly,
B. B. JOHNSON

Johnson ruled with a firm hand, as John always knew he would. Even the president's best friend, Comiskey, suffered two player losses. Big John Katoll, a pitcher, was suspended for a "minor" offense, throwing a ball at an umpire's head, but with good control. Bill Shugart, a shortstop, was black-listed for serious offenses, and left the game that year. McGinnity's late-season suspension was hailed by papers partial to the National League as "a sure sign that Joe will jump back to Hanlon." Even at this risk, Johnson backed up his umpires.

The Orioles' first year in the American League was not a howling success, nor was it the dismal failure claimed by historians who, of course, were obliged to accept partisan news as fact. The baseball guides report Baltimore's paid attendance for the 70 home games as 141,952. Newspapers reported a profit of $15,000. This is hardly supported by the total receipts at home and abroad of $52,860.38. Of this sum, $11,183.82 went to visiting teams, on the basis of the then prevailing rate of 12½ cents for each paid admission. Actually, then, attendance was a little below 90,000 for all home games.

The corporation's operating loss was only $7,926.40, and many of the competing clubs in both leagues would have rejoiced at such a figure. However, the Orioles would have shown a handsome profit, had they not been obliged to build a new plant while old Union Park remained idle.

14

JOHN McGRAW's transfer from Baltimore to the New York Giants in July, 1902—from the American League to the National —was wholly unexpected by press and public. Sports writers of the day combined the few available facts with partisan surmises, and as a result, John has been called many uncomplimentary names in history books and in newspapers from which most of the books are written and rewritten. He has been accused of trickery, trapping Ban Johnson and the American League, deserting his Baltimore friends and backers, selling out to the National

League at a big price, and whatever traitorous terms could be heaped upon his unprotesting head.

All of this is untrue, as I shall show. He never flinched or protested, for the sole reason that baseball could be helped only by vigorous competition on the field and rivalry between two strong leagues. John was the key that unlocked the door to this situation, and not too soon, either. National League owners were engaged in a suicidal struggle that threatened the very existence of baseball as a game and as a business.

The facts have been buried over the years as a salve to individual pride and so-called National League prestige, which was considered important to the pioneering league at the time. As a hard-playing National Leaguer again, John never felt free to correct the impressions as time went by, not even to Sam Crane, his old friend and the sports writer who compiled John's book of anecdotal memoirs for publication in 1923. The details remained locked in an old red-leather trunk that had no key.

The fact is private papers show quite clearly that Ban Johnson and John McGraw never were enemies, mortal or mild; they never even had a row. Johnson was not only aware of every move that John McGraw made in 1901 and 1902, but actually advised him on how to make them!

As to desertion, it must be recalled that the National League first deserted John McGraw in 1899 after his greatest season as player-manager. His name was the biggest and most electrifying in sports because of his unmatched playing skill and inspired leadership. But twelve club owners ignored this vital fact in their jealous strife and financial frenzy, brought about by interlocking interests and overlapping ownership. Desperately reducing their ranks from an unwieldy twelve to eight, the National League also deserted Baltimore, cradle of scientific baseball, fountain of brilliant history and unflagging enthusiasm. They abandoned fertile territory and the young man from Truxton who symbolized the Oriole spirit, and then they fought against continuation of Baltimore baseball under any auspices.

As I have recorded, John was resigned to playing no baseball at all in 1900. Conditions surrounding his and Wilbert Robinson's eventual decision to sign a St. Louis contract after the season opened may be correctly termed subterfuge, but it wasn't trickery. John's complete disgust with National League men and methods was common knowledge through his open efforts to launch the new American Association. Also, his insistence on a one-year contract at St. Louis, without the reservation clause, was indication enough that he wanted to be free of obligation at the end of the season.

After he had signed and reported in mid-May, he literally knocked himself out trying to win in St. Louis. He collided with the grandstand in July while chasing a foul fly and was carried off the field unconscious. He could play baseball only one way.

The necessity of an American League team in New York City was frankly admitted in the earliest talks with Ban Johnson and Charles Comiskey in Chicago that year. Getting into this vital but well-protected territory was always a hope, but there was no way to plan it beyond a risk of financial suicide through open competition. The National League knew that the American could never regard itself an equal without a New York franchise.

Ban Johnson's method was to play a waiting game while keeping his own league strong through competition and efficient operation. The weaker would have to give ground, and the National League, torn by inner strife, couldn't get stronger. The big break came when John T. Brush stopped fighting Andrew Freedman and joined him in the summer of 1901.

The Baltimore Orioles' financial picture, which I have detailed, was reflected by all fifteen other big-league clubs. Most of them enjoyed better attendance, but with correspondingly higher salary lists and plant operating costs. The Robison brothers were depleting a fortune made in Cleveland traction to finance a St. Louis Cardinals team that was all but wiped out of players.

In addition to young Donlin and Keister, who left with John and Robinson, they had lost two great pitchers, Cy Young and Jack Powell; the matchless Bobby Wallace; "Snags" Heidrick, a .339 outfielder; and two all-time catching stars, Lou Criger and Ossie Schreckingost. The waning strength of the National League may be gauged by the fact that this decimated St. Louis team finished fourth behind Pittsburgh, Philadelphia, and Brooklyn in 1901.

In the wake of this blow came the news that Ban Johnson had interested a St. Louis brewer, Zach Tinker, in taking 50 per cent of an American League club for $50,000. With that deal set, Johnson prepared to move Henry J. Killilea's team from Milwaukee to baseball's ghost town. They would play in Chris Von der Ahe's old and empty Sportsman's Park, only an outfielder's throw from the National League field. Rumor became a fact when Charles Comiskey appeared later in the year and signed the lease for the American League.

Johnson's ability to interest strong capital was a frightening factor. By careful and judicious management, for which he had a demonstrated talent, Johnson threatened to go along for years, despite deficit operation. One of his strongest backers was a Cleveland mining and shipping millionaire, Charles W. Somers. He owned the Boston Red Sox and had loaned money to guarantee the operation of at least one club, Cleveland. No one denied that both leagues were losing money, but the American League could borrow more.

Significant at the time was the fact that Boston, Chicago, New York, and Cincinnati were second-division teams in the National League in that order, and that owners of these clubs were closely allied through minority stock interest in the New York Giants.

The most powerful club owner in baseball, if not the wealthiest, was Andrew Freedman, despised and disparaged since he pulled a surprise coup to get control of the Giants in late 1894. This historic and priceless franchise in the nation's largest city, fought over like a bone among dogs, was characterized in print as "... positively the rankest apology for a first class ball club that was ever imposed upon any major city...." Freedman's growing power had many channels of effect, not the least of which was control, through lease or option, of all available sites for new baseball parks in Manhattan, Bronx, Brooklyn, and Queens. One lease alone, that on historic Manhattan Field, 155th Street and Eighth Avenue, cost $15,000 per year. With a threat to abandon the property, he demanded that the National League share this rental burden. The League refused, but Brush and Soden paid part of the cost to protect their Giant interests.

First indication that Brush had definitely decided to line up with Freedman came in June, 1901, when he got in touch with John at a supposedly secret meeting and skirted the idea of returning to the National League under the "most ideal conditions." Ban Johnson and John quickly capitalized on this display of weakness by indicating that it had succeeded in causing a breach between them. The method was bald charges and countercharges in the newspapers. The man soon to be my husband was accused of "startling crimes and treason to the American League." I noted earlier that it had caused my first concern for him, and also that he had asked me only to believe in him. I believed without question or doubt.

Approaching John McGraw with a proposition was common practice between baseball seasons. As I have said, his presence in any big-league city usually produced an impromptu meeting with a club owner and an offer to play, or manage, particularly in New York. Once he made a hurried trip to New York solely to see a promising Baltimore colored boy from Druid Hill Avenue, Joe Gans, lose a twelve-round match to the lightweight champion, Frank Erne. The trip, made in early March, produced headlines because Andrew Freedman had met him again. Through 1899 and 1900 there were at least a half-dozen meetings with John T. Brush, whose movements were always characterized as "secret."

The meeting of late June, 1901, brought another appeal and a promise of the fine New York setup, if John would interest two or three other American League managers and players in deserting the younger league. John said that it might be done, whereupon he reported the meeting, as he did all others, to Johnson.

Since Brush had spoken in New York's behalf, Ban Johnson felt that the time was right for creating overconfidence. Just as John had bewildered the National League with his trumped-up rumor of peace in February, Johnson created a rumor of trouble in his own ranks. John kept his promise to "interest" others, but he did it through a newspaper friend, John H. "Andy" Anderson, of the Baltimore *Herald*. One of those Andy spoke to was Jimmy Manning, part owner and manager of the Washington club. Then came the "blast" from Chicago on Friday, July 26, 1901:

> President Johnson today declared he had information that John J. McGraw was flirting with John T. Brush or other National League magnates regarding jumping the American League. He also declared that James Manning, manager of the Senators, and George Stallings, manager of the Detroit Club, had been approached by a Baltimore emissary. Johnson said

he had known for some time that Baltimore was figuring on a double cross, but that the American League was ready for it.

"I know what is doing down there and am fully conversant with the scheme, and I want to say right now that I don't care how quick Baltimore goes over, bag and baggage, to the National League. We want no Benedict Arnold in our midst. We know that two of our men have been approached and we are sure it is McGraw who is backing the scheme, but they cannot hurt us."

James Manning, here [in Chicago] with the Senators, said:

"I might have learned more of the scheme if I had listened, but I choked off the man quickly and would not listen to it. I am with the American League first, last and all of the time. It is useless for any emissary, either of Baltimore or the National League, to make any proposition or suggestion to me. They know where I stand."

Charles Comiskey, of the White Sox, said:

"The worst McGraw can do is to disrupt the Baltimore Club. The American League is firmly built and is the result of a number of years, and no one man can break it up."

Manager McGraw was seen this afternoon at Cleveland by a representative of the *Herald* in regard to the report given out by Ban Johnson that the Baltimore manager is engaged in an attempt to wreck the American League, and styling McGraw as "the Benedict Arnold guy of the League."

"So the 'Julius Caesar' of the League calls me a 'Benedict Arnold,' does he?" said McGraw. "I should like to know upon what evidence he bases this assertion. I think I have the interests of the league quite as much at heart as he. I have my good money invested to a considerable extent and I am anxious that the league should meet with all success.

"What has Johnson at stake? He is paid an annual salary to do our business, and what right has he to make baseless assertions about his employers? I am frank to say that I believe there is too much one man power in the league, and that the affairs of the organization are being run in the interests of one particular clique.

"As to Stallings and Manning being approached, let Mr. Johnson give his proof."

This situation quickly simmered to a boil, as expected, for the writers partial to National League interests heralded it as the biggest possible break for their cause. Both Johnson and John McGraw were properly indignant during interviews, but not during correspondence. The 1901 season had scarcely ended on September 28 when "Benedict Arnold" received the following memorandum from "Julius Caesar":

J. J. McG.

The matter of postponing the fall meeting until some time in November has been under consideration. To hold the meeting at this date would force us to disclose our hands too early in the game. Then again the public has turned its attention to foot ball, and there is little interest now in the affairs of the game. I will notify you by wire if there is a postponement. With kind regards, I am—

Yours Truly—
B. B. Johnson

Through the fall of 1901 and early 1902, maneuvers within administrative baseball were like those in chess, though all the pieces were never in evidence at one time. The rumor of ill-feeling between Johnson and McGraw served its purpose, for John met many people with "encouraging" messages from New York, and usually in secret. Interspersing these clouded contacts were rumors that confused the situation and gave comfort to both sides in what would be called today a war of nerves.

On October 22, 1901, John T. Brush wrote from Indianapolis to Pat Powers, president of the Eastern League, denying the existence of territorial protection. The National Agreement had lapsed after ten years in force. President Young, of the National League, concurred. Whether by blunder or design, this pivotal decision materially aided and encouraged the American League. It was notice to all concerned that minor-league players and territory were open to raid, and it guaranteed privation for minor leagues. Baseball was thoroughly disorganized.

The news took the promise and steam from a projected meeting of the newly formed National Association of Professional Baseball Clubs scheduled for later in the month. The minor leagues were thoroughly abandoned, and remained so until March when Ban

Johnson signed a protective agreement with Tom Hickey, president of the American Association.

The faction so long hopeful of easing or forcing Andrew Freedman from baseball received greatest encouragement from the New York City election of November 5, 1901. A fusion or coalition ticket was successful in halting the four-year reign of the Democratic Tammany Hall machine, in which Freedman was a power. Fusion forces elected a new mayor, Seth Low; borough presidents of Manhattan, Brooklyn, and Richmond; a district attorney for New York County; and four justices of the supreme and city courts. Freedman's close friend, Richard F. Croker, resigned as Tammany leader and returned to Europe, where he lived in splendor.

Baseball facts and rumors flew wildly as a result of both gossip and design. They had to be fitted together in the manner of jigsaw pieces. Chess and jigsaw—it was that and more. The element of double cross was always a threatening factor. All that John McGraw had worked for in Baltimore—financial security, property, business success, integrity, friendships, fraternal associations (he had joined the Eagles), and the girl he was to marry on January 8 —all was more or less at stake. One false move, or even a hasty one, could sink his overloaded little craft. It was a struggle for survival on the part of several individuals and factions. Many sincere baseball people were caught in a violent storm of their own making, and each would necessarily sacrifice the other to reach shore.

It was and still is a business. It is a man's world. Perhaps a mother's savage defense of her brood might be likened to a man's battle to salvage wealth, position, pride, power, or whatever was in jeopardy at the time. I have never felt hostile to any phase of it or to any person connected with it. Knowing far less at the time than I do now, I was confident that John McGraw would survive and that I would be proud of him.

Responsibility for any phase of the American versus National struggle is of secondary importance. Just who was half right or all wrong I couldn't and wouldn't say. I do know that John McGraw kept in constant touch with his league president Ban Johnson, on every development and meeting and proposition. The jigsaw puzzle was still incomplete, and John was playing the waiting game when we left on our wedding trip on January 8 for

Washington, Savannah, Palm Beach, St. Augustine, and a few way stations. John arranged for the Orioles' 1902 training trip, and his plans of "business as usual" were properly publicized. Upon our return, the following letter from Ban Johnson awaited him:

American League
Professional Base Ball Clubs
1206 Fisher Building
Chicago

Chicago, Illinois
Jan 24th 1902

Mr. John McGraw
Baltimore, Md.
Dear Sir:—

It is well that you have been beyond reach of the New York party in the last ten days. I must again urge you to be very guarded in your dealings with the New Yorker. Betrayal of confidence or even broad intimations would occasion you much embarrassment in Baltimore. This is something that cannot happen, however, if the proper safe guards are thrown up. Affairs are in such shape, I believe, that compliance with any reasonable demands we may make can be enforced. From the trend of events in the last two weeks, I can say with much positiveness, that Freedman is behind the overtures that have been made to you.

I would suggest that you express no special interest. If any advances are made let them come entirely from the New York end, and insist upon a clear definition of their attitude. The American League will enter into no alliance, nor can we with safety accept and house a National League discard. The American has earned too good a reputation to jeopardize its standing with the public by an affiliation with a faction or an individual of the National. No one can deny us the right to embrace any legitimate opportunity to improve our circuit. By complying with the above suggestions you will follow safe lines, and the proposition can be handed me in such shape that it can be worked out to a satisfactory end.

I understand all along that there was no demand for Jennings at Baltimore. Further I appreciated the fact that you could not give him serious consideration after the talk we had in Chicago last fall. The publication, however, was premature and a thing to be regretted. Griffith remarked to me in the presence of a newspaper man: "Will the American League permit Jennings to come back after the way he ditched us last summer?" I replied in the negative. As far as my information goes Jennings has never made any overtures to an American League club. Unnecessary "branding" is something that should always be avoided. With kind regards, I am—

Yours Truly—
B. B. Johnson

The Jennings matter concerned Hughie's failure to "jump" from the National League to the American. Everyone expected him to rejoin his Oriole flock. Instead he followed his transfer orders from Brooklyn to Philadelphia. John explained to President Johnson in Chicago that poor Hughie could never play top-flight baseball again on account of his arm. It had failed to respond after medical treatment.

"He can't hurt us playing over there," John confided.

And so Hughie, still a winter student at college, wasn't unnecessarily "branded"—not even a Benedict Arnold in reverse. In fact, he went to the American League some years later as manager of the Detroit Tigers.

The difficulty and delay in the "New York situation" lay in a stalemate that had developed in the National League as a result of John T. Brush's switch over to Freedman's side. Those two, with Robison of St. Louis and Soden of Boston, were opposed by the owners of Brooklyn, Philadelphia, Chicago, and Pittsburgh. They were deadlocked in matters of policy and presidency.

Despite Tammany Hall's city-wide defeat in the municipal election, Andrew Freedman still held the upper hand in New York baseball, and he could turn the tide either way. His Giant team was less than average in personnel and was made worse by indifference and rebellion, which was encouraged by absentee ownership. The game itself was at the lowest ebb New York fans had ever known. All the awful things hoped, and perhaps planned, for

Freedman's team had been realized. He was shorn of everything except money and power.

Unfortunately for the rest of baseball, Freedman gave no hint of his plans, and he could materialize any one of several. He could sell the team and ball park for at least $150,000. He had turned down an offer in that amount from A. G. Spalding and James A. Hart, owners of the Chicago National League club. One ominous possibility was that he might sell his Polo Grounds leasehold to the American League for profit or spite. The Giant franchise and disorganized team, of course, would be turned back to the National League, which would have no available playing space in New York, since Freedman had firm control of all desirable sites.

Significant, as later developments showed, was the election of John B. Day, former owner of the club, to membership on the Giants' board of directors at Jersey City, November, 1901.

John McGraw's secret appointments with the New York emissary continued through February. Meanwhile, the shaky Baltimore Orioles were refinanced. John J. Mahon, a political leader and contractor, bought control, loaned the club money, and assumed Syndey Frank's role as president. With that, Mr. Mahon's son-in-law, Joe Kelley, left Ned Hanlon in Brooklyn and became an Oriole again. John lost a couple of players—Donlin to Cincinnati and Jack Dunn to New York—but he gained more. In addition to Kelley, whom he always called one of the all-time greats, he signed Dan McGann, Billy Gilbert, Jimmy Sheckard, and a few others, chiefly National Leaguers. He took a good squad to Savannah for several weeks of training, during which time his meetings on the New York situation were suspended. They picked up again as soon as the season began.

Opening day in Baltimore, on April 24, 1902, was in sharp contrast to the previous year, chiefly in attendance. Fewer than 2,500 turned out to see the Orioles score 6 runs in the first inning off Connie Mack's rookie left-hander, Eddie Plank, to win, 6–2.

Two days later the Orioles were beating the Red Sox in Boston for the season's opener before a record crowd of 15,000. They were packed into standing room on the field, and 8,000 were turned away. It was a splendid testimony to American League baseball and the popularity of Jimmy Collins, Red Sox manager. Enthusiasm reached such a peak at one stage of the game that

4,000 fans raced onto the field. Players of both teams worked at clearing the diamond of fans and debris, and then went on with the game. A near riot broke out again in the ninth inning, when Boston scored 4 runs to win, 7–6. John was put out of the game by Umpire Connolly for "kicks," and Joe Kelley played third.

The fact that the American League was going right on and also drawing good crowds helped accelerate John's many conferences with the New York representative, who was now an official of the Giants, Fred Knowles. Another factor that helped break the deadlock was the successful transfer of the Milwaukee team to St. Louis. Zach Tinker, the brewer failed to back the club, but Ban Johnson obtained financing and installed Ralph Orthwein as temporary president. A year later Robert Lee Hedges, of Cincinnati, manufacturer of "Banner Buggies," took over the franchise and presidency and attending headaches. There was no question about Johnson's ability to place a team anywhere he felt was advisable. He had yet to take a backward step.

The full year of waiting paid dividends, for the National League cracked first. What had started as a simple proposition involving desertion in July, 1901, had been nurtured and molded into a gigantic and complex deal by spring of 1902. Following President Johnson's advice, John had the situation just about ready to turn over to his superior.

He was now discussing his own transfer as player-manager, the sale of the Giants, the financing of Cincinnati, and a compulsory admission of an American League team into New York City. At one point John was requested to take over the Polo Grounds concessions as part of "management," but he refused on several grounds. One was that he had no desire to be general manager, since the team-building would be a major job. More important, a perfectly good concessions manager had operated the sale of score cards and edibles for several years. He was Harry M. Stevens, the jolly man with the red coat from Columbus, Ohio, and then Pittsburgh. He had worked hard to parlay an idea into big business.

"I don't even run the concessions in Baltimore, Mr. Freedman," John said. "We let it out to Cassedy and Klosterman. In Stevens you have the best man in the business here, and you ought to keep him."

By mid-May and after many secret meetings in New York, Philadelphia, Wilmington, and even at Freedman's country home at Red Bank, New Jersey, all aspects of the deal were settled.

The one expendable franchise in the American League, Baltimore, would be moved into New York as an interleague rival of the Giants.

John J. McGraw would move to New York as player-manager of the Giants.

In return for selling his control to John T. Brush, Freedman would select the American League ownership and turn over a suitable space for building a ball park.

Pending actual contract signing, plans would be set in motion to finance a $70,000 indebtedness of Brush's Cincinnati club.

The main strength of the Orioles would be placed in the National League.

Baltimore stockholders would be satisfied by means of cash or a satisfactory equivalent.

President Ban Johnson would arrange the legal technicalities involving friendly repossession of the Oriole franchise for subsequent transfer to New York.

Another delay came as a result of John's slashed knee in late May, but he was up and around in early June pushing himself against doctor's orders. Despite a stiffly bandaged knee, which made him limp, he kept an appointment at Gravesend race track, Brooklyn, with Frank Farrell, known as the "Pool Room King."

Farrell's rooms had little or nothing to do with billiards. They were betting institutions for off-course wagering and perfectly legal at the time. One of his busiest emporiums was at Sixth Avenue and 30th Street, New York, and connected with a prosperous saloon. A half block down 30th Street, at 137, was Captain "Big Bill" Devery's Nineteenth Precinct station house. Eight years later it was moved across the street to number 138, its present site, and eventually renumbered the Fourteenth. Through Tammany politics, if nothing else, Farrell and Devery were close friends.

Action on the New York deal accelerated from this meeting at Gravesend. In addition to being a member of Tammany, Farrell was a co-owner of race horses with the wealthy Fleischmann brothers, Julius and Max. Their father, Charles, had founded the fabulously successful yeast company in Cincinnati, which expanded so fast that a large plant was opened for yeast and the distillation of gin at Peekskill, New York.

Through Farrell, the Fleischmann brothers agreed to enter the Cincinnati picture as purchasers of the Reds, lock, stock, and debts. Julius, the older, was only twenty-nine, but a thorough sportsman and very popular in Cincinnati, so much so that they elected him mayor, youngest in the city's history, and gave him a second term. The purchase price gave Brush a start toward buying the Giants from Freedman for $200,000. The National League owners backed him for the remainder. Farrell, Devery, and other loyal Tammany members set in motion a plan to take over and finance the American League franchise, though Devery never appeared as a board member in the incorporation papers.

With all points settled, John obtained confidential advice from John M. Ward, the ballplayer attorney, and ironed out all wrinkles from his proposed contract with Andrew Freedman and the Giants attorney, Cornelius J. Sullivan. The document was made a "rider" to the standard baseball contract, with certain paragraphs of the latter crossed out and supplemented under separate agreement. The contract included a "good conduct" clause. I hasten to add that this was included only to serve as proof to the opponents of Sunday baseball that manager and players were "under control." The contract is enlightening in many ways, particularly in the matter of material rewards. John McGraw did not "line his pockets" with money, nor did he "get rich by selling out the American League," as has been written so often and which he made no effort to correct. He executed a big deal for the purpose of establishing healthy competition in baseball's largest city. Of least importance at the time was the money consideration, $6,500 a year as playing manager, and only $4,000 if he failed to play!

John became an employee of the Giants as of Tuesday, July 1, 1902. The New York *World*, a morning paper, carried a three-column story the next day stating that John J. McGraw would "open negotiations with Andrew Freedman for the job as manager." Soon other papers were printing news and views of the big baseball switch.

Meanwhile, John managed the Orioles through the next two weeks, for he could not take over until the remainder of the plans and agreements had crystallized. Finally all was ready and, on July 16, John and John T. Brush appeared for a late evening meeting at 26 Bank of Baltimore Building. There in the office of Joseph C. France, Andrew Freedman's legal representative in Baltimore, the Orioles were made expendable.

Through shares held by John, Wilbert Robinson, and Father John G. Boland, a Baltimore priest, John J. Mahon was able to sell 201 of the 400 outstanding shares to Mr. France, who bought them in the name of the Giants. This gave the New York club control of the Orioles.

As Giant manager, John selected Joe McGinnity and Jack Cronin, pitchers; Bresnahan, a catcher; and Dan McGann, the first baseman. Taking no chances, John had procured earlier in the day a note on Hotel Stafford stationery that he has treasured all his life. It read:

Baltimore, Md.
July 16th 1902

I agree to play Base Ball for the New York Base Ball Club the balance of the season 1902 for the sum of Two Thousand Dollars $2,000. I also agree to sign for the season 1903 for Four Thousand Dollars $4,000. Salary above mentioned to be paid in semi monthly installments. I further agree to live up to all club rules training dissopation etc.

JOE McGINNITY

John T. Brush then selected two players for Cincinnati, Cy Seymour and Joe Kelley. A prime condition of the deal was that Kelley would get the Cincinnati managing job, and Mr. Mahon made certain that the condition was carried out for his son-in-law. The six players were notified in the morning and left to join their new teams. John and Mr. Brush returned to New York.

Ban Johnson, waiting in Washington, appeared early in the morning of the seventeenth to take over. He called a meeting of the minority stockholders, Harry Goldman, Sydney Frank, Theodore Straus, and Myles Brinkley. Exercising a provision of the American League constitution, he took an immediate assignment of the ball-park lease. He then ordered the scheduled game played with St. Louis and appointed Al Selbach as captain. Wilbert Robinson had not yet returned from Hudson, Massachusetts, where he had gone to attend his mother's funeral.

Six players, not including John, from a roster of fourteen left only eight. The Orioles could not field a team. President Johnson ordered the game forfeited and then served the minority stockholders with a show-cause order demanding reason why he should not take over the franchise "to protect the stockholders." Goldman and Mahon were "ordered" to appear before the league board of directors, after which Johnson wired nearby teams for the loan of players so that the schedule could be completed.

On Friday, July 18, a quorum of the league's board of directors met at the Rennert Hotel and declared the franchise forfeited. The American League could now move it at any time to New York free of legal complications. Wilbert Robinson was "exonerated" and named manager of the team. In exchange for his Oriole stock, he was given John's half of the popular Diamond Café, of which John had been ordered to divest himself in his contract.

Harry Goldman assumed the post of business manager and then, with Sydney Frank, arranged the formation of a new operating company. State Senator Olin Bryan became counsel for the new club. President Johnson outlined a plan for continuing the schedule to the end of the season. He then journeyed to Atlantic City for a rest.

As you can see, no one, not even the baseball player, was bilked, double-crossed, or suffered loss. John Mahon was reimbursed for his investment and loans. Father Boland, one of the pastors of St. Vincent de Paul's on Front Street near Lafayette, and one of John's oldest friends, was paid in full for his "rooting interest" stock. Robinson received the Diamond Café. Joe Kelley finally got his managing job. Goldman, Frank, and others got Oriole Park, which they sold to Ned Hanlon less than four years later for a handsome profit.

True, John McGraw got only a modest contract to manage the Giants, but he also got an opportunity beyond price. Greater than gold, too, was the satisfaction of having delivered baseball from bondage to the threshold of its greatest ascent.

I am not sure that it ever made up for the abuse he took and the brand he had to wear for the rest of his life. He never complained. More important to him was that the "New York situation" had been solved at last. Baseball was no longer at war. Of Ban Johnson, John could only say publicly, "He picked on me and I couldn't stand his umpires." Beyond that, he never referred to the incident and struggle. He was too busy making a dream come true under new and challenging surroundings.

Of John McGraw, President Johnson was more wordy, though a bit ambiguous, in his statement as he departed for Atlantic City:

> The McGraw-Baltimore incident is closed. It took a long time for the patrons of baseball in Baltimore to learn McGraw's peculiar curves and angles, but they learned fast. The National League sent a good, kind angel in the form of Freedman's certified checks and the angels had wings enough to carry McGraw away. So Baltimore and the American League rejoice.

And so, we went on to New York City and the Giants.

15

EXCEPT FOR RIDICULE and vilification, baseball history contains little information about Andrew Freedman, his work and wealth. Since he was John McGraw's first New York employer, I feel that more should be known about this controversial man. Most interesting to me is how he managed to become a power so absolute in organized baseball.

He was born in New York City on September 1, 1860, of average parents. He had a younger brother and sister, Daniel and Isabella. He attended St. Aloysius Academy, and graduated from the College of the City of New York. As a law student, he developed an interest in real-estate law, and then in the changing values of city property. At twenty-four he worked for a wholesale dry-goods house, after which he went into real estate with one Simon H. Stern. He dealt actively in high-priced footage on Fifth Avenue, and in the comparatively cheap and obscure acreage of the Bronx. One of his early Manhattan deals was selling the 2,500-seat Academy of Music on East Fourteenth Street. It was adjacent to Tammany Hall, which he had joined as a loyal Democrat when twenty-one.

Freedman's warmest friendship in Tammany was with Irish-born Richard F. Croker, seventeen years his senior and already a favored brave. Croker's aggressive methods as a teen-ager, when he promoted prize fights and led the notorious Fourth Avenue Tunnel Gang, won the admiration of Boss Tweed before that Tammany leader's fall in 1871. Croker formed an alliance with Tweed's successor, John Kelly, and through key appointments, grew rapidly in political stature and power. When he married, Croker selected Freedman as his best man. By the time leader Kelly died in 1886, Croker and Freedman had cemented a close personal and political friendship. Croker succeeded Kelly as chairman of the all-important Finance Committee, which meant automatic leadership of Tammany Hall. Henceforth, Freedman was a member of the same committee and many inner councils. He could have held any of several top offices in the Hall and elective or appointive posts in city government, but he accepted none at all.

He was a rather good-looking man, robust and of medium height. He avoided participation in sports and took his exercise in walking. Unless excited or incensed, he spoke with a light voice, but the words were sharp and direct. His mouth was firm beneath a black and generous mustache. His dark hair, naturally curly, was parted in the middle. His large, gray, almost arrogant eyes, reflected a quick and violent temper. He harbored a fear that someone might discover, or even suspect, his few deeply hidden sentimental quirks, and this, contemporary friends explained, accounted for some of his "barking dog" qualities.

At the time John first knew him, Freedman lived in an apartment at Sherry's, then on Fifth Avenue and Fifty-fourth Street. He also maintained a country retreat at Red Bank, New Jersey, which John visited. He was a fairly heavy eater, though something of a gourmet. One of his favorite dishes was the French carrots which Louis Sherry grew in his cellar for preferred guests, and Freedman was one of them. His tailoring was extremely neat and fastidious. He wore expensive but tasteful jewelry and usually carried one of an assortment of gold-headed canes, which he occasionally swung during an outburst of tempestuous debate. He never married.

Freedman always said that his interest in baseball really began when he was appointed receiver for the bankrupt Manhattan Athletic Club, though he had watched the M.A.C. games on Manhattan Field as a young man. But all Tammany Hall was baseball-minded, chiefly because John B. Day, the Giants' pioneering owner, was an active member. Another reason was Joseph Gordon, Day's brother-in-law, and a prominent Tammany Democrat. He had owned the pre–National League Giants when they were called the Metropolitans. He had also held many appointive offices and was elected to the State Assembly in 1888.

Day's Giants played their games on the original Polo Grounds at Fifth Avenue and 110th Street. Later he built a grandstand at 155th Street and Eighth Avenue at the end of the elevated line. As I noted before, the rival Brotherhood League built next to and north of Day's park in 1890. When the league disbanded at the end of one season, Day took over the abandoned field and grandstand, which, after many changes, is the Polo Grounds of today. Manhattan Field is the parking lot.

The year 1894 brought several pivotal developments to New York City, Tammany Hall, and Andrew Freedman. All of them influenced the course of baseball in the New York area.

Most important, I suppose, was the celebrated investigation of the Lexow Committee into municipal affairs. I do not presume to judge or venture an opinion. I report only the events as they occurred. The end result of the investigation was the defeat of key Tammany Hall candidates at the polls. William L. Strong was elected mayor on a "reform" ticket. Dick Croker resigned his leadership to John C. Sheehan and sailed for Europe, where he had stored considerable wealth.

Second in importance was belated action, after long official argument, on plans for a New York City subway. The London underground had been a decided success for almost thirty years. A Manhattan subway was authorized under the Rapid Transit

Act of 1891, and a Rapid Transit Commission was appointed in 1894 with Alexander E. Orr as president.

The third development, resulting from the second, was Freedman's purchase of control in the Giants through the co-operation of his fellow member in Tammany Hall, John Day, and one Eddie Talcott, a young Wall Street operator and betting commissioner. As already noted, the move was made quietly and ostensibly as a purchase for James A. Bailey, circus impresario and partner of P. T. Barnum. Freedman's small blocks of minority holdings, obtained from Talcott, and with the help of Day, became part of the majority when combined with those purchased from A. G. Spalding. Day gradually lost control after the Brotherhood war, and ran the Giants only through the friendly co-operation of other stockholders—the Spalding brothers, Soden, of the Boston club; Brush, owner of the Cincinnati Club, etc. But at the end of 1894, Freedman was in unchallenged control, with Soden, Brush, and J. Walter Spalding, brother and partner of A. G., holding a minority position.

The deal involved no more than $50,000, if that much. The Giants were Temple Cup champions, but only by virtue of that awful four-straight victory over the celebrating Orioles. Freedman not only helped Day financially, but kept Giant ownership in "friendly" hands. More important, baseball was bound to prosper as a result of New York's expanding rapid transit system.

But Freedman's troubles began the moment he snatched control of the Giants from the multiple grasp of the outlanders. He had differences with managers and employed three in 1895. He openly charged favoritism toward Brooklyn in the scheduling of games by the National League, for it was common knowledge that Charles Ebbets, of the Brooklyn club, did most of the work on the schedule for President Young. Freedman was rebuffed in the make-up of league committees. A. G. Spalding was also "reprimanded" for selling his stock to Freedman with a motion by Frank Robison and Brush to give the valuable baseball manufacturing contract to the Overman Wheel Company.

Brush made at least two determined efforts to buy out Freedman before the start of the 1896 season. The first was secretly through a minority stockholder, William B. Wheeler, of New Haven and Yale University, who replied with a firm, "No!"

Approached directly, Freedman countered with an offer of $50,000 to Brush for his minority stock. The Cincinnati owner refused and then offered $50,000, $60,000 and $65,000 which amounts Freedman scoffed at each time.

Richard Croker returned to America and, during 1896, visited many of the big-league cities and ball parks with Freedman. This gave rise to the claim that Croker actually owned the Giants. Freedman dismissed the accusations, along with the growing vilification, and went about his business, which was far beyond the knowledge or suspicion of club owners and press.

His visit to Baltimore, for instance, was to meet with John R. Bland, president of the United States Fidelity and Guarantee Company. He emerged from the meeting with a deal to place New York City casualty insurance, official and otherwise, with Bland's company through a New York setup to be headed by Freedman. The Giants' owner was interviewed later in Cincinnati on pertinent baseball affairs and in the company of Dick Croker, but the prime reason for his visit was not baseball. He was there to meet with George B. Cox, Cincinnati political boss, on the placement of that city's casualty insurance. Ten years later Freedman's income from this field alone had reached $100,000 annually.

Proper study and delineation of major developments in New York City would have disclosed Freedman's growing power in business, finance, and politics. The so-called Western faction of club owners chose to battle him through league councils.

The unfortunate Rusie case is an example. It started with Freedman's stubborn insistence that the fines totaling $200 could not be returned. The Giants had suffered through the young man's defections. (He had won 23 games, but lost 22.) Freedman's proffered contract was refused. After a year of idleness, Amos showed an eagerness to pitch in 1897. Freedman tendered the same contract. Rusie demanded not only the return of fines, but reimbursement for legal fees in the amount of $5,000 owed to Hawkins and Smith, Indianapolis attorneys.

Freedman laughed. The league grew apprehensive, for Rusie demanded his release so that he could play with another baseball team. Freedman refused his release, claiming that he was needed by the Giants and showing the contract for $3,000. Rusie then took his case to the United States Circuit Court at Trenton, New

Jersey, since the Giants were a New Jersey corporation. The National League had to step in to defend its "Articles of Agreement" against Rusie's claim of unfairness under the reservation clause (Paragraph 19) and a demand for the right to pitch for any other club. Colonel John I. Rogers, of the Philadelphia Club, headed counsel for the league.

The case was heard in late March, and judicial opinion was reserved. Before a decision was rendered, the National League owners decided to reimburse Rusie for most of his legal costs. He signed a Giants contract on April 21 for the same salary he was offered a year before. Freedman did not return the fines, nor did he contribute a cent toward the pitcher's legal fees.

The league suffered another blow in the same month with New York's passage of the Raines Law, which ended Western dreams of Sunday baseball in New York and Brooklyn. The statute was part of the all-important move to create a Greater New York. The city of Brooklyn, and counties of New York, Queens, and Richmond, and Bronx borough (it was not a county until 1914) were to be joined into one gigantic city on January 1, 1898. This would give the new "Greater London" a close fight in the race to become the world's largest city.

Since it would be called New York, erstwhile Brooklyn city would be a secondary borough with a secondary baseball team. When asked if he would demand the elimination of Brooklyn from the National League, Freedman replied indignantly:

"Certainly not! Should the Brooklyn Gas Company go out of business just because of consolidation?"

Freedman's next giant step was taken late in midsummer of 1897, when he went to Europe and returned with Dick Croker. John C. Sheehan quickly stepped down as leader of Tammany Hall and fifty-four-year-old Croker stepped up. He studied the well-laid plans for the campaign to elect New York's first greater-city mayor, rolled up his sleeves, and went to work. Millions awoke on the morning of November 3, 1897, to find that Tammany Hall Democrats had regained city-wide power through the election of a ticket headed by Robert A. Van Wyck as mayor. And the term, for the first time, would be four years!

Freedman spent only a small amount of his time administering the Giants' affairs, and none at all worrying about them. He met each thrust in league councils with a firm parry, and usually countered with a damaging riposte. When Charles Byrne, Brooklyn president, announced an intermediate ticket price of thirty-five cents, for "covered bleachers," Freedman said he would raise *all* grandstand seats to seventy-five cents and continue paying the visiting club the prevailing twelve and a half cents per head. Byrne died late that year, and Ferdinand Abell backed Charles Ebbets as club president.

The new Brooklyn leader tackled the "Freedman situation" with a daring plan, which resulted in bringing the best of Baltimore hitting and pitching to Brooklyn in an out-and-out syndicate operation for the 1899 season. He fielded one of the strongest line-ups in the history of the game, led by its best manager, Ned Hanlon. Many were certain Freedman's Giants would be so overshadowed that the fans would clamor for the new Superbas to represent New York City.

Though Rusie won nearly fifty victories in two seasons after his return, the Giants sank steadily in the club standings each year. Even the venerable Cap Anson as manager failed to help the team or the attendance in 1898, the war year. Freedman suspended Rusie for habitual rule-breaking, chiefly of training. Loyal John Day stepped in to manage through most of 1899, but the Giants, torn by growing indifference and dissension, were door mats on the field. The reinforced Brooklyn team won the most games, though John McGraw's Baltimore "leftovers" drew the biggest newspaper space and attendance.

Freedman, returning to New York in late September from a vacation in the White Mountains of New Hampshire, was quoted as saying:

"Baseball affairs in New York have been going on just as I wished and expected them to go. I have given the club little attention and I would not now give five cents for the best ballplayer in the world to strengthen it."

For this apparent indifference, Freedman was castigated in the sports pages. One incensed writer said:

> Freedman is like a spoilt child when opposed. He will, metaphorically, throw himself on the floor and kick up his heels and refuse to play. He needs a spanking, and the press

has spanked him hard, but like the parson's son, he refused to be good, and the other magnate boys have gone over to his yard to play, and taken with them all kinds of sweetmeats to conciliate their pouting playmate.

While Ebbets and Hanlon were basking in the glow of their somewhat hollow victory, Freedman was working with others to revive the Rapid Transit Commission, which had lain dormant for six years. Ebbets, Brush, the Robisons, and Dreyfuss were busy with new and secret plans to reduce the National League to eight teams, but Freedman was studying the transit deadlock between two stubborn factions.

New York's streetcar lines were owned by William C. Whitney, Thomas Fortune Ryan, and others. George Gould and Russell Sage controlled the elevated roads. Neither company would "tunnel under" the other in any way. The reason was obvious. A subsurface line would be rapid enough to render both streetcar and elevated lines obsolete.

William Barclay Parsons designed the subway. City engineers and surveyors under the Van Wyck administration laid out routes for the first twenty-two miles of underground. They charted many more miles of temporary routes up and down Manhattan, under rivers, and over into Brooklyn. Andrew Freedman already knew every block of city real estate and every foot of the proposed lines. The subway contract involved expenditure of $50,-000,000 by the city for construction and $25,000,000 more for equipment. Bids were finally invited exactly six years after appointment of the Rapid Transit Commission.

The award went to an obscure contractor named John B. McDonald, whose only distinction, besides a "solid jaw, thick chest, and brawny arms," was construction of the Jerome Park Reservoir. He would have to employ as many as 10,000 laborers at a time, a condition he could easily meet. The stumbling block was a compulsory deposit of $1,000,000 in cash to the city, and a performance bond of $15,000,000. McDonald had almost no capital at all—just some good ideas.

Freedman took the contractor to see August Belmont, whose late father had been on the presubway Transit Commission. Young, asetic-looking August was American representative for the Rothschilds, European bankers. He was a Tammany Democrat. His brother, Oliver H. P., was a member of both Tammany Hall and the United States Congress from the thirteenth District.

Belmont quickly arranged for the million-dollar cash deposit and the heavy bond. He formed the Interborough Rapid Transit Company. Freedman participated heavily in this corporation and another, the I.R.T. Construction Company, to do the digging, blasting, and building. The scope of Freedman's activities and mushrooming wealth is reflected by his holding directorships in the Forty-Fourth Street Realty Company, Central Theatres Leasing Company, Fifth Avenue Coach Company, Dobbs Ferry Traction Company, Park Carriage Company, New York Railways Company, Interborough-Metropolitan Company, New York and Queens Railway, Subway Realty Company, New York Terminal and Dock Improvement Company, and others. Of course, most of the casualty policies and indemnifying went through his New York office in the Hanover Bank building at 11 Pine Street.

Though he remained in the background financially and politically, Freedman's subway and realty coup was one of the most spectacular in New York financial history. Profit on construction of the first twenty-two miles, which took four years to complete, was estimated at $8,000,000. Shares in Belmont's I.R.T. Company, with a fifty-year franchise, ballooned in value overnight. The Brooklyn subway extension, which he also obtained, was later built for $11,000,000 on credit of $3,000,000 extended by the city. The company's worth, on the basis of subway rights for the immediate future alone, was estimated at $50,000,000. And the subway revenue for ten years after the opening on October 27, 1904, exceeded the most optimistic figures. The operating profit was simply a bonanza.

As you can easily see, Freedman was able long in advance to tie up every available piece of real estate near proposed subway outlets on which a baseball plant might be built. And he did. No matter where rival baseball prospectors went, the patch of land was out of reach through option or lease. As I have noted, he forced Messrs. Brush and Soden to share the $15,000 annual rent on unused Manhattan Field.

It is interesting, if not significant, that the subway line planned to run under Fourth Avenue, Brooklyn, and started in 1909 on an outlay of $16,000,000, sped right past Charles Ebbets' Washington Park at Third Street. The express stations had been placed at Pacific Street and 36th Street by the city planners many years before. They were two miles apart and equidistant from the baseball field. Even the local stop was far from the turnstiles.

By the time the line began service, Ebbets had surrendered up to 50 per cent of control in the ball club to the McKeever brothers to help finance the construction of a new park, Ebbets Field, in Flatbush. It opened in April, 1913, a few blocks from the Prospect Park station of the old Brighton Beach elevated line. But even without the benefit of subways, Ebbets Field holds the National League attendance record for a single season. It was set in 1947, a pennant-winning year, and would indicate that a winning team will always be a greater influence than a subway station.

The effect of Andrew Freedman's influence in baseball was felt with increasing force as the embattled owners failed to dislodge or even weaken his position in New York. They were further harassed in 1901 by the Ban Johnson competition in Boston, Philadelphia, and Chicago. The prestige of John McGraw and Wilbert Robinson as American Leaguers in Baltimore was heavy throughout the country. The loss of 111 players to the rival league, and the further loss of gate receipts, promised nothing less than failure or bankruptcy for at least half the National League clubs.

The owners had personal wealth in varying degrees, but Andrew Freedman's affluence was easily equal to all of it. More important, he could afford to operate the Giants at a substantial annual deficit, while none of his rivals could do so without depleting personal fortunes.

Just a hint of Freedman's ability is gained from his handling of a single trusteeship. Judge Gildersleeve appointed him a committee of one to administer a fund of $2,000,000 for Ida M. Flagler, divorced wife of Henry M. Flagler, developer of Florida. Under a few years of Freedman's stewardship the fund grew to $5,000,000.

The lone ray of hope for the anti-Freedman forces in a disastrous year came on November 5, 1901, when Tammany Hall's four-year reign ended at the polls. A Fusion party backed Seth Low to victory in the mayoralty race over Edward M. Sheppard.

The margin was relatively small, but the sweep was city-wide. William Travers Jerome became district attorney, and Mayor Van Wyck was badly defeated in a bid to become Supreme Court Justice. Richard Croker resigned his Tammany Hall leadership to John F. Carroll and prepared to live in Europe again.

The sports pages of the day heralded the election results as a key triumph for the anti-Freedman forces, forgetting that the election wasn't retroactive. Nothing could wipe out the gains of four previous years. The gigantic subway project was a fact and the beginning of a city expenditure that would total a billion dollars within the next fifty years.

Besides, three club owners already were "playing in Freedman's yard." Unable to lick him, Brush had joined him, bringing in Frank DeHaas Robison of St. Louis and Soden of Boston. The three met with Freedman in one final effort to solidify their individual positions. The scene was Tower Hill, Freedman's country place at Red Bank, New Jersey. Historians have called the place "baronial," but it was merely a large and comfortable suburban house on a substantial section of wooded grounds. Freedman's part in the meeting has been called "Machiavellian," perhaps an easier description than to write that three club owners had decided to abandon their former associates in the now futile anti-Freedman cause.

Out of the Red Bank meeting in November, 1901, came the fantastic scheme to incorporate the National League into a gigantic syndicate trust, with preferred and common stock, gate receipts prorated, and player contracts common property through corporate affiliation. Whether this was to be permanent or a temporary expedient to protect the league from Ban Johnson is not for me to say. But it was a bona fide plan and well publicized at the time.

More important to all concerned with baseball now or ever, it marked the greatest distance club owners ever strayed from "the boy and the baseball." Both were completely forgotten and forsaken. The thin and precious golden thread that holds the game together—a boy's indestructible desire for competition on the field—was ignored. Thoroughly abandoned were the little Jack McGraws of Truxton, the red-cheeked Amos Rusies of Indianapolis, the Babe Ruths in the industrial schools for boys, the barefooted Honus Wagners in the tree, the joyous kids playing stick ball in the city streets or in the pastures of America.

With eight National League club owners divided and deadlocked at the December meeting of 1901, nothing could be done. Freedman, Brush, Soden, and Robison wanted the syndicate plan adopted with the aging Nick Young as president. Hart of Chicago, Rogers of Philadelphia, Dreyfuss of Pittsburgh, and Ebbets of Brooklyn wanted the revered A. G. Spalding elected president. They argued and balloted for many hours and failed to break the deadlock. After more than twenty ballots, the syndicate faction left the room. The four remaining hurriedly elected Spalding president "unanimously."

It was more than an illegal election; it was a travesty of all parliamentary procedure. Andrew Freedman regarded it as a personal affront. His rage was nearly apoplectic. More than all else, this unfortunate "election" of Spalding moved Freedman to carry the deal with John McGraw and Ban Johnson to a conclusion. And so the Giants' secretary, Fred Knowles, was ordered to step up the secret meetings, which I have already recounted.

All chance of conciliation ended a few weeks later when "President" Spalding appropriated the National League books and records by subterfuge. Freedman obtained a permanent court injunction against Spalding as "president" and forced a return of the league records. He also forced adoption of a Board of Control, consisting of Soden, Brush, and Hart, to run the League in place of a president. With this, Freedman's power in the National League was complete.

When Andrew Freedman added his name to John's contract on July 1, 1902, his ownership of the Giants virtually ended. The signing was concrete expression of agreement on the over-all deal, which materialized step by step through the next nine months. The three major baseball developments to be synchronized were:

The National League, through membership assessment, would finance most of Brush's purchase of control of the Giants for $200,000. Cornelius J. Sullivan, one of Freedman's attorneys, or John B. Day, would remain on the Board of Directors. Sullivan was still a director ten years later.

Brush would turn his Cincinnati club over to a syndicate in

that city for a substantial cash consideration and assumption of $70,000 in debts owed by the club. The new owners of record would be Julius Fleischmann, mayor of the city, and his brother, Max; George B. Fox, Cincinnati political boss; and August Herrmann, a protégé of Fox's and head of the Water Works Board.

The Fleischmanns, wealthy through manufacture of yeast and gin, were incurable baseball enthusiasts. In addition to running their Hudson River plant near Peekskill, New York, they operated semiprofessional leagues across the river in the summer and turned out many good minor-league players. One of their summer-hotel stars in 1900 was a kid named Miller Huggins, who, after playing with St. Paul, turned up with the Fleischmanns again at Cincinnati in 1904. A prime feature of Catskill resort baseball was Julius Fleischmann playing the outfield in regular competition. Unfortunately, one of his stars confided, he played "like a yeast manufacturer."

The Fleischmanns' former racing partner, Frank Farrell, would have a share in the new American League club in New York, which would be headed by Andrew Freedman's old Tammany friend, Joseph Gordon, brother-in-law of the loyal John B. Day. Thomas F. McAvoy, Tammany leader in the Twenty-third District, would not only have a piece of the new club, but would get the excavation plum for the new baseball park. Thus, before stepping out of baseball, Freedman took care of a few political and personal friends.

Whether he was all or any of the terrible things he has been called in print and behind his back, I am in no position to say. Vilification is to be expected, John always explained, when you have something that other people want and can't buy or earn. Except for occasional meetings, or a note of congratulations, Freedman had nothing to do thereafter with the Giants. John Day was a regular attendant, though, even when he had to be brought to the Polo Grounds in a wheel chair.

Freedman lived on in Louis Sherry's apartments, and in late November of 1915 he suffered a stroke of apoplexy. He lingered on in his suite, helpless for three weeks, and died on December 4, mourned at least by his brother and sister. Undoubtedly there were others, for he was active in many fields. He was a trustee

Chicago, Ill., Jan.24th, 1903.

Mr.John F. Hedges,
Baltimore,Md.

Dear Sir:

It is well that you have been beyond the reach of the New York party in the last ten days. I must again urge you to be very guarded in your dealings with the New Yorkers. Betrayal of confidence or over hasty intentions would occasion you much embarrassment at Baltimore. That is something but do not hamper, however, f the proper safe guards are thrown up. Affairs now to such shape. I believe that compliance with any reasonable demands we may make can be enforced. From the trend of events in the last two weeks, I can say with much positiveness that the same is behind the overtures that have been made to you.

I would suggest that you express no special interest. If any advances are made let them come entirely from the New York end, and insist upon a clear definition of their attitude. The American League will enter into no alliance, nor can we with safety accept and house a National League discard. The American has earned too good a reputation to jeopardize its standing with the public by an affiliation with a faction or an individual of the National. We can and will the right to embrace any legitimate opportunity to improve our circuit. B complying with the above suggestions you will follow safe lines, and the proposition can be handled so in such shape that it can be carried out to a satisfactory end.

2.

I understood all along that there was no demand for Jennings at Baltimore. Further I appreciate in fact that you could not give his services consideration after the way we had in Chicago last fall. The publication, however, was premature and a thing to be regretted. Griffith removed to me in the necessity of a newspaper man. Will the American League permit Jennings to come back after the way he treated us last summer? I replied in the negative. As far as my information goes Jennings has never made any overtures to an American League club. Unnecessary "branding" is something that should always be avoided. With kind regards, I am

Yours truly,

(signature)

The Ban Johnson letter of policy and advice in the final steps of the negotiations that brought John McGraw to the Polo Grounds and the American League into New York.

The McGraws relaxing in their Edgewood Avenue home.

of the Long Island Railroad, Society for the Prevention of Cruelty to Animals, Metropolitan Museum of Art (his Red Bank home contained $250,000 worth of paintings), and the American Museum of Natural History. He was a member of many clubs—Lawyers, Bankers, National Democratic, Railroad, Opera, Lotos, Turf and Field, Coney Island Jockey, Red Bank Yacht, and the Automobile Association of America. He was fifty-five years old.

And he willed his entire fortune of four million dollars to charity. Half of it was set aside and the income assigned to his brother and sister until their deaths, at which time it was to be added to the initial two million dollars of endowment for an unusual retreat. It was the Andrew Freedman Home for aged and indigent persons who "at one time have been in good circumstances but who by reason of adverse fortune have become poor and dependent."

The Board of Directors, numbering twenty-five who serve "without salary or fee," obtained incorporation papers under a special charter on March 9, 1916. The board included Val Snyder and John B. Day, Giants directors; Judge Gildersleeve; Richard Croker, Jr.; and many personal friends. Only two of the original list of administrators remain at this writing, Alvin Untermeyer and Charles B. Guggenheimer. James A. Farley has served on the board for a number of years.

The first World War delayed building, but the board purchased considerable land on the Grand Concourse, Bronx, and, while waiting for the war's end, sold parcels for a total that exceeded the entire purchase price by $20,000. And still they had a full city block left. The home, of white granite on a landscaped plot, opened July 15, 1924. It contains twenty-four pairs of single rooms, each pair separated by a bath, and fifty-two larger rooms, each with a bath, for couples. Admission is by application through a committee of the board. An applicant must be sixty years old and not over eighty, but, once admitted, may remain without expense of any kind as long as he or she lives. The average age of the 136 guests is 79. The home's charter has been duplicated nearly thirty times throughout the country. Particularly interesting is a paragraph in the conditions as outlined by the founder's will:

Whenever a husband and wife are received into such home or homes, provision shall be made for their dwelling together therein. There shall be no restriction as to the form of worship which shall be observed on the part of any of the inmates of such homes and every reasonable opportunity shall be afforded for the free and undisturbed observance of the religious rites to which they have been accustomed in accordance with the tenets of their faith.

Thus directed the "Machiavellian" Andrew Freedman.

16

THE VICTORIA HOTEL, at Fifth Avenue and 27th Street, was quiet, roomy, and comfortable. George Sweeney, the manager, gave us a parlor on an upper floor where you could barely hear the clop-clop-clop of horse-drawn coaches on the busy avenue, and our new life in New York began.

John McGraw, of course, was no stranger to the city, which he had visited many times as a player in summer, and on business meetings, sporting events, and secret errands between seasons. Even I had seen a bit of the city the year before. My parents had taken me to the Panama Exposition in Buffalo, just before the assassination of President McKinley. My first New York visit was memorable for two reasons: John had come over from Philadelphia to greet us at the old Broadway Central Hotel, cradle of the National League; and my mother had bought me a stunning red coat at Stern Brothers' store, which was then on 23rd Street.

But on this trip in July, nearly a year later, we practically tiptoed into town, and John's stern admonition still rang in my ears. I was cautioned against talking to anyone about baseball, especially newspapermen. And even as he said it, the papers were headlining a variety of insinuations. The city's total of twenty daily papers, morning and evening, featured John McGraw's "jumping" the American League in Baltimore, his "bitter row" with Ban Johnson, and the league president's veiled charges, and John's callous "desertion" of old and trusting friends in Baltimore.

I tried not to read them, but I couldn't help hearing small newsboys on the street corners greeting the late-afternoon sports-minded crowds with lurid declarations that, I'm sure, were not in the stories at all.

"It sells papers," John said with a wry smile. "And it builds interest in the baseball team. People might get curious and go to the Polo Grounds to see what it's all about. Once there, they'll forget everything but the ball game."

"Well, I just don't like the charges to go unanswered," I said.

"Neither do I," he replied, and his face sobered. "But it's a small part of something more important. Everything will be all right. From now on, all we have to do is play baseball. And we will, harder and better than anybody else."

That wasn't news. John McGraw couldn't play any other way. What always amazed me was how he could find the answer, the solution, to all of his troubles through victory or merely hard play on the baseball field. Looking back through the years, I think it was most significant, and also a bit on the fantastic side, for I doubt that anybody ever took over a more hopeless situation than the one he assumed in New York City on July 19, 1902.

More than mere lack of skill had put the Giants in last place by fourteen games. The situation had a sinister appearance. Key players simply were not interested in anything except their salary checks. "One less day till payday!" was a cry frequently heard after a ball game, won or lost. "Wish it would rain tomorrow and choke off the game," said one player, "but stay pleasant over Sunday." The hope was for a rainy Saturday, and a clear Sunday, when no baseball was permitted.

To a real ballplayer, these words are unthinkable. To most of the hapless Giants in early 1902, the expressions were part and parcel of a thoroughly demoralized group of ne'er-do-wells. Despite the presence of some worthy players, all were known as knockers, shirkers, and loafers in the sports pages. Ringleaders were openly accused and named. When released or transferred, Giant players would quickly talk and tell of the shameful conduct on the field and in the clubhouse. Of course, the demoralized team was said to reflect the character and incompetence of the despised owner, Andrew Freedman. Detailed accounts of Freedman's tempestuous outbursts have been pointedly publicized, but little is told of players singing and whistling merrily in the clubhouse after losing ball games.

Little or nothing is said of the older players' mysterious dislike of Christy Mathewson, then only twenty-one years old or the reason for the unhealthy antipathy. He was a great pitching prospect always. John remembered him from Norfolk, Virginia, just down Chesapeake Bay from Baltimore, and how he had won twenty-one games there while losing only two. John had close touch with the minor-league teams in the area, through friends and from spring exhibition games.

The Mathewson story was supposedly a mystery, for Norfolk had sold his contract to the Giants in midseason of 1900 for $1,500. Christy lost in his first big-league appearance on July 17, thanks to Brooklyn's hard-hitting line-up and five New York errors. After the loss of two more games, Freedman canceled the deal and returned the player to Norfolk. There he continued his winning ways to total twenty-one for the year.

More important, those three appearances in a big-league uniform made him subject to draft. John T. Brush, owner of Cincinnati, part owner of New York, and a member of the Rules Committee, drafted Christy for $100. Brush then transferred the player to New York in exchange for the suspended and disillusioned Amos Rusie, who never pitched again. The Norfolk Club protested the $1,400 loss, charging subterfuge, chicanery, and unprintables. The cries were increased during 1901 when Christy appeared in regular turn with dramatic results. He won his first eight games, half of them without allowing a run. He turned in three shutouts in succession. His attempt at nine straight victories resulted in a 1–0 defeat by St. Louis. But he appeared in 40 games for 1901, pitched more than 330 innings, and turned in 20 victories for the year, including a no-hit game in St. Louis.

There could be no justifiable reason for baseball players disliking that kind of pitcher unless they were encouraged somehow not to like him. It was certainly part of the bold revolt among the players. Christy finally admitted openly, "I cannot win with them behind me!"

Manager Horace Fogel put him on first base, and he couldn't

win with them in front of him. Jack Hendricks, a rookie transferred to Chicago, told of the shameless treatment of Matty by ringleaders, whom he identified. He declared that they threw badly to him at first base, bouncing balls and pulling him off the bag with ridiculously wide throws. He played three games at first base, and three in right field for a group called "the rankest apology for a first-class team ever imposed upon any major-league city."

This "team" went west in July and won only three games while losing twelve. A four-game series at Cincinnati, played while John, Mr. Brush, and Ban Johnson were working night and day to complete the Baltimore deal, is interesting, if not revealing. The Reds beat the Giants, 6–0, on July 14, with Bob Blewett, an experimental rookie, pitching. Christy Mathewson played left field. He pitched the next day and lasted only two innings. Jack Dunn committed an error, and George Smith, acting manager, committed two. The Reds won 10–2. They also won the following day, 7–2.

Then came the news of the big transfer, Kelley and Seymour to Cincinnati, and McGraw, with four stars, to New York as manager. Mathewson started on July 17, pitched with his "old-time form" and won, 6–3. The Giants played errorless baseball behind him!

More than 10,000 traveled to the Polo Grounds to see John appear as playing manager of the Giants for the first time on Saturday, July 19. The subway, of course, wasn't open, though the streets were. Here and there in Manhattan were signs of some gigantic mole pushing a path under the avenues, and the newspapers contained daily accounts of digging progress.

Most fans of the day used the Sixth Avenue elevated to reach the Polo Grounds. Game time was at four o'clock and the "El" ran a baseball special from Wall Street that made only one stop, 42nd Street, on the way to the Polo Grounds. Also, an excursion boat steamed up the Harlem River on days of games. This picked up patrons from the Second and Third Avenue elevated terminals at 116th Street and, for a quarter, provided a leisurely ride up the river to a dock just south of the wooden one-lane vehicle bridge from Harlem to the Bronx. It was also a heavy transfer point to the New York and Northern Railroad that ran through the Bronx and Westchester.

Other patrons drove along the Speedway from the west and north to be discharged at the top of Coogan's Bluff. There they descended a stairway to the turnstiles. General admission was 75 cents, and box seats $1.25. The first 100 to appear at the bleachers got in for 25 cents, and all above that number paid 40 cents.

The game drew a surprising number of fans in carriages, both hired and private. Horse-drawn coaches charged a dollar for the first mile, with each additional mile 40 cents, and something like 30 or 40 cents for each fifteen-minute waiting period. Split up among three or four fans, this was not considered expensive. Moreover, a number of baseball-minded hackies would make an attractive flat rate for the ride to the game and back. Once there, the carriages and fares were herded behind a rope that stretched around centerfield from bleacher to bleacher of the horseshoe-shaped wooden structure. The clubhouse and dressing rooms were in center field then, as now, but at the street level.

From time to time in this account, I have mentioned the late Harry Stevens, whom John first met in Columbus, Ohio, in 1891. He had started there with a hundred pounds of raw peanuts, which he roasted and bagged and sold, along with printed score cards of the game. When we reached New York, he had developed the concessions business into a rapidly growing enterprise. He provided generous wedges of pie for ten cents. A frankfurter sausage in a split roll was ten cents. These were later popularized as "hot dogs" by the great New York cartoonist, "Tad" Dorgan. The printed score cards, carrying the line-ups and considerable advertising, were five cents. A hustling staff of vendors plied the wooden grandstand tempting the eager fans.

Waiters roamed the aisles in black coats and neat white aprons. They carried trays each bearing from fifteen to twenty large glasses filled with glistening beer. At ten cents a glass, the lager disappeared fast among the thirsty and hungry.

All this was part of the vivid baseball scene that I remember when we entered New York, almost holding our breath and secretly wondering if we had made any kind of mistake by leaving Baltimore. For the record, here is the first Giant line-up, with John as playing manager:

Jim Jones, lf.
John McGraw, ss.
Dan McGann, 1b.
Steve Brodie, cf.
Bill Lauder, 3b.
George Smith, 2b.
Libe Washburn, rf.
Roger Bresnahan, c.
Joe McGinnity, p.

I wish I could report that John hit a home run in the ninth—
or any inning—to win the game. He didn't. He made one hit
and scored a run. Joe McGinnity had one fairly bad inning. The
villain was John's freckle-faced roommate of old, Hughie Jennings. As first baseman for Philadelphia, he took particular delight in making John's debut in New York a failure. Hughie made
a key hit during the five-run rally that gave Philadelphia the
game by 5–3, and he shouted raucously at John:

"G'wan back to Baltimore where you belong, Mac!"

No two men, or boys, revered each other more deeply than did
John and Hugh, and yet they were capable of such sadistic mutual
treatment. Of course, John would have taken even greater delight
in beating Jennings, irrespective of their personal feelings. It is
something that only the true baseball player can understand.

John began to plan changes in personnel upon taking over at
the Polo Grounds. One of the first made was the hiring of mustachioed Thomas J. Murphy, the faithful and skilled Baltimore
grounds keeper who had worked so long at Union Park and then
in the Orioles' American League park. John McGraw's baseball
was based on speed and alertness. He needed the best-kept ground
in the league, and Murphy provided it. An elderly, quiet, married
man, he was proud of his work.

The Giants' headquarters, located in the St. James Building, at
Broadway and 26th Street, were only two blocks from our hotel.
John was able to visit the office on his way to the Polo Grounds,
which he liked to reach at 10:00 A.M. each morning and no later
than 10:30. In those days the Madison Square section was more
or less in the center of things. Most of the theaters were in the
Broadway and 34th Street area; it was the same with the big stores
and the restaurants. Delmonico's had moved above 42nd Street,

but was replaced by Martin's, one of the best dining rooms, just a block down the street from our hotel. From our window we could see workmen reaching the top of the latest skyscraper, the Flatiron Building, erected on a small triangle of land at the south side of 23rd Street where Broadway crossed Fifth Avenue.

Of twenty-three players on the New York roster when John reached town, nine were made available for outright release or exchange. He talked deals everywhere on the next road trip, which found me in Baltimore. I used his absence as an excellent reason for spending two weeks or more with my folks, and to do some shopping at O'Neill's. This brought me a mild outburst of McGravian wrath when we met again.

"You're a New Yorker now!" he exclaimed and made misunderstanding impossible. "I'm a New Yorker. They pay us money, and we should do as much of our spending with them as possible. The best stores are here, so do your shopping here. Always try to spend your money where you make it."

Not only did I follow his orders in shopping; I went the limit. Later in the year John T. Brush became majority owner by taking over Andrew Freedman's holdings. The deal required many days and meetings in New York and Red Bank. John returned from the St. James Building one evening to report that it was just about finished.

"A few shares are available, if anybody wants them," he said.

"How many?" I asked.

"Four."

"How much a share?"

"Two-fifty apiece, a thousand for the four."

"I'll buy them," I said. "I'll invest in John McGraw's future."

He looked over at me and smiled. "All right, you can have them," he said, and thanked me for the expression of confidence.

I still have those four shares, which makes me, next to Connie Mack, of the Athletics, baseball's longest continuous shareholder—good heavens! What on earth am I saying?

Coincident with the transfer of majority control in the Giants from Freedman to Brush was the organization of the Greater New York Base Ball Association, Inc. This company was capitalized at $100,000 to take over and operate the American League franchise, which president Ban Johnson had repossessed by default in the friendly action at Baltimore on July 18, 1902. Stock ownership was held by seven men, most of whom were personal or political friends of Andrew Freedman.

Chief backer was Louis J. Weil, a capitalist of West 14th Street. Chief builder was James J. Wallace, whose offices were in the St. James Building, long headquarters of the Giants. Two contractors were shareholders, William H. Hurst, and former Police Inspector Thomas F. McAvoy, who was Tammany Democratic leader for the Twenty-third District, in which the new team would have home grounds. A fifth stockholder was Samuel A. Byers, a real-estate operator, long active in uptown properties.

The last two participants were Frank Farrell, poolroom operator with whom John had held a key meeting at the Gravesend race track in early June, 1902. Even as the American League club was being organized, Farrell's former racing partners, Julius and Max Fleischmann, were refinancing Brush's Cincinnati Reds for George Cox, Cincinnati political leader, and his protégé, August "Garry" Herrmann, head of the city's Water Works Board.

With Farrell as vice-president, the seventh stockholder and president of the new corporation was Joseph Gordon, Tammany Democrat (Pontiac Club) and brother-in-law of John B. Day, then a member of the Giants' board of directors. Gordon was Superintendent of Buildings for New York City in 1901 by appointment, and an assistant for many years. He operated a prosperous coal and wood business.

With the new club's financing arranged, Freedman "released" one of the many real-estate parcels under his control and large enough to contain a baseball playing field. The site selected was bounded by Broadway, Fort Washington Avenue, 165th and 168th Streets. In two years a subway train would reach that area.

The plot of ground, scene of Billy Sunday's religious revival fourteen years later, and now bearing the great Presbyterian Medical Center, was a mountain of rock. The contract for excavating some five thousand cubic yards of stone and shale went to one of the stockholders, District Leader McAvoy. After removing the rock, he filled the area with a layer of dirt or loam that he obtained from the subway excavating downtown.

Several weeks later the new American League team, nicknamed the Highlanders because of the ball-park location, went into spring training under the management of Clark Griffith, whom Ban Johnson had obtained from his old friend and Chicago owner, Charles Comiskey. They were in Macon, in the central part of Georgia. The Giants, under John McGraw were in old and familiar Savannah, quartered this time at the De Soto Hotel.

With Andrew Freedman's passing from the baseball scene, an era was over, and a new one had begun. John McGraw had only one supreme purpose in mind: to build a winning team of Giants, one that would dominate by sheer power of skill and the will to win. Baseball in New York City was at its lowest ebb. But the glowing embers in the ashes of administrative fire needed only a boy and a baseball to fan them into a conflagration.

John McGraw was that "boy and the baseball," who, in my opinion, could be neither destroyed nor denied. Defeat was his mortal enemy. He was a force that knew only one compromise: victory. All else was of minor importance, for without victory, without a team of fighting, hustling players to create that victory, baseball had no meaning for him. By the same token, life without baseball also had little meaning for him. It was his meat, his drink, his dream, his blood and breath, his reason for existence.

17

WE SAT IN the lobby of the De Soto Hotel for hours, days it seemed, each staring when the other wasn't looking. She had gray eyes and dark brown hair. She was dressed rather nicely, I thought. This was not a catty reaction. It seemed fitting and quite in character, because she came from a somewhat strait-laced family in Lewisburg, Pennsylvania, where they had always lived.

And she was a Sunday-school teacher, which also made her suspect. I caught her staring at me a few times, thinking narrow thoughts, perhaps, if I was any judge of appearance. She was the wife of a player, and I was the wife of the player's manager. She was spending her honeymoon on a southern training trip, a mere bride, while I had spent my own honeymoon in this very city some time before.

While this great dissertation was going on in my youthful head, the object of my mental meandering was doing a pretty good job on me from across the lobby. I wore a new dress that was generously sprinkled with sequins, and the very latest thing in New York. Also, on my left hand was the dazzling engagement ring that reflected my husband's pride and affection. It represented something else to the bride across the lobby. She actually thought, "Only a hussy would wear a ring like that!"

Thus began a lifelong friendship with Jane Stoughton Mathewson, Christy's bride of a few weeks. Soon we were shopping together and laughing at our mutual suspicions. While the men were practicing, we would stroll down Bull Street to Forsyth Park where the early spring azaleas were budding and all of life seemed green and new and full of hope.

I told John of Jane Mathewson and of our happy visits, and I asked what kind of person her young husband was. I knew he was big and bulky, blond, and with big, smiling, wide-apart blue eyes. John had played baseball with him, and they had talked. What about him?

"Looks like he can pitch with his head as well as his arm," John replied, and he honestly believed that answered my question.

The Giants' spring training was marred by only one incident, or accident. John's weak left knee buckled again. He had played thirty-four games as a Giant in 1902. Now the injury reappeared during sliding practice, and he limped through the remainder of the training, doubtful again of ever taking part in a game.

Reaching New York, the happy McGraws and Mathewsons rented a ground-floor furnished apartment at Columbus Avenue and 85th Street, only a block from Central Park, with the elevated line convenient for a ride direct to the Polo Grounds. We had seven rooms, which cost $50 a month. John paid the rent and gas bill and Christy paid for the food which totaled about the same, since the men traveled half the summer.

Such an arrangement, that of baseball pitcher living with manager, would be hazardous today. But that year, 1903, John was thirty and mature. Christy, only twenty-two, was a quiet, soft-spoken boy, though he carried his part of conversations.

He had attended Bucknell College, pitched brilliantly, and played football. He could have graduated easily, but he wanted to start out in professional baseball. He had an unusual mind, a quick mind, and the stubbornness of a person with a trained mind. He had the ego of a great competitor and a deep-rooted belief that every opponent was his inferior. He did not smoke or drink, and he asked to be excused from playing baseball on Sunday because of religious training. He was nearly six feet two inches, with two hundred pounds of well-conditioned body. He read a lot.

Most interesting was his memory. It was almost photographic. He could remember dozens of cards that had been played in a game, and a cribbage score. He played checkers by numbers. That is, the squares were numbered in his mind from one, two, three, four in the opponent's king row, and then five, six, seven, eight for the second row, down to twenty-nine, thirty, thirty-one, and thirty-two in his own king row from left to right. And he could talk about the most common opening, Old Fourteenth, or its countless variations as long as you would listen.

When he played checkers, his response to a move was drawn from his memory of the proper defense. It wasn't even necessary for him to see the board at checkers or chess, which enabled him to defeat eight or ten really good players while blindfolded.

John's own memory was somewhat fabulous in his sphere of interest, baseball rules and technical shortcomings. He had trained his mind to remember what all pitchers threw best, and what type of pitch batters could hit easiest. He had studied style, idiosyncrasies, weaknesses, and favorite methods. He could reconstruct a full ball game, pitch by pitch.

All this he poured into Christy Mathewson's retentive mind as they lived together, went to the Polo Grounds together each morning at ten o'clock, practiced together, dressed together, played together, and fought side by side on the field.

"I never had to tell Christy anything a second time," John once said. "In addition, he watched Joe McGinnity closely. We made a science of studying batters. Within a few years he had charted nearly every ballplayer in the National League, just like his variations of the Old Fourteenth opening. He also began working on his control. By watching McGinnity, he picked up the idea of the change of pace pitch and perfected it. Sensing the need of reserve strength in a pinch, he seldom wasted energy early in a game. When a hit meant a run, or the game, he was as close to invincible as any pitcher could get."

We hadn't been in the Columbus Avenue apartment more than a month when the call came from the hospital. I found John in the emergency operating room and doctors struggling to halt a nasal hemorrhage. During pregame batting practice, players yelled, "Look out!" He turned to look, and a thrown ball smashed his nose, felling him, stunned and bleeding. The ball had been caught and thrown in from the outfield by Luther Taylor, a right-handed pitcher, who could neither speak nor hear, and was known as "Dummy." He was miserable with remorse over the accident.

John insisted upon returning to the Polo Grounds and the game. The doctors scoffed at the idea, but John won permission to leave for Philadelphia next day with the team.

"I'm going, too," I announced.

"You'd better stay here," John insisted. "I'll be all right."

The nose was broken and the severed cartilage had ruptured an artery. The bleeding had stopped, but it could start again without warning, and did in Philadelphia, by the way. The doctors backed me and John finally agreed to let me make the trip.

"Then tell Christy to stay," he said. "No use leaving Jane alone in the apartment."

This story will be unbelievable to many who knew only one side of John McGraw. Perhaps they will insist that the ball hit him in the head, softening his brain. Actually, it helps explain his thinking, even with a nose full of pain.

Neither Jane Mathewson nor I liked to be alone in somebody else's ground-floor apartment. Christy would certainly remember it, if he went to Philadelphia. No pitcher can do the club or himself any good when his thoughts are back in another city with a frightened bride. Morale could best be preserved by leaving Mathewson home.

Many baseball men have singled out as most important John McGraw's ability to weld a conflicting assortment of personalities, some good, some fine, some odious, into a winning combination. He did it through understanding and then exercising full control. He permitted no flouting or defiance of that control. Leaving

Christy Mathewson home because his bride "didn't like to be alone" was part of his genius for understanding.

He displayed it again some years later by fining this same Christy Mathewson $500 for playing poker with his teammates for high stakes.

"Anybody else would be fined twenty-five or fifty," John said to the man he revered and called the greatest of all pitchers. "But you know better, Christy, and the fine is five hundred."

Mathewson was certain to win any competitive contest eventually. The other players couldn't match his skill, and if they did and had better luck, he had the perseverance and patience to outlast them. Regardless of money, beating the other fellow was a basic, spiritual thing within Christy's nature, just as it was in John McGraw's. Christy recalled this side of John McGraw to an army officer of his battalion in France during World War I.

"You wonder how a man who had been so much to me, and I to him, could do such a thing," Christy sighed in recollection. "But he not only fined me the five hundred; he made it stick. I never got it back."

Not getting back the fine was another unkind cut to Giant players. Few knew of the ten-dollar bills, the twenties, and even fifties, that John slipped into players' lockers at home and mail boxes on the road, usually out of his own pocket. Each was a silent expression of thanks for an occasional extra effort, for an unusual pitching or hitting performance.

Over the years John became fairly well known for his tongue-lashing of Giant players, sometimes with a fine, and always without regard for his personal likes or dislikes and mutual feelings. The relationship had nothing to do with play on the field or desire to win the ball game.

Because of John McGraw's unyielding, autocratic methods, and the varying characters that only he could assemble, the morale of his Giant teams was usually in a delicate state, but invariably high. His penchant for vocal vitriol, cutting sarcasm on the bench and field, and his aggressive challenge to all in sight or sound, including umpires and club owners, may have tightened team morale, but it never weakened team spirit. Players didn't know what to expect next, and played their heads off to prevent it.

But it was always his team and his personal responsibility, and nothing on earth was more important than its success. To play for John McGraw, you first had to play to win. Secondly, you played as he told you to play, and asked questions later, because he knew far more of the game than you ever hoped to. Whether you were blessed with greatness or mediocrity, you played your best under his directions and according to his decisions. If they were wrong decisions, he, and no one else, was to blame.

Jane Mathewson and I took our housekeeping seriously, including the cooking, in 1903. We led normal lives, fed the men well, and left them alone to talk their baseball. They were happy in their scheming, because the Giants were a winning team. Their happiness was the cause of ours.

We couldn't realize, of course, that they were making baseball history by sheer force of personality and determination. Nothing else, in my opinion, can account for the Polo Grounds miracle of 1903 and 1904. A few men, barely a half-dozen, made the pendulum of miserable failure swing back toward victory and financial success. At the core was John McGraw. Around him whirled athletic greatness and a faith in his methods that almost defies belief in this so-called enlightened age.

But what else could spur men to give so far beyond their ability? No riches had been offered. No threats had been made. Who has the understanding or the words to explain it? It can only be felt by those who did it, and they have never talked much about it.

The Giants of 1903 played 139 games. Joe McGinnity and Christy Mathewson pitched in exactly 100 of them, a few times in the same game. The work of the rough-handed ironworker from Indian Territory was so far above ordinary endeavor as to bring a catch in your throat. This was the man who had huddled with John in a corner of Union Station, St. Louis, one chill night in February, 1901, and placed his baseball future in John's hands with only a verbal assurance that all would be well. Eighteen months later he had pledged his all on a piece of hotel stationery.

In 1903 he completed 44 of the ball games he started, and he pitched in a total of 55. He worked 434 innings, facing 1,658 batters. He won 31 victories and suffered 19 defeats. On August 1, 8, and 31 he pitched and won both games of double-headers. He had attempted this "Iron Man" feat twice for John in Baltimore, two years before, during the September drive, but could win only one of the two games each time. In 1903 he was not to be denied, and his untiring double-duty arm brought glory and fans to the Polo Grounds to revive almost forgotten legends.

Christy Mathewson's pitching was hardly less impressive. He worked in fewer games, 45, and innings, 367, but he struck out 267 batters. The last-place Giants of 1902 won only 48 games. The second-place Giants of 1903 won 84, of which McGinnity and Mathewson accounted for 61. Younger Roger Bresnahan, catcher, first baseman, infielder, outfielder, and pitcher, if they needed one, turned in the best batting average of his life, .350 for 111 games. George Browne, who became a star after his transfer from Philadelphia to the Giants the year before, was still a star in the outfield with a batting average of .313.

But all of them—McGann, Gilbert, Mertes, Babb, Lauder, the veteran Van Haltren, and even surly "Niagara" Frank Bowerman —played to the hilt every minute in their positions. The Giants clinched second place in the National League by beating the three-time champions, Pittsburgh, in the next to the last game of the season. The winning pitcher was red-headed Leon Ames, twenty-one, discovered and sent to John by his old Truxton friend and sponsor, Bert Kenney.

Believing that Boston, American League champions, would not risk an interleague test, John challenged championship Pittsburgh to a post-season series, like the old Temple Cup competition.

"The Pittsburgh team is so far superior to Boston in the other league that there is no comparison," John said in a statement to the press. "I'd like to see Fred Clarke's team make them look foolish, but I'm afraid the series won't come off. My proposition therefore is for Pittsburgh to play five games with the Giants, with all proceeds going to the players of both teams."

But the two league champions, Pittsburgh and Boston, met in a postseason series for the best five out of nine. Pittsburgh won three of the first four, and then lost four straight. To New York fans, however, this was all secondary to the fact that the "rankest apology" team had become a relentless and charging aggregation of ballplayers fighting tooth and nail for victory. Overnight this most ridiculed club in baseball had restored public confidence in New York. And a good thing, too, because the new American

League team had made a good showing in the first season on the hilltop by finishing fourth.

The Giants played nine or ten profitable postseason exhibition games, after which the Mathewsons left to spend the winter in Lewisburg. John and I moved back to the Victoria Hotel. He went to the office daily to plan changes in personnel. He released the veteran Van Haltren. He strengthened the infield by replacing Babb and Lauder. John got Bill Dahlen from Ned Hanlon at Brooklyn, and a youngster, Arthur Devlin, a graduate of Georgetown University, who had played well for two seasons at Newark.

John McGraw always said that a fast, sure infield, with good reserves, would handle three-fourths of the fielding chances, especially with curve-ball pitchers. He would recite the percentage and make it quite simple, which I am unable to do.

John had written Joe McGinnity to find out if he planned to boil out at the Hot Springs bath, or perhaps go south a little early. Since Joe had pitched one of the hardest seasons on record, John rather hoped he would forget the ironworks and Indian Territory for once and rest up. But Joe replied on January 5, 1904, as follows:

Dear Friend Mack,

Received your kind letter. Glad to hear from you and would like to come for a month, but don't think I will be able to get down this year as it costs too much for me to stand. So I will try to get in shape here this spring. I have not been well for the past two months, but I am getting all right again now. Well Mack, we look to have a Ball Club for next year and if you can get them in shape in the Spring and get a good start we will win a game now and then. That is what helped us out last year. I suppose you are having a good time down there. I would like to spend a month there, but I can't stand it this year. So I will not get to see you before we report. But will start in to work the first of the month and will try to report in Good Shape. So Mack, if you have time, drop me a line and tell me the news. With best regards to all, hoping to hear from you soon, I remain,

As ever

Joe McGinnity

The opening of the 1904 baseball season was reminiscent of the old days in Baltimore and an almost forgotten era in New York. The game, scheduled for Washington Park, Brooklyn, on Friday, April 15, was threatened by an early morning snowstorm. Fortunately the flakes stopped falling at ten o'clock, leaving white streets that were soon cleaned by the sun.

The mechanical age reared its head when Charles Ebbets, Brooklyn Club president, abandoned the old-fashioned horse and carriage for a pregame parade through the streets. He engaged two large gasoline-driven vehicles for the dignitaries. They drove over to Madison Square as thousands cheered, picked up John, Mr. Brush, and other New York officials, and then continued with an impressive, though slightly noisy, parade down Fifth Avenue, over the Brooklyn Bridge, and to Fourth Avenue and Third Street. There the biggest crowd in Brooklyn's baseball history was jam-packed in the flag-draped bandbox park. Unfortunately the speeches and music and presentation of municipal officials and floral tributes delayed the starting time until four o'clock. By that time it was cloudy, and an arctic chill shrouded the scene.

But the excitement kept the fans from actually freezing after the opening pitch. George Browne hit a single. Devlin sacrificed. McGann singled, scoring Browne. McGann took second on the throw-in and scored on Mertes' hit. Christy Mathewson had a two-run lead. It was halved by his wildness a few minutes later when Brooklyn batted, but the Giants got back the run in the second on Mathewson's single. He went on to win the first of his thirty-three victories for the year.

Christy pitched one more inning than in 1903, but lost only twelve times. Most encouraging, John said, was his base on balls record. He walked but 78, against 100 the year before.

Marvelous as Christy was, the story of the year again was the Iron Man, "who had not felt good" during the winter. This easy-going, sidearm, curve-ball master pitched more than 400 innings for the second straight year. He appeared in 51 games, giving him and Matty a 2-year record of working in 199 games, and winning 129 against only 32 defeats. For 1904 they turned in baseball's all-time best, a combined total of 68 victories and only 20 losses!

The affable Iron Man's work was a supreme tribute to faith and loyalty. In 1903 he had pitched and won three double-headers during the month of August. His headline-making achievement in 1904 was a string of fourteen consecutive victories, and a total of 35 for the year. With only eight defeats, this gave him a percentage of .814, by far the best in baseball.

Up on the hilltop tragedy happened on the last day. Clark Griffith could have won the American League pennant with the Yankees, had they taken a double-header from the Boston Red Sox. They won the second game, but in the last inning of the first game, and with two out, Jack Chesbro, pitching his 55th game and trying for his 42nd victory of the season, wild-pitched and lost the game, plus the pennant.

The Giants staged a runaway race ahead of the Chicago Cubs. They finished with 106 victories, 13 games in the lead. Except for the veteran Jack Dunn and Bill Marshall, who played infrequently, the Giants had no .300 hitters. Even Mike Donlin, whom John reacquired in July, hit only .280 after the switch from Cincinnati. It was the pitching all the way—McGinnity, Mathewson, then Luther "Dummy" Taylor with 21 victories, and George "Hooks" Wiltse, pitching his first year for John, with 13. Those four accounted for 102 of the 106 wins. It was a tremendous pitching staff, backed up by a young, fast, and sure infield. Once the Giants took the lead on July 13, they were never headed.

To those who insist that John McGraw was completely without sentiment, I offer the first game of September 22, 1904, as refutation. John had four versatile catchers, Bowerman, Bresnahan, Jack Warner, and the pinch-hitting rookie, Bill Marshall. But the catcher in the first game was an old Giant hero of the John B. Day era, James Henry "Orator" O'Rourke, who received a rousing reception and a large floral horseshoe from old fans. Despite his fifty-two years, he caught the entire nine innings and made one base hit in four times at bat. In the absence of radio and even leased-wire telegraph, no one knew that the Chicago Cubs had lost in Philadelphia, making the Giants' pennant a mathematical certainty, but John suspected it might happen. He was doubly glad, for the popular Jim O'Rourke had caught the pennant-clinching ball game, his last in a big-league uniform.

Immediately after victory, plans were announced for a gigantic Giant benefit and civic celebration. A special performance was arranged for Sunday, October 2, at Klaw and Erlanger's New York

Theater, Broadway and 45th Street. John T. Brush bought the first box for $5,000. Purchasers lined up for the cause, and the subscription fund grew rapidly for the gala night.

The New York *Journal's* young cartoonist, Thomas Aloysius Dorgan, known as "Tad," devoted a seven-column drawing to the team on the stage. He caricatured them dressed in rented tuxedos and had everybody in it from John to "Buster" Wilson, the mascot. Tod Sloan, the famous jockey, was a witty master of ceremonies. Dave Montgomery and Fred Stone, of *Wizard of Oz* fame, skipped an engagement in Boston to help out. Other contributors were Digby Bell, Dan McAvoy, Gus Edwards, Miss Grace Cameron, and Miss Helen Bryon and her entire company. State Senator Brady called them "Champions of the World." The theater really rang when the final act was introduced by silver-voiced Joe Humphries, the young sports announcer. John accepted a large loving cup in behalf of the team. Then he was showered with personal mementos, a watch charm set with sixty-eight diamonds from Louis Mann and other stage friends, a set of diamond cuff buttons from Harry M. Stevens, and less brilliant items bestowed with equal pride and affection. The receipts of the benefit totaled $25,000, which went to the team.

As soon as Boston was declared the American League winner, John made known the fact that his team would not play them in any postseason series.

"It is a minor league," he said in several different ways, "and the Giants would outclass them."

Actually, he would have given the equivalent of a right eye to meet and beat them, but John T. Brush had struggled long to set up a permanent program for postseason competition between the leagues' winners. He wanted no shambles, such as had eventually killed the poorly arranged Temple Cup Series. Since the so-called Brush Rules were neither ratified by the two leagues nor complete, he chose to pass up the postseason competition and gamble on a bigger and better series in the future.

But once again John McGraw was obliged to bear the brunt of recrimination. His remarks of calculated contempt, freely uttered at the time, were written into the record, official and otherwise. Also once again John acted in a good cause. Healthy interleague competition really dates from October, 1904, when, from his pinnacle of baseball achievement, he defied the American League to become strong enough and "worthy" to compete with his Giants.

18

JOHN TOMLINSON BRUSH was one of the most courageous of men. The last two decades of his life, his busiest and most controversial years, brought a progressive paralysis that handicapped him physically with increasing severity and finally put him in a wheel chair. But nothing ever stilled his active mind or lessened the fighting qualities of his tireless heart.

He was born on June 15, 1845, in Clintonville, Ohio. Orphaned at the age of four, he lived with his grandfather in Hopkinton, Massachusetts, about twenty-five miles west of Boston. He began work in a Boston clothing store when he was seventeen, and a year later, 1863, he enlisted in the First New York Artillery. He served with distinction until the Civil War's end, but rarely did he mention the subject, even in his own home.

He returned to the clothing business after the war, and during the trying days of reconstruction, he clerked in several large eastern cities. In 1875, at the age of thirty, he opened his own dry-goods and clothing establishment in Indianapolis, Indiana. Prospering from the start, he became active in civic and fraternal affairs. The Masonic order drew his special attention and energies. He took his Blue Lodge degree in Indianapolis, where his membership remained. He was a Knight Templar in Rapier Commandry, a member of the Scottish Rite bodies. He received his thirty-third and last degree as a merited honor for proficiency and zeal.

The first Mrs. Brush, the former Agnes Ewart, died in 1888, leaving a daughter, Eleanor. Another daughter, Natalie, was born of a second union in the mid-nineties, and I believe her mother, Mrs. Elsie Lombard Brush, is still alive at this writing.

Brush backed the Indianapolis Club in the National League for three years, 1887–88–89, during which time the team finished eighth once and seventh twice. When the senior league needed help in 1890 to end American Association competition in Cincinnati, Brush took over the holdings for practically nothing from the harassed Aaron S. Stern, who had patterned his baseball operation after Coney Island methods.

Brush was a formidable leader in league councils and a shrewd committeeman. His eye was always on New York as a site for his baseball operations, and perhaps the clothing business as well. There is little doubt that he would have reached New York and exerted his influence sooner but for two setbacks: the beginnings of his long and torturous paralysis, and Andrew Freedman's unexpected stock-control coup at the end of 1894.

He worked on the Brush Rules to govern postseason competition unceasingly through the winter of 1904–1905 and presented them to the National Commission by mid-January. Except for minor changes, particularly the spreading of larger gate receipts to other first-division clubs, the rules are the same for the prosperous World Series nearly a half century later.

After completing the plan, Brush spurned a challenge from the New York American League team to a spring exhibition series. The Giants ruled metropolitan baseball, and neither Mr. Brush nor John had any intention of sharing influence.

The year 1905 was a long, hard, and memorable one, but it began with John returning to the Victoria Hotel one evening early in February wearing an expression of quiet satisfaction.

"Well, Hughie made it," he said, with a half sigh.

"Made what?" I asked. Jennings had returned to Baltimore as manager of the Orioles in 1903 after Harry Goldman had put them into the Eastern League.

"He's a lawyer," John said. "He's admitted to the bar. Hughie's a lawyer!"

Mind you, many baseball players of the day had achieved higher education, but Hugh Jennings, thirty-five, had started late and with little of everything except courage and determination. And it was in a day when professional baseball players carried something of a stigma to travelers in the upper circles of society. Individual players commanded respect here and there, but the craft as a whole was regarded as something to be avoided.

The 1905 Giant team was his best, John always insisted. He would go through the roster and explain how and why each player rated above his counterpart on other great teams. The players could really fly. John held a field day in Memphis, Tennessee, on the way north from the Georgia training camp, and the results amazed even him. George Browne ran the thirty yards from the batter's box to first base in three seconds flat. Billy Gilbert covered the distance in three and one-fifth seconds. Mike Donlin and Sammy Strang, a utility player and pinch hitter obtained from Brooklyn, tied as the third speediest when they were timed in three and two-fifths seconds. But Roger Bresnahan, a catcher, made it in four seconds, as did young Arthur Devlin, who usually caught Roger in impromptu races.

John was certain that he had the fastest team in baseball. The players were certain he had the very best team in either league, and didn't care who knew it. All scented victory from the start, even though McGinnity threatened to hold out all year. He demanded an extra $2,000 claimed as lost through Mr. Brush's banning California exhibition games the previous fall. The team enjoyed the highest morale as the season opened against Boston at the Polo Grounds on Friday, April 14. To keep it high, John hired the first of many old Orioles, "Boileryard" Bill Clarke, who had caught for Baltimore several years before. John needed no catching, and Clarke, aged thirty-seven, was through as a player, but he figured to help the young pitchers. Of course, no mention was made of sentiment.

John McGraw had been a controversial figure over the years, but always when he was playing with or leading an outstanding team. He has never been attacked in print or in executive councils when he was confined to his bed by illness, or to the second division by a poor team. When his methods pressed upon the boundary lines of what today is known as "good sportsmanship," I have not offered an alibi, nor have I attempted to excuse him.

The idea of deciding baseball's destiny, game by game, or season by season, through the thrown or batted ball was an obsession with John McGraw. Psychologists might call it a fetish. He countenanced no other method and fought to decide everything on the field, because there alone he was master of his fate. No doubt existed in his mind that the baseball and the bat preceded all else in this growing and prosperous game. He learned the rules before he could read them; he knew the language of the players who had dreamed and suffered to learn as he had. In the play of the game, the rowdy and the gentleman spoke a common tongue.

Under John McGraw a sour-natured Bowerman could teach and help a gentlemanly Mathewson, as Frank did after John took over in 1902, yet neither had anything in common otherwise. Mathewson would instinctively rise to surrender his seat to a lady in the subway or streetcar. Bowerman once raced a lady for a campstool on a Brooklyn–New York ferryboat and got there first. When she slapped his face in anger, he called her a bum sport and had her arrested for assault.

A Joe McGinnity could write a colossal falsehood to Secretary Fred Knowles about salary—as he did when Knowles failed in November, 1903, to send him the contract agreed upon—and yet bite his tongue off before he would lie to John. A "Bugs" Raymond drove other managers to distraction with his impossible habits. Yet he could pitch for John, and did, winning eighteen games one season in a Giant uniform that was constantly soaked with honest, but alcoholic, sweat.

In the play of the game, the urge to win, the willingness to take his constant, sharp-tongued direction, and to put the many little steps to victory above all else, they were as one. And they were never more so than in 1905.

The historic break between Pittsburgh and the Giants occurred in mid-May of that year, but it actually started in July of the previous season, 1904. John and his Giants began to do the wholly unexpected, seriously threatening Pittsburgh's three-year domination of the National League. The first visit of 1904 had been uneventful, but the second produced a cascade of vicious libel in the newspapers. It was best described by Allen Sangree, who traveled with the Giants for the New York *Globe*. He wrote from Chicago on July 21, 1904:

I sat in the press stand (Pittsburgh) during the four games alongside the official scorer, a cautious, careful man who knows his business, is an ardent rooter for the home team, but dispenses justice. Neither from him nor any other of the experienced baseball writers did I hear a word of complaint about McGraw or anyone else on the team. Indeed, it was generally commented that the club behaved itself remarkably well. McGraw only took the coaching line a few times and then had little to say. The relations between the Giants and Pirates were friendly also, and the most captious critic could find no fault with the former's behavior. In view of this just read one of the several nasty articles that appeared daily in the Pittsburgh press, topped with a scare head, but very wisely lacking a signature:

"No National League baseball team that has appeared here this season has shown so rowdy a spirit as that exhibited by the Giants on the present trip. The buzzing of the pennant bee about their ears has probably turned the heads of the most of the metropolitans, and they are as stuck up as a country beau out with his best girl."

The full quotation ran at great length, and contained bold insults to Christy Mathewson, who was referred to as "Sis" because of his tenor voice. It accused Matty of foul language and vituperation. It charged that Bowerman had invited a jail sentence by locking Manager Clarke in a New York hotel room previously and beating him, which also libeled Clarke's well-known courage and fistic ability. The story went on to tell how:

". . . Muggsy McGraw is as loud-mouthed as he can be and the expressions he uses to occupants of the grandstand are not all within the bounds of propriety. It is really a shame that the regular patrons of the game at Exposition Park should have to be subjected to the talk of one whose swell head, over the prospects of winning the National League pennant, has caused him to lose sight of the fact that he owes a lot to the people."

The story further stated flatly that John had a second time "turned the air blue with an outburst of invective" and that he had kept it up along the streets, shouting at passing fans. Sangree then closed with:

Some of the other artists were even more scurrilous, and the best newspapermen in the town were annoyed at the series of tirades.

"These things are either inspired by a personal enemy of McGraw's or someone associated with the management," said one well-known sporting writer. "It seems utterly improbable that 'Barney' Dreyfuss would countenance such a method of roasting a rival, so it must be one that has it in for McGraw, because nothing that he or the team has done on or off the field calls for such rot as this."

Returning to New York with clippings of the published abuse, John met with Mr. Brush and attorneys. It was a legal matter, and not only because of the libel; the accusation was a threat to his three-year contract with the club.

Brush had long fought against rowdyism and foul language on the field as a means of breaking down resistance against Sunday baseball in the east. A clause against rowdyism and foul language had been put into John's contract by mutual consent as proof that club and manager were desirous of controlling this odious aspect of baseball. John had readily agreed to the stipulation, for his position on the matter had long coincided with the stated demands. He had willingly agreed to control outbursts among his players, just as he had agreed to all other terms of his contract.

A copy of the document was on file in the National League office. The conditions were fairly well known. Thus, the Pittsburgh attack might have been aimed at creating evidence that John had violated his contract. If believed, the trumped-up story was grounds for suspension, or even abrogation of the contract. Fortunately it was too bold and overdrawn for belief. The vicious attack on Mathewson was ridiculous. Why were such reports written only in Pittsburgh? Mr. Brush offered legal assistance to seek civil redress.

"No, thank you," John said finally. "I'll handle it myself. The newspaper isn't to blame, but some writer or a person behind the writer is. I'll find out."

The published abuse appeared in varying degrees for the remainder of the 1904 season. The Giants' visits to Pittsburgh threatened trouble, but the Pirates finished fourth, and New York won the pennant. That made the city easy to forget.

The inevitable occurred in 1905 during a Pittsburgh-Giants game at the Polo Grounds, following four straight victories over the Cubs, three by shutouts. John questioned an umpire's decision in no uncertain terms. He was ordered off the field. His temper mounted, and when he had finished, his tirade included the Pittsburgh president, Barney Dreyfuss. There was no stenographic transcript of the outburst, but Mr. Dreyfuss, charging he had suffered "personal and unprovoked verbal abuse," lodged official complaint against John with the National League president, Henry Clay Pulliam.

A week later John was fined $150 and suspended for fifteen days for verbal abuse of President Dreyfuss. A special meeting of the league directors was called for June 1 to "try McGraw for making allegations of crookedness and control of umpires against Mr. Dreyfuss."

Harry Pulliam was only thirty-six years old at the time. He was a handsome young man, of slight build, nervous temperament, dark hair, and alert brown eyes. He came from a fine Kentucky family, graduated from the University of Virginia, and served in the Kentucky legislature. He was secretary to Zach Phelps, of the Louisville Club, in his early twenties. He helped the Colonels through stormy days and, when Dreyfuss bought the club, he remained as secretary. Later Dreyfuss made him president. After the park burned, Dreyfuss, as previously stated, transferred his interests to Pittsburgh and Pulliam went as club secretary-treasurer. The Pirates enjoyed great success in 1901–1902–1903.

But you may recall that Andrew Freedman, before selling out in 1902, had forced the National League, in lieu of a president, to accept a Board of Control, consisting of Arthur H. Soden, of Boston; John T. Brush, new owner of New York; and James Hart, of Chicago. At the 1903 fall meeting of the league, Hart led in abolishing the Board of Control, proposed young Pulliam as president, and succeeded in having him elected.

Within a year the Pittsburgh "situation" had developed, with John and the Giants a target of unprecedented viciousness in the press. His smoldering rancor may be held inexcusable by some, but it was understandable. His carefully built baseball team was in jeopardy. They were a fast, hard-running, hard-playing team, playing the best and most "inside baseball" seen since the Orioles of Ned Hanlon's days. Fortunately they also had a sense of humor usually found among winners.

"We couldn't go into Pittsburgh that year," John has recalled, "without having some kind of run-in with the fans. The newspapers would announce, 'the rowdy Giants, accompanied by representatives of the yellow press, got into town this morning.'

"We used to suit up at the old Monongahela Hotel and drive to the game in open carriages. Exposition Park was then in Allegheny City, across the river. To reach the bridge, we had to pass a public market, and our dark uniforms made attractive targets. After the game we had to repass the market where the razzing started back and forth, especially after winning. We usually won in nineteen-five, though one of the games was lost by forfeit in the ninth when I refused to continue until an umpire said whether a runner sliding into third was safe or out. He actually refused to make the call.

"But one day we had to dodge handfuls of gravel, loose pieces of brick, and anything throwable all the way to the bridge. Then came the market, and the razzing, and our razzing right back. After that the vegetables—potatoes, onions, tomatoes, and even ancient cantaloupes.

"Joe McGinnity rose in his carriage as peacemaker and the carriage swayed. As he lurched over, four big tomatoes hit him squarely on the seat of the pants. It was the funniest thing we'd ever seen, but not to Joe. We were a one-suit team, and dry cleaning was unthinkable, if it even existed. It was a long road trip for McGinnity.

"Sammy Strang, in another carriage, was hit on the head with an overripe cantaloupe. Others had got in the way of so many vegetables that people at the hotel thought we had played a ball game in a garbage dump. But it couldn't stop us from beating Barney Dreyfuss and his ball club. We played all the harder."

John and Mr. Brush were in Boston with the Giants for the Decoration Day series when word of the fine and suspension came from Pulliam. Both entered Superior Court and applied to Judge Sheldon for an injunction to restrain Pulliam from fining or suspending on the basis of stated charges. This was not "laundering linen" in public. The press was given definitely to understand that John had accused Dreyfuss of certain dishonest acts. If true, the accusations were most reprehensible and libelous. Mr. Dreyfuss needed only to rustle up a few witnesses from the thousands at the Polo Grounds, including his own team, to support his claim.

The Pittsburgh club took no such action. Instead, the League Board of Directors met in Boston on June 1 and acquitted John of the charges. Moreover, the board censured Dreyfuss for "engaging in an altercation with McGraw in public."

Judge Sheldon issued a temporary restraining order on the ground that John had not been given a hearing by President Pulliam before suffering the condemnatory fine and suspension on May 27. Pulliam replied to this the next day with a public denouncement of John T. Brush for seeking by common law to defeat the very baseball legislation that he, Brush, had fostered at a previous National League meeting. A week later the league president was obliged to announce that new anti-rowdy laws were needed by baseball, and that he would refund all fines above $10 inflicted upon players prior to the McGraw injunction.

Meanwhile the "boys with the baseball" were making more important history on the field. Two of the Giants, pitchers Leon Ames and Dummy Taylor, were undefeated for the season. As the schedule went into June each had won nine straight games. Ames was the first to break, and it was his misfortune to lose his try for ten in a row at Pittsburgh. Taylor failed to win his tenth at Cincinnati a week later.

Sandwiched in between these two heartbreakers was Christy Mathewson's no-hit classic pitched against the Cubs in Chicago. He opposed the great right-hander Mordecai "Three-Finger" Brown, so named because of a missing first finger on his pitching hand. Matty had pitched a no-hit game against St. Louis in 1901, but this was a far more masterful performance. He struck out two batters and walked none. Only two Cubs reached first base, both on errors. Brown was almost as remarkable, for he allowed only one hit until the ninth, and lost by a score of 1–0.

Each series on that memorable first western trip produced a recollection, and John always laughed at the last one, a defeat in Cincinnati. Hooks Wiltse managed to swallow his cud of chewing tobacco while pitching. He tried to finish the game, grew deathly sick, and left, but not before he had given up enough hits to lose it.

Back in New York we had more troubles. The Mathewsons took us driving in their new car, a beautiful machine with black leather upholstery and polished brass kerosene lamps. Mitchell, the chauffeur, lost control while driving through the woods of Westchester. The car plunged off the dirt road and into a sand bank, spilling us all.

We held our breath for ages it seemed, until Jane waved from her cramped position in the front seat and announced that she was all right. She was pregnant at the time, and we just couldn't believe she was uninjured. Mitchell drove back to the city with greatest care, and Jane reported the next day that all was well.

The Giants' lead over the despised Pittsburgh Pirates increased. They sped down the homestretch, led by Christy Mathewson, on the way to his third season of 30 or more victories. He finished with 31, giving him a 3-year total of 94. On account of his slow start, Joe McGinnity won "only" 21, which put his 3-year total at 87. Matty and McGinnity! In 3 seasons they appeared in 288 games, pitched 2,236 innings, and fashioned 191 victories.

They accounted for 52 of the team's 105 victories in 1905. The remainder came from Red Ames, 22; Dummy Taylor, 16; and George Wiltse, 15. It was league domination with a vengeance.

The irrepressible Mike Donlin finished third behind Cy Seymour and Honus Wagner in the race for batting honors, with .356, the best of his life. Roger Bresnahan was the team's other .300 hitter. He batted two points above that mark. Arthur Devlin led the league, and even Honus Wagner, in stolen bases with 59. As expected, the Giants ran wild on the bases. Sandow Mertes stole 52; the veteran Bill Dahlen, 37; Donlin, 33; George Browne, 26; Strang, 23; McGann, 22; and Bresnahan, 11.

They moved into the first and perhaps the greatest of all World Series against the Philadelphia Athletics. Every game was a pitching masterpiece, and all five games were shutout victories. It was a personal triumph for Christy Mathewson who pitched three unforgettable victories, turned in twenty-seven scoreless innings, and walked only one batter. Joe McGinnity pitched the other shutout for New York, and also lost a 3–0 game to Chief Bender.

Each Giant received $1,142 and a diamond-studded gold button, emblematic of their World's Championship. John McGraw received a new three-year contract, with no extra clauses this time, calling for a salary of $24,000 per year!

19

NEW YORK FANS and sporting circles took John McGraw and his Giants to their hearts and heads in 1905. Expressions of gratitude and enthusiasm were almost beyond description or belief. The fans weren't quite as raucous or rowdy as the Oriole partisans of eleven years before, but they were just as sincere, and the joy lasted longer.

Popularity is not the word for it. The game and the team were an ideal outlet for an interest that had had no channel of expression. The new century had ended the life and the period of Queen Victoria, symbol of quiet demeanor. The sports-minded Prince of Wales, racer of horses and friend of John L. Sullivan, had become England's ruler. The yoke was off. Sports enthusiasm and participation grew fast.

But baseball was almost without competition in the widening struggle for interest and patronage as the only big spectator sport. Mounting attendance at the Polo Grounds and growing publicity aroused curiosity and envy in the entertainment world. The schedule offered more than seventy "performances" a season, equivalent to a ten-week run on Broadway. The second and fifth games of the 1905 World Series drew a total attendance of 50,000 at the Polo Grounds. That equaled the capacity of all the so-called Broadway theaters for a single night, and few of them sold out regularly.

Actors, entertainers, restaurateurs, sportsmen, gamblers, and men-about-town joined the dyed-in-the wool baseball fan. Jerry Cohan used to bring young George M. to the Polo Grounds. Weber and Fields, Ray Hitchcock, Willie Collier, Macklyn Arbuckle, Wilton Lackaye—the list is endless. They could rise at noon, eat a leisurely breakfast and amble to the Polo Grounds by the new subway, have a midafternoon snack there, and even find someone who wanted to wager. All this before the four o'clock starting time. They could have an exciting afternoon, and still reach Herald or Times Square in time for dinner and their theater curtain at 7:30 or 8:00.

Thus, John McGraw's Giants and the entertainment world overlapped. His stature increased. He was an important person, because he knew more about the game than anyone else. There could be discussion, but no arguing baseball with him. His very presence in a gathering obviated dispute on any phase of baseball, beyond an opinion of whether one player was better, or faster, or tougher, than another.

Since his position in baseball and New York was assured, John opened a billiard parlor on Herald Square in partnership with Tod Sloan and Jack Doyle, a sports-minded young man whose integrity had already made him a favorite holder of stakes and wagers on sporting events. Patronage was assured by John's phenomenal success in baseball and Sloan's fame in America, France, and England as the greatest and most colorful jockey since "Snapper" Garrison. Also, little Tod had captured the heart of beautiful Julia Sanderson, of Springfield, Massachusetts, a Broadway musical comedy star in her teens.

Another such captive was tiny Mabel Hite, a Baltimore girl, who had gained a degree of stage fame. The conqueror was Mike Donlin, the breezy but brilliant Giant center fielder. John wasn't happy about the union, especially when Mike announced their plan to become actors.

"They'll be actors, all right," John muttered. "Bad actors!"

Louis Mann, one of the earliest stage personalities to board the Giants' bandwagon, was a steady visitor at the Polo Grounds for the next quarter century. He talked baseball incessantly and recruited fans from the Broadway scene, especially from the Lambs Club, long the headquarters of the entertainment fraternity. It was inevitable that both John T. Brush and John McGraw would be taken in as members, and so they were. Brush lived there for many years.

A studious boy entered the baseball scene about that time. I recall him carrying schoolbooks, wearing short pants and black stockings, slicked hair, neatly polished shoes, and hustling on errands for John T. Brush, who was obliged to use a wheel chair almost constantly. The boy, Edward T. Brannick, was a product of a West Side section of New York where all boys grew up to be either good or bad. Eddie, of course, grew up to be good. He was born at 453 West 48th Street in a flat above McEntegart's saloon.

His uncle was working in the old Madison Square Garden, not far from the Giants' office, setting up a stage that was to hold a mechanical scoreboard. As a service to fans, Mr. Brush engaged the Garden and installed Coleman's scoreboard so they could follow the August road trip of his red-hot 1905 team. Eddie went down to help his uncle, because "it was practically working for the Giants."

Eddie toiled under the platform, pushing the mechanical figures back and forth to simulate the movements telegraphed back from the road games. His diligence and zeal each day impressed Mr. Brush, who asked if he would like to work in the Giants' office. What a question to a teen-ager in 1905!

"In nineteen seven," Eddie once recalled, "Mr. Brush told me Mr. McGraw needed a boy to take care of the baseballs, which had been disappearing much too fast, and to be with him on the bench at all times to do errands. I was that boy, and I was to be at the Polo Grounds at ten the following morning.

"Next day I rushed through my duties for Mr. Brush at the office, and got uptown about fifteen minutes late. I explained to Mr. McGraw, and he almost took my head off.

" 'I don't care what Mr. Brush wants you to do,' he barked. 'When I say ten o'clock, I mean *exactly* ten o'clock.'

"From that moment I knew who my boss was, and I also knew who was boss of the Giants—Mr. McGraw!"

During these early years in New York, especially 1904–1905–1906, John and I had no regular home. To be near the Polo Grounds, we took a room at the Washington Inn, at 155th Street and Amsterdam Avenue. Roger Bresnahan and his beloved Addie also had a room there in 1905. That same year a fresh-faced young man named Harold Chase came to town and lived at the Inn while playing first base for the Highlanders. He was a bright and attractive boy of twenty-two, alive with youthful love of the game. John often talked baseball with him.

The new subway made transit rapid to the downtown area, but after the baseball season, we took quarters at the Victoria or the Breslin and later the Imperial. The Mathewsons rented a furnished apartment of their own in 1906, for that was the year their baby made his appearance in the world. He was a fat and chubby boy with light hair and blue eyes. They named him John Christopher, and we felt very proud of a great pitcher's tribute to his manager.

When John left town with the Giants, I invariably packed a bag and returned to Baltimore for a visit with my folks. At first these trips were inspired by loneliness and a feeling of strangeness in New York. Not until several years later did I realize that they also had value to my family. My sister Jeannette had married Charlie Schryver, and I soon realized that my parents missed us. I could also see that my father's health was failing. Arthritis and rheumatism crippled him late in 1905. He took trips to spas and resorts without benefit. He grew helpless early in 1906 and then died. But I continued my "commutation" to Baltimore.

The Giants of 1906 started off with a rush of victories and enthusiastic patronage. Then the young Chicago Cubs picked up where Pittsburgh had left off as arch rivals. Frank Chance, a catcher when John first saw him in 1899, was first baseman and "the Peerless Leader." The city of Chicago took the Cubs to their hearts just as New York fans had embraced the Giants. Under a new owner, Charles W. Murphy, the Cubs were a fast and hustling team, as their 116 victories of 1906 and 107 in 1907 indicated. But John always pointed to a few key happenings on the Giants to support his belief that "the Cubs didn't win—the Giants lost."

First there was Christy Mathewson's siege of diphtheria in early 1906, and he had to be removed from his wife and baby. He pitched a hundred fewer innings than ordinarily. Following that, the Giants' best hitter, Mike Donlin, slid into third base at Cincinnati, jammed his heel, and was carried off the field with a broken leg. He played only thirty games that year. The next year, 1907, he held out all season and made good his promise to go on the stage.

The veteran Dan McGann suffered a broken arm, and it was a long time healing. Roger Bresnahan was hit on the head by a pitched ball and had to be kept from the line-up for extended periods. Bill Dahlen slowed down to a walk at shortstop, and John needed speed. After finishing fourth in 1907, he made his first big trade as a Giant manager. He sent Dahlen, McGann, Bowerman, Browne, and a young pitcher, Cecil Ferguson, to Boston for the veteran manager–first baseman, Fred Tenney, and a young short-stop, Al Bridwell, hitting .225. The trade of five Giants for two from the league's weakest club was deplored by fans and writers.

But behind the trade were many weeks of study, floor-pacing, and speculation. John was completely rebuilding the Giants. He had several young and green players produced by his one-man scouting staff, "Sinister" Dick Kinsella, of Springfield, Illinois. One was a happy-go-lucky kid from the mines at Caseyville, Illinois, named Lawrence Doyle. He was not quite twenty-one when John first saw him in July of 1907, and in his very first game he made four or five misplays. John thought back to his own errors and misery at Baltimore in August, 1891, noted the boy's forced smile, and kept Doyle in the line-up.

Later that year an eighteen-year-old boy from Watertown, Wisconsin, Fred Merkle, came to the Polo Grounds, again on recommendation of Kinsella. After trying him a few times at second base, John turned him over to McGann to coach at first for the rest of the year. Another infielding youngster scouted and drafted from a Pennsylvania league that season was twenty-two-year-old Charlie Herzog, a Baltimore boy. And out of sheer senti-ment, he drafted a twenty-year-old pitcher named Otis Crandall simply because he pitched for Grand Rapids, the club that gave John his first real baseball contract in 1891. These were the youth-ful question marks in a daring plan to rebuild, executed quietly, because real baseball fans cannot sympathize with the transfer or release of a favorite player. That is good and admirable, but it never wins pennants.

"The first indication that a player is slipping comes from his legs," John always said, and on the best of authority, because it happened to him. "When I notice that an infielder or an out-fielder has lost that quick spring of youth in going for a ball, I immediately begin looking for his successor. It would be stupid to wait until he has lost a lot of games for me.

"I let a lot of good players go, yes. But I have never yet discovered any method of getting a crack player without giving up a good one and sometimes a great one in exchange. I may have a crack player who is not absolutely necessary to the machinery of my club. I will trade him in a minute, if I see a chance to get the one man who completes the cogs for my machine. That is why I have brought back former Giant players, not merely once, but sometimes twice."

John saw Bridwell as a sure-handed shortstop whose hitting would improve. He not only admired Fred Tenney as a player; he respected his skill as a manager. Fred was thirty-six years old, but John had known his good character and habits from the early 1890's. He was always in the best of physical condition. He devised the 3–6–3 double play (1b. to ss. to 1b.) in 1897. He was capable of playing only to win in any uniform. Tenney came to the Polo Grounds as a pivotal veteran who held together and in check a wild assortment of mavericks. Their carefree spirit was best expressed later by the deathless chant of Laughing Larry Doyle, the Caseyville mine boy:

"It's great to be young and a Giant!"

John McGraw had a special incentive to win after 1907, though the ordinary urges were more than sufficient. Hughie Jennings had left Baltimore late in 1906 to succeed Billy Armour as manager of the Detroit Tigers. He had two good outfielders, Cobb and Crawford, and two good pitchers, Donovan and Mullin, and he managed an otherwise fair team to Detroit's first American League pennant. He often spoke of joy to be had in meeting and beating his old friend in a World Series!

Christy Mathewson was a storybook pitcher in 1908. "Old Gumboots," a nickname traceable to his knock-kneed walk, won every heart in town. He worked and won as never before, appearing in fifty-six ball games, more than one third of the Giant's total. He proved to be one of the greatest "team" players.

The Giants caught fire again, ignited by the five youngsters, Doyle, Herzog, Bridwell, Merkle, and "Otie" Crandall, none of whom was past twenty-two years of age. Sprinkled among them were the veterans—Fred Tenney at first, Mike Donlin, who had returned for a great year, in the outfield; Cy Seymour, whom John had bought from Cincinnati late in 1906; Arthur Devlin at third base; and Roger Bresnahan, who caught 139 games, and with shin guards for the first time.

The team also was ablaze at the plate, and finished with a batting average nineteen percentage points better than the Chicago Cubs. Chance's team got off to a great start, as was expected, but the Giants drew up to them in late August and took the lead in September with the Pirates making it a close three-way fight.

The first and most important climax of that unforgettable season came in the tenth inning of a scoreless tie between Pittsburgh and Chicago on September 4. Manager Clarke was on third base and Warren Gill on first in the home half of the tenth. Hans Wagner singled off Three-finger Brown. As Clarke scored, Gill turned from his journey to second base and raced for the clubhouse. Artie Hofman, Chicago center fielder, threw the ball to Johnny Evers, who raced over and touched second base. He demanded that Umpire Hank O'Day declare Gill out to end the inning and nullify Clarke's run.

His claim was based on Rule 59, which read:

> One run shall be scored every time a base runner, after having legally touched the first three bases, shall legally touch the home base before three men are put out; provided, however, if he reaches home on or during a play in which the third man be forced out or be put out before reaching first base, a run shall not count. A force-out can be made only when a base runner legally loses the right to the base he occupies, and is thereby obliged to advance as the result of a fair hit ball not caught on the fly.

Wagner's base hit had forced Gill off first. He did not run to second. Evers got the ball while still in play and made a simple force-out.

Umpire O'Day claimed he did not see the play. Evers, a brilliant and fighting infielder, exploded, shouted his rage and demanded that Gill be called out. O'Day refused. The Cubs returned to their hotel, and the team owner, Charles Webb Murphy, filed an official protest with the National League President, Harry Pulliam. He demanded that Evers' claim be recognized, the rule enforced, and the game replayed.

Pulliam refused the protest. He dismissed the claim and ruled that the game was a Pittsburgh victory by 1–0.

The entire nation was at fever-pitch over this three-way baseball race, for the defeat sent the Cubs into third place. Nineteen days later they were playing at the Polo Grounds before a large and excited crowd after taking the first two of a four-game series. Now it was the ninth inning with the score 1–1 and two out. Moose McCormick was on third. Nineteen-year-old Fred Merkle was on first. The batter, Al Bridwell, single cleanly into center field, almost hitting base umpire, Bob Emslie, who fell to the ground getting out of the way. McCormick scored the winning run. As he crossed the plate, Merkle, halfway to second, turned and raced toward the clubhouse.

Again Artie Hofman recovered the ball and threw it to the infield. John McGraw has described the play many times:

"Evers did not get the ball. It rolled through the happy, milling spectators and past third base. A substitute Chicago pitcher, Floyd Kroh, seeing Hofman making wild motions and pointing, rushed from the dugout and got the ball. Joe McGinnity ran out too, snatched the ball from Kroh's hands and threw it into the right-field stands. That's why I have always said Evers never made the put-out.

"And why was an unannounced Chicago player on the field?

"His mere touching of the ball rendered it dead. Besides, Jack Hayden, one of the Chicago outfielders, had gone to the clubhouse, thinking the game was over. The Cubs did not have nine players on the field, and no play of any kind was possible.

"But Evers appealed to Emslie, now upright and brushing the dirt from his uniform, and he ignored the plea. Evers then switched his appeal to O'Day who was walking from the plate, mask in hand, and removing spare balls from his pockets. Evers grabbed one of the balls, ran to second base, stepped on the bag, and demanded that Merkle be called out on a force play and McCormick's run nullified.

"No decision or gesture of decision was made, and we expected none. Frankly, nobody paid much attention to the squabble, because the new rule carried no weight. We even joked in the clubhouse about Evers' effort to put one over, as he had tried in vain to do in Pittsburgh. And that ended it."

I hasten to add that John had only admiration for Evers and

his heads-up baseball. He could hardly feel otherwise, since he had played that way throughout his own career.

The nation's telegraph wires burned throughout the evening. Crowds stormed offices of newspapers setting headlines to feature the strange finish of this game, which had a vital influence on the close pennant race. With excitement still mounting next morning, a reporter called upon O'Day at his hotel to ask if the situation had been cleared up. O'Day said that the runner, Merkle, was out because he had to reach second base to avoid a put-out.

"But that left the score tied," the reporter reminded. "Why didn't you order play resumed?"

O'Day paused, and then said, "I called the game on account of darkness."

Actually, O'Day had been summoned after the game to the New York Athletic Club, then at 59th Street and Sixth Avenue, where the National League President, Pulliam, lived. The result of the game remained in question, but few believed the Cubs had won. How could Merkle be out on September 23, if Gill wasn't out on September 4?

Pulliam vacillated. He entertained Chicago's demand for a forfeit of the game. While withholding official decision as to whether the game was won, lost, or tied by the Giants, he assured the New York club that a play-off wasn't necessary. As a direct result, only one game was played with the Cubs the next day, September 24, and Christy Mathewson won it easily. Had Pulliam acted with the power at his command, the disputed game could have been settled by a double-header.

The Cubs left town, and the matter was allowed to simmer until the Giants, with Leon Ames struggling to regain his power after a siege of malaria, began to lose their lead. When it appeared there might be a two- or even a three-team tie, Chicago demanded that Pulliam enforce the rule calling for contending teams to play the full twenty-two games with each other. Pulliam then held an executive meeting in Cincinnati. Heading a three-man board, he ruled, after a day and two nights of hearing "evidence," that the New York–Chicago game of September 23 would have to be replayed. Pittsburgh's 1–0 victory over Chicago on September 4 was allowed to stand.

The 1908 race ended with the Giants and Cubs tied for first

place. Pittsburgh was third, a game behind. The Cubs appeared at the Polo Grounds on October 8 for the play-off before the largest crowd, 26,000, ever jammed into the park. Naturally, the number claiming to have seen the game has increased over the years. Police lines were broken, and even the sports writers were deprived of their assigned seats by belligerent early arrivals. This resulted in forming the Baseball Writers Association the next year.

Even the players were at explosion pitch. As the Cubs finished batting practice, Joe McGinnity went out to start New York's fielding workout, and Chance refused to leave the plate. McGinnity pushed him, and Chance punched Joe in the jaw. Players converged quickly to fight it out with fists, and a riot was narrowly averted. Two men were pushed from the crowded elevated structure beyond center field into the street and killed. Two spectators slid off the grandstand roof during the game and miraculously fell to the field unhurt. Jane Mathewson, carrying two-year-old Christy, narrowly escaped injury in the crush through the help of the police on duty.

Mathewson started for the Giants and struck out two Cubs, and Herzog threw out the third. Jack Pfeister took the mound for Chicago, hit Fred Tenney and walked Herzog. He caught Herzog off first, and got Bresnahan out. Donlin limped to the plate and doubled to right, scoring Tenney and sending the crowd into ecstasy. When Seymour walked, Chance replaced Pfeister with Brown. The Cubs scored in only one inning, the third, but made four runs. Brown was invincible, except in the seventh, when the Giants filled the bases. They could score only one run on a fly ball. The Cubs fielded under the worst conditions. Cushions and pop bottles flew from all sides. But they won the game and "John's pennant." The 4–2 defeat dropped the Giants into a tie for second place with Pittsburgh.

The matchless Christy had won 37 games during the year. He had walked only 42 batters in 416 innings. It was by far his greatest season, perhaps the greatest year that any pitcher ever failed to enjoy. That such a great and conscientious moundsman had to lose with the big prize so very close caused John McGraw many sleepless nights. This great competitor had won exactly 200 victories for the Giants in eight years!

But it wasn't only Christy. John had gambled heavily on his

young and green players. Their morale, once the highest, was shaken. Sports writers everywhere berated the teen-age Merkle as the goat of the September 23 game. He was accused by writers and fans alike of making the biggest boner in baseball history. And what moved John almost to uncontrollable fury was the official decision, belatedly announced by the Pulliam office:

"We can, therefore, come to no other conclusion," it said in part, "than that the New York club lost a well-earned victory as the result of a stupid play of one of its members."

Stupid indeed! Was Warren Gill stupid for not completing the ninety-foot journey to second base on September 4? Was Umpire O'Day stupid for "not seeing" the very same play, which, if called in accordance with Rule 59, would have penalized the Pittsburgh Pirates and Barney Dreyfuss?

Because of unfeeling fans, who for years shouted "Bonehead!" and "Don't forget to touch second!" from many grandstands and train platforms, John McGraw never forgot this rank insult and injustice to one of his younger players. He couldn't forget the irreparable damage it inflicted upon Merkle. He saw the player weep in the clubhouse and heard his pleas of, "Get rid of me, Mac. I don't deserve to play on the Giants!" John began the long job of rebuilding the boy's shattered confidence by raising his salary $500.

Another galling aspect of the 1908 defeat was losing the chance in a lifetime to meet and beat his old Oriole roommate, Hughie Jennings, in the World Series, for Hughie had won his second straight pennant with the Detroit Tigers.

With Merkle the whipping boy for an administrative catastrophe, attention was conveniently distracted from a complete rupture of feelings behind the official scenes. The Giants and Pirates had been at swords' points since December, 1903, when Barney Dreyfuss succeeded in having his protégé elected president to replace the three-man Board of Control. Pulliam's premature fine and suspension of John in 1905 and public embarrassment in civil court had widened the breach. Mr. Brush had opposed the Pulliam candidacy for three years, and Garry Herrmann had joined him. Brush refused to vote at all in the annual league meeting of December, 1908. The president was re-elected by a 7–0 ballot, but Brush's feelings were no secret.

Pulliam had been enmeshed by a most unfortunate emotional

situation, hardly of his own making. Whether he ever should have been placed in the thankless job is hard to say. He was of nervous temperament and a thorough gentleman. Seemingly he lacked the objectivity necessary to rule with an iron thumb, as Ban Johnson had long ruled in the American League. His setback in a Boston court could and should have been avoided in 1905 by studying his rules of fine and suspension before openly blackening the reputation of any manager or player with a punishment that could not be supported by proof.

The pressure mounted daily through the winter. At the February, 1909, meeting in New York, the club owners gave Pulliam a leave of absence "for reasons of illness." He remained away from the baseball scene through the spring and part of the summer. What he did or thought in those dark days has never been recorded. It is not pleasant to contemplate even today.

On the evening of July 28, the telephone switchboard operator at the New York Athletic Club noticed a signal flash from Pulliam's room. Unable to get an answer, she sent an employee, Thomas Brady, to see what was wanted. Brady found Pulliam sprawled on a divan, clad only in his underwear, and a ghastly wound in his head. A five-chamber revolver was on the floor containing one live cartridge and one exploded shell. A bullet had plowed through his head from the right temple, shooting out both eyes, but he was still breathing.

Dr. J. J. Higgins, the club physician, said he had been struggling on the floor or the couch for at least two hours. He spoke to Pulliam, asking why he had shot himself. He asked it again and again. Pulliam was unconscious, but made two replies, "Why, what shot?" and "What shot?" There were no notes. Friends or relatives could not account for the tragedy.

Harry Pulliam, only forty years old, lived through the night and died at 8:10 the next morning. He was taken to his native Louisville and laid to rest in Cave Hill Cemetery on August 3. Most of official baseball attended the funeral rites.

John McGraw did not go. He was traveling with his Giants from Boston to Chicago. Mr. Brush did not feel physically able to make the trip.

20

THE LEGEND OF John McGraw as "anti-umpire" has been built over the years by convenient omission of how anti-McGraw the umpires were on memorable occasions. John was anti-anybody whose carelessness, ignorance, or ineptitude influenced victory or defeat in a ball game by setting himself up as more important than base hits, runs, and errors. This factor, and no other, was the actual basis for all of John's recorded outbursts of temper and violence on the ball field.

When he and his team took the field, everyone on the other side, including the bat boy, was his mortal enemy for the next two hours or so. Had I, his wife, sat on the opposing bench, I would have been counted with those whose duty it was to defeat him. And woe be unto any umpire who began calling close ones against him. He wanted at least half of them, and hoped for a fraction more, in case his luck was bad the next time.

To my knowledge, John never questioned an umpire's integrity. He regarded incompetence or ignorance as far worse. He could understand and deal with dishonesty. Incompetence was like a collar button under the dresser; he just couldn't cope with it.

Perhaps his worst umpire trouble came at Cincinnati in June, 1917, and when he was trying to beat the very man and player he held in highest esteem, Christy Mathewson. Christy had wanted to be a manager, and John had released him to the Reds in mid-July, 1916. A year later John was busy with the task of making Christy wish he had never taken the job, and also with trying to hold first place against the Phillies.

Trouble came in the ninth when Hal Chase, Cincinnati first baseman, shouldered Art Fletcher as he ran by and the contact prevented a double play. This was not a rolling block from a slide into second, such as we see today; it was bold interference. Having the ball, Fletcher was entitled to the ground he occupied. Rule 56 said so, and interference was a violation.

Fletcher appealed to Ernie Quigley, the base umpire, who ignored the protest, as did the plate umpire, William "Lord" Byron. The winning run scored an instant later, and John rushed out to air his opinion of such officiating. According to later testimony, Byron foolishly accused John of "being run out of Baltimore!" That brought the punches. Matty Schwab, Cincinnati grounds keeper, rushed out, and Bill Rariden, Giant catcher, intercepted him with a pummeling. Even Christy Mathewson himself wouldn't have been spared. Police and other players finally restored order. John was suspended indefinitely by League President John K. Tener, a former governor of Pennsylvania, and also a former big-league pitcher.

"I'd give a hundred dollars," John exclaimed, still enraged, "to tell that Tener to his face what I think of him and his National Commission!"

Reporters, present as he stormed, asked if he could be quoted. He told them to make it as strong as they wanted and they did. But every word made the situation worse. John was in trouble for the physical contact with Byron, and for the aspersion on the league president and the National Commission. He denied the printed account, and the reporters, principally George Herbert Daley and Sid Mercer, demanded a hearing in defense of their written words. John withdrew the denial after realizing that he hadn't read the story. President Tener fined him $1,000 for the assault on Byron.

Mercer was satisfied, but they didn't speak for a year or two. In addition to being a good reporter and a companionable young man, Mercer was a skilled competitor at three-cushion billiards, John's favorite game. Mercer was one of his toughest opponents on the road and at the Lambs Club in New York. John finally extended the hand to "make up."

Umpire rows have always made excellent newspaper copy, especially when the reporter's team was losing. Since the Giants handed out far more defeats in National League cities than they had to absorb, the lurid reports of fights, tongue-lashings, Napoleonic belligerence, rumors, Oriole legends, half-truths, and, on occasions, bald libel, were often substituted for accounts of local defeats.

John McGraw knew that a controversial manager and team would create more discussion and paid admissions than a colorless group of baseball mechanics. He understood the entertainment aspects of baseball better than any other player, manager, or club owner. He proved it by commanding maximum newspaper space, paid admissions, personal popularity and unpopularity.

Far more important is that he proved it with victories and pennants through aggressive, scientific baseball. Never at any time could the entertainment factor or field controversy encroach upon the prime importance of those base hits, errors, runs, and victories.

John McGraw's fault, if it can be called a fault, was thinking and living baseball twenty-four hours a day. He doubted that any umpire kept up religiously with the annual rule changes, as he had from his earliest boyhood.

How could they with a living to earn in some other field six months of the year? As umpires, they were poorly paid in view of the time and integrity demanded, and the constant abuse they had to endure. John's salary as Giant manager in 1910, for instance, was ten times that of the highest-paid umpire, Hank O'Day, on the National League staff. Bill Klem, discovered and sent to the league by Jim "Orator" O'Rourke in 1905, was paid only $2,500 a season five years later. Nine regular umpires in 1910 received a total of $15,000 in salary. Each drew less than $1,000 expenses for the six months. They paid out of pocket for all but railroad fare.

They also had to pay fines. President Tom Lynch, a former umpire himself ("Dirty" Doyle closed his eye with a punch), took over Harry Pulliam's vacated job for 1910 and quickly brought umpires to taw. Jim Johnstone got nicked twice for sizable sums that year. "Uncle Charlie" Moran, just starting in, paid one, as did Steve Kane. And even Bill Klem, working his sixth season for the league, had to pay President Lynch a fine. The nature of the violation is of no interest here. Even Klem's fine of $100, levied by League President John Heydler, another former umpire, in 1920, is less important than that a ranking umpire was officially reprimanded and fined, revealing him as definitely fallible and more or less human. When they put ignorance or laziness above the game itself, they were simply inhuman to John McGraw, a contemptible lot who would destroy the very game to which he had devoted his entire life.

A celebrated quotation is one that John McGraw supposedly said to Bill Klem: "I'll have your job for this," and Klem's dramatic reply, "If my job depends on that, sir, you can have it!"

Whether true or not—and it may be—it always makes good and colorful reading. To match this legend, I offer umpiring history that occurred at the Polo Grounds on April 25, 1913, when the Giants were starting after their third straight pennant. Philadelphia was a strong contender. The score was 0–0 in the Giants' half of the tenth with none out and the bases full. Moose McCormick, the batter, singled cleanly over shortstop and Merkle scored the "winning run."

The plate umpire, Klem, refused to allow the score, because *his back was turned to the pitcher when the hit was made!*

There is neither excuse nor reason for an umpire to be out of position when a play is made. His eye must be on the ball always when it is in play. But there was no McGravian outburst, riot, or assault, even when Klem ordered the fans off the field and the runners back to the bases. McCormick hit the next pitch into a double play. Another Giant ended the inning. After a scoreless eleventh, Klem called the game on account of darkness.

By the time John completed his long-range plan to rebuild the Giants in 1906–1907–1908, Roger Bresnahan was managing the St. Louis Cardinals. For his contract John received "Red" Murray, an outfielder, and Arthur "Bugs" Raymond, a right-handed spitball pitcher who used 86-proof saliva. Raymond was thoroughly unreliable off the mound, and yet John saw in his baseball interest the one channel that might inspire him to normal behavior.

Called Bugs by everybody, he lived up to the nickname without effort, and usually without realizing it. His eccentricities and misdemeanors made good newspaper copy and clubhouse tales, so many, in fact, that I don't see how he could have performed them in three years with the Giants. Only one of the seasons, 1909, was a good year for him. It was his first, and baseball people always offer this example of understanding and success with Raymond, who won eighteen games, as proof that John "could get a good season out of anybody!"

Sadness came with the departure of the Iron Man, Joe McGinnity, released to take over the job as manager of Newark for 1909. Unbelievable as it sounds, during the next two years Joe pitched in 116 games, worked well over 800 innings, and won 59 victories. He was still pitching minor-league baseball in 1925 at the age of 54! Truly, an Iron Man!

John McGraw surrounded himself with youthful hope of the speediest kind. Besides the colts previously mentioned, he found twenty-year-old Fred Snodgrass, a California outfielder; Joshua Devore, an Ohio outfielder, also only twenty; and John Tortes Meyers, a catcher, and an Indian, from Riverside, California. Nicknamed "Chief," he was genuinely fond of good music, had a fine baritone voice, a keen sense of humor, and a wife named Pearl. He called her "Dearie" and claimed she was his boss. He had attended Carlisle Indian School and Dartmouth College.

While there were other trials and errors among the young personnel, the last of the new crop to arrive before 1910 was Arthur Fletcher, another Kinsella discovery from Collinsville, Illinois. No, there was one other, a shy and rather handsome third baseman from Los Angeles, and also twenty. John brought the blushing youth into the Polo Grounds clubhouse in 1909 for an introduction to the team before a ball game.

"This is our new infielder," he announced. "Boys, meet Arthur Shafer."

Big Cy Seymour, an old Oriole in word and deed, responded first with, "We're all damned glad to meet you, Tillie!"

Then came the chorus!

"Yes, sir, Tillie, glad to see you!"

"Make yourself t'home, Tillie!"

"Good luck, Tillie. . . . Save your money, Tillie. . . . Get the last bounce, Tillie . . . Tillie . . . Tillie . . . Tillie. . . ."

There were disappointments, chiefly from the parade of young pitchers. Names like Dickson, Buck, Parsons, Klawitter, Rudolph, Drucke, Faust, Marquard were constant headaches through 1909 and 1910 as John waited in vain for these pitchers to "arrive." Mr. Brush had paid his old friend, Bill Watkins, of Indianapolis, a large sum for left-handed Marquard's contract. He was known as the "Eleven Thousand Dollar Lemon."

But a Chief Meyers replaced a Bresnahan, an Art Fletcher succeeded a Bill Dahlen, a Larry Doyle went in for a Billy Gilbert, a Merkle for a Tenney, a Herzog spelled Devlin at third, though Charlie could and did play everywhere except first. These twenty-year-olds were by no means ready for the big leagues, though putting on the Giants' uniform was big help. One St. Louis sports writer explained it this way in 1909:

Johnny McGraw owes not a little of his success to detailed instruction for his players. McGraw has a habit of getting hold of good, raw material—that is, material that has natural speed, good hands and eyes and gameness. McGraw puts this kind of material through a course of sprouts that is calculated to make players out of them or prove they have no ability. He makes them practice various styles of batting for hours at a time, and also how to get away fast from the plate. In teaching men how to slide he has a load of sand dumped around the base, so that the men will not be injured.

An interviewer asked John a year later if inside baseball, which they had discussed at length, injured a batter's average and spoiled his chances of leading the league in hitting.

"Yes, it most certainly does," John replied. "We have batters on our team who are hitting around two-fifty. They might be in the three-hundred class were it not for the prescribed effort required of them almost every time they go to bat. I permit no deviation from instructions.

"With first base occupied, it is almost mandatory that my batter hit to right field, so that the base runner will have a chance to reach third base, instead of only second with the hit into left. Then, when the defensive club shifts to play for that maneuver, we may suddenly switch tactics by a sign from the bench. This orders the batter to place the ball into left field. He has been trained to do this.

"I'd like to use fewer signs, or do away with signals entirely, but I can't with so many young pitchers and fielders. The veterans can be directed by a wave of a hand. They know about what to expect or do. It's a slower process with these boys. And it's sure. It may hamper them a little at first, but soon it becomes part of their natural skill, and they will be outstanding because of the firm foundation in tactics and strategy."

John started ordering certain pitches by signs from the bench shortly after reaching New York. By 1905 he was calling every pitch for all except Mathewson to take full advantage of his knowledge and memory of rivals' hitting strength and weakness. Had players remembered, as Christy usually did, John wouldn't have pre-empted pitcher or catcher.

When the system of signaling from the bench worked in isolated spots about the infield and to batters in the early 1900's, John extended it to include almost all of the strategy. The young players believed firmly in his knowledge and eagerly obeyed. That they played better and more interesting baseball, even when losing, gave them a feeling of competitive superiority and security. Several of the young Giants sometimes forgot or disobeyed.

Most renowned is Sammy Strang, a pinch hitter and happy-go-lucky fellow who was fined $25 in 1905 for hitting away when he was ordered to bunt. The story became a legend, because Strang's hit was a home run. More important to John McGraw than the run or the game was that Sammy had jeopardized a carefully prepared system. Instead of sulking, Strang helped John develop the delayed steal early in the century. This was a simple strategy, based on a move to steal, stopping to create complacency on the part of the pitcher, and then, when the pitcher turned his attention and effort to the plate, streaking for second.

To give his signals, John sat on the dugout bench, usually at one end, and leaned on a fungo bat, holding it at the end to brace himself as naturally as possible. The position of his hands at the top, or handle end, carried the sign. Both hands gripping, left above right, right above left, folded at the top, one on top, one gripping —it went like that. The meaning could be reversed every other inning, every third inning, etc.

The first-base coach was the checker or verifier, and no player was certain before a game that he wouldn't be sent to the first-base coaching box for relay or checking. In fact, if John suspected any Giant player of carelessness or rusty memory, he simply sent him out as coach to confirm or erase the suspicion with a few well-chosen signs.

John's calling of signals was the basis for assorted terms, many uncomplimentary, used to describe his somewhat autocratic firmness on the field. He was called Napoleonic, or Bismarckian, or a master mind, a Svengali, a mailed fist, a field czar, a strutting Caesar, and so on. Today he would be labeled a dictator, a commissar, a premier, or whatever happened to be the most recognizable sobriquet to convey the idea of unswerving and dominating power over procedure.

A wealth of clubhouse stories illustrate how far he would go to preserve his so-called domination. They tell of him chasing the unfortunate Phil Douglas around the locker room, up the stairs, and right into the street, shouting his rage, brandishing a small souvenir bat that he kept on his desk. Phil had only tried to seek relief from one of John's suspensions, and the mere sight of the pitcher's face supposedly produced violent wrath. Personally, I think he put on a show as the only way of impressing Douglas.

Once players stripped down after a defeat, and two of them decided to ride out the storm by hiding in the shower. No one was permitted to leave during these critical harangues, which were made longer when he had to reach into the past for some half-forgotten shortcoming to make sure that every ear on the club was reddened by the tongue-lashing. While this particularly long siege continued, the two chilled and naked players suffered a far worse punishment in the shower. Turning on the hot water was out of the question, and so they simply shivered until John stormed from the clubhouse.

Was it wrong? I don't know. With no instruction book to guide him, he had to devise his own system. All originators are usually despised and ridiculed at first and sometimes destroyed eventually. Had he not fought back tooth and nail, John McGraw couldn't have survived even his first full year on the Orioles.

All I know is that today virtually all baseball teams are run by signs on defense and offense. I watch the game on television, and I hear the announcer say:

"Now Joe has stepped out to rub dirt on his hands. He is looking down to Manager Whosis at third base to see whether he should hit this next pitch or take it. Now he has his sign. He steps back in. The catcher is looking over to the dugout to see what Manager Whatsis wants thrown. Now the runner on first has his sign. He's ready...."

But none of the sixteen big-league managers is a Napoleon... a Svengali...a master mind. In fact, I haven't even heard one called a dictator or a commissar!

21

THE REBIRTH of the New York Giants came at Marlin, Texas, about twenty miles southeast of Waco. The year was 1910, and it marked one of the earliest uses of a big-league training camp to popularize a resort. More properly the camp was at Marlin Springs, a spa two or three miles east of the town. It seemed a greater distance to the players who had to walk to and from camp as part of their training.

John McGraw walked it too and also kept in shape by playing in the exhibition games. Physical conditioning wasn't easy, because he enjoyed the relaxation of beer and conviviality after reaching New York. Players caught riding back to town simply had to run around the big training grounds from three to five times. Tom Murphy, the Baltimore and New York grounds keeper, used to go down ahead of the team to fix and groom the big field.

One of John's oldest teammates appeared at the Marlin camp in the person of Henry Fabian, the Cedar Rapids outfielder who got stuck in the mud near third base during the exhibition game with Cap Anson's team in 1891. Years had passed since their last meeting, and Fabian was close to tears of joy. Never an outstanding player, he had made great personal and financial sacrifice before admitting it, and things had not gone well for him in Texas. John hired him to help with grooming the grounds. When Murphy grew old and fell ill, Henry took over the job of Giants' head grounds keeper in New York.

No keeper of the sward in the shadow of Coogan's Bluff was more conscientious in his work or more jealous of its appearance. John never forgot Henry's first sight of the fans leaping from the grandstand and racing across his beloved grass.

"Get back! Get off—get back!" he screamed, and gesticulated wildly. "John . . . Mac . . . John—look at 'em! They'll ruin my grass! Get off *my* grass—get back, all of you!"

It was a job to restrain Henry, who was about to call the rest of his crew for a finish fight with the public.

"Take it easy, Henry," John cautioned. "The fans have walked over this grass for years, and they'll be walking over it long after you and I are gone. You might as well start getting used to it."

But Henry never got used to Burleigh Grimes, his personal enemy for many years. In retaliation for Henry's annoying jeers during a game, Burleigh would select the greenest spot around the pitcher's mound and there dig a fresh divot with his spikes.

"He does it to plague me!" Henry insisted. "A spitball pitcher doesn't need dirt. He uses spit."

"Between spitballs, Henry," the pitcher said, "I use dirt, and it must be nice and fresh."

John also took on Arlie Latham in 1909 as combination coach and court jester. Though forty, Arlie played a few games. He had been a third-base star on the great Comiskey St. Louis teams beginning in 1883, and with one of the cheeriest personalities the game ever knew. At the age of nearly ninety, Arlie was still drawing chuckles as custodian of the Yankee Stadium press box.

Wilbert Robinson first appeared in a Giant uniform at Marlin in 1910, and the two old Orioles were back together helping each other after a lapse of eight years. Business at the Diamond Café dwindled fast after the disappearance of big-league baseball from Baltimore in 1902. Robbie had done some coaching and catching as a minor-league Oriole under Jennings and then Jack Dunn, and had worked in a meat market between seasons.

John felt that Robinson, who had a way with pitchers, could help solve the Giants' pitching problems, especially Rube Marquard. Besides, it was good to have old friends around. Later that year he hired Willie Keeler, who was over the hill, as a pinch hitter.

A young and inquisitive sports writer for the New York *Morning Telegraph*, Heywood Broun, was particularly interested in the 1910 reunion of McGraw and Robinson. Barely twenty-two and fresh out of Harvard University, his persistent questioning of the legendary Baltimore days brought to light a long-hidden record: Robinson's seven hits in seven times at bat on June 10, 1892. People had long thought it just another "Oriole fish story," but Broun believed it, wired the news north, and had it verified. Only then did it go into the records.

John doubled his scouting staff at the time by hiring a second hunter of players while Dick Kinsella was still beating the bush in the Midwest. "Sadie" McMahon, the Oriole immortal, had been a good judge of spirits, which hastened his decline as a great pitcher. Perhaps he might be a good judge of spirited ballplayers. John took a chance, and Sadie had a badly needed job.

"I may not send you much, Mac," he promised, "but whatever I recommend will be good."

Sadie almost didn't send anything. I don't know how long he searched—all of a year, I guess. Finally he sent one outfielder, a small, fast fellow who hadn't hit much at Utica, New York. Despite the catcalls and demands of the Polo Grounds fans to "get rid of him," John kept the boy on, and finally Sadie's only discovery, George Burns, made good. He played at the Polo Grounds for twelve seasons.

It was at Marlin, also in 1910, that John first split his team into A and B squads and played simultaneous exhibition games, an innovation at the time. Regular rosters were limited to eighteen and rookies, to be cut loose later, made the two teams possible.

John used Mathewson, Crandall, Doyle, Devore, Murray, Seymour, Devlin, Merkle, and Snodgrass as the backbone of his group. He sent Wilbert Robinson out in charge of Herzog (traded to Boston that year), Shafer, Fletcher, Tenney, Bridwell, and Art Wilson, a promising young catcher. Except for Wiltse, the pitchers under Robbie's care were strictly rookies. The two teams spread out, playing exhibition games as often as they could be scheduled, and many of them were for charity. Several were held for the benefit of the Public Schools Athletic League in Dallas at the end of March, 1910.

John also intensified his efforts to get his players out of the cheap and claptrap hotels and into the best of living conditions on the road. Heretofore, baseball patronage was scorned by the best of inns and accepted only occasionally. John felt that if his Giants could promote a mineral springs resort and be housed in a fine hotel like the Arlington at Marlin, they were good enough for any place in the big-league cities.

The Giants had finished third behind two powerhouse teams, Pittsburgh and Chicago, in 1909. When he caught and passed the Pirates in 1910 to finish second, John knew that his carefully laid plans would succeed. Mathewson, of course, was the key to his pitching staff, for this tireless worker kept on winning twenty-five or more games year after year. Two veterans were behind him, Ames and Wiltse. Crandall was the best of the youngsters.

As the Highlanders finished second, Mr. Brush and Frank Farrell agreed to play a postseason series under the same conditions that would govern the World Series between the Cubs and Athletics. The Giant-Highlander clash went seven games, but the issue never seemed in doubt. Mathewson dominated all four victories. He won three complete games, and saved Louis Drucke's victory by pitching the last three innings. He walked only one batter in the thirty innings.

Led by Josh Devore, who stole six, the Giants totaled nineteen stolen bases for the series. Paid admissions totaled more than 100,000 and the receipts went over $80,000. Each Giant received $1,110.62, and Art Fletcher used his money for marriage, a honeymoon, and a start in housekeeping with his childhood sweetheart, Blanche Dieu. Fletcher became a great player, manager, and coach, a family man, and a director of his home-town bank.

"The nineteen-eleven team stole the pennant," John once said. "Mighty few ball clubs were faster than that combination. The players got the notion that they could steal on anybody, and they nearly broke Roger Bresnahan's heart. The Duke wasn't doing too well anyway as St. Louis manager—no money or scouting— and the Giants made it worse. We handed the same treatment to Bill Dahlen, who had left us to manage Brooklyn in 1910. On one trip West we arrived in Chicago with a club in rags and tatters— had to telegraph for new uniforms—nearly every player had slid out the seat of his pants.

"We had patched and patched until the principal feature of our pants was safety pins. Josh Devore's clothes barely hung on him. Doyle, Merkle, Murray, and Herzog, traded back from Boston, were in no better shape. The telegram for new uniforms got wide publicity, but it was no fake. On the day we sent the wire at Chicago, Josh Devore slid into second and couldn't get up. His pants had actually come apart. Players had to surround him and walk him off the field. There was nothing left to pin!"

During the month of May, 1911, the team was so hot it set fire to the Polo Grounds. At least, that's what the sports writers claimed when a fire broke out behind third base during the night and burned much of the left-field pavilion. Luckily the team had just finished a home visit. Returning from the west, they accepted the hospitality of the Highlanders and played one home stand in the bandbox park on the hilltop.

The Polo Grounds stands were repaired and during the winter Mr. Brush spent a half-million dollars enlarging and modernizing the old park. Called Brush Stadium, it rivaled the two other "firsts" in concrete and steel baseball plants, Forbes Field at Pittsburgh, and Shibe Park in Philadelphia, both opened in 1909.

New York's joy was unconfined when the base-running mavericks brought the 1911 National League pennant home. John's billiard room on Herald Square was the repository for a flood of telegrams from his Broadway friends—George M. Cohan, Sam Harris, Louis Mann, John McCormack and his manager Dennis McSweeney, De Wolfe Hopper, Jim Corbett, Joe Humphreys, and practically all the members of the Lambs Club. There was a particularly touching and welcome telegram of appreciation from John T. Brush, and a warm note from Andrew Freedman.

Second only to the speed and expert fielding play of the youngsters, was the emergence of Richard "Rube" Marquard, the "lemon," into a peach of a pitcher. He won 24 games, which, with Mathewson's 26, represented more than half the team's total of 99. Robinson had again proved a master of developing pitchers.

The World Series of 1911 was no less thrilling than the regular season, and the only one I saw complete outside of New York. I always watched the Polo Grounds games, but going to another city with my husband was a snare and a delusion. I never saw him, and I doubt that he knew I existed. He remained close to the players. I scarcely saw him in 1911 when I went to Philadelphia in a party with the Cap Hustons, later part owner of the Yankees, and the Stevens family.

A word about the 1911 Series: The Giants lost, but again Mathewson was superb. He took the first game by 2–1 before the largest Polo Grounds crowd up to that time. Marquard lost the second in Philadelphia, and then Mathewson had the third game "won" 1–0 in New York with Frank Baker at bat in the ninth. A third strike came over and down. Baker swung and missed. The ball hit the heel of Chief Meyers' glove, bounced away and to the dugout, exactly like the Mickey Owen passed ball thirty years later. The umpire ruled that Baker had ticked the ball. Maybe it was unfortunate, because Baker hit the next pitch out of the park to tie the score, and the Athletics won in the eleventh.

John claimed a little hard luck, but dismissed this with a further claim that Connie Mack had put together one of the really great baseball teams. He felt no shame at the loss, and the Series set a new money and attendance record. Each player on the losing Giants received almost $2,500.

It was the first of three fantastic years crowded beyond belief with unforgettable moments of happiness, triumph, tragedy, travel, wealth, death, and life. John McGraw rose to unparalleled heights and influence in baseball. Despite defeat by Connie Mack in 1911 and 1913, and by the Red Sox through two Giant fielding lapses in 1912, the Giants virtually dominated the game in style of play, personality, speed, aggressiveness, color, and three successive National League victories.

Wilbert Robinson coaxed another pitcher into big-league maturity, Charles Tesreau, named "Big Jeff." His enormous bulk made him resemble Jim Jeffries, former heavyweight boxing champion. Tesreau, an overpowering right-hander, never had a losing season in the big leagues. And Rube Marquard, the "lemon," opened the 1912 season with 19 straight victories, a record that still stands.

But another pitching life slipped away the same year, 1912. Bugs Raymond, released the previous year, collapsed and died in a hotel room at Chicago. He was still brooding over being out of baseball, and the recent death of his two small daughters. He was only thirty years old.

John T. Brush had broken his hip during the summer, and his health failed fast. He managed to see another pennant brought to the enlarged Brush Stadium, thoroughly justifying his faith in John McGraw, the team, and the public's willingness to patronize a winner. The Series with the Boston Red Sox went eight games, on account of a 6–6 tie in the second game. With victory barely a put-out or so away in the final minutes, first Merkle and Meyers got mixed up on a foul fly, and then Snodgrass made his memorable muff of a fair fly that permitted the winning runs to score.

One of John's last personal contacts with Mr. Brush came in a telegram a few days before when the Giants clinched the pennant. It read:

Congratulations. Gratitude and high appreciation goes with this, my dear John, over your magnificent work which culminates today in the capture of the National League pennant for the season of 1912. All honor to you and the team that you have welded into a wonderful baseball machine.

John T. Brush

Mr. Brush started for California a few weeks later in his private railroad car, hoping the California sunshine would help his fast-tiring body. But life slipped from his grasp on November 25, before he had covered a third of the distance. He was brought back to Indianapolis for interment. There all baseball congregated to pay tribute to one who had fought since earliest childhood against seemingly hopeless odds.

But he had left behind proof that the battle was worth while financially as well as for the love of the game. He died a millionaire. His department store flourished in Indianapolis. He had a large home in that city, another in Florida, and an estate in New Jersey. He left control of the prosperous baseball club to his wife, with supervision under the direction of his son-in-law, Harry Hempstead, who was elected president.

The whole nation had become Giant-conscious, and fans everywhere couldn't get enough news of them. New York sports writers, riding on the crest of the new popularity, wrote columns and full pages dramatizing the varied personalities of the team. Jack Wheeler, an enterprising writer for McClure Syndicate, became the first ghost writer by reporting the 1911 World Series under Christy Mathewson's by-line. Next year the articles were published in a book by Putnam's under the title *Pitching in a Pinch*. Wheeler later headed his own syndicate and after that the North American Newspaper Alliance.

For several years John had been lending his name and knowledge to a number of instructional books issued by Richard K. Fox, who published the *Police Gazette*. After the 1912 Series, the theaters clamored for personal appearances, and he agreed to a winter tour of the vaudeville circuit. The weekly salary was somewhat fantastic, but from this he paid an agency fee and his expenses. His total income for the full year was between $50,000 and $60,000. It was also the first year of income tax, which was quite modest—less than 10 per cent on $100,000, I believe. You could afford to earn large sums.

Bozeman Bulger, a baseball writer for the New York *Evening World*, worked with John on the vaudeville material. Bulger had a keen sense of humor that meshed with John's. They went over all the humorous tales and devised a fairly funny monologue.

Here again John pioneered with a fund of original stories from his vast experiences. His acting friends of the Lambs Club coached him on delivery, stage presence, articulation, applause waits, entrances, and exits. But behind it all was his own sense of humor and the simple tales of the baseball field and personalities.

The tour was a complete success. The baseball writers in each city interviewed him in the dressing room, and published his views on winter baseball topics. My one regret was that John barred me from his opening at B. F. Keith's Colonial in New York and all the other shows as well. His excuse was that he would feel silly and nervous with me in the audience.

After our visit to my family in Baltimore for the 1911 holidays, we started the new year by retracing the pioneering footsteps he took in Cuba twenty-one years before. We went to Key West, Florida, by train and across the gulf by boat. Though he was accompanied by a wife and most of his National League champions, Havana writers hailed him as *El Mono Amarillo*, the Yellow Monkey.

Cuban independence was only ten years old, and freedom came hard. As late as 1909 General Enoch Crowder had been obliged to quell insurrection on behalf of the United States. But now public works had been instituted by the regime of President Miguel Gomez, and some of the hovel neighborhoods had begun to disappear. Roads were improved. Transportation vehicles, both public and private, were swift and modern. Cubans enjoyed a yacht club off Marianao, several nice bathing beaches, a thriving casino, great shipping, and even motion pictures.

A sudden rise in white population, almost a third, had been brought about by a thriving commerce, chiefly with the United States. Sugar plantations had been enlarged. Workers were earning steady wages and spending money. The unforgettable poverty and peonage were gradually being replaced by a proud and independent, self-governing people.

A welcome oasis for food and companionship was the American Club, on the corner of the Prado and Virtudes, a few blocks north of the site of what is now the beautiful capitol building. They served a daily lunch and substantial dinners in the evening, followed by formal dances and social games. The club contained a well-equipped gymnasium and other facilities.

Christy Mathewson was always a prime attraction under these conditions. John took him to the Lambs Club in New York many times for an evening of cards or checker and chess demonstrations against the club's experts. Competitors and onlookers were always amazed, somehow, that a "mere" ballplayer could have such double-barreled skill. And the people at the American Club fitted into the pattern as the men engaged in various card games.

The rise of baseball activity and interest in Cuba, was rapid, considering its early start. While Carlos Ayala was the first and foremost organizer, a young student named Nemesio Guillo had returned from the United States with a baseball and a bat as early as *1857!* This information came from José Massaguer, another Cuban youngster who had entered St. John's Military School at Ossining, New York. He discovered the Giants and John McGraw in the early 1900's and made baseball rooting and writing his career. As sports editor of *El Mundo,* he laid the foundation for much of John's success with winter exhibition games, and even more for his enjoyment and popularity on the island in later years.

When we reached Havana in 1912 several baseball parks were in steady use, and John was busy seeing all of them. The biggest and best was Tropical Stadium, built and operated by the Tropical Brewery in the junglelike park alongside its beer factory, and just across the Almendares River. The Giants played most of their exhibition games on those grounds with Christy Mathewson heading an all-star attraction. In later years it was the site of several big-league training camps.

Cuba had a pitching counterpart to Christy, a tall Negro named Mendez and known even in 1912 as the "Black Mathewson." He always looked best against the Giants. Without mincing words, John bemoaned the failure of baseball, himself included, to cast aside custom or unwritten law, or whatever it was, and sign a player on ability alone, regardless of race or color.

John settled for players who were undeniably Cuban, for the Giants trained regularly in Texas, and he understood the significance and severity of segregation laws. At no time did he wish to offend ordinances or the people who lived by them 365 days of the year. As a result of his return to Cuba, John signed several boys of promise, Emilio Palmero, a left-handed pitcher; José Rodriguez, a flashy first baseman; and Angel Aragon, an infielder, whose son was signed by the Giants twenty-nine years later. They weren't the first Cubans to reach the big leagues. At least three preceded them by a few years, Armando Marsans, Melo Almeida, and Manuel Cueto, thanks to a visit in 1910 by Frank Bancroft, long business manager of the Cincinnati Reds. Just as we arrived in 1912, the Philadelphia Phillies, managed by Charlie Dooin, were leaving. One of the Phillies was a bowlegged, grinning, and happy infielder named John Lobert, who later became one of John's favorite players and lifelong friend.

While the Giants won again in 1913 with 101 victories, giving them a three-year total of 303, the biggest news was John's signing the big Olympic champion, Jim Thorpe, an American Indian, on February 1. Because he had played semipro baseball one summer in North Carolina, the Amateur Athletic Union president, James E. Sullivan, declared Thorpe a professional. He had won two all-around championships at Stockholm, Sweden. He had been praised and decorated by King Gustaf V of Sweden, but all his prizes were returned to the Olympic Committee.

John rushed to sign him as both player and gate attraction. Far from being a big-league player, Thorpe was a splendid athlete with great reflexes, hence strong possibilities. He would undoubtedly learn, and earn his keep while learning.

The second big news came on May 9 as the result of a previous meeting in Chicago. After a performance at the Palace Theater one night, John went over to "Smiley" Corbett's place in the Loop. There he met Garry Herrmann, of the Cincinnati Club; John Bruce, National Commission secretary; and Charles Comiskey, owner of the White Sox.

After exchanging greetings, Comiskey called him aside, and

said, "Say, John, what do you think of taking our teams on a trip around the world, splitting expenses?"

"When would you want to start?"

"At the end of next season. We'll tour until March."

"All right, I'll go," John said and they shook hands.

That was the deal. They had nothing in writing, though they met later and discussed having Mathewson, Meyers, Walter Johnson, and other stars, appear in American games before sailing.

There is a question as to which was more trouble, organizing the global trip or reorganizing Jim Thorpe. The Indian was thoroughly uninhibited, gullible, and fair game for the fun-loving Giants. Throughout the summer Thorpe had plenty of money from his bonus and salary, fairly high for those times. And so he courted his girl, Iva Miller, when he could, and otherwise by mail. She was one-sixteenth Indian.

Jim had first attended Haskell Institute in Kansas and then the Carlisle Indian School in Pennsylvania. Knowing that Indians were supposed to be protected or supervised, the Giant players appointed a supervisor on the Giants. Whom could the government trust more than another Indian, John Meyers? The Chief was "it," only they neglected to tell him.

Thorpe learned of it in such a way that Meyers was suspected of self-appointment. Then they confided that the Chief was opening Jim's mail from pretty Iva. Thorpe simply exploded when he actually found one of his precious letters in the Chief's locker. The blast took place when John was in his office at the ball park. It consisted of the wildest yells ever heard on or off the prairie. Fortunately no one but workmen was in the ball park that morning, for John rushed out to investigate the yelling and found Chief Meyers running for his life or scalp with Thorpe definitely on the warpath.

Clad only in Turkish bath towels, which each carried in his hand, the two Indians were racing up and down the aisles, around the big grandstand. Meyers was screaming protests of innocence. Thorpe shouted threats at the culprit who had tampered with his mail. But he failed to catch Meyers. Anyone seeing the spectacle could only laugh, and John enjoyed it.

"Looks as though the wrong Indian competed in the Olympic Games," John chuckled, and returned to his work.

The World Series ended on October 11, and was something of a rout of all Giants, except the matchless Mathewson. He pitched two games, winning one with a ten-inning shutout and losing the other by 3–1, when Eddie Plank gave the Giants only two hits. Within a week John completed all his club business, which did not include the transfer of Charlie Herzog (again) with young Grover Hartley to Cincinnati for Bob Bescher, the base-stealing wizard. John arranged to let Wilbert Robinson go, when Bill Dahlen resigned as manager of the Brooklyn Superbas. Robinson had the inside track at the latest most modern baseball plant, Ebbets Field, which had opened in April.

John never stood in the way of any player who had a chance to manage. He could hardly spare a catcher of Bresnahan's caliber in 1909, but no one was more deserving of the opportunity than the Duke. Gradually "McGraw boys" were filling the posts, and soon he would be surrounded by former students of his methods, each trying to batter him down.

The trip around the world was extremely well-planned. Comiskey and John contributed or underwrote one-half of the total cost as a personal obligation. In that way, John could invite whom he pleased. One of the first on the list was his old benefactor at Truxton, Bert Kenney. He had long since paid Bert the $70 advanced in those darkest hours at Olean. But taking Bert Kenney on this trip, one chance in a lifetime, figured to reduce an obligation that John always felt could never be wiped out entirely. Another old friend accompanied us in the person of Father McNamara, one of the priests at St. Ann's, "our" church on York Road, Baltimore.

Comiskey and his White Sox manager, Jimmy Callahan, selected the American League umpire, Jack Sheridan. John invited Bill Klem, even though Bill's carelessness had cost him a victory on April 25. Klem was young and firm and a showman on the field. He would give the games color and authority. John was responsible for his expenses, though Bill paid the cost, about $1,100, of taking his charming wife, Marie.

The American League playing contingent included Tris Speaker of the Red Sox, Sam Crawford of the Tigers, and Urban Faber, Jim Scott, Joe Benz, Andy Slight, Tommy Daly, and Buck Weaver, all of the White Sox; "Tip" O'Neill, the writer, came along as secretary. Ted Sullivan was the lecturer and master of ceremonies. And there were two Chicago newspapermen, George Axelson of the *Record-Herald*, and Joe Farrell of the *Tribune*.

In addition to Jim Thorpe, John brought Laughing Larry Doyle, Fred Merkle, Bunny Hearn, George Wiltse, and Mike Donlin of the championship Giants. From the Phillies he enlisted Mike Doolan and John "Hans" Lobert, both infielders. The St. Louis Cardinals contributed Ivy Wingo, Lee Magee, Steve Evans, and Jack Bliss. Germany Schaefer came from the Senators, Walter Leverenz from the Browns, and Dick Egan from Brooklyn.

The addition of Donlin was somewhat touching. Despite the twelve years of trouble he had caused, what with holding out all one year and threats and divided interest with the stage, refusal to keep in playing shape, and public defiance that delighted sports writers, John couldn't forget that on the ball field Mike had always been a great outfielder and hitter who played to win. Now he was all but licked by misfortune, poor health, and recent tragedy. His tiny wife, Mabel Hite, had died during the year, and John felt that the trip would be a welcome diversion. He even gave him a Giant contract after we returned. Mike was in uniform for thirty-odd games in 1914 as a substitute and pinch hitter. He made only five hits in about thirty tries. But the long voyage helped him over a rough spot.

Here was something of an object lesson of what can be done with youth without trying, but we seldom pay much attention to free lessons in this world. Right on the same ship was another lesson in the making, giving us a career that was ending and another beginning. Jim Thorpe had married Iva, a sweet and pretty girl. The trip was their honeymoon. We were scarcely across the Pacific when John lost patience with carefree Jim's refusal to behave himself.

"If it weren't for your wife," John scolded, "I'd send you right back to your reservation by the next boat!"

Another honeymooning couple were Grace and J. Louis Comiskey, son of the Old Roman. Seventeen ladies made the trip, all wives except little Margaret Callahan, Jimmy's nine-year old daughter, who wanted to bring back a little Nagasaki baby as a Japanese doll.

While Comiskey and John were prepared to share all expenses

in the event of a 100-per-cent loss, they planned well to forestall possible deficit by opening the trip with a schedule of thirty-six exhibition games in cities of the Midwest, South, and far West. Attendance at these games was so good that the trip was guaranteed against heavy loss before we sailed from Vancouver, December 3, on the yachtlike *Empress of Japan.*

A month before that, however, the journey was overshadowed for me personally, and for John, too, when my mother died suddenly in Atlantic City. We were in Texas when the call came, and I wanted John to go on with the tour alone. Of course, he refused, and Mr. Comiskey insisted that we take care of things in Baltimore and return together at any time before the scheduled departure.

While the passing of a mother is not wholly unexpected—mine had been ill—our hopes somehow always give us a false belief that the inevitable never will happen. And so, I'm to be forgiven if I say that, while the trip around the world was a fantastic thing, it could not be the joyous experience for me that I had planned.

We left from Vancouver for a twenty-three-day trip across the Pacific that should have taken only ten days for the seven thousand miles. I have no first-hand reports of the Mayflower voyage, almost three hundred years before, but I doubt it was as rough as ours. For ten days an eighty-mile wind was recorded, and even the entire crew suffered from seasickness.

Like any trip around the world, of 38,000 miles, it would require a separate volume to cover all the interest and excitement and laughter aboard ship and on land. December found us playing games in Yokohama, Kobe, Nagasaki, Shanghai, Hong Kong, and Manila. We spent the last two weeks of December, including Christmas, at sea, reaching Brisbane, Australia, on New Year's Day. We played at Brisbane, Sydney, Adelaide, Freemantle, and Colombo in January, and spent the last week steaming through the Indian Ocean and up through the Red Sea for Suez and on through the historic canal.

February brought the warm waters of the Mediterranean and the sunshine of north Africa, Italy, and the French Riviera. We played games at Cairo, Alexandria, Naples, Florence, Monte Carlo, Nice, Marseille, and Paris. We spent February 8 and 9 in Rome, but played no games. The time was spent in visiting the historic ruins and what was to me and most of us, especially Father Mc-

Namara, the high spot of the trip. We had an audience with His Holiness, Pope Pius X. He was small and venerable but quite alert and wholly cognizant of our mission in behalf of baseball. He seemed so active that none could suspect he would pass to his reward within the year and remain a symbol of rare understanding and progress to the Church.

It was a peak of realization in more ways than one for me. Here was the "boy and the baseball," spreading the message around the world. Here was the little fellow from Truxton, who had carried the precious baseball in his hip pocket "like a permanent tumor of the buttock" as he performed the holy services as an altar boy for the itinerant priests from Cortland. Now he stood before the Prince of God, representing a game to which he had devoted his every hope and dream and ounce of energy. For this childhood vision he had fought and shed his blood, risked his name and his life and his chance at material wealth.

And here he stood before Pope Pius X with the baseball, not in his hip pocket, but embedded in his heart, and with his friends, his wife, his early benefactor, a priest of his church, an umpire with whom he would soon be quarreling fiercely again, an unbridled Indian from the American plains, a broken spirit from Broadway night life. . . .

This was John McGraw, the boy with the baseball, now forty years old. He had appeared before Japanese royalty, Australian governors, East Indian princes, khedives, starched ambassadors, and beribboned military chiefs. He would appear before the English royal family and shake hands with young King George V. He would tread the soil of his father's native Ireland. He would be hailed, with his fellow travelers, arriving in America on the *Lusitania*; feted and wined and dined in a gigantic all-night banquet at the Biltmore Hotel, New York, and favored with unprecedented renown.

But I remember best and most often the boy and the baseball, journeying from the humble altar at Truxton, New York, to the hallowed ground in St. Peter's as one more step in his determination to live out a childhood dream.

22

THE WORD "home" became a six-room reality in 1910 when we moved into a fifth-floor apartment of a building at 301 West 109th Street on the corner of Broadway. For the next eleven years a chain of unforgettable memories was forged, chiefly from an endless parade of visitors and friends that represented every imaginable walk of life.

It also represented the animal kingdom, thanks to a friend in Massachusetts who specialized in raising Boston bull terriers. We hadn't been in the apartment long before John brought one home. He was small, wide-eyed, and quivering.

"The poor thing," I said. "What's his name?"

"Truxton, of course," he replied with a hint of impatience.

Somehow I was supposed to guess that a John McGraw dog couldn't be called anything else. I learned it as a fact when the first terrier eventually went blind and picked up a piece of poisoned meat on Riverside Drive. John appeared with another as a replacement, and he was named Truxton. So were the third, fourth, and fifth—yes, over the years he had five Boston bull terriers all named Truxton.

Each was cute and precious. They were most enjoyable one at a time. More than that in a city apartment was another matter, as John learned one morning during a phone call from Grand Central Station. He had just arrived from a series in Boston and called with what he thought was the happiest news. Upon hearing of the latest canine misfortune, his kennel friend in Massachusetts had set a new high in generosity.

"Blanche," he announced, "I've brought home five of the cutest—"

"Five what?" I gasped.

"Wait till you see them," he exclaimed. "Five of the cutest little Boston terriers. Warm some milk, tear up a couple of blankets—"

"You go find four friends, John McGraw," I said firmly, "and get rid of that many dogs. If you have no friends, there won't be any here, either!"

Frankly, I don't think any man in his right mind would bring five puppies to a city apartment, but I couldn't take any chances. I had to make sure he didn't bring his puppies into the house, because there's no defense against them. I might add that Truxton number six was a large black and brown Airedale that almost broke up our home, and Truxton number seven was a wild and defiant wire-haired fox terrier that should have been named Mike Donlin. He specialized in getting out after midnight and arousing a wide radius of Westchester neighborhood with the most prolonged and senseless barking I have ever heard.

I stood at the door or tiptoed out, calling softly many a night, pleading and threatening under my breath, but Truxton number seven would back away and bark even louder. While this was going on, John McGraw made such helpful contributions as, "Don't lose your temper, Blanche." "Remember, he's only a dog." "He means well, Blanche." "That's his way of playing." "*Now* you know what I went through with poor Bugs Raymond." Not once did he ever try to get that crazy thing back in the house.

Of course, the dogs worshiped him. They tolerated me and the household help, but John was always something special to them. He represented fun, surprise, titbits sneaked from the dining table during meals, roughhouse, and enjoyable teasing.

For many, many years our mornings in New York began with: "Well, it's Truxton against the world!"

Since dawn the terrier's sharp ears had been awaiting that announcement. It was a signal, and there followed a violent scratching as Truxton's little legs and feet thrashed to work up some friction and momentum on the linoleum and then on the hardwood floor of the hall. But he kept at it, snorting, panting, and racing.

Reaching our room, he would have enough speed to negotiate a fifteen-foot leap through the air and onto our bed. Sometimes he would overshoot the landing strip and make a perfect four-point contact with me as the runway. Legs still thrashing, he'd right himself, direct his snorts of delight at his beloved master, and then shower him with what I suppose were dog kisses.

When John wheeled out of bed before announcing that "Truxton was against the world" for another day, the terrier's activity centered around trying to do something for him. He'd pick up a slipper, or drag trousers from a chair, or simply race out into the hallway and back in again, shivering with dog joy. Though neither understood the other's language entirely, a sparkling conversation usually ran through the next hour, or until John sat down to his breakfast.

He liked good food and enjoyed it all over the world, but he seldom varied his breakfast menu in America. It consisted of orange juice, scrambled eggs not too soft, bacon, buttered toast, and coffee. Our cooks broiled plenty of bacon and asked no questions. It always disappeared. And always parked on the right side of his chair as he scanned the many newspapers was one of seven Truxtons. As he read and ate, his right hand would descend at intervals until all the bacon had been consumed between them.

John claimed he could drive a car, but he seldom took the wheel. We had automobiles ever since learning to enjoy them with Mr. Brush. He and John shared ownership of a C.V.I. with seats of upholstered leather in bright red shortly after we came to New York. Cars were fairly expensive, except the so-called utility models, like the Brush (no connection), the Regal, Maxwell-Briscoe, and others. A Brush Runabout was priced at $485, with rumble seat and toolbox $20 extra. Maxwell-Briscoes sold for $600 up, and the Regal for $900. The Chalmers and Winton limousines cost $3,000. John had a Winton of his own and a racy-looking Rambler.

He had a man drive him to the club offices, first in the St. James Building, which also housed the National League offices; then to 200 Fifth Avenue, and after that to 15 West 44th Street, just off Fifth Avenue and a block east of the Lambs Club. His last office was at 100 West 42nd Street, at the corner of Sixth Avenue.

With a car to be called, the Truxtons, particularly the first, had the most fun. It was part of the waiting game after John had shaved himself and had breakfast. The phrase was, "I think it's time to *get the car!*" The little terrier could pick those three words out of any context. John always tried to conceal the words in casual comment and never succeeded.

The little legs flew again, this time for the door. Of course, he couldn't open the door. He'd run back again, whining and complaining. He'd return more frantic than ever, because the emergency was mounting. Only he could *get the car*.

"I wish I had the car," John would say. "What happened to Truxton? Where on earth is the car? I need the car!"

Well, he enjoyed hearing the thrashing feet and snorting and pitiful whining, but I couldn't for long. It was too tantalizing and unfair, and so I'd open the door for the little dog, unless the cook had weakened first. Out into the hall he'd fly and down the stairs. John McGraw would be at the window, waiting to see the little thing race across the street to the garage. If the door was closed, the garageman soon answered his angry barking. Presently he would emerge, sitting proudly on the front seat beside the chauffeur. John would reward him with a gentle patting and put him into the hallway with thanks and a fond good-by.

Home must have given John a feeling of security and perhaps thanksgiving, for we hadn't been in the apartment more than a year or two before he began his series of little books. They were a sort of vest-pocket diary, though he kept only names and figures in them. Prosperity always attracted the less fortunate. If they didn't meet John at the ball park, they would catch him at the race track or the billiard room, which he maintained until the first World War, or by phone at his home.

Soon after each New Year's day he would start jotting with all the determination of a person keeping a fresh diary. He would write a name or an initial, and then the amount he had loaned. These weren't the so-called touches that a man of affairs forgets as soon as the unfortunate had departed. John kept only account of fair-sized sums, and, with feminine curiosity, I'd say:

"Where's last year's book?"

"Inside. Why?"

"Inside where?"

"Oh, inside . . . the desk . . . it's somewhere. Why?"

"Do you want me to write any letters or make any phone calls?"

"Oh, no, these are all good. That's why I keep the account."

He presumed they were perfectly good debts, as the borrower had assured him, but in his heart he had no intention of ever doing anything about delinquence. He was being a "good businessman" by keeping such accounts, and the jotting went on, month after month, year after year. The old book would be put aside casually, and a new one started. I used to look at them and try to figure, but I couldn't make head or tail of names or amounts. He misplaced a little book on one occasion and began searching through the drawers of desks, cabinets, bureaus, and vanities. That was when he discovered my hidden lipstick, and also when I heard a good sample of the McGravian wrath and impatience.

"It's bold to wear this stuff," he snapped. "Besides, you don't need it. It makes you conspicuous. If you want to be stared at, do it right. Go to Henry Dazian's down the street from the Lambs, and he'll fix you up with a flashy costume nobody can help noticing. But this rouge and stuff makes a girl look cheap."

He was the same about women smoking, and not because he himself never smoked. He simply idealized femininity as it was and especially those he cared about. I've seen him watch women puffing on cigarettes all over the world, and I don't think he ever felt comfortable at the sight of it.

His little vest-pocket diaries were filled each year with assorted sums due, and were put aside without comment. He had no rancor over them, and to my knowledge, he never dunned anybody. One morning in later years he opened a small package at breakfast. Reaching into the tiny wooden box lined with cotton batting, he brought forth a glistening lump of gold the size of a thimble.

"Stanley Boler!" he exclaimed. "Look at this. A nugget, real gold, from Stanley Boler!"

"It's beautiful," I said, looking close.

"And you say nobody ever pays me back—"

"I never said any such thing!"

"Well, you probably thought it plenty of times," he went on, strictly for the benefit of his own conscience. "Why, I only loaned Stanley—how much *did* I lend him? I've got it in the book."

"What year?" I challenged.

"Why. . . ." he struggled to remember. "The year he went out to start his mining out in—wherever it was. Anyway, it was no more than twenty-five dollars. And look at this, real gold, and it's worth a thousand dollars."

He was the happiest man in creation, for here was vindication of his liberal philosophy. The nugget was actually worth about seven or eight hundred dollars, and John packed it carefully in the box and carried it to the Polo Grounds. There he proudly displayed the lesson of bread cast on the waters, or something, showed it all around, and put it in his locker. That was the last he saw of it. He came home empty-handed and reluctant to discuss it. His excuse was that whoever took it probably needed it.

During my work on this volume I returned to my apartment after an out-of-town trip and found a letter, which to my amazement contained a substantial check and a note of apology. I can't, of course, identify the sender, but the substance of his note was:

> John loaned me this more years ago than I like to admit. But it was never convenient to pay him back. Then, when I had enough, I ran into some tax troubles, which have just been cleared up. Now I can pay, and I am happy to do so in the name of a great man and a greater gentleman.

This was not the first remittance, but it was the largest by far, and somehow the most touching. Like Stanley Boler's nugget, it made up for all those who, for reasons which John never questioned or even mentioned, were unable to repay him. And somehow, I am sure he never gave the loans a second thought.

Of course, John McGraw had no monopoly on liberality, for it is common in baseball and rarely publicized. The game is hazardous in every way, and the unfortunates always outnumber the lucky. Baseball does its best, officially and privately, to provide legitimate work for those who need it. Many clubs carry scouts and coaches, and whomever else they can fit in, when they are not strictly essential. More important is that the needy ones gave something to the game.

They appeared at the Polo Grounds over the years, and work was found for them whenever possible. Big Dan Brouthers served as a Polo Grounds watchman for a number of years. Amos Rusie reappeared and worked on the turnstiles. There was employment for Jim Mutrie long after his handle-bar mustache had whitened. Bill Dahlen was part of the plant operation late in John's tenure. Smiling Mickey Welch worked on the gate, and even Charles "Silver" King, one of Mickey's toughest pitching rivals who won 144 games in four years in the early eighties, shuffled in and took a job as one of the sweepers at fifty cents an hour when that was a fair wage.

This is the part of baseball that creates a secret pride in the heart of anybody who has been a part of it. No club does any more than another, because each does as much as it can.

I never knew the exact nature of John McGraw's financial

philosophy, and I never worried about it. He gave me everything I ever asked for or failed to ask for. I wanted for nothing, and so I never questioned his income or what he did with it. Naturally, I had a wife's concern that his generosity might hurt him, yet I had no fear that it would hurt me. I did wonder from time to time if the endless loans or gifts would drain his patience, and I am happy to say that they never did.

I recall objecting only once to his generosity and I didn't fully appreciate the circumstances. All I knew was that the tailor had just made and delivered a fine new suit for John at what was then a fairly high price. His wardrobe was never lavish, and, like many men in his station, he had to be dragged into tailor shops. Hence I looked forward to going out with him in the new suit.

I heard him talking with this evening caller in low tones at the door. Just who it was I never learned and didn't care at the time. But I grew suspicious when I noticed John hurrying through the living room and then rattling things in his closet. Sure enough, he returned with a suit on a hanger. He had *the* suit, a pair of shoes, and a guilty look.

"Just a minute," I said. "You're certainly not going to—"

"This fellow's got a job to take over first thing tomorrow morning, Blanche," he whispered, and shushed me with his finger. "He can't go in any old suit. It's an important job. He's got to look nice."

And I watched the good suit disappear into the night with the stranger, though he was probably an old friend of John's. My husband looked neither left nor right as he hurried past me and into his workroom, where he could escape further discussion of the matter.

His ever widening circle of friends and the growing number of hardship cases simply became part of his living pattern. Sometimes he would take a western trip with a doctor's orders not to give any dinners or hold any parties. When that happened, the hotel clerk received a number of envelopes for prospective callers on the first day in each city. They contained notes of regret, or simply notes of varying denominations. No one ever knew how much, least of all John himself, but this sort of thing went on from the time fortune began to favor him financially until he was only a memory.

He was what is known in the entertainment or restaurant world as a check grabber, and, surprising as it seems, his penchant or determination sometimes caused embarrassment. His party frequently included men whose pride of hospitality equaled his, at least temporarily. They would excuse themselves and slip away to catch the dining captain for payment of the check.

Those proud souls never tried such a trick twice. Not only was the self-proclaimed host denounced, but John would also accuse the waiter of double-crossing him. He'd berate the captain and announce to the proprietor that he would never patronize his confounded place again. Restaurateurs soon understood him, and no one in a McGraw party could possibly get the check.

In places like Mother Leone's, when it was over at Seventh Avenue and 38th Street, just below the Metropolitan Opera House, the question of who was host never arose. Mother Leone's boys learned fast, for we were steady consumers of their fine Italian food long before World War I, and John's last public appearance was at a dinner in Leone's, which had moved ten blocks uptown in the early 1920's.

Though we ate Italian food most often at Leone's, we patronized all of them—Rosie's long before she moved to 51st Street, Guffanti's, Zucca's, Enrico and Paglieri's, and of course Mori's just below Greenwich Village. We dined out frequently, and leisurely, because it was the best way for John to "taper off" the hypertension of the day's game. His favorite theater entertainment was still the lighter type, which we found at the Casino, the New York Roof, Hammerstein's, Lew Fields' new Winter Garden, and the Hippodrome, then the largest theater in the world. That distinction belongs to Havana now, I believe. When the Palace opened, we were regular weekly patrons for many years until the demise of fine vaudeville.

The Highlanders outgrew their bandbox park in 1912 and prevailed upon Harry Hempstead to accept them as tenants for one year only, 1913. Like the man who came to dinner, they remained on. The yearly rent was substantial, but never needed by the landlord. He didn't forget that the American Leaguers had housed the Giants during a time of emergency in 1911. Mr. Hempstead was happy to reciprocate for the single year.

Then came the Federal League competition in 1914, bringing

severe dissatisfaction and unrest among big-league players. They had been organized into a brotherhood by Dave Fultz, a former player and an astute lawyer. To combat all this, the Highlanders needed revenue from the Saturday and holiday crowds. Unable to get it in the small hilltop park, they remained on through two years of competition from a third league. This was followed soon by America's entrance into World War I, which put a new park out of their reach. At one period before 1920 the Yankees had no lease and were actually on a month-to-month basis.

John McGraw had heard the echoes of the Players' League in 1890. He had been a key factor in the success of the American League. Naturally he watched and felt the progress of the Federals with deepening interest, and not a little apprehension. They had millions in capital. They were luring stars with attractive offers, but not nearly as many as the Johnson league had signed in 1901. The reason lay in prosperity and few player grievances. The advent of new and massive parks in Philadelphia, Pittsburgh, New York, Chicago (Comiskey Park), Brooklyn, and another contemplated by Jim Gaffney in Boston was a major obstacle to competition at the gate. Still, Johnson had done it with the capital of Charles Somers.

And then John came home one evening to announce that the Federal League wouldn't and couldn't succeed. I reminded him that they had only started, and probably had lots of money.

"I know," he said. "They offered me some of it—a lot of it. They offered me more money than I ever saw in my life."

"Saw?" I asked.

He nodded. "They had it, ready for deposit," he sighed. "One hundred thousand dollars . . . deposited in cash to my name . . . just for signing. I'd get a big salary, too."

You cannot realize what such a sum meant in those days. Wheat was under a dollar a bushel wholesale, and corn a little more than fifty cents. Flour was $4.00 a barrel. Coffee was eleven cents a pound. The best steer beef sold under eight cents a pound. Steel beams for construction were $27.00 a ton. Anthracite coal was $5.00 a ton in New York. Gold was $20.67 an ounce. The offer was an opportunity to be a man of wealth and independence no matter whether the new league succeeded or failed.

"The thing won't last," John said finally. "It can't last. The hundred thousand wouldn't be spent to build the Federal League, because I couldn't contribute that much. The money would be spent to destroy the National League, or at least land a hard, low blow."

He paced the floor with small, nervous steps.

"Well, you can't help baseball by destroying any part of it. So, I turned them down!"

23

FOR THE SECOND time in twelve years John McGraw saw the personnel of his carefully built team come apart at the seams. But the Giants of 1914 and 1915 neither collapsed nor sank. In the first of the two years they played .600 or pennant-winning ball until after July 4, and less than .500 ball for the rest of the season. They slowed down to a trot while the Boston Braves, fired by the tempestuous George Stallings, galloped up from last place on July 15 by winning eight of every ten games. During the final two weeks, while the Giants were winning eight and losing nine, the Braves won fifteen against a single defeat and took the pennant easily.

Tesreau and Mathewson won 50 victories, but Marquard and the youngsters disappointed. Wiltse was through. Only one regular, George Burns, hit above .300 and he made it with three points to spare. Yet he led the league in stolen bases with 62, while Bob Bescher, obtained from Cincinnati for his specialty while we were on the World tour, stole only 36.

It was time for a change, and John knew it, but the search for younger players had become keener throughout the nation. New and stronger names were necessary to meet the new and stronger competition in his own ball park. At the end of 1914 Frank Farrell had sold the Highlanders to another Tammany Hall member, Jacob Ruppert, Jr., whose wealthy father, founder of the brewery, had recently died. Ruppert's partner was an engineer, Tillinghast L'Hommedieu Huston. The team was now known as the Yankees, and their new manager was the popular Wild Bill Donovan, whose pitching had helped Hugh Jennings win three pennants in Detroit.

The Giants finished last in 1915 for the first and only time as a McGraw team. More important than the finish was that Christy Mathewson had reached the end of the pitching trail. There would be other Giant greats on that rubber, but none could possibly compare with him. John's biggest job from then on was to keep Christy set apart as something special in his mind. As a result, John never compared his later pitchers with the immortal Matty.

Most unusual about the last-place finish, and a fact rarely mentioned, was that the Giants were only 3½ games out of the first division. Fourth-place Chicago won 73 and lost 80, while the Giants won 69 and lost 83. Furthermore, Larry Doyle won the batting championship, and Fred Merkle, batting .299, had played the outfield sensationally for an emergency period. When Marquard failed again, John sold him to Brooklyn in late August.

But the end of the year brought the end of the Federal League opposition, and the distribution of playing strength. John got two outfielders, Benny Kauff and Edd Roush; an infielder, Bill McKechnie; and a battery, Rariden, a catcher, and Fred Anderson, a pitcher. With that, he sent Chief Meyers to Brooklyn on waivers, giving Wilbert Robinson the very battery he had coached to fame, Marquard and Meyers.

When the Giants opened up the 1916 season with eight straight losses, John began to telephone, write letters, and plan for wholesale changes. The ice-cold team suddenly became hot. They won four games at Pittsburgh, two at Chicago, four at St. Louis, three at Cincinnati, four at Boston—seventeen in a row.

Another slump followed, and John continued with his plans, which centered around Christy Mathewson. He could have remained in New York forever as a coach, but he wanted to manage, and John arranged it. On July 20 the Giants' greatest player was transferred to Cincinnati with the ex-Federals, Roush and McKechnie. In exchange John finally got Charlie Herzog back again to bolster and pep up his infield, and Wade Killefer, a catcher. A few days later Christy signed a three-year contract to manage Cincinnati. Within a week he reappeared at the Polo Grounds before a large weekday crowd that was definitely pro-Mathewson.

John didn't mind losing this one. The Giants treated Cincinnati unmercifully all year, winning 16 of 21 games played.

The departure of the Mathewsons emphasized more acutely than ever the passing of time, and I decided to take my first mid-season road trip with a baseball club. The cities were interesting, but I think my mind was on Cincinnati. Also, I was certain of eating with my husband only at breakfast. Twice he wasn't even on hand for that. He had people to see, calls to make. He was arranging to transfer players. The Giants were running cold again. On our last day in Pittsburgh John traded Merkle to Brooklyn for Lew McCarthy, a catcher. Two days later in Cincinnati he sent Larry Doyle to Chicago with two rookies for thirty-year-old "Heinie" Zimmerman, a native New Yorker, and a third-basing veteran of World Series with the Cubs in 1908 and 1910.

For the first time I really saw the effect of a trade upon a player who was loathe to leave. Laughing Larry Doyle was in tears. He had coined the chant, "It's great to be young and a Giant." Now he was neither. "Batting champion one year, traded the next," he cried.

John assured him that including him in the deal was necessary, and that he would be a Giant again as soon as possible. There was more to Doyle's reluctance than sentiment. He had small children, and his wife was not too stable. Though he told the press he wouldn't join Chicago, he reported and batted .436 for nine games.

These scenes were never easy. One of the most difficult came in June, 1927, at Chicago, though John had remained in Cincinnati. He arranged to trade Eddie Farrell, Kent Greenfield, and Hugh McQuillan to Boston for Zack Taylor, a catcher; Larry Benton, a pitcher; and Herb Thomas, an infielder smaller than Eddie.

Farrell had graduated from the University of Pennsylvania and was studying or had completed his dentistry course. His childhood had been spent only a few miles south of Truxton, and his life-long dream was to play ball for John McGraw. His distinguished college baseball career had pointed to the Giants, and he had played with them as substitute through 1926. His hitting, his infield play sparkled. The news of the trade almost felled him. He took the quickest train to Cincinnati for a meeting in John's room at the Gibson Hotel.

"You can't do this to me, Mr. McGraw," he protested.

"I'm not doing anything to you, Eddie," John said. "I had to put you in the deal. They demanded you instead of cash."

"But you don't understand, Mr. McGraw. All I ever wanted from baseball was to play for John McGraw, for you. I . . . I can't put out anywhere else. All my life—"

"Oh, yes, you can, Eddie," John soothed. "A real ballplayer puts out for the game itself, not just for one manager."

"You don't understand—"

"I understand this, Eddie: I need you here and I'll bring you back—soon as I can."

Little Farrell was shaking his head and fighting the tears. John doubted that a real ballplayer could put identification with one team or person above the play of the game. He kept his word and brought Eddie back to the Giants in 1929, almost two years later to the day. After watching him in amazement for a week, he called Eddie into his office, and said, "Something definitely is wrong. You have no speed, no pep. You're not the player I had here two years ago."

As Eddie had predicted, the spark was gone. He had tried, but the urge to "put out" simply wasn't there. He was traded to St. Louis for 1930 and was with Chicago before the season ended, missing a World Series. The Yankees took him on as utility infielder in 1932, and he reached the Series that year, but he was never the old Farrell again. He was released next season and entered dentistry, which he practices today in Newark, New Jersey.

It was good to see Jane in Cincinnati, but after a few guarded phrases in visits to her apartment at the Alms Hotel, we decided the city just wasn't for us. Ten-year-old Christy had just recovered from an appendicitis operation, and looked it. Jane knew a nice, quiet lake with living quarters in upper New York State. If we returned to New York right away. . . .

So, we sort of jumped the team, after saying good-by to the men, returned to New York, and left immediately for a short holiday at Jane's lake. Christy took his team to Pittsburgh and then to Chicago for Labor Day. John took the Giants to Boston for the same week end. That was my first and last road trip during the season with the club. It was much more fun and relaxing at the lake, talking, fishing, watching little Christy.

Immediately after Labor Day the Giants caught fire again.

Ferdie Schupp, the little left-hander, defeated Brooklyn, and the longest string of victories in the history of baseball was under way. Rube Benton pitched a one-hit shutout in the first game of a double-header against Boston at the Polo Grounds on September 30 for their twenty-sixth in a row. Schupp won six, including a one-hitter; Tesreau, seven; Perritt, four; Benton, five; Sallee, two; and Ritter and Smith, one each. Seven of the last eleven victories were shutouts, and yet the Giants gained no ground on the league leaders during the streak. The New York *Times* said editorially:

> This belated but not unappreciated triumph of the Giants has been accomplished without the one thing which has always been held to be most essential in the game. They have good pitchers, but not a Matty or a McGinnity in the lot. What they have most of all is good management. All honor to them and their manager.

But at Ebbets Field on October 2, their manager didn't believe the Giants were doing their best to defeat league-leading Brooklyn. The Braves were beating the Phillies twice in Boston, and a Brooklyn victory would nose out the despised Philadelphia team, champions of 1915. John watched their antics with growing rage. Another old Oriole teammate and friend, Wilbert Robinson, was about to win a National League pennant. Nobody would be happier about it than John McGraw, but not until *after* Robbie had won against the strongest opposition. You don't let up ever until the game is over, until the flag is cinched. Preferring to see Brooklyn win, rather than Philadelphia, his Giants weren't bearing down.

With a few well-chosen remarks to individuals and the team as a whole, John stormed off the bench and out of the Ebbets Field dugout in unmistakable protest and rebuke for all to see.

Barney Dreyfuss headed a movement to haul John on the carpet for an explanation or apology during the National League meetings in December at the old Waldorf-Astoria. This symbol of gracious living was then located at 34th Street and Fifth Avenue, site of the present Empire State Building. While the outraged officials convened in nearby meeting rooms, John visited with reporters, managers, coaches, and scouts, with or without jobs, in the long, red-carpeted corridor known as Peacock Alley.

It was no secret that certain officials of the National League were not pleased with John's success and prominence, which was neither new nor inhuman. I don't remember John ever being pleased when someone else won the pennant. But I doubt that he would have put legislative moves ahead of the game itself, as the rule makers did in reducing player limits in order to curtail the number of rookies he might look at in the spring or carry during the year. When that ruling hurt other clubs, the player limit was raised again. Then John's method of leaving earlier for spring training than other clubs was attacked. He liked to evaluate the young players first thing and weed out the hopeless, study the promising, and integrate those ready—all before the known quantities reached camp.

Managers were never allowed in executive council, and so John continued to wait at the Waldorf each day. Somehow the "apology forces" failed to summon enough votes, and he was never obliged to elaborate on why he walked out on his own team in Brooklyn for not doing its level best. When the club owners passed the rule forbidding training before March 1, at the December, 1916, meeting, John circumvented the penalty quickly, with the help of Mike Donlin.

Mike had become a promoter of sorts, and suddenly emerged with a barnstorming scheme. He lined up several players from National League teams, including those run by "anti-McGraw" forces, for a trip to Cuba. He completed his barnstorming group with all the young Giant players John wanted to see. By sheer coincidence, of course, John was in Cuba during February and saw his hopefuls or hopeless under competitive conditions for more than two weeks. He had Donlin ship the desirables to Marlin, where the Giants began training, in accordance with the rule, on March 1.

That was one of the happiest camps, and remembered most by players and writers, who seemed to come from all over. One of the biggest and best was Charles E. Van Loan, known as the father of baseball fiction. Another unforgettable in camp that year was Al Schacht, a skinny New York boy, who had a lame pitching arm and a trusting nature. When Art Fletcher pointed to a certain bath booth as containing the culprit who had doused little Al with ice water, Al took another bucket of ice and water and doused the occupant of the booth. Out walked a red-faced but shivering John J. McGraw, who knew, of course, that the rookie had been duped.

John remembered Al as an eager little fellow who had run errands for him and the players at the Polo Grounds. He brought him and his useless arm to training camp, and Schacht was a barrel of fun even then. One day Al went the way of all baseball flesh and hitched a ride back to town. He was whistling and dangling his feet off the rear of the wagon contentedly when he looked over to see John walking the distance as part of his own training.

Al's gargoyle face broke into a wide grin. He waved. John waved back. Al held up one hand with his fingers extended—five times around the park, yes? John simply held up *both* hands with fingers extended—*ten* times around the park, positively!

"Was I lucky!" Al has recalled. "If he hadn't been wearing shoes, he'd have held up his fingers and toes—twenty times around the park!"

High spots of the 1917 training period, and augury of things to come, took place in Dallas, where John and Hugh Jennings had brought their teams for a big game of the New York–Detroit barnstorming trip. Ty Cobb was the American League's outstanding star and a prime gate attraction. Arriving late at the park, he kept 5,000 Dallas baseball fans waiting to see him in pregame practice. Most annoyed at this was Art Fletcher, who had become a spirited Giant in his own right from a shy, hesitant stenographer and business tyro. Before really entering baseball as a profession, Fletcher kept his job at Ingersoll-Rand in Illinois for two years in deference to his family. To join spring training, he would move up his summer vacation, and in order to play the first season in Dallas in 1908, he obtained a six-month leave of absence from his stenographic duties. He was a quiet boy and self-conscious, especially of his prominent chin. He had the Spalding people sew a special collar on his Giant uniform and he always played with the collar standing up to help hide his chin.

And here was this same ex-stenographer taking charge of the tardy American League firebrand in Dallas. Since Cobb had surrendered the 1916 batting championship to Tris Speaker after nine straight years, Fletcher went into an ex-champion routine at second base. Herzog embroidered the verbal attack at shortstop. Reaching first base on a pass, the enraged Cobb shouted, "I'm comin' down!"

He made good on the next pitch. Herzog took the throw and rolled into a cloud of Texas dust. Suffering a gashed thigh and shredded pants, Charlie leaped on Cobb, and the fight began. Fletcher dived in and caught a portion of Cobb's thinning hair. Both managers rushed out with other players and pulled their chattels apart.

John accosted Cobb in the Dallas hotel that evening and gave him a severe tongue-lashing publicly for his bush-league display of courage with spikes. Herzog went to Cobb's room later and almost suffered a broken back, according to reports (and this feud has many versions of varying accuracy), when Cobb bent him backward over the front of a bed. Cobb may have "won" that encounter, which was only a beginning, for Herzog and Fletcher intensified their verbal attacks.

"They're crazy," Cobb complained to Jennings. "And somebody may get killed."

Cobb was genuinely fearful that real harm might come out of the feud, because he had fought and beaten just about everybody except the Herculean Charlie Schmidt, Detroit catcher. The climax came at Wichita Falls, Texas, when Herzog, impatient for a show-down, entered Cobb's room again. Fletcher and little Benny Kauff waited outside the door while the greatest of baseball fights took place. Furniture was overturned and bedlam let loose as the punches flew for many minutes. There are several versions of the battle, and declarations of who "won."

"Nobody won," John always said. "There was no referee. Charlie came out of the room on his own power and played ball the next day."

Cobb left the tour, though not in fear. He went to Cincinnati and there finished his training, but each day's mail for the next two weeks brought him a post card from Fletcher, Herzog, or Kauff, carrying as much derision and sarcasm as the United States mails would permit.

Another high spot of the spring was John's fifth contract as manager of the Giants. Mr. Hempstead joined the team in the south, and they discussed another long-term arrangement. The World War was reaching a peak. Our military intervention was imminent. John needed a feeling of security in order to hold the team together and make postwar plans. The result was a five-year agreement at a comfortably high figure. The salary was exaggerated in the news reports out of Waco, Texas, but that was only because actual salaries of players and managers are never discussed officially.

More important, it gave the baseball world, and particularly the players, to understand that John McGraw was in sole charge of their destiny on the field.

The Giants kept up the fighting pitch throughout the year, hustling from start to finish. A left-hander, Ferdie Schupp, reached a one-season zenith with 21 victories, though he had threatened the year before by allowing less than an earned run a game in almost 150 innings. The outfield was fast and batted well. George Burns hit over .300 and stole 40 bases. Benny Kauff led the team with an average of .308 and Zimmerman batted close to .300. Defensively the infield, with Walter Holke at first, Herzog at second, Fletcher at short, and Zimmerman at third, was not only fast, but thoroughly experienced.

This team won John's sixth pennant in New York, and by a wide margin. War cast a cloud over the World Series, but it was a financial success. The White Sox won the first two in Chicago, and then Benton and Schupp pitched shutouts at the Polo Grounds. Returning to the west, the Sox won the fifth, and then the sixth in New York.

Both teams made costly errors of omission. Red Faber won three victories, but gained greater renown by trying to steal third base with Buck Weaver there waiting to score. In the last game, Heinie Zimmerman tried to run down the speedy Eddie Collins for a "boner," which it wasn't, John said, because Bill Rariden, our catcher, wasn't in position for Zimmerman's throw.

Nothing could ever make up for a defeat on the diamond, but John always thought Clarence Rowland, manager of the White Sox, came closest to it after the Series when he said publicly:

"John J. McGraw is the grandest man I ever met in baseball. He is the gamest sportsman and the best loser I ever saw and that's saying a lot. When it was practically assured that we would win, long about the eighth inning, John sent word over to me to keep my club together and leave the field in a body with the Giants. He explained that he wouldn't answer for what some of the disappointed New York fans might pull off if the players straggled out one at a time. I think that was one of the whitest acts I ever heard of, coming from a man that must have been bitterly disappointed."

The war curtailed the next season immediately after Labor Day. The Giants finished in second place behind the Boston Braves with a record low attendance of 256,000. Then baseball was forgotten until the war's end, which came two months later. One of everybody's favorite players and a Giant, Harvard Eddie Grant, was killed on the battlefield with the armistice only three weeks away. Many of the eligible players had entered the service, including managers. Christy Mathewson had resigned at Cincinnati to accept a commission in the Chemical Warfare Division.

Having seen the Giants through one of the roughest periods, Harry Hempstead expressed a desire to sell stock control of the club, which he voted for the heirs of his late father-in-law. John scurried around for buyers, particularly among his moneyed friends, for he considered the Giants a fine investment. I had thought so sixteen years before. My stock, bought at $1,000, was worth $3,000, and had always paid a dividend.

John talked to Harry Sinclair, the oil man, who had helped finance the Federal League. With this avenue not completely closed, he worked up considerable enthusiasm with George M. Cohan and Sam Harris. They were fabulously successful partners, theater owners, and baseball fans from way back. George had written the stirring hit song of the war, "Over There," and was starring in *A Prince There Was*. Both listened to the exciting situation and went into a serious huddle.

Meanwhile Magistrate Francis X. McQuade, long a friend of the Giant players and management and one of the earliest and hardest workers for Sunday baseball, wandered into the Astor Hotel. There he encountered a New York City police captain, William Peabody. Judge McQuade mentioned the fact that the Giants were for sale. Out of this meeting came a contact with Charles A. Stoneham the Wall Street broker, racer of horses on New York tracks, and a baseball fan.

Mr. Stoneham was a man of action, but never in his life did he move faster, for he had received a tip on the Giants from another source. Overnight he took the situation in hand, and the purchase went through almost before Cohan and Harris came out of their huddle.

But it was big business and the most valuable property in baseball. A million dollars obtained stock control of about 1,300 shares. Judge McQuade took 70 shares at a cost of $50,000. And John also bought 70 shares. These, plus my four, and a few shares that John obtained from Mr. Brush in 1910, made him a big-league club owner for the second time. With Mr. Stoneham as president, Judge McQuade was elected treasurer, and John was elected vice-president of the New York Giants.

That January evening we took the longest and most enjoyable hansom cab ride of our lives. We rode around and around and through Central Park for hours, it seemed. And it also seemed as if we were back in Druid Hill Park, Baltimore. The future seemed that rosy.

24

WITH THE WAR at an end and freedom everywhere a fact, southern climates and semitropical strands called in a voice that could be heard loudest in northern temperatures. Florida was discovered as a resort and playground, and the island of Cuba an oasis in every sense of the word. The prohibition movement, launched in Congress and the Senate during wartime in 1917, was heading toward national acceptance as the year 1919 opened. Cuba prepared in earnest for those who planned to evade liquor restrictions at the cost of international travel.

For many years we had enjoyed the hospitality of a Havana catering to visitors who drank in moderation. In our earlier visits John had discovered the daiquiri cocktail at La Florida restaurant on Monserrat and Obispo. He also discovered its congenial and sports-minded proprietor, Constantino Rabalaigua, who later became famous as a one-man judiciary for sports arguments. In John's honor the proprietor-bartender concocted a rum drink called "Jota Jota" (pronounced "hota") for John's initials, J. J. It is still sold today.

Wines and cocktails were part of gracious living in the United States before the first World War. I never sat at the celebrated "Round Table" at Jack's, on Sixth Avenue and 42nd Street, or patronized the notorious Battling Nelson bar up front, but I met hundreds who did. You would have to see and know and, hence, understand the place that alcoholic beverages in moderation occupied in American living during the early part of the century. Where overdone, it became a harmful nuisance in any walk of life.

Havana has always boasted a number of fine spots to dine, and I recall *El Sitio* (The Place) out toward the edge of the city and very early the *Dos Hermanos* (Two Brothers). There José Massaguer helped stage the testimonial dinner to John on the eve of his departure for the States in February, 1916.

The threat of prohibition in America altered this more or less simple mode of epicurean enjoyment. Cuba was suddenly host to a number of restaurateurs who simply transferred their places of business to Havana. One of these was an amiable Spaniard, José Abeal, of New Orleans. He located just around the corner from the American Club and welcomed a distinguished patron. We were more impressed by his *arroz con pollo*, made with less saffron than usual.

John teased the proprietor a lot, chiefly because of Señor Abeal's apparel. Center of attention was his *camisa*, or shirt, which José insisted was a *blusa*, or blouse. More important to John were the balloonlike sleeves, which José called *mangas*. Containing tucks and frills they flapped and were supposed to be colorful. To John they were a hazardous nuisance, especially when Señor Abeal's sweeping *manga* upset a glass.

"Take off those sleeves, Joe," John said impatiently. "How can you attract business when you keep slopping up the place with those sleeves?"

When José Abeal tried to laugh it off, John kept at him and called him Dirty Joe, or plain Sloppy Joe. At the American Club he talked about "going around to Sloppy Joe's." He invariably greeted José with, "How's Sloppy Joe tonight?" Soon the strangers began to appear and inquire timidly, "Is *this* Sloppy Joe's?"

And so it went, a simple kidding nickname that provided fun and laughter until Señor Abeal grew serious and created a crisis. He wanted to show appreciation by making John his permanent guest.

"Why, you'd go broke in a week," John scoffed. "I'd bring the whole American colony here every night and eat and drink you right out of business."

"But, John, listen—"

"You listen," John exclaimed. "Either I pay, or I don't come to your sloppy joint. I'll find a clean place!"

Abeal acquiesced as an alternative to possible anonymity. John continued visiting Sloppy Joe's and lived to see it have branches. Abeal has since passed on, but the famous bar continues, operated by three brothers-in-law of the original *El José Lodoso*.

While John McGraw may have gravitated to these characters a bit now and then, they never failed to find him. One of the best and most enjoyable in Havana was a two-gun scamp from Texas named H. D. "Curley" Brown. He had built race tracks and casinos in Texas, and he saw tremendous possibilities in Havana. The city saw possibilities in Curley, and let him build the Cuban-American Jockey Club. Hard by it, he built and operated a gambling casino, and then ran into difficulty.

At the trial he claimed it was self-defense. Speaking with a Texas drawl and considerable twang, he explained that this Alberto Piedra tried to collect what was called a "special tax," but to Brown it was a plain shakedown. When Alberto reached for a handkerchief, Curley moved faster. No one had ever outdrawn him in Texas, and no one was going to beat him to the gun in Havana. He let the tax collector have it. Unfortunately, the victim was the son-in-law of Juan Montalvo, former Secretary of State. Curley drew a three-year sentence. President Zayas pardoned him in early 1922 before the term had been served.

But his track went up for sale while John and his new boss, Charles A. Stoneham, were there, and that's how they took over the operation of a race track and casino. Neither of them really wanted it, but they enjoyed most afternoons there anyway. Why not buy? And so they did.

Even Christy Mathewson had a memorable visit to the track, though not in the ordinary sense. John staged a special race to see whether he or Christy could pick the faster mule, and for side bets. With the finish only a few yards away, Christy's mule was far ahead but happened to see an open gate that led to the stables. He stopped and turned. The jockey pulled his head and slapped his rump and dug his boot heels into the animal's ribs. But the mule wanted no more racing. While he stood there, trying to get out the gate, John's mule "thundered" down the stretch and across the finish line.

"Don't ever bet on mules, Mr. Mathewson," John cautioned and held out his hand for payment. "They're not reliable."

Christy returned from France in February and immediately went to work as coach of the Giants. John had hired Pat Moran, former manager of the Phillies, the previous year, but Pat became Cincinnati manager after the sale of the Giants, leaving the post open. John took the team to train at Gainesville, Florida, and there resumed an old friendship with Lou Burkhim, manager of the 1891 team of nomads.

Much has been written in previous pages about the factions for and against playing baseball for paid admissions on Sunday. New York, Brooklyn, Boston, Philadelphia, and Pittsburgh were the idle spots. New York led the way in removing the barrier after many years of seeing players or promoters arrested for taking up collections, or merely for playing benefit games.

A pivotal date in the development of Sunday baseball in New York State, April, 1918, is virtually unknown, for few have heard of it in relation to the statute. That was the day, however, when the following preceded the law first submitted to the Legislature:

To the Governor and Members
    of the Senate and Assembly,
State of New York
Gentlemen:

I hand you herewith copies of various interviews, letters, news comments and editorials of New York State newspapers, which are self-explanatory, relative to and having direct bearing upon Senate Bill Nos. 866, 1281, 1402, entitled

AN ACT TO AMEND THE PENAL LAW IN RELA-
TION TO GRANTING TO LOCAL AUTHORITIES
THE POWER TO REGULATE SPORTS ON SUNDAY.

Respectfully submitted,
ROBERT R. LAWSON
Ninth Senate District.

Behind the law by a Republican state senator from Brooklyn was a well-ordered survey of opinion from civic leaders, representative clergy, top officers of feminine groups, and letters of endorsement from mayors of many large cities throughout the nation. City Magistrate Francis X. McQuade, appearing before the Senate Committee, said in part:

"I appear here today to voice my sentiments in favor of Senator Lawson's bill permitting Sunday baseball. I have been a city magistrate for the past seven years and during that time a great many violators of Section 2145 of the penal laws have been arraigned before me.

"Can you conceive of a law which would make your son a criminal just because he batted a baseball in an open lot on a Sunday afternoon? Can you think of anything that we might do on the Sabbath that would tend to uplift the morals of the community any better than the playing of a baseball game? Whether an admission fee is charged or not does not make any difference."

John McGraw and Christy Mathewson were arrested for playing a benefit baseball game at the Polo Grounds for an admission, in August, 1917, and hauled before Judge McQuade. He not only dismissed them, but denounced the law to arresting officers.

But the Lawson Bill, approved and ready for passing, never came up for vote. Later in the year it was evident that Republican Governor Whitman would be succeeded by Democratic Al Smith, and he was, on November 5. Republican Bob Lawson lost out in the Ninth District, too.

Immediately after the first of the year, the substance of the bill was reintroduced under the sponsorship of Democratic Senator James J. Walker, and put through both Senate and Assembly as the "Walker Sunday Baseball Law." Governor Smith signed the bill. The pen used for signing was affixed to an engrossed resolution of congratulations and thanks and presented to Magistrate McQuade by the Governor. New York City's first Sunday baseball game was held at the Polo Grounds on May 4, 1919, before 36,000 delighted fans. Magistrate McQuade threw out the first ball, which he retained.

Eventually McQuade became a bitter critic of John McGraw in the Giants' board meetings, in public, and in the press. Feelings became harsh and ugly, and we were hurt deeply at times, but it could not alter the fact and record that Judge McQuade foresaw the benefit of Sunday baseball and had the courage to fight for his convictions. Whether it was the Lawson Law or the Walker Law, the public and the club owners and the players have since profited immeasurably because of it.

Though the Yankees drew only 6,000 fans for their first Sunday game two weeks later, baseball attendance at the Polo Grounds for both clubs was trebling. The two Colonels, Ruppert and Huston, had lured little Miller Huggins from St. Louis in the National League a year before, and were ready to spend a fortune in a postwar race for playing strength. Since the military had decimated the sand lots and minor leagues, scouting for players meant nothing. There was only one answer: pay money for the best.

The St. Louis Cardinals had gone through the wringer during the war. Mrs. Schuyler Britton had sold the club to a group of civic-minded citizens organized by Branch Rickey, who had then served in France with the Chemical Warfare Division, Mathewson's outfit. The plight of the 1919 Cardinals was best depicted by Rickey himself before the Celler Committee at Washington, D.C., October, 1951. The following is from Rickey's testimony during the study on monopoly power:

"Now, it is not a joy continuously to experience the emotions of defeat. I did not like it. But there was nothing I could do about it. We had a park for which we had paid $175,000, by selling stock in a new corporation to the citizenship of St. Louis. We owed $175,000. And we finished in last place in 1918. And I said to myself, 'What can I do about it? I have no money. We have a reserve list of twenty-three players,' only three of whom were with the club two years later, for they did not rate. Clubs usually finish last on merit, because they do not have enough good players.

" 'How can I, then, get more players? I have no money. I have an acquaintanceship in college circles, because I had been the coach of a large university for some years.'

"I was nonplused about it. And Mr. McGraw came to me and threw on the table a beautiful deal, where he would give me five men, and he would take Hornsby. And he even wrote out the batting order for me, how my team would line up."

John failed in this first attempt to get Hornsby, who was far from being an outstanding player at the time. He had played three seasons with the Cardinals, compiling batting averages of .313, .327, and .281. His high promise was obvious to the trained baseball mind, and he was the one, John assured his new boss, Charles Stoneham, to form the core of a winner. If Rickey wouldn't take five players for Hornsby, certainly badly needed cash would do the trick. The second meeting took place after a Polo Grounds game and in the back room of a café on Broadway just below 125th Street. In attendance were Rickey and a New York banking friend, Mr. Stoneham and John.

John explained that the new owner of the Giants and his associates were anxious to bring a star to the Polo Grounds and take advantage of a postwar surge of interest, ensure Sunday attendance, and so on. Hornsby seemed like a good bet, though a gamble. The Giants were ready to transfer a considerable chunk of capital to St. Louis in exchange for the player in question. Everybody would be better off.

"We'll pay a hundred thousand dollars!" Stoneham said.

Rickey seemed unimpressed. After an appropriate pause the offer was raised to $150,000. Here the parties fell into a discussion of tangibles and otherwise, a sort of stall on both sides. Mr. Stoneham's patience began to drain low. He was ready to go higher, but he certainly wanted a little reaction to the dollars being tossed around. Suddenly he jumped the offer to $200,000, a sum that represented 20 per cent of what he had paid to own the Giants.

"I don't think I can take it," Rickey demurred, and the reply was exasperating.

"Well, will you take two hundred and fifty thousand?" Stoneham exclaimed.

"No—"

"What do you mean no?" Mr. Stoneham demanded. "What will your stockholders think when they hear you've turned down a quarter of a million dollars for *one* player?"

"I don't know," Rickey replied. "I don't see how they could be pleased. That amount would get us into the clear. But I'll tell you what I'll do."

All remained silent and expectant as the thirty-eight-year-old Rickey paused.

"You have a player I'd like," Rickey continued.

"I think that can be arranged," John said.

"Not so fast, Mr. McGraw," Rickey cautioned. "This is a young player. I doubt that you know he's on your club, though I suppose you do. He's green and he's only played a few games."

"Who is it and what about him?" Stoneham asked impatiently.

"His name is Frisch," Rickey said, "and I'll give you fifty thousand dollars for him right now—"

"What's going on here!" Mr. Stoneham exclaimed. "You haven't got fifty thousand dollars. You haven't got a quarter, Rickey. What are you trying to do, insult us?"

Stoneham had lost almost all his patience. He didn't know that Rickey would "pay for" Frisch out of money obtained for Hornsby. Stoneham was using his own money, lots of it, and here was the head of an impoverished ball club, working as both president and manager and getting paid for neither job, offering a fortune he didn't have. And McGraw had spoken so highly of this Rickey, too.

"Look, this is the last!" Mr. Stoneham said, leaning over a table which they surrounded. "I'll give you two hundred and fifty thousand dollars cash for Hornsby, and you can keep him till the end of the season. If the Giants are lucky enough to win the pennant, we'll add another fifty thousand to the price."

John said quickly, "You can't do that, Charlie!"

"Don't tell me what I can't do!" the harassed man exclaimed.

"Charlie, you've got me wrong," John soothed. "I meant about Hornsby playing against us and then making an additional payment."

It was instinctive to a ballplayer. It would be easy for a businessman to understand anywhere but under the harassing conditions of this, his first player deal. Calm was quickly restored, and the offer pegged at $250,000. Rickey talked around the point of the young player, Frisch, but John wanted no part of that. His hopes for the twenty-year-old Fordham athlete were high and he was very much aware of his presence on the team. Finally the meeting broke up with cool pleasantries and no results beyond the exchange of two second-stringers.

The next day's *Evening Sun* carried the headline over a story by Wilbur Wood stating:

GIANTS OFFER $300,000 FOR ROGERS HORNSBY

It couldn't be denied, but few believed such fantastic figures. Presently John began to scheme all the harder, because the Yankees had made their first bold move in the purchase of Carl Mays, one of the American League's best pitchers. The Red Sox received about one-fourth the sum offered for Hornsby. This was confirmation of John's suspicions: a major deal between the moneyed Yankees and the Boston Red Sox, which had been bought on long-term credit three years before by Harry Frazee, the theatrical producer.

This deal was worked out through the fall and announced early in January, 1920. The Yankees paid Frazee $525,000, of which $125,000 was for baseball's home-run king, Babe Ruth, once of St. Mary's Industrial Home for Boys, at Wilkens Avenue and Caton, Baltimore. The $400,000 was regarded as a loan, secured by a mortgage on Fenway Park. It would be "paid off" in the future. Since that kind of money from gate receipts alone was in the realm of the impossible, John was pessimistic.

"It means that little by little," he sighed, "Frazee's whole team, or the best part of it, will wind up in the Polo Grounds as Yankees right under our noses. And seven years ago Hempstead and I thought they'd use our ball park just for one season!"

25

OF THE ENDLESS challenges that crammed John McGraw's baseball life, those arriving with the 1920 decade were greatest. Each in itself was an emergency, and as a group they comprised a backbreaking burden that made a servant of his mind day and night. And he was not yet fifty.

His first responsibility, of course, was to baseball through competition on the field, and secondly to Charles A. Stoneham, who had assumed corporate control of the Giants. It was a financial risk as well as an investment. The bankruptcy of Charles W. Somers is a tragic example. He had helped finance the American League, and it survived because he had backed two clubs. But he failed for two million dollars in 1915. With him sank his Cleveland baseball team, minor-league clubs, and his Great Lakes shipping and mining interests.

Though the Federal League "surrendered," after 1915, the settlement terms were a drain on organized baseball's financial resources through the World War period. Branch Rickey's plight at St. Louis in 1919 was not unusual, and few had Hornsbys to sell. Unable to interest new capital, second-division clubs depended solely upon paid admissions to exist. And some simply couldn't.

Baseball helped itself a little as 1920 began by raising admission prices to a point commensurate with postwar operating costs. Bleacher tickets went to 50 cents. A rise in per-capita assessment to the visiting club was an invitation to replace these benches steadily with regular seats calling for a higher tariff. Admission to the pavilion, or covered bleachers, was put at 75 cents, with general admission $1.00. Box seats were $1.50 and $2.00, with "war tax" of 10 per cent added. Today it exists as amusement tax.

Prosperity in New York benefited all clubs. All baseball suffered from the lack of it. Higher attendance meant greater revenue to the visiting team, but the "spending war" staged by the two Polo Grounds clubs did much to keep at least three or four of the foundering afloat. The sale of one player for $50,000 in those days could do it. The transfer of money for players never affected the rugged character of competition on the field. In fact, the players sent to a second-division club from the Giants occasionally caused John to mutter petulantly, "Why didn't he play that way for *me?*"

When John failed to get Hornsby in 1919, he traded the contract of Ferdie Schupp, the southpaw pitcher, to Rickey for that of big Frank Snyder, a catcher. Snyder hit only .250, but Schupp won sixteen games for Rickey the next year, one of his best. Had he remained and pitched that way for the Giants in 1920, they'd have won the pennant.

Another result of failing to land Hornsby was the purchase of Arthur Nehf, the left-handed pitcher, from the Boston Braves in late 1919 for a considerable sum. Nehf's record with a poor club was fair. It improved when supported by good defense and hitting.

The popular belief that John McGraw "bought" pennants can be refuted in a paragraph or two. Buying a pennant would naturally mean buying star players. He bought only *three* recognized stars, and no two in the same season. The first was Dave Bancroft, the shortstop, in early June, 1920. He sent Art Fletcher and Wilbur Hubbell, a right-handed pitcher, to Philadelphia with considerable cash. Fletcher lost his father and brother after the 1920 season and remained out of baseball a year.

Bancroft proved his value three weeks after joining the Giants by hitting six singles in six times at bat against three pitchers on his old Philadelphia team. He hit either left-handed or right, depending upon the type of pitching. He was an intelligent, resourceful playmaker, and capable of giving John as good a game of three-cushion billiards as any nonprofessional.

In July of the following year, John gave a pitcher, a catcher, an outfielder, and cash to Philadelphia for Emil "Irish" Meusel, an outfielder who hit right-handed, but hit hard and often. As outfield insurance, he obtained thirty-year-old Casey Stengel, also from Philadelphia, for a few younger players.

Six months later he brought back little Heinie Groh, the third baseman, from Cincinnati. Heinie had been with him as a rookie in 1912. To get him back John gave a fortune to the Reds and then paid Groh a very high salary. Henry was a steady .300 hitter at Cincinnati, but never as a Giant. In fact, he was quite disappointing in his first year at the Polo Grounds, 1922.

While Bancroft, Meusel, and Groh were key players, they were a minor part of the whole team, numerically and otherwise. John built his record-breaking Giants with care and amazing patience and essentially with rookies, like Earl Smith, the catcher; George Kelly, who was a long time "arriving," as was Ross "Pep" Youngs. Both Young (the *s* was seldom used) and Kelly were rookies with the Giants in 1917 and had to be optioned for experience. Frank Frisch came out of Fordham in 1919 on the recommendation of Arthur Devlin. He pinch-hit for Hal Chase on June 17, against Grover Alexander, and failed in a losing cause. A week later Heinie Zimmerman got married, and Frank replaced the benedict at third base for his first play in a Giant uniform.

Three stars, a half-dozen rookies coaxed and coddled and taught, a few veteran pitchers, and a veritable parade of trials and tribulations—those were John McGraw's Giants of 1920–21–22.

Second in importance to producing a strong and colorful winning team of Giants was the necessity of keeping that team in the eyes of the public, and keeping the eyes of the public on the team. This has been erroneously attributed to John's so-called ego and desire for the limelight. Spectators pay to see a good and colorful team, never a manager.

Corporate survival in baseball depended upon paid attendance. Victories were the best panacea for an empty ball park, but the New York sports writers were the liaison between team and public. Prior to 1920 virtually all of them followed the Giants. Newspapers could not afford to assign a staff man to both teams, and sometimes not even to the Giants.

Baseball has long made a practice of inviting writers to accompany teams to spring training and for road trips at club expense. Most papers accept this hospitality, though some do not. To the club it is merely an expenditure that otherwise would be earmarked for display advertising in those papers. More important, it carries no obligation, for the baseball correspondents write and publish unbridled opinions, and I can say that again. But it is healthier this way. The public would and should distrust any writer who withholds a legitimate news story for any reason. Breaking a confidence of manager or club official, of course, is in another realm.

Prior to 1920 the Yankees would take a road trip with one sports writer sending back different stories to six or more New York newspapers. The Giants went west with a full complement of top-name writers. The arrival of Babe Ruth at the Polo Grounds changed all this. He was a big daily story, and the new spending policy of the two colonels, Ruppert and Huston, promised headline material. A sharp division of by-line sports writers followed. Presently the Giants were struggling for sports-page limelight that had been theirs exclusively for nearly twenty years.

Babe Ruth simply took over the headlines in 1920 by hitting at least one home run every third day to total 54 for the year. His batting average was .376. The next year he did even better by totaling 59 home runs, and hitting for an average of .378. And in 1920 the third-place Yankees outdrew the second-place Giants at the Polo Grounds by more than 100,000 paid admissions!

I go to such length because all three top executives of the Giants —Mr. Stoneham, John, and Judge McQuade—have been unfairly

Managers McGraw and Rowland at the opening of the 1917 World Series in Comiskey Park, Chicago.

Andy Reese struggling to pass catcher Hartnett while Clyde Beck tags him to prevent tying run in key game of 1928 pennant race. "No interference," ruled Umpire Bill Klem, left.

charged with "ordering" the Yankees out of the Polo Grounds. Being minority shareholders, neither John nor Judge McQuade could do any ordering out. Mr. Stoneham owned the club. The situation was obvious to all concerned. It had been a touchy problem in meetings between the two leagues, long before Mr. Stoneham became owner. As an indication of this, I quote a story by Sid Mercer, published early in 1920.

Plans for a modern baseball stadium with a seating capacity of at least 40,000 are now being considered by officials of the New York American League Club, and building operations may be under way within a very short time, so that the Yankees will be assured of a home of their own next season.

The site of the new plant was selected by Colonel Jacob Ruppert several years ago. It is in Long Island City, just beyond the Queensboro Bridge Plaza, where traffic flows in and out of Manhattan and Long Island. The Yankees would have been playing there long ago but for the war which halted building operations.

The semi-official announcement that the Polo Grounds would be played exclusively by National League teams after this season is not a surprising development. A separation of the two local clubs has been forecast ever since control of the Giants passed into the hands of Charles A. Stoneham, John J. McGraw and Judge McQuade last winter. Propositions by Colonels Ruppert and Huston to maintain the Yankees at the Polo Grounds under a long-term lease have been turned down politely but firmly. Without desiring to be discourteous to a business rival, the men who operate the National League team want the place to themselves. The Giants have long been an institution in New York and would be in danger of losing their identity as the "home team" if they should encounter a bad season while the Yankees were winning.

Probably one of the conditions that convinced the owners of the Giants that the American League should no longer be identified with the Polo Grounds was the idleness of McGraw's team on two Sundays while the Yanks were playing to big crowds here. Sunday attendance has been averaging crowds of 22,000. A week ago the Giants laid off in Blue-Law Boston while the Red Sox appeared at the Polo Grounds, and yesterday they Sundayed in Philadelphia idleness while Walter Johnson entertained a large crowd here. Of course, the Yankees have this idleness problem when the Giants are home, but the Giants own the park.

Not until two years later did the Yankees obtain satisfactory grounds, and they located just across the Harlem River on the old Astor Estate land, which was one of the parcels tied up by Andrew Freedman twenty years before. Thereon rose the great Yankee Stadium, thanks to three prosperous years, 1920–21–22, at the Polo Grounds. Just as John and his associates had believed and predicted, everybody was better off, competitively and financially.

While Brooklyn and Cleveland decided the World Series, John was completing his exhibition schedule for Cuba. Adding Babe Ruth, whose 54 home runs made him the outstanding attraction, guaranteed success for the 1920 Cuban trip. Operation of the race track and the nearby casino added to the fun and the excitement.

We had the most laughter and relaxation in our rooms at the Chibas Apartments that year. Not far away were John Lobert and his wife. They had made the trip around the world. Lobert was known as "Hans" because he resembled Hans Wagner somewhat, though Lobert would always add, "Until I pick up the bat." He had been a fine and aggressive player, and John liked him as a warm, shrewd, and humorous fellow with a deep sense of loyalty.

It was at the Chibas Apartments that John McGraw somehow found a Chinese chef named Ching, though he and Hans always referred to him as "Solly no lice." He was an exceptional cook and co-operative, and he would make any recipe delicious. Obeying my secret instructions to minimize starches, he never cooked enough rice. At almost every meal Ching had to apologize, "Solly, no mo' lice." With this, John and Hans would come close to hysterics and forget their appetites.

They taught Ching to cook corned beef and cabbage, and for the two winters he served us, that delicacy made us the envy of the American colony. John's heated arguments with the immigration officials in his two-year effort to get Ching into the United States made him frustrated and furious.

"How did he get in here?" John would demand. "And how will he get out? You can't keep a man like this prisoner!"

They explained the laws and clauses of the exclusion act over and over to him, but all John could think about was having Ching cook in our new home on Edgewood Avenue, in Pelham, New York. But there was no way of getting him out of Cuba legally. John was swamped with "friendly" offers to spirit Ching across the gulf for $500, but he always fought off the temptation, thank goodness.

The Havana and Almendares teams were no match for the Giants, especially with Babe Ruth hitting long drives for the Giants. John tried to even things by having George Kelly pitch against Palmero, Hernandez, Fabre, and Acosta, but the Americans won almost every day. The fans didn't care. They turned out in large numbers to see "Los Hee–gantes" and "El Bambeeno," as they called them.

Another source of enjoyment were the Sunday specials at Oriental Park, "our" race track. I don't know what humans had raced against horses in Cuba before. Two great Olympic sprinters, Chet Bowman and Jesse Owens, ran against them later. Hans Lobert would race anything. He had been one of baseball's fastest runners. In the great field day at Cincinnati in 1910, when Sheldon Lejeune made the record baseball throw, Lobert circled the bases in record time, 13 4/5 seconds.

Though nearly forty, he raced a motorcycle and later a thoroughbred horse. He also ran against a mule. He never lost, because he knew exactly how much handicap to take or give from a standing start. It all added up to fun by day.

At night there was fun at the casino, and John presented all the wives of the guests with a green chip worth $25 to start on. A few smart girls simply cashed the chip and watched. There was good food and excellent music at the casino, but I could never get John to dance more than once around the floor, and then only if the band would play "When Irish Eyes Are Smiling." His stiff collar would wilt and he'd beg off with, "It's just not for me, Blanche."

He never got enough of a favorite song. He would listen to it over and over again. Chauncey Olcott was a distinguished singer, especially of Irish ballads, but John would simply order him to sing "When Irish Eyes, etc." and poor Chauncey obeyed. The two Macs, John McCormack and his manager, Dennis Mc-Sweeney, visited us often. The golden tenor voice was at John's disposal for any of the classics from his father's native soil, but unless McCormack first sang "When Irish Eyes," there was no concert. They seemed to love him for his audacity.

John had a special friend, Frank Belcher, a basso profundo from the Lambs Club. Frank had been a vaudeville soloist and his specialty was "Philadelphia in the Morning." When he retired from vaudeville and an occasional Victor Herbert operetta, Frank became a prosperous cigar salesman. His prosperity, I hasten to add, stemmed chiefly from a nonsmoker, John McGraw, who bought thousands of dollars worth of cigars every year from Frank. If you were a friend of John's, you knew where to buy your cigars . . . or else.

In this way, John always had his favorite singer available. Frank had a range for whatever distance, long or short, you wished the song to be heard. His booming basso could rattle windows, or hum with a kitten's purr. And while he sang, no man in the world was happier than John McGraw.

Of course, his pride in Belcher's singing provoked the needlers to action, and Judge McQuade used little Jimmy Flynn as a rival to Belcher. Flynn, a hunchback, plugged songs professionally—on the stage, at the six-day bike races in the old Madison Square Garden, and anywhere a song could be made popular. He enjoyed competing against Belcher when Judge McQuade paid him to stir up a little good-natured trouble with ballads in silvery tones that often moved his listeners to tears. Then the men would guess aloud that this was certainly better than any bass voice. Why, he could outsing poor Frank Belcher the best day or night. . . . John McGraw either settled the matter then or stalked from the presence of such tone-deaf idiots.

Frank was a middle-aged bachelor, rather portly, with dark hair and large, soulful brown eyes. John used to plague him unmercifully about his chronic bachelorhood, and why he should do something about it. Frank responded to a dinner invitation one Thanksgiving Day at Edgewood Avenue. After the meal, John began teasing about his bachelor state and finally said sharply, "Just why is it you *won't* get married, Frank?"

"I am married," Belcher replied solemnly.

"When did you get married?"

"This morning." He reached into his pocket. "Here's the certificate."

For once John McGraw was speechless. He examined the fresh document with unbelieving eyes. Then he turned on his old friend savagely.

"You fool! Where's your wife? Why didn't you bring her here?"

"You didn't invite her," Frank said quite soberly. "I'm joining her a little while after dinner—"

John rose quickly, and both of us packed him off as fast as we could to join his poor bride of a few hours.

Moments of the annual Cuban excursions were frivolous at times, and intentionally so. This type of holiday was never more necessary than during the fall and winter of 1920–21. The first three months of the previous baseball season had brought the shocking realization that Mathewson was sick. Long before Christy went to the specialist in July, John was pacing our bedroom floor at night, telling himself, sometimes aloud, that the steady and deepening cough wasn't true. Christy had done a good coaching job on the Giants with Jeff Tesreau. He belonged in the Polo Grounds, both as a symbol of the deathless past and as a silent spur in the hide of any player who failed to hustle.

But the doctor said that Christy must drop his work and move with his family to Saranac Lake in upper New York State. He would get better, with care, rest, and the fighting heart that had turned the tide of so many losing battles. The reassurance failed to relieve John's emotional strain the rest of the season, for Christy was not yet forty!

Hughie Jennings resigned his job at Detroit on October 15, and became a Giant coach two weeks later. It was a good business deal for both, but it also brought the two old Orioles together again. Dan Brouthers was a Polo Grounds watchman. Wilbert Robinson had just signed a three-year contract with Charlie Ebbets. They formed the nucleus of the visiting old Orioles who called on Willie Keeler once each year in Brooklyn where he was confined to his sister's house by a bad heart.

The cares mounted, professional, financial, and personal. I was glad we had taken over the large house in Pelham. I was happier buying a lot of furniture and hanging curtains and making a new and comfortable home for a man deeply concerned over the misfortunes of his old friends. Buying furniture for ten more rooms was fun, but also a problem. Our master bedroom was very large. Adjoining was a dressing room and double bath. The furniture looked lost and so I bought two beautiful twin beds, which helped fill the room.

"What happened to the bed?" John asked.

"Well, John, it seemed that the two beds—"

"Send them back. Get the other bed."

"But I've bought and paid for these!"

"Give 'em away. Get the other bed."

He turned and walked off, leaving me no alternative. It was quite a job, returning the twin beds and getting less than I paid for them, and then paying a premium to buy back the double bed as a valuable antique!

Our first formal gathering at the new Pelham home resulted from a casual invitation to the new commissioner of baseball, Kenesaw Mountain Landis. As a young Ohio-born Indiana lawyer, Landis got a political start through appointment as secretary to Walter Q. Gresham, a power in Indiana affairs, who had been Secretary of the Treasury under President Arthur. Gresham became Secretary of State under Cleveland in 1893 and hired Landis, a Democrat. Sometime later Landis saw fit to become a Republican, and President Theodore Roosevelt saw fit to appoint him to the federal bench for the Northern District, Illinois, in 1905, at an annual salary of $6,000.

Landis had handled the Federal League litigation with wisdom and understanding in 1916. His knowledge of baseball and forthright decisions on the bench made him a natural selection for the one-man job of supervising organized baseball. Supervision was deemed necessary and wise after it was learned that eight of the Chicago White Sox had conspired to lose the 1919 World Series to the Cincinnati Reds. This was the lowest blow that baseball ever received. John felt wretched over the inexcusable weakness of players, and worse at the thought that it had affected his friends. The pioneering Charles Comiskey owned the White Sox, and an old Oriole teammate, Kid Gleason, was manager. John had engineered the managing job with Cincinnati for Pat Moran.

John saw the Landis election as a move to strengthen central authority over both leagues in baseball. Not long after the new commissioner took over, John said publicly:

"I am convinced that the greatest constructive baseball move of recent years was the placing of authority in the hands of a commissioner—and making Judge Kenesaw M. Landis that commissioner."

Of course, the dinner to Judge Landis at Pelham had nothing to do with official baseball. John and Brandon Tynan, the actor, saw to that. Conversation was mostly about the old days, on the stage and ball field, in both New York and Chicago, where Landis had struggled as a discouraged young attorney at the turn of the century.

The evening was a success from start to finish, and I'm sure the real reason was a gem in the kitchen, Mildred Jefferson, our new colored cook. She had pride in achievement, and her physical appearance was a living advertisement of her skill. She was assisted by a tall and gangling colored boy, Edward James, who tempered John's disappointment over failing to get Ching out of Cuba. John found him in San Antonio, or perhaps he found John. Edward was barely sixteen, but his height and sober face made him seem much older. He could drive a car and do just about anything asked of him. More important, he was always willing, regardless of the day or hour.

Mildred and Edward converted the house into a perpetual mecca for our ever widening circle of friends. John found intelligent off-field companionship in Dave Bancroft, whose sense of humor was keen. I think John laughed more with "Banny" than any other player, and Dave's laughter was strident and piercing. His wife, Edna, was the best of company. At the time of their marriage in 1910, Dave was just past eighteen and I believe Edna wasn't quite seventeen.

The night owl, though, was Charles Stengel, whom everybody called Casey, because he was born in Kansas City. He was a bachelor during his three seasons as substitute outfielder with the Giants, and treated John as one. They talked through countless nights in the kitchen. What on earth they gabbed about I never learned. Each blamed the other. John confided that Casey could talk your head off. In the morning Casey would pay tribute to

John's old baseball stories, and how he couldn't get a word in edgeways.

Of course, it was just an excuse to stay up all night. They spent most of the time in the kitchen, because it was nearer the food. Casey liked to cook bacon and scrambled eggs, which he did two or three times a night, and John liked to eat them. Truxton, the Airedale, did all right, too. In the morning Mildred would open the food chest first thing, shake her head, and telephone Weisbecker's market for supplies, muttering:

"The peas are gone again. How can that Mr. Stengel eat so many raw peas?"

New York City became the capital of the baseball world in 1921, when the Yankees and Giants duplicated the 1906 feat of the White Sox and Cubs in Chicago. The Yankees finished their season in New York and became sentimental favorites while the landlords were out on the road, struggling to overcome an insurmountable lead held by the Pirates. The high spot of the year came when the Giants rose to the occasion and won a succession of victories. The shock to Barney Dreyfuss may be gauged by the fact that he had already built special bleachers and field boxes to accommodate his first World Series crowd since 1909.

But John took greater delight in telephoning Saranac Lake after Pittsburgh games. In the quiet of his room at the Schenley Hotel, John painted a play-by-play picture with words: "You never saw such hitting, Christy ... everybody.... Yesterday Smith caught and murdered the ball.... Today I put in Snyder against Cooper and he hit.... Kelly'll hit over three hundred this year.... Imagine that, Christy.... Remember how he was laughed out of the park five and six years ago, and how old uncle Bill Lange begged me not to give up?...

"It was Nehf again today.... He pitched like a master, Christy. ... We can take this Pittsburgh crowd sure now.... Frisch and Young both hit today.... Frisch has really made it.... Bancroft pulled a beauty on Charlie Grimm.... We've beaten Cooper and Adams and Hamilton.... They don't have much left.... We'll pitch Toney tomorrow.... Call you tomorrow night.... Take it easy.... Tell Jane hello ... and young Christy...."

And after the pennant had been clinched, all New York turned out to fill the Polo Grounds in tribute to the absent Christy

Mathewson. It was his day, and all receipts were turned over to the Giant immortal, not as charity, for Christy had saved and invested his money wisely. It was simply part payment for what he had meant to fans, to players, to manager and management, and totaled $52,500. What Christy had meant to baseball and the Giants could never be paid for with cash.

The 1921 World Series was the third in succession and last to be decided on a basis of five out of nine. It was the first with Commissioner Landis in full control, and the Yankees had full control of the Giants in the first two games. Carl Mays held them to five hits (Frisch got four) and no runs in the first game. Waite Hoyt pitched a two-hit shutout in the second.

Then the flood gates opened, and the Giants took control. They hammered four Yankee pitchers for twenty hits and thirteen runs, eight of which came in the seventh inning. Phil Douglas beat Mays in the fourth game, squaring the series. Nehf lost another close one to Hoyt, but the Giants took the last three on timely hitting and superb pitching by Fred Toney and Jess Barnes, then by Douglas and finally Nehf.

All attendance and financial records were broken. More than 250,000 paid over $900,000 to see the eight games. Each Giant received $5,265, and each Yankee $3,510. The share to the Commissioner's office was enough to pay the Landis salary of $50,000 for two and a half years. Both New York clubs drew a bonanza in profits, for the players shared only in the first five games, the number necessary for victory.

This was the second profitable year of the new Giant dynasty, and there was no doubt about the superiority of John McGraw's team. It was a strong club offensively and defensively and lacked only outstanding pitching to make it one of the greatest. Nehf was the "stopper," but the right-handers could win the big games. During the next few years John searched all over, tried countless prospects and veterans. He traded on hopes and hunches, but failed to find the pitching strength he sought.

The Giants of 1921–22–23 won because they could outhit the opposition and back up their spotty pitching with defense as accurate and speedy as the Polo Grounds ever saw—infield, outfield, and behind the plate. They had no fear of right-handed or left-handed pitching. Two of the game's best switch hitters, Bancroft and Frisch, gave the batting order unusual offensive mobility. Two experienced catchers could be alternated, because Earl Smith batted left-handed and Frank Snyder right.

The Yankees won the American League pennant in their last season at the Polo Grounds, 1922, after a hard fight with the best of all St. Louis Browns teams, spear-headed by George Sisler, who batted a record .420. On the day before the first game, John went to the clubhouse and had one, brief, heart-to-heart talk with his players. He said:

"You can beat these fellows. I don't think there is any question about it. We have a big advantage in that they are favorites. Not once since we started our last drive have you pitchers failed to come through when called on, and the rest of the team has backed you up. You can do it just as well in this series. All you've got to do is play ball just as if you were playing a regular game in mid-season. There is no difference. The team that gets impressed with the idea there is a difference will become self-conscious and lose.

"All I ask you is, forget those odds of seven to five against you. Those figures merely represent the opinions of the sports writers. Get out there and play baseball just as you have all season. I'll do the directing and if anything goes wrong, I'll take the responsibility."

The favored Yankees were outpitched, outhit, and outplayed in a manner that is unbelievable today. Little Art Nehf beat them in the first and last games, though not easily. Jack Scott, a veteran, and young Hugh McQuillan, both right-handers obtained after the start of the season, won the other games. The Yankees didn't win at all. They came no closer than a ten-inning, 3–3 tie, and many writers called it a victory in four straight, first since 1914.

"I signaled for every ball that was pitched to Babe Ruth," John recalled and always with delight. "In fact, I gave the sign for practically every ball our pitchers threw. They preferred that I do it. It was no secret. You could see Snyder or Smith turn and look at the bench before signing to the pitcher.

"This was not done in any slipshod or guesswork manner. We pitched only nine curves and three fast balls to Ruth throughout the series. All the rest were slow balls, sometimes called change-ups. Of those twelve pitches, eleven of them set the big fellow on his ear. He got one foul. And we usually crossed him up by curving with men on bases. He got only two hits in seventeen times at bat, and the whole team of Yankee sluggers made but eleven runs in forty-six innings.

"Best of all was the new play we pulled on them. It was a cut-off play, the Bancroft cutoff, because he was ideal to pull it. With a runner in scoring position, usually at second, and a base hit to the outfield, the fielder whipped the ball in hard as though throwing to the plate to prevent the run. But the throw was always low, and right at Banny. He caught it, conceded the run, and played for the hitter rounding first or heading for second. We broke up three dangerous rallies that way. We caught Bob Meusel in the last game with it, and won the game by trapping Wally Schang on it a few minutes later."

Success and complete domination of baseball brought John a five-year contract, which, with record salary and bonus, made his annual income thoroughly commensurate with his unparalleled position in the game.

Though his team-building was closer to perfection than ever, John McGraw dared think of replacements. He not only thought of them; he planned them, and far in advance. An episode in Memphis, Tennessee, where the Giants stopped for a traditional exhibition game in April, 1922, is an example. John answered a knock on his door at the old Peabody Hotel, and there stood a living declaration of independence, William Harold Terry, twenty-three, of Memphis. Discouraged with pitching minor-league baseball, he had taken a job making storage batteries and then with an oil company, played independent ball, and bought a home for his pretty wife at 204 South Willett Street. Kid Elberfeld, manager of Little Rock signed him in late 1921, and then Terry changed his mind. He just didn't want to be a minor leaguer. Elberfeld "sold" his contract to John, with explanations. After a brief greeting, John said:

"They tell me you're a great hitter."

"Did they also tell you I'm a great pitcher?" Terry countered.

"Never mind the pitching," John scoffed. Then he confided:

"I'd like you to play at Toledo. Roger Bresnahan is the manager and part owner. He's the boss. He's one of my oldest friends. He knows more baseball than you'll ever learn. I'm going to have a first-base problem in New York sooner or later. Work hard at it and don't worry about advancement. I'll have you up as soon as I can. Is that all right?"

It was all right, and they shook hands. Terry played the position and hit well. He fought off the urge to pitch. The next year he was outstanding with a last-place club. He was the best defensive first baseman in the Association and hit .377. Bresnahan gave up control of the club in midseason, and George Whitted, the outfielder, managed. When he quit in August, John telegraphed during the heat of his own big-league pennant race and recommended Terry as manager for the rest of the season. Terry actually ran the Toledo team for several weeks in 1923, and then reported to the Polo Grounds. He played two games at first base and pinch-hit once.

During 1922 John paid a high price for the best prospect in the Pacific Coast League, Jimmy O'Connell, a twenty-year-old outfielder. He paid another large sum to his old friend, Jack Dunn, successful owner-manager of the Baltimore Orioles, for John Bentley, another left-handed pitcher who could hit well. He paid Kid Elberfeld very little for a spindly jack-rabbit infielder named Travis Jackson, who was only eighteen when he wore his first Giant uniform. But this was ancient compared with the pink-cheeked Chicago high-school boy, Fred Lindstrom, who was only sixteen when John turned him over to Roger Bresnahan at Toledo late in 1922. Fred played the infield with Terry all of the next season.

Another interesting Giant acquisition came in late August of 1923. A young baseball-minded bank clerk, Frank Lawrence, who operated the Portsmouth, Virginia, club, picked up a big little fellow named Lew Wilson during the minor-league meetings at Louisville in December, 1922. Wilson had hit well for two seasons at Martinsburg, West Virginia, but no one wanted him because he seemed fat. He was about five feet six inches, weighed over two hundred pounds, and was deceptively built. Lawrence took him for his Portsmouth club, and he set the Virginia League afire in 1923. By midsummer everybody wanted this .388 hitter. Lawrence put a price of $25,000 on his contract, and nobody wanted him again.

John wired Lawrence to visit New York in August. In the Giants' 44th Street office the conversation centered around nineteen-year-old Kent Greenfield, a right-hander, who had won nine and lost twelve for second-division Portsmouth. Lawrence set his price and the deal was closed.

Then the bank clerk said, "Come on, Mr. Mac, let's talk about Wilson. How much are you going to give me for him?"

"You've been asking too much," John said. "You can't get that kind of money. He's a bush-league ballplayer."

"No, Mr. Mac," Lawrence said soberly, "he's only playing in a bush league. Lew is a major leaguer right now and only twenty-two. If he keeps in condition, Mr. McGraw, he'll stay in the line-up and go all the way. He's got color and power. I'm so sure of him, I'll make this proposition: You pay me five thousand cash. Then give me one thousand dollars for every point he's hitting above three hundred next July first."

"That's not fair," John argued. "He'd make good by hitting two ninety-nine, and you'd only get your five thousand. He's worth more than that right now."

John prevailed upon him to take $11,000 cash and two low-classification players. Lawrence agreed, because the trading dead line was only a few days away. After that he couldn't deal, and the player would be subject to draft for $2,500.

As you know, Wilson was a Polo Grounds sensation for much of the 1924 season. George Herbert Daley, sports editor of the New York *World*, staged a nickname contest, and Lewis emerged as "Hack," for Hackenschmidt, since his muscular development reminded everyone of that celebrated Russian wrestler. On the morning of July 1, 1924, Wilson was hitting in the neighborhood of .370, and Lawrence wrote, "How much of the seventy thousand dollars do you think you owe me, Mr. McGraw?" John wired for him to come to New York.

"A deal is a deal, Frank," he said, "but you must have some players to sell."

"I haven't any Wilsons," Lawrence sighed. "Wish I had."

"I have no reports on your Portsmouth club," John said, "but I'll buy a couple of players anyway."

Lawrence sold two contracts for a sum that came close to making up the $10,000 difference in what he had "lost" on Wilson. The players, bought sight unseen, were farmed out and eventually released.

A gauge of John's daring program of reconstruction in the midst of his greatest period of baseball supremacy was the San Antonio camp of 1923. Playing personnel numbered fifty, not counting unsigned players trying out. It was a record at the time, though today it is considered normal. And for every Terry or Jackson or Lindstrom, there were fully a half-dozen phenoms whose names were quickly forgotten.

John now had well-meaning friends everywhere in the nation—former teammates, old players, self-appointed scouts, grateful beneficiaries of his secret generosity. Each "tipped him off" to another Matty, or a Wagner, or a Cobb. The cost of these tips was enormous, but one of them succeeded occasionally, and made the whole effort a rewarding experience.

By the end of 1923, John was ready for several major replacements. Dave Bancroft went to Boston to become manager, accompanied by outfielders Bill Cunningham and Casey Stengel, whose three years of substituting and World Series homers would never be forgotten. In exchange John received Joe Oeschger, a right-hander, who had pitched the twenty-six-inning scoreless tie against Cadore in 1920, and Billy Southworth, a veteran outfielder.

This trade was unfairly heralded as an example of John's ingratitude to Bancroft and Stengel, but not by the players themselves. Anyone who had heard Banny's laughter so often in our Pelham home or waited out Stengel's nocturnal visits in the kitchen would know otherwise. To have played for John McGraw now was a badge of distinction, a guarantee of preferred managing or coaching employment. Just as the Baltimore Orioles had gone out to make history as managers—Kelley, Jennings, Dunn, Robinson, Gleason—so were the disciples of John McGraw's methods launching forth. Thus far it was Bresnahan, Dahlen, then Herzog and Mathewson. Fletcher was managing the Phillies, now Bancroft the Braves. Within two years John had Casey Stengel managing and developing his young players at Toledo.

The Giants' domination of the National League in 1923 and 1924 was overshadowed, but not diminished, by losses to the Yankees and the Washington Senators in World Series. Few historians point out that the Giants were in first place for two full seasons almost without interruption. They took two brief tumbles early each year—less than six days all told. But from May 1 to the end of each season, they were always out in front.

And during this period the Giants had no batting champion, no home-run champion, no base-stealing king, and no pitcher who won twenty games. Indeed, no pitcher in that two-year period won more than sixteen victories! But the team had the big run-scorers in Frisch and Young. Meusel and Kelly batted them across. The Giants had the most total bases for their hits. And they led defensively in things like fielding average, fewest errors, etc.

At the end of the 1924 season John McGraw's Giants had won their tenth National League pennant in 22 years. They had won four straight championships for the first time in league history. Charles Comiskey's four Association flags in the late 1880's was the only thing like it. Cap Anson, Frank Selee, Ned Hanlon, Fred Clarke, Frank Chance, and John himself had tried for the fourth in the National League. All had failed until 1924 when John brought the Giants, and the Giants brought John, to the very pinnacle of baseball fame and good fortune.

It was a justifiably happy party that left immediately after the World Series for a Giant–White Sox exhibition trip to Europe.

26

TWO WEEKS after the final put-out of the 1924 World Series, we landed on the British Isles with a party of nearly eighty baseball troupers. Despite his sixty-five years, Charles A. Comiskey headed the American Leaguers, who were mostly Chicago White Sox. John McGraw proudly presented his Giant stars, winners of four straight pennants. These two baseball pioneers had brought their teams to play at Stamford Bridge, London, ten years before as the final stop of a triumphal round-the-world tour. Now they wanted to see if the game could be accepted. None of the thirty-odd players received more than expenses. Receipts above basic costs were pledged to charity.

I'm afraid we got more enjoyment out of England than the

Britons obtained from baseball, but that's understandable. Our group included many wives and several honeymoon couples. Casey Stengel had married Edna Lawson in mid-August, and I never saw a happier pair. Ross "Pep" Young, our little right fielder, and Walter Huntzinger, a pitcher, were Giant benedicts. Dave Bancroft brought his Edna, Heinie Groh his Ruby, and Frank Frisch his Ada. The Art Nehfs, the Emil Meusels, the Hugh Jennings, and several couples on the Chicago White Sox made supreme enjoyment unavoidable.

European travel that year was the heaviest since the end of the World War, principally on account of the Eighth Olympiad, held at Colombes Stadium in Paris during July and August. Before leaving Europe, John bumped into countless American friends who had spent from four to six months just holidaying around the continent.

Thanks to the understanding Xaverian brothers at Mount St. Joseph's in Baltimore, our nephew, Sindall Schryver, was able to go along with us. He was my sister Jeannette's son by Charlie Schryver, who had died barely three years after the boy was born. Sindall was fifteen years old and my responsibility, but the whole baseball party sort of took him in tow. He was everywhere on shipboard and on land, and he remembered more facts from our month in Europe than he ever retained from books in a similar period. He donned a Giant uniform for every game, and he was right in the front, grinning, when members of the British royal family appeared for introductions.

The British newspapers and magazines devoted space generously to the exhibition games, particularly those at Stamford Bridge in London. Tom Webster, widely syndicated cartoonist, drew several spreads of caricatures on the exhibitions. Charles Graves, pen-and-ink satirist of the *Illustrated News*, gave the contests an American-like treatment.

But when it was all assembled, I wasn't sure that English people really wanted to like baseball. They were warm and receptive, and the games drew large crowds in London. However, I feel that these attendances resulted primarily from the staggered patronage of the British royal family, beginning with the Duke and Duchess of York. King George V and Queen Mary attended the final game on November 5, accompanied by the Prince of Wales and Prince

Henry. Introductions to the teams were handled by Frank B. Kellogg, United States Ambassador to Great Britain.

From this meeting John obtained the autograph of George V on a baseball which carries the signatures of three British rulers—George V, Edward VIII, and George VI. Eventually I hope to see it signed by Elizabeth II and displayed at the Baseball Hall of Fame in Cooperstown, New York, with other historic curios.

There was a universal tongue-in-cheek quality to the reports by the English writers. Writing in the *Morning Post*, A. C. M. Croome insisted upon comparing the game with cricket. B. Dennison devoted too much of his lengthy account in the *Daily Telegraph* to the actions of the coaches, chiefly Hughie Jennings and his somewhat famous cry of "Eee-ya-a-a-ah!" The *Daily Chronicle* wanted to know why a brass band wasn't used to "liven things up." The *Daily Express* reported that Hughie's outcrying had caused the Duchess of York to chuckle for an hour, and that 10,000 people were almost deafened.

The *Evening Standard* ran a long story by G. Bernard Shaw that described his boredom in boring detail. The general tone of Shaw's story failed to reflect his high position in British letters. He compared the players' sliding actions to a game of puss in the corner, and he used a fan's casual remark to get in a plug for his recent *Back to Methuselah*. He did pay tribute to John, though with his tongue in both cheeks, when he wrote:

> They were not proud, these heroes, and I shall never forget that Mr. McGraw, in whom I at last discovered the real and authentic Most Remarkable Man in America, shook hands with me. He even shook hands with the Duke [of York]. But though he was very nice to us, there is no denying that he played us both right off the stage.

The most welcome sight in the British printed word came from the pen of Sir Arthur Conan Doyle, creator of the Sherlock Holmes tales. He wrote an appeal to the editor of the London *Times* for sympathy and understanding of baseball, not as a replacement for cricket, football, or tennis, but as a means of widening the enjoyment of British youth in a democratic sport. He said in part:

As one who has sampled most British sports, it seems to me that in those Press comments, which I have been able to see, too much stress is laid upon what may appear to us to be a weakness or a comic aspect in the game and not nearly enough upon its real claim on our attention.

If it were taken up by our different Association teams as a summer pastime, I believe it would sweep this country as it has done America. . . . What we need now is a central association which would advise and help the little clubs in the first year of their existence.

The tour shifted to the continent, where games were played in the mid-November chill of Colombes Stadium, Paris. A succession of difficulties at this point brought an official end to the exhibition tour. Most important was a decrease of both temperature and public enthusiasm. A live-wire publicity man might have helped ensure the games against poor attendance. The risk of winter, and resultant poor patronage, coupled with the difficulty of transporting our large party to Berlin and Rome, made continuation to those cities inadvisable. The baseball stars were given expenses for another two weeks and ordered to reassemble later in Paris for the homeward journey.

While the players and wives traveled in varying directions on the continent, John and I made our headquarters at the Grand Hotel. We took side trips into Brussels and points of interest in the Low Countries. Word of our presence in Paris got around, thanks to Sparrow Robertson, a Parisian sports figure, and it seemed as if everybody found us either at the theaters, our hotel, or the American Bar. We encountered Damon and Ellen Runyon, and Mr. and Mrs. Frank Graham spent many hours with us, all enjoyable. The Grahams, I believe, were on their honeymoon that fall.

The trip had many rewards, but the most satisfying, to me, came from the words of Charles A. Comiskey, who continually praised John McGraw to the press. From his Wisconsin lodge, Mr. Comiskey said:

While memories are still fresh in my mind of the greatest baseball tour ever made, I would like to register a tribute to

one of the greatest sportsmen in the country, John J. Mc-
Graw. I do not think that Mr. McGraw received full credit
for what he did on the memorable trip of the Giants and the
White Sox around the world. Could I have a year to pick a
partner for a journey of the kind we just finished, I could
not possibly find a better man than John J. McGraw.

If I should ever make another trip, I could ask for no greater
favor than to have John J. McGraw as a partner.

The years have given a frank expression, such as this, even
greater warmth, for the third generation of Comiskeys is operating the historic White Sox of Chicago. Charles A. died in late
1931, and J. Louis headed the club for seven years. Then his
widow, Grace, took charge with the skilled help of Harry Grab-
iner, who accompanied us to Europe in 1924. She has two children, Dorothy and Charles II, to lead the club, assisted by an able
general manager, Frank Lane.

The Florida postwar resort and land boom had flowered for at
least three years when the Giants began training there in February,
1925. St. Petersburg, a bare and sandy peninsula of Pinellas County
when John visited Florida almost thirty-five years before, had
become a thriving resort solely because of big-league baseball
publicity originated by one Al Lang in 1914. Now Bradenton,
southward across Tampa Bay from St. Petersburg, and Sarasota,
nine more miles to the south, were making belated efforts to capi-
talize on the value of their west-coast sunshine in the conditioning
of athletes. Sarasota had already prevailed upon the Ringling circus
interests to establish a winter quarters, and John Ringling, nominal
head of the multimillion-dollar traveling entertainment, had invested heavily in local real estate. Today there stands on Long
Key four stories of reinforced concrete, shell of a proposed super
hotel. Even Ringling invested beyond economic safety.

It was a foregone conclusion that John would eventually meet
a real-estate promotional group. As "King" of the Sarasota Orange
Blossom Festival in 1925, he was tapped. This was not unusual.
Over the years John's ever ready cash had spurred the hope of
gold and silver miners, oil drillers (The Little Giant Oil Well!),
sporting-goods dealers (Honus Wagner's store), and many more
channels never again heard from. Some were investments; others

were called that to excuse the dreamers or down-and-outers who borrowed his money. While the Florida real-estate deal was an investment, it was supposed to be like all others mushrooming throughout the sunshine state.

Phocion Howard, a breezy, likeable, and optimistic cane-carrier, introduced John to Louis M. Polakow and Israel B. Perlman. Polakow was from Chicago and reached Sarasota by way of Jacksonville, where he had hired a secretary. The project was no more than an idea with options on acreage; at one time so were schemes like the fabulous Coral Gables promoted by the Fishers, and Miami Beach, promoted by Henry Flagler. Why, John could remember Florida back before either was even an idea!

Polakow and Perlman could obtain suitable land, a sizable chunk, extending back from frontage on Sarasota Bay. You had to have water front for the yacht club and boat landings. Ringling's gigantic project southwest across the bay on Long Key, costing millions, had its own exclusive boat landing with direct access to the azure Gulf of Mexico. The Polakow-Perlman land was part of Section 17, located not in Sarasota, but Manatee County, where the fading records of the promotional shambles lie today.

The operating company was called the McGraw-Pennant Park Corporation, and the biggest name in baseball was used as an eye-catcher and sales come-on. John's original investment was about $5,000. This was matched by several others, chiefly race-track friends, among whom were Tim Mara, Whitey Beck, Coley Madden, and Maxie Blumenthal. Even a few Giant baseball players went in on it. Surveyors laid out a wide boulevard in the shape of a figure eight. Avenues and side streets were named for New York Giant immortals of the past and present. The remainder of the invested capital was used to advertise heavily in the newspapers of big-league cities. The ads were so worded as to picture John in the role of a Pied Piper and personally guaranteeing the project, its completion, and delivery of deeds. New York papers carried full-page ads in January, 1926, and smaller ones were seen in Cleveland and Chicago.

The land assembled by Polakow and Perlman comprised several parcels, largest of which was owned by one Bertha H. James and priced at $184,569. After three transfers, a $52,000 parcel belonged

296

to W. B. Shelby Crichlow. These and smaller holdings were "bought" for $307,431 by the McGraw-Pennant Park Corporation, and a blanket mortgage taken out against purchase for exactly $307,431. A substantial part of this was handled through the Trust Company of Sarasota, in the adjoining county.

Except for brokerage fees or commissions, apparently little or no cash changed hands at any stage of the transfer, and the property was put up as security. The record shows that the corporation paid Manatee County $396.86 in taxes. A crew of live-wire salesmen began at once to sell—sell—sell. One prominent Sarasota broker was particularly active in disposing of lots. His and other commissions were not only substantial; sometimes they equaled more than half the buyer's down payment. Many bought for quick, speculative resale. The money taken in by the corporation went for a few sidewalks, sign posts, more advertising, and a couple of offices. No corporate stock was ever distributed to investors. Nothing was paid off against the over-all mortgage. I know that John received neither money nor stock for his $5,000.

Most important was that buyers of lots received no deeds. They couldn't because title was heavily encumbered and no one filed a plat, or plan of the streets and lots, with the county officials in behalf of the corporation. The record shows only that the land changed "ownership" in bulk for stated sums, and the sums are truly bewildering. Before one piece of acreage reached corporate ownership, it was sold by an individual to a company for $10,000, then to a third party for $18,000, then to a fourth party for $52,000, and to a fifth party for $1.00.

John demonstrated his own naïve faith in the future of the project and in Sarasota as a training site by purchasing a fine winter home at the north end of the city near the Bradenton line. His sizable building costs made the value of the house and grounds $35,000. We never lived in it, and I got as far as buying curtain material when the so-called Florida boom stopped booming in the spring of 1927.

Real-estate promotions all over the state collapsed and fell like punctured balloons. Backers, participants, and corporate officers simply withdrew with a shrug, and the last one holding the deed to property either struggled on or let it go. Paper losses were enormous. Actual losses, while real, were not too staggering and fairly common. Speculators who had gone too deep suffered in proportion to their greed.

The blanket mortgage on the Polakow-Perlman property was foreclosed by the holders. The McGraw-Pennant Park Corporation, having no land to sell or deliver, was out of business. Like all others in real-estate promotions John was willing to take his modest losses. With shocking unexpectedness, however, he became a marked man. Those who carried on the business of Pennant Park had used his name through the United States mails for advertising, soliciting, and selling. To his amazement and embarrassment, his name, and his alone, now bore the brunt of the blame for the entire speculation, including money spent for title transfers, lush brokerage fees, heavy commissions to live-wire salesmen, and newspaper advertising. However much had been taken in from "buyers" and regardless of how it was spent, John McGraw alone became responsible on a legal technicality. All others were protected by the elasticity of law relating to officers of bankrupt corporations.

Lawsuits appeared rapidly and from all directions to harass him for the next several years. Justifiably indignant buyers who couldn't even walk upon the land they had "bought" ignored the fact that John got none of their money. He was within reach through the federal statutes governing use of the mails, and they reached. John's lawyer met the various claimants and discussed settlement. Some were understanding. Others were adamant. It was a ceaseless worry, a sword of Damocles over his head, a financial millstone around his neck. And yet he complained very little and showed no bitterness. He berated no one for the folly, and he paid ... and paid ... and paid ... almost to the end of his days.

One night after a telephone call, he crawled into bed in our Pelham home with the heaviest of sighs and murmured, "Well, the last one is paid. Thank God that's over." He lay down for the first night of uninterrupted sleep in many years. The Sarasota venture had cost him nearly $100,000 from his own pocket. No one else had refunded a penny.

John McGraw seemed to thrive more upon defeat than triumph. He regarded victory as a matter of course—a rightful heritage. Defeat was a catastrophic exception, calling for immediate and

298

drastic measures. It had to be temporary, like personal setbacks, and soon all else would be rosy and normal again.

The finger of tragedy reached out to touch him with greater frequency and severity in later years. Willie Keeler's passing on New Year's Day, 1923, was a heavy personal loss, even though the annual visits of old Orioles prepared them for Willie's departure.

This blow was lightened somewhat a few weeks later when Christy Mathewson was able to leave Saranac Lake to head a syndicate and take over operation of the Boston Braves. His associates, both New Yorkers, were Emil Fuchs, a former city magistrate; and James MacDonough, a builder. It was a big undertaking. Responsibility involved some credit financing, but at least Christy fought his way back to baseball as he had promised. He was an excellent good-will "front" even though the job called for hard work. He had started his professional career at Taunton, Massachusetts, in 1899 at the age of eighteen. Next year he pitched sensationally at Norfolk, Virginia, where he was "discovered" and sold to the Giants by the manager, who was John F. "Phenomenal" Smith, a star pitcher of the 1880's. Christy had always been popular in Boston as a Giant, even when winning.

We were all together again a year later in St. Petersburg, Florida, where the Giants played an exhibition game with the Braves. The Columbus Avenue honeymooners—Jane, Christy, John, and I —sat in an unpainted sun-drenched grandstand and watched Dave Bancroft lead the Braves against Hugh Jennings, who coached the Giants. We went on to our fourth straight pennant that year, but Christy's Braves did poorly. Bancroft fell sick and spent several weeks in the hospital. The team finished last. With a two-year paid attendance totaling under 400,000, the Braves reported a loss of more than $100,000. Christy worried and worked too hard and returned to Saranac for further struggle with his lung condition.

Late September, 1924, brought John another shock that sprang from an unbelievable situation just as the Giants clinched their fourth straight flag. He didn't know Commissioner Landis was in New York until the message came summoning him to the old Waldorf-Astoria. There he and Mr. Stoneham found that the Judge had grilled Jimmy O'Connell, the outfielder, and Cozy Dolan, hired as coach for 1923 when Jeff Tesreau left to teach baseball at Dartmouth College.

The Giants had scored their fourteenth victory in twenty games with the Phillies in 1924 and clinched the pennant at the Polo Grounds on Saturday, September 27. Late that night Henry Sand, the Philadelphia shortstop, went to the room of his manager, Art Fletcher. He reported that O'Connell had asked him before the game if he favored the Giants and then, if he "didn't bear down too hard," there might be $500 in it as a reward. Fletcher, of course, telephoned Landis at once.

To John's amazement, the twenty-three-year-old O'Connell had admitted making the offer and had implicated Dolan. Intense questioning of Dolan brought out a single exasperating reply: "I don't remember . . . I can't recall." Both player and coach were barred from the World Series, and from baseball forever.

There is no way to figure why anyone, even a dishonest person, would be naïve enough to offer a mere $500 to a single player with a .235 batting average as a means of ensuring participation in gate receipts that were to pass a million dollars. It was a mystery then and remains one to this day. Other Giants were questioned, but nothing developed beyond O'Connell's inexplicable proposition and Dolan's repetitious "I don't remember . . . I can't recall."

In two years John had brought O'Connell to the doorstep of stardom. His reward was the loss of a heavy investment and a sure .300 hitter. Dolan had been a substitute third baseman on the Giants in 1911 and part of 1912. The coaching job was more to help an old player out of work than anything else. Now Cozy was disgraced, jobless, and beyond help. He had a hard time getting along after the scandal. He appealed to Landis, to the Giants, and to John directly, but of course nothing could undo the harm he had done to baseball.

John sent out a hurry call to Roger Bresnahan, and the Duke came on to be Giant coach. This seemed right, Jennings, Bresnahan, and McGraw together again.

When Hack Wilson hit only .239 in 62 games the next spring, John sent him to Toledo on option, subject to recall. A major-league club was allowed eight such options at the time. Somehow "Sunset" Jimmy Burke, manager of the Mudhens, spurred the pudgy outfielder to his very best. Playing and batting furiously on a sixth-place team, Wilson finished with an average of .343 for 55 games. Notice of recall was sent to Toledo while the Giants were failing in their race to catch Pittsburgh. John hadn't found his twenty-game pitcher, and a lot of good Giant hitting was wasted. Led by Bill McKechnie, the Pirates won their first pennant since 1909 with New York second. John's nine-year record, from 1917 to 1925 inclusive, was five pennants and four seconds!

Joe McCarthy, manager of Louisville, won the Association pennant and also a contract to manage the Chicago Cubs the next year, 1926. While he was busy ending Baltimore's domination of the Little World Series, a telephone call came from Pittsburgh. It was the Cubs' general manager, William Veeck, father of the modern Bill Veeck. Chicago had finished last in the National League race, "earning" first pick in the draft to be held soon after the World Series. Did McCarthy like any particular player?

"Yes," Joe said, "draft Wilson of Toledo."

"Wilson!" Veeck exclaimed. "Why, he's on option from New York."

"Just call out his name and see what happens."

Veeck followed instructions at the draft meeting later, and plenty happened. John had attended the World Series in an effort to help his old rookie infielder, McKechnie, figure a way to defeat young Bucky Harris and the Washington Senators, if the rain ever let up. He and Mr. Stoneham rose in the draft meeting to protest that the option renewal on Wilson had been dispatched, though not on or before September 15, as specified in the rules. The player was draftable, yes, but only on a slim technicality. The Giants' intentions were definite, and a clerical error had caused the delay.

But fifteen club owners saw no margin for error. Commissioner Landis recognized Chicago's right to draft Hack Wilson for $5,000, biggest bargain in baseball history. He hit .321 for the Cubs, led the league in homers for 1926 and 1927, and again in 1930 with 56, a league record even today and only four shy of Babe Ruth's all-time high. While hitting .356 in 1930, he broke Hornsby's league mark for batting in runs with 190, still a record. His salary rose to more than $30,000 a season. Jimmy Burke, Toledo manager, who tipped off McCarthy to the lapsed option, was immediately rewarded for his alertness with a big-league coaching job that lasted seven seasons. He collected nearly

$100,000 in salaries and World Series shares as McCarthy's head coach on the Cubs and later on the Yankees.

Casey Stengel, released by Boston late in 1925, had managed Worcester in the New England League for a few weeks. John arranged for him to succeed Burke at Toledo, and there Casey's managing career really began. Two years later Toledo fans had their first pennant in twenty-five years of American Association history. Casey remained a playing manager until his fortieth year and helped develop several fine rookies for John at Toledo.

While Forbes Field reverberated with the cries of the crowd at the first game of the 1925 World Series, Christy Mathewson's gallant struggle was drawing to a close. News that the end was only a few hours away reached the press box just as Pie Traynor hit a fifth-inning homer, the Pirates' only run. Walter Johnson's great victory was thrust into the background as hard-bitten sports writers fell to describing the passing of a man who personified a whole baseball era. None expressed his feelings better than the white-haired realist and sports editor of the New York *Herald-Tribune*, W. O. McGeehan, in the first and last paragraphs of his column:

> PITTSBURGH, Oct. 8—While the captains and the kings of baseball were gathered here last night after the first game of a world series there died at Saranac the best loved of all the baseball players and the most popular of all American athletes of all times—Christy Mathewson.
>
> If baseball will hold to the ideals and the example of Christy Mathewson, gentleman, sportsman and soldier, our national game will keep the younger generation clean and courageous and the future of the nation secure.

Knowing of Christy's desperate and losing battle for several weeks failed to ease our grief at his passing. Through it all Jane Mathewson, left with a teen-age son, displayed an inner courage that has always been a lesson in fortitude. John was tight-lipped and silent, for he had received still another blow. Hughie Jennings couldn't coach any more. Feverish and losing weight, he had returned to his Pennsylvania home near Scranton to spend the next two years fighting what appeared to be the same foe that had conquered Matty.

Losing these precious people was bitter and soul-trying to John McGraw, and yet he never uttered a word of question. He had seen it, suffered it enough to regard it as a pattern containing sufficient giving to compensate for the cruel taking away. Perhaps you couldn't always recognize the gifts, but they arrived, just as the victories always appeared to end a losing streak. You simply had to believe that compensation was on the way. Having faith late in 1925 wasn't easy, for how was he to know that a sixteen-year-old boy held any kind of answer to the mystery of the eternal giving and taking away?

And yet, in those final days of September, when Matty and Hughie were leaving him forever, the youngest of all his players stood in the doorway of his Polo Grounds office, hat in one hand, light straw bag in the other, and with sharp, brown eyes staring from a boyish face.

"Mr. McGraw," he said, "I'm Melvin Ott. Harry Williams sent me."

27

WILL ROGERS was a Giant baseball fan from the day he reached New York as an aspiring vaudeville monologuist and rope-twirler in his early thirties. His favorite was the left-handed pitcher, George "Hooks" Wiltse. George had married Della Schaffer after his first season in New York, 1904, and lived a quiet life for a Giant of 1910–11–12.

Most of the other players lived at the Hotel Braddock on 126th Street, or the Colonial at 125th at Eighth Avenue, where the famous or infamous Tonges bar could be found with too many Giant feet on its rail. Handier to the impatient was Eddie Terp's saloon, near the Polo Grounds. Rogers once reached town in the early days, and couldn't locate any Giants to see and appraise his new act at Hammerstein's. He found Wiltse at home, of course, but with a bad cold and sore throat. He couldn't eat, and John had permitted him to rest by skipping a few games. Rogers pleaded until finally Wiltse agreed to attend Will's big-time *première* "just for a few minutes, though I shouldn't."

George sat through Rogers' new act, repressing his cough and aching to get back home. He forgot that John McGraw always kept track of new acts until they came face to face in the lobby.

"Good evening, George," John greeted. "Glad to see you well again. We lost a double-header to Philadelphia today. Be out early tomorrow. You're pitching against Brooklyn."

Will Rogers was out early, too, interceding in Wiltse's behalf by putting what he called sense into John McGraw's head. His harangue, delivered with the best Oklahoma twang, fell on deaf ears. Wiltse pitched and suffered and wheezed and coughed through nine innings. Thanks to some good Giant hitting, he won the ball game and went back home to bed. For many years Rogers tried to prove John wrong in making Wiltse pitch, but John would shrug and say, "Anybody who can sit through your acting is healthy enough to play baseball."

Rogers never won his point during twenty years or more of visits to our home, usually during the baseball season. With his built-in grin and ready humor, he was most companionable and humble beyond belief. After we had taken the house at Pelham, his visits became more frequent, but the added incentive was Edward James, who concocted chile con carne in a manner that Rogers called the best in the world. Our kitchen became the chile headquarters of the East. Usually Rogers would telephone from Dinty Moore's and ask me if Edward was there. I'd tell him yes, and that I'd order beans from the market right away. It was always casual and always fun.

Mildred tried and I tried, but we could never make the chile come out as Edward did, though we'd use the same ingredients. To serve four people, he diced three tablespoons of salt pork. You can use suet or bacon, but Rogers said salt pork was best. He assembled a quarter cup of chopped onions, a pound of ground beef, a half teaspoon of salt, one and a half tablespoons of chili powder, a can of tomatoes (size 2½), and one pound of pinto or kidney beans cooked in advance until tender.

Edward melted the salt pork in a large iron skillet. He added the chopped onions and cooked them until they were a golden

304

brown. He added the chopped meat and salt. He stirred and stirred and cooked the meat until it was brown. Then he added the chili powder and tomatoes and let it simmer for a half hour, at which time he added the cooked beans, a cup of pineapple juice, and simmered it all for two hours more. Rogers liked the chile served with slices of raw sweet onion and Uneeda Biscuit.

When Will brought along a Texan, such as Amon Carter, the Fort Worth publisher, he'd have to invite Frank Snyder or Pep Young, or both, to make it a real Lone Star affair. They'd all proclaim Edward James the greatest of chile masters when the party included what Rogers called "chile haters." He recognized no degree. You either liked chile or hated it, and the despised chile haters were herded into the breakfast room. Reduced to a meager fare of broiled chops or steaks, they were completely ignored by the chile eaters holding forth and laughing with "mine host" Rogers in the dining room.

The key to this enjoyment and relaxation was Edward James with the car and the chile skill, and Mildred Jefferson in the kitchen. Edward was always ready to drive anywhere, at any hour. After the ball game, John would telephone to say that he and perhaps one or two at the most would be home for dinner. Mildred followed my instructions for the meal, but always with an eye on Edgewood Avenue.

"Here they come, Mrs. McGraw," she'd call. "But a taxicab is following mighty close."

John and his original guests would be in the limousine, and the taxi would contain from three to five others. When we weren't prepared for that many at dinner, I'd simply get into the big car and we'd continue on to Travers Island, summer home of the New York Athletic Club, of which John was a member. The food and service were excellent, and his friends always had a good time.

Because Edward James was unmarried, John felt free to keep him nearby with the car at all hours of the day and night. I faced a major problem when Edward came to me with a look of agony and a confession that he had fallen in love with a cute and vivacious colored girl from the Eastern Shore section of Maryland. Realizing the importance of his irregular hours, Edward was loath to do anything that might jeopardize the work and employer he loved more than anything else, until he met his girl.

So I told Edward to get married, and we'd keep it a secret. John never knew that his loyal chauffeur, butler, valet, chile master, and faithful friend was married. He remained with John at all hours when the team was in New York. When John traveled with the Giants, I packed Edward off to live with his wife. He memorized the National League schedule at the start of each season and never missed a date.

I say that John never knew, but I'm not positive, because his eyes missed very little. One of our favorite dishes was fried chicken, and it was Edward's, too, especially the white meat of the breast. Once John held the serving fork suspended over the platter, looked up into Edward's face, and said:

"I'm a fair man, Edward. I'll give you these two legs and a good second baseman, if you'll go out to the kitchen and bring me one of your breast pieces."

Convinced that John knew chicken anatomy, as well as baseball, Edward served *all* the fried pieces thereafter.

Spring training of 1926 at Sarasota brought John face to face with another major rebuilding job. Key to the situation was little Pep Young, a favorite of almost everybody. For the first time in ten seasons he had failed to hit .300, and the drop from his all-time major-league high of .355 was 86 percentage points. John wasn't worried about the average; he expected it in all players. His concern centered around Pep himself. Despite the presence of a baby girl, the recent marriage hadn't succeeded. Pep wasn't feeling too well mentally or physically. The club physician suspected an organic disturbance.

Irish Meusel, the hard-hitting left-fielder, was approaching thirty-three, which explained his accelerating loss of speed. Southworth, just thirty-two, hadn't played or hit up to his capabilities. On account of Bill Terry's success as a hitter and first baseman, John used George Kelly in both infield and outfield in 1925 to utilize his long-ball hitting, but he lacked speed. All of John's young outfielders, Al Tyson, Otis "Blackie" Carter, and Al Moore, were right-handed hitters, but very green. His best left-handed hitter, Terry, had refused to sign a contract or report.

He had an abundance of catchers, and Bresnahan to coach them. They were headed by the veterans, Frank Snyder, thirty-three, and Grover Hartley, nearly thirty-eight. The youngsters were Hugh McMullen, Paul Florence, Jim Hamby, Jack Cummings, and Mel Ott. Big Florence, twenty-five, and Ott, eight years younger, hit left-handed. John watched all of them run and throw and catch and hit for several days. Then he took aside the boy from Gretna, Louisiana.

Harry P. Williams, an oil man, who supported a sand-lot team as a hobby, had written enthusiastic letters about this boy, his high-school playing, and his persistence on the sand-lot team. Harry had been a McGraw fan and friend from the old days when he courted and later married the beautiful Marguerite Clark. She was playing in *The Wild Rose* with Eddie Foy and Elsie Ferguson the year John took over the Giants. Williams called the boy a catcher, but just turning seventeen you can be anything. At that age John was a 105-pound pitcher.

"Have you ever played the outfield?" John asked.

Ott nodded. "I like to play—anywhere," he answered.

John had seen him swing a few times at the Polo Grounds. He brought the bat around level and with authority, indicating power.

"Go out and shag flies with Pep Young for a few days," John directed and motioned toward the outfield. "Watch him and follow him and see what you can do out there."

Thus began one of baseball's most brilliant careers that led straight into the Baseball Hall of Fame at Cooperstown, New York, twenty-five years later.

The Giants' difficulties, instead of decreasing, rose during the five weeks of training at Sarasota. Groh suffered a broken arm. Nehf sustained a fracture of his most important finger, the first on his pitching hand. The finger was inflamed, and the nerves acted up long after it had been set. Terry remained in Memphis, refusing to report until he received $1,000 more than the club had offered. And the continuing lack of pitching promise, except in young Fitzsimmons, wore John's patience thin. He was sharper with the players on whom he depended most—Frisch, Meusel, Kelly, and Lindstrom.

Mel Ott went to bat in the big leagues for the first time on April 27, 1926, during a game at Philadelphia. Terry, still holding out, was under automatic suspension ten days after the opening of the season, a league rule. Ott pinch-hit for Jimmy Ring in the seventh inning, facing Wayland Dean, and struck out, swinging. The Giants won the game, but John considered it an omen. He telephoned Memphis that night, though Billy Southworth did the talking. Terry got his $1,000, was reinstated, and left to join the club immediately. John used him mostly in the outfield and as a pinch hitter, and Terry turned in his most disappointing year.

Reaching St. Louis on the first swing through the west, John sold Nehf's contract to Cincinnati. Though the pitcher's finger was still inflamed, his arm was well, but in need of work. He was certainly not the old Nehf, but he was far from through. His broken finger was no secret to the rest of the league, and his failure to pitch for the Giants was a matter of record. Later he proved his value by totaling twenty-five more big-league victories after 1926 and pitching in a World Series, his fifth, in 1929. He was disappointed, probably shocked, by the deal, but that was an old and normal reaction of players leaving the Giants.

On the day of Nehf's departure, Groh left to join Casey Stengel in Toledo. There he played 105 games and batted .300 for the first time since the year he joined the Giants. Within another month John traded Southworth to the Cardinals for Clarence "Heinie" Mueller. He recalled Florence from Indianapolis and sent them Hartley.

The general uncertainty of player status frayed nerves as the season progressed. The uncertainty of the pitching didn't unfray them. Hugh McQuillan, practically useless on the mound, made himself more so by slashing his right (*the*) thumb. The glass in the framed picture of his girl broke as he was removing it from his suitcase. When Travis Jackson slid into the plate at St. Louis and rolled over in agony with torn tendons in his knee, Andy Cohen, an infielder, was recalled from the minors. On the second western trip John had a severe verbal fracas with Frank Frisch before the players in the Cincinnati clubhouse. After a continuation of the row in St. Louis, Frank's nerves exploded. He packed his bag, quit the club without notice, and returned to New York, leaving John bewildered and disappointed.

Frisch rejoined the team when the Giants resumed play at the Polo Grounds, but the spell was ended. John couldn't forgive him for breaking just when his co-operation was needed most. They stopped speaking and communicated through coaches, or signs

GAINESVILLE BASE BALL CLUB.

CHAMPIONS OF FLORIDA 1891.

Florida pioneers of March, 1891. John McGraw, seventeen, stands at rear left. The nomadic Al Lawson is in front of the silk-hatted manager.

First of several Silver Jubilee celebrations for John McGraw in 1927. Above at Venice, Florida, March 12. McGraw is in center background, standing. To his right, seated, Bozeman Bulger, New York Evening World, toastmaster; at his right, standing, L. D. Reagain, publisher of the Sarasota Times, sponsor of the dinner; then John Ringling, of the circus family; Samuel Gumpertz, of Sarasota; William J. Burns, of police and detective fame; and (profile) L. D. Worthington, Mayor of Venice. At the Mayor's right shoulder is Nap Rucker, famous Brooklyn southpaw; surrounding foreground table (profile) Jim Tierney, then Giants' secretary; clockwise: Roger Bresnahan; Fred Lindstrom; Dick Vidmer, New York Times; Will Murphy, New York Daily News; Rogers Hornsby. Identifiable to the right are Wally Pipp (gray suit); Art Fletcher; Bob Shawkey; Stoney McLinn, Philadelphia sports writer; and Rube Marquard. Behind Pipp can be seen George "Monitor" Daley, New York World; and half-hidden by pillar, Wilbert Robinson, Brooklyn manager.

from the bench. The Giants fell before the late-season rush of Pittsburgh, St. Louis, and Cincinnati. Then freshman manager, Joe McCarthy, came on with his rookie draft prize, Hack Wilson, hitting like a demon, and the Cubs pushed the Giants into the second division for the first time since 1915. John sent Snyder to St. Louis for the waiver price and released Meusel unconditionally.

The season produced only one bright spot: the seventeen-year-old Mel Ott, batting sixty times and mostly as a pinch hitter, turned in an average of .383.

Across the Harlem River, the Yankee Stadium rang with the cheers of another World Series throng. Miller Huggins had rebuilt a disorganized seventh-place Yankee club into a pennant winner, and Rogers Hornsby had managed the fourth-place Cardinals into their first National League championship. Though he scored a brilliant victory in seven games over the Yankees, Babe Ruth, and the new slugging star, Lou Gehrig, Hornsby's days in St. Louis were numbered. He had protested late-season exhibition games so heatedly that President Sam Breadon couldn't tolerate him on th club. John accommodated Mr. Breadon with a recalcitrant of his own, and on December 20 the famous Hornsby for Frisch deal was made. John added Jimmy Ring, the pitcher, to make sure Frisch wouldn't consider himself equal to Hornsby.

As soon as Bill Terry had signed a two-year contract, George Kelly was sold to Cincinnati. Since Pep Young had not improved physically, only the fragments of another Giant era remained. John had a single purpose now: another pennant. Each of his moves from this point on was aimed at that goal.

We were in Havana when he engineered the three-cornered deal with Brooklyn and Philadelphia that brought Burleigh Grimes, the spitball pitcher, to the Polo Grounds. "Old Stubble-beard" was a rough and tough campaigner, as Henry Fabian, the harassed groundskeeper, claimed. He had a spotty record with Brooklyn, but he was a worker, and John never lacked hope.

John McGraw's "Silver Jubilee Year" got off to a head start on March 12, 1927, at Venice, Florida, a beautiful Gulf coast development about twenty miles south of Sarasota. It was another dream of sunshine and wealth that turned into a financial nightmare at the expense of the Brotherhood of Locomotive Engineers. Millions of the union workers' treasury were poured into the project before officials at headquarters in Cleveland called an abrupt halt and left it to the tropical wind, sun, and storms.

At the time of the testimonial affair, Venice was a small but thriving resort and the promised land for retired railroaders. It looked sound and safe with a fine hotel, stores, and beautiful homes. A quorum of John's friends, old and recent, was easily assembled. Wilbert Robinson had the Dodgers at Clearwater. The Braves and Yankees trained in St. Petersburg. The Phillies were at Bradenton, and Connie Mack's Athletics to the south at Fort Myers. The party was long, and the speeches short. The guest of honor received a handsome silver set with a large tray. Robinson and Mack made the presentation.

The year was made even more memorable on June 1 when John led the Giants onto the greatly enlarged campus of St. Bonaventure's College at Allegany, New York. The spirit of Father James lived again in the person of Father Thomas Plassmann, O.F.M. As head of the college for many years, he had rekindled with his understanding and leadership the Old Oriole legends. John found a large athletic ground to be christened the McGraw-Jennings Field by a baseball game between the Giants and the Bonas under the captaincy of Frank Early.

Fans totaling 7,000 poured in from the surounding hills and saw the Giants win, 11–2, with Hornsby, Jackson, Lindstrom, Mel Ott, Edd Roush, Fitzsimmons, Terry, and others, but the star of the day was "Yetes" Eachz, of the campus. Playing shortstop, he turned in four put-outs, five assists, three double plays, and made two hits in five times at bat for a losing cause. Cy Kritzer, now an outstanding sports writer, pitched for St. Bonaventure's. A dinner followed, and all the Giants were made honorary alumni.

But even this was surpassed seven weeks later on the actual date of John's first game as manager of the Giants in 1902. A large committee had met with Mayor Jimmy Walker at City Hall some time before to formulate plans for the day.

Present at this meeting was the gracious Connie Mack, who said to the committee, "There has been only one McGraw, and there has been only one manager—and his name was McGraw."

The Polo Grounds ceremonies on July 19 were preceded by a luncheon at the Commodore Hotel. The high spot of this gathering came when John A. Heydler spoke. He was a baseball pioneer, first as a printer and writer, then as league secretary. Now he was National League president, and he recalled solemnly:

"When John McGraw came from Baltimore to New York, the National League was tottering. It was close to bankruptcy. The fight being waged by the new American League threatened the very life of the old circuit. But McGraw saved the situation. He put New York back on the baseball map. He built the Giants into the most powerful machine in baseball."

Later John stood in the center of the little kingdom he had fashioned. Surrounded by flowers, dignitaries, music, flags, and fans, he heard the thousands of voices cheer his name and deeds. A quarter century before he had been surrounded by a small arc of wooden grandstand, wide stretches of bleacher benches, occupied by thousands of disillusioned skeptics sitting in judgment of a brash outlander.

Those stands had been replaced by a horseshoe of steel and concrete during the winter of 1911–12. Eleven years later another reconstruction project costing a million dollars had produced one of the most modern steel and concrete ball parks in the world, seating more than 50,000 and extending completely around the historic baseball field.

Now he was in the midst of pomp and ceremony and flowers... Mayor Walker, Admiral Byrd, John Heydler, Commissioner Landis, Colonel Jacob Ruppert, silver-voiced Joe Humphries, who had introduced him from the stage in October, 1904; and at his right side, leaning unsteadily on a cane, was the gentle man who had helped John more than he ever realized, Hughie Jennings, with only six more months of life remaining.

It was the right year to win the National League pennant, though John recognized no wrong year. He had assembled an outstanding team of high-salaried stars. He had brought his former rookie, Edd Roush, from Cincinnati. His infield was dazzling, comprising Terry, Hornsby, Jackson, and Lindstrom. His catching was weak, and the May–June slump forced him to deal for a battery, which he got from the Braves by sacrificing Eddie Farrell with Kent Greenfield and Hugh McQuillan. He obtained Zack Taylor, a catcher, and Lawrence Benton, a promising pitcher. By looking closer he could also see a new outfielder, Herb Thomas, 5 feet 4½ inches. He had Burleigh Grimes, whose 10-year pitching record showed 163 victories and 140 defeats, plus World Series experience. Yet read what Grimes said ten years later when he was managing Brooklyn:

"I worked for McGraw only one year, but in that season I absorbed more baseball than I had learned in all the years before—and since.

"I learned, for example, the entire theory of curve-ball pitching in just about five minutes, and after McGraw had explained it to me in his clear, concise fashion. I could have kicked myself around the ball park for not having got the general idea myself.

"McGraw showed me that right-handed hitters had to pull a curve to the left side of the diamond, because their bats were all the way around when they made contact with the ball. Suddenly the science of pitching took on a new meaning. Balls hit to left meant more double plays, fewer runners advancing from first to third on singles, more victories for the team and more money in the bank for me. Fifteen years of experience and experimentation had not taught me a simple, obvious piece of strategy, but McGraw laid it on the line for me cold—and in five minutes."

Burleigh won nineteen games for the Giants that season, and John missed the pennant by a scant two games. Important losses in May and early June were too much of a handicap despite a good September drive. Pittsburgh finished first, and St. Louis second, only a half game ahead of the Giants. In February of the next year Grimes was traded to Pittsburgh for Vic Aldridge, a fifteen-game winner and a past master of curve-balling, which John favored. Grimes quickly put his new knowledge to use. He pitched against the Giants five times in 1928—twice at the Polo Grounds and thrice in Pittsburgh—and won every time. His 25 victories gave him the biggest season of a career that totaled 270 games won.

We were in Havana on January 10, 1928, when the deal was made sending Rogers Hornsby to the Boston Braves in exchange for Frank Hogan, a huge catcher, and Jim Welsh, a left-handed-hitting outfielder. Immediately all manner of mystery and intrigue was injected into the transfer, particularly by sports writers.

John enjoyed the millions of words written about the Giants. They were sorely needed with another season approaching. The Yankees had outclassed seven American League clubs in 1927.

Babe Ruth had set a new record of sixty home runs. Miller Huggins had taken over the headlines by winning the World Series in four straight games. The Hornsby deal turned the spotlight abruptly in January, but not without a sacrifice. In a frantic effort to interpret "sinister" reasons, Hornsby was unjustly accused of fighting with every member of the Giants on the field and in the front office, and everyone was accused of fighting with poor Hornsby. It was the widest assortment of alternatives ever lavished upon the sports public.

Mr. Stoneham declared with emphasis to Bozeman Bulger for the record that he had had no quarrel as reported with Hornsby. The statement that Hornsby was traded "for the good of the team" was not intended as a reflection on the player, his skill, character, or penchant for betting on horse races. The deal was a matter of policy that John explained repeatedly over the years: he would give up any player to improve his club where that improvement was needed. He needed a hitting catcher desperately, and he needed left-handed hitting in the outfield.

Pep Young had been taken from the lobby of a Philadelphia hotel early in 1927 to a hospital and passed away six months later from a combination of dropsy and uremic poisoning at the age of thirty. Mel Ott was not ready, as his fielding and batting average showed. Roush was approaching thirty-three, and his throwing arm was not strong. Welsh was only twenty-four and could run, hit fairly well, and throw. John sacrificed Hornsby, a great hitter but a thirty-two-year-old infielder, for two players in their early twenties. Big Frank Hogan was not yet twenty-two.

Hornsby, a great competitor, announced to Ken Smith that he would lead the league in hitting at Boston, and he did. That seemed conclusive proof to the fans of a hidden motive behind the deal, but it was almost meaningless to John. Hogan caught 124 games, batted .333, and pinch-hit well. Welsh hit .307 for the same number of games. The batting championship is an individual thing, as John said in trading Larry Doyle in 1916. From 1920 through 1925 Hornsby won six straight batting championships, but his team failed to win the pennant in any of the years. The records of fifty years show that only eight batting champions in each league led their teams to a pennant in their season of triumph.

Only twice, 1909 and 1931, have the batting champions of both leagues met in the World Series.

To my knowledge there was nothing of a so-called sinister nature behind the Hornsby switch to Boston. It is true that he quarreled with someone or anyone, including the Giant players, when John put him in charge of the club during periods of absence, but this is not indicative of anything except Hornsby's nature. It was also a well-known characteristic of John McGraw's nature. Perhaps the most absurd of all explanations was that John was "jealous of Hornsby." He had only profound respect for Hornsby, as a great batter and, more important, as a player who thought only baseball and played it to the hilt.

A result of the deal, though not a factor, is that it brought desperately needed help to a foundering baseball operation. Christy Mathewson's death was a heavier blow to the Boston club than many believed. A kind and gentle man, wholly inexperienced and unskilled in baseball operation, Judge Fuchs was left to carry on as president. His financial plight was fairly serious as 1928 began, and later in the year it was considerably relieved by the sale of Hornsby's contract to the Chicago Cubs. Hornsby helped with the details during a road trip in August. The deal, announced in November, gave Boston three pitchers, an infielder, and a catcher, plus cash in the exclusive neighborhood of $200,000.

This is a side of baseball that club owners rarely divulge for fear of bringing the baseball picture out of focus, but here's one:

John scheduled a Giant-White Sox spring exhibition game at Norfolk in 1928 to help his Virginia League friend, Frank Lawrence, discoverer and seller of Hack Wilson. Lawrence had turned over the operation of his Portsmouth team to a friend while he tackled the Norfolk situation at his own expense to save the league. John awoke at the Monticello Hotel to see a heavy rain and no sign of a letup. He met Lawrence in the lobby looking drearier than the weather.

"Cheer up, Frank," he greeted. "We'll try again next year."

Lawrence shook his head sadly. "There may not even be a this year, Mr. Mac," he sighed. "I need three thousand dollars to keep this club going till June. I figured on at least a thousand from this game. Why does a thing like this happen to me?"

John was already reaching into his pocket. He produced $3,000 in cash and stuffed it into Lawrence's hands.

"Pay this back when you can, Frank," he said. "But make sure it comes from baseball, not your personal funds. Baseball will be stronger if you force it to pay its own way. I'm giving you baseball money, and I want only baseball money back."

There was no check, receipt, or note—only faith in a young banker who loved baseball. It was mid-June before John heard from Lawrence. The Virginia League couldn't finish the season.

"I want to straighten out that loan, Mr. Mac," Lawrence called. "But you said I can't pay it personally."

"That's right," John replied. "You'll be back in baseball again. Don't worry about it."

"But I'd feel better with it straightened out. Suppose I give you my two best Norfolk players. They're not big-leaguers, but they could go pretty high in the minors. Will that square it?"

John said that would square it. Lawrence mailed the two contracts and one player went as high as the American Association. A few years later Lawrence was back with his Portsmouth team in full flower as part of the Piedmont League, and it has flowered ever since. The young man who discovered Hack Wilson is now president of the American National Bank in Portsmouth. It is not surprising that he was at Wilson's side when death called for a penniless and repentant physical wreck. He transported Hack's remains to a West Virginia cemetery and, without fanfare, defrayed the cost of the burial. Only two weeks before, Wilson had appeared on the television show, "We the People," and with obvious physical distress, told of his losing battle with liquor, sickness, and poverty. He was only fifty-one.

The year 1928 was a banner one in all ways except the most important: winning the pennant. John finally developed the outstanding pitcher he had sought so long. It was Larry Benton, the curve-balling right-hander, the Giants' first 20-game winner since 1921. He worked 310 innings, pitched 28 complete games, and won 25 while losing only 9 to lead the league in percentage.

A second 20-game winner appeared in the person of Fred Fitzsimmons, pitching his third full year as a Giant. You might even consider the rookie left-hander, Hubbell, as a 20-game winner that year. John reached into the Texas League, where Hubbell

315

had won 12 games for Beaumont, and outbid the Yankees and Cleveland. Carl started against the Pirates at the Polo Grounds on July 26, but also against Burleigh Grimes, and lost, 7–5. Before the season was over, Hubbell had won ten victories in eight weeks, and another Giant player's march to the Cooperstown Hall of Fame had begun.

After a shaky start, quieted by a couple of pitching changes, the Giants became a typical McGraw club. Andy Cohen was carried off the field on the shoulders of a joyous crowd on opening day at the Polo Grounds. John had his hard-hitting outfield, with Ott in right, Welsh in center, and Lefty O'Doul in left. All hit well over .300. Terry hit .326, and Lindstrom .356. Cohen hit .274, and Jackson .270 and with about equal power. Hogan was the big surprise, for he batted .333 and caught 124 games. In fact, Hogan caught more than 100 games for five years and hit .300 or better in four of them.

John always felt that the 1928 pennant was "taken" from him on Thursday, September 27, in the first game of a double-header with the Chicago Cubs, who were out of the race. The Cardinals, leading the Giants by a half game, were playing a single game in Boston. The Giants had a chance to tie.

Young Hubbell had started against Nehf before 30,000 fans. It was a close game, and when the Cubs went ahead, 3–2, old Jack Scott, returned by Stengel from Toledo, pitched. With Andy Reese on third as the tying run, Nehf fielded a ground ball and threw to Clyde Beck, at third. Reese was caught in a run-down play. Gabby Hartnett, the Chicago catcher and a slow runner, took Beck's throw and forced Reese back toward third before tossing. Then when Reese tried to run toward the plate from Beck, Hartnett was straddling the line. He failed to backtrack and was plainly in Reese's path.

Under Rule 54, Section 5, the regulations clearly stated:

> The base runner shall be entitled, without liability to be put out, to advance one base except where more are specified in the following cases:
> (5) If he be prevented from making a base by the obstruction of a fielder, unless the latter have the ball in his hand ready to touch the base runner.

There was no question of judgment. There were 30,000 witnesses who saw Hartnett run down the base path, throw the ball, and then block Reese's return. News photographs at the time clearly showed Hartnett over the line, Beck holding the ball, and a bewildered Reese actually pushed by the slow-footed Hartnett. In the heat of the 1952 pennant race, a catcher blocked Jackie Robinson in an identical run-down play at Ebbets Field, and the plate umpire immediately ordered Robinson to score the run because of interference!

But on September 27, 1928, William J. Klem, the plate umpire, declared that Reese *had not* been impeded. John protested to President Heydler and had copies of the photograph submitted as proof. Heydler refused to overrule what the umpire claimed a "judgment" play though he had viewed the obstruction from the press box.

True, it was only the tying run, and even winning, added to Joe Genewich's 2–0 victory in the second game, would have only tied the Cardinals for the league lead. But John McGraw never asked more than an even chance, which is what he started with in every game he ever played. He always insisted he was deprived of the 1908 pennant by an umpire's blunder, and he insisted that an umpire's blunder cost him a pennant twenty years later.

It is the same umpire, Klem, who permitted his name to be used over a story in a national magazine in April, 1951, that said:

> But John McGraw *on* the field was a detriment to baseball until the day he resigned as the Giants' manager. They said his departure was for 'reasons of health.' Actually, it was because of front-office ennui brought on by John's endless arrogance, bickering and plain bad manners.

Klem was a dying man when this was written, and he barely lived to see it published. I'm sure he was sorry when it appeared.

But I prefer to look back upon the first day a young and handsome umpire named Albert Stark, called "Dolly," worked with the Giants in a Southern exhibition game. Tremendously impressed with the young umpire's actions, his promptness, and take-charge air, John wrote immediately to President Heydler, praising the new official and complimenting Heydler on getting him.

Neither John nor Dolly ever spoke, on the field or off, until three years later when Stark, incensed at a ribbing from the Giant bench and suspecting the manager, took off his mask and ordered John right out of the ball game.

Though he tried just as hard through the next three years, John never came close to a pennant again. The Giants' hitting was all anyone could expect, and the fielding was in the Giant tradition. John obtained good players—Critz, O'Farrell, Leslie Mann. Baseball immortality was developing in right field as Mel Ott batted and fielded with the very best, and also at first base where Bill Terry was inviting comparisons with Chase and Sisler and hitting with championship skill.

The pitching remained uncertain, even though Fitzsimmons and Hubbell improved. The unusually high batting averages indicated the use of a livelier baseball, and that factor reduced the subtlety in pitching.

Roger Bresnahan left to enter business in Ohio after 1928. Hans Lobert, who had helped Roger, accepted a chance to manage in the Eastern League. John took on Dave Bancroft as coach and a sort of assistant manager. We returned to San Antonio for training again, and the Bancrofts livened up things in the house at Pelham after the season had opened. Of course, it wasn't the same as before; nothing ever is, but you seldom realize it with time gliding by.

It took a telephone call one Thanksgiving Day to make us realize how lucky we were, even losing pennants on an umpire's "judgment." It was Larry Doyle, and he was close to tears.

"I hate to bother you, Mac," he murmured, "but I don't know what to do. It's not me so much as the children. I just can't let them go hungry ... and there's nothing more to ... to sell."

That included, the silver, presented by admiring fans when it was great to be young, and a Giant. Mismanagement of salaries and savings and an unfortunate domestic situation had victimized one of the happiest of ballplayers. John sent for them immediately, and Larry came with the three growing children. We gave silent thanks that he had called. John put him to work as a sort of trunk supervisor for the Giants, and part-time chauffeur, which lasted until he needed medical care ... another lung condition.

Some time later Doyle went to Saranac, and there discovered

that love actually is in some human hearts and that Giant fans and officials are blessed with good memories. It always seemed ironic, though, that lovable Larry should eventually use the same bed at Saranac endowed in the name of his old roommate, Christy Mathewson.

Another memorable visit, but not as tragic, was that of Iva Thorpe, and her three children, Gale, Charlotte, and Grace. Her first baby, Jim, Jr., had died in infancy. They were the cutest girls, and they loved our Airedale, Truxton the Sixth. He was a wonderful playmate for all three until Iva noticed them scratching their heads. It was embarrassing, and I felt terribly sorry for her. Then both she and I began scratching our ankles. It was quite a joke to John until he began scratching his ankles.

An enormous band of dog fleas had set up housekeeping in the deep pile of the carpeting in the sun room! We didn't know where to begin and the extermintaor refused to guarantee results.

"No tellin' where they start or end," he said gloomily. "Depends on how many years they been—"

"Just a minute!" I exclaimed. "This is *not* a normal condition in our home."

He shrugged and began work. Iva went to work on the children. I wanted to exterminate the dog, but John would have none of that, and spoke as though his precious Truxton had been victimized. He would always take the part of the dog. Years before, when we lived on Broadway and 109th Street, he was the same when the Boston bull terriers would die from time to time for various reasons.

"How is it," he once said, eying me, "they always die when I'm on a road trip?"

It was a month before the exterminator said the fleas were gone, but positively. Meanwhile, we enjoyed Iva's long visit, and the children enjoyed themselves when they weren't scratching. Iva raised the children after the divorce, and did an excellent job. Today she is a proud grandmother, and remarried and is living quite happily.

Some four years had passed since Frank Frisch left for St. Louis, and during that time John and he hadn't spoken. Oh, I suppose they yelled things at each other across the field at the Polo Grounds or Sportsman's Park, but it's possible their mutual stubbornness prevented even that. To John one of his favorite players had become a "krauthead," which disturbed him far more than Frank's being a part of the new spirit of St. Louis that was dominating National League baseball. The same Branch Rickey, who was president and manager of the impoverished Cardinals ten years before, was winning his fourth pennant in six years.

It happened quite suddenly one evening just as we had finished dinner at the New York A. C. clubhouse on Travers Island. I saw Frisch several tables away. I leaned over to John and said, "There's Frankie Frisch over there; I'm going to invite him to call on us tonight."

John nodded, and I think he smiled. I went straight to the other table. Frank saw me, rose, smiled, and seemed embarrassed. I gave him a cheery hello and held out my hand, which he took.

"Frankie," I said, "Mr. McGraw and I want you to call on us tonight. You know where we live, for you've been there before." When he fumbled for a reply, I talked right on, "Now, Frankie, we'll be waiting, and you won't disappoint us, will you?"

He murmured a promise, and I left wearing my best smile. I think Frank's words and feelings best describe the result of my inspiration.

"When I left the club a half hour later that night," he recalled to a friend, "I felt like a doomed man on his way to execution. I drove to the Edgewood Avenue house, parked in the driveway, walked slowly across the lawn, and even paused before ringing the bell. The door opened almost at once, and there stood Mc-Graw, in his shirt sleeves and with his arms outstretched. He grabbed my hand and pulled me into the house.

" 'Come on in, Frank,' he said. 'I've just been putting some bottles of wine on the ice.'

"Mrs. McGraw was in the kitchen, making sandwiches. She stopped and came out to take my hat and coat. And the next two hours were the most enjoyable I ever spent in my life. The subject of baseball was never mentioned. The whole talk was about life and living and homes.

" 'Frankie,' he said, 'get away from New York. Buy a place in the country. When I bought this place in Pelham, I never expected to occupy it, for I thought I could never live anywhere but in New York City. It wasn't long before I couldn't get away from the office fast enough to get home. Take my advice; buy a home in either Pelham or New Rochelle. You'll never regret it. My only regret is that I didn't do it ten years sooner.' "

Frank bought a beautiful place in New Rochelle not long after. For many years he had lived at 3211 Perry Avenue, in the Bronx, but he quickly became attached to the suburban life and horticulture. An uncle, Henry Seagroat, maintained large greenhouses in Berlin, New York, east of Albany, and what Frank couldn't grow in his garden spot, he obtained from Uncle Henry. He is justifiably proud of the home he has made for himself and his charming wife, Ada. We were always proud of Frank, even when not speaking, for we knew of his family life, which is one of the finest stories yet to be written or divulged.

We had another nonspeaking problem, Bill Terry. After his two-year contract for 1927–28 had expired, Terry was a holdout every spring. The Terry problem might have been solved, and at a saving, by giving him the two-year contract he asked for annually, but Terry received a one-year contract at a substantial increase. Then he played harder, or at least better, than the year before. He hit .372 in 1929, and .401 in 1930 to set a league record for base hits, 254, and became the only .400 hitter in New York Giant history.

Terry's batting average dropped 52 percentage points the next year and his salary was cut $5,000. He resented the reduction, because he had missed the batting championship by .3486 to .3489. But a nationwide depression, not the lower average, dictated the lower salary. Attendance had declined everywhere. All this time neither Terry nor John spoke, even on the baseball field. Occasionally during the season we would pass him alone or with the pretty Mrs. Terry. He would tip his hat, bow slightly, and say with unmistakable emphasis:

"Good evening, *Mrs.* McGraw."

They had to speak in March, 1932, when Terry, still holding out, came down from Memphis to see us in New Orleans, but it was brief and cutting and to the point. "How much?" and "No."

"Listen," John said coolly, "go out and trade yourself. If you can get me Frankhouse, I'll O.K. the deal now."

"Make your own deals," Terry growled, chewing his cigar. "I get enough blame just playing first base."

While Frisch was a krauthead, I believe Terry became a knucklehead or some such cranial monstrosity. Meanwhile, no one knew the extent of John's personal problems as the 1932 season began. He had to abandon the first western trip early in the swing. Bancroft handled the team.

It was on Wednesday, June 1, 1932, after a 4–2 defeat by the Phillies at the Polo Grounds, that John beckoned to the player he hadn't spoken to for about a year and a half. Staring and defiant, Terry was ready for the blowoff. He entered the office and started to close the door. John told him to leave it open.

"Stand with your back to the door," he said. "I don't want to close it, and I don't want anybody to know what we're saying."

Terry stood as directed.

"I'm retiring from this job," John said in that disarmingly quiet voice of his. "If you want it, you can have it. Now, don't give me your answer right away. Take your time and think it over."

Later Terry said that he had played harder than ever before in his life during the nonspeaking period, to show John McGraw that Bill Terry was the bigger man of the two.

"But at that moment," he said, "I never felt smaller, and he showed me in ten seconds what a really big and genuine man he was. I was overcome, but not completely, because I had sense enough to draw in a deep breath and say, 'I'll take it!' "

Except for a few words of details, that was it. There would be a meeting later with Mr. Stoneham, and an announcement soon after. John cleared off his desk, closed the drawers, picked up his hat, and descended the stairs leading to the long green field surrounded by the massive framework of steel and concrete.

It had been a long and exciting journey . . . thirty years, lacking a month, since he signed. But it was the right thing to do. So much had changed . . . it was almost bewildering. He wheeled around and started out to meet Edward James, waiting with the car. You could see the big Yankee Stadium across the Harlem River. He paused. The old wooden clubhouse and steps were about here. He used to sit there in the sun before the ball game, he and Keeler and Jennings, pounding the beef to put in their spiked shoes ... so long ago ... and exchange smart quips with Ed, the Irish cop and a rabid Giant rooter. Ed guarded the horses and buggies behind the center-field ropes, and after the game he bodyguarded Fred Knowles when he took the day's receipts up the 155th Street hill to the Washington Heights Bank on Amsterdam. The cop ... Mulrooney ... he'd sure be surprised at the news. Mulrooney, the Polo Grounds cop ... he was Police Commissioner now....

That's how much everything had changed.

28

ANNOUNCEMENT of the change in Giant leadership was made on June 3. To John's great regret, it pushed aside one of the major feats of batting history. Fate picked this day for Lou Gehrig to hit four home runs in a single game against the Athletics in Philadelphia. Only two others had done it, Bobby Lowe and Ed Delahanty, nearly forty years before, and neither against the Orioles. And the retirement news made it a secondary story!

If John thought only Ed Mulrooney, the former Polo Grounds cop, would be surprised, a nation of well-wishers had news for him in every conceivable form of communication, including, of course, the telephone, which we had to have disconnected temporarily at Pelham. The letters ... telegrams ... and hand-delivered notes. They came from the highest in government to the crudely penciled messages from derelicts who purloined hotel stationery for conveying their feelings and left them at the Giants' office because they didn't have the price of a stamp.

It was impossible for John to acknowledge even a small portion of them. He was loath to pick out some and neglect the grubby fellow he had never seen. And so, I'd like to reprint one brief letter here as thanks and to represent the thousands who wrote with such unforgettable sincerity and feeling.

From a "boy and a baseball":

Most of what was written of John McGraw's physical condition in the late years was excusably wrong, because medical reports were not available. Few could believe that he could retire voluntarily, because of his bulldog refusal to quit any situation without licking it. Well, there are some things we simply haven't the power to lick, and one of them is organic disintegration.

John never recovered from the broken nose suffered in May, 1903, when he turned his face into the flight of a thrown baseball. Arteries were severed and poorly reconnected. Over the years it gave him trouble, and in early 1922 he postponed the trip to Cuba to undergo a corrective operation. After that a streptococcus infection set up what they call St. Anthony's fire, or erysipelas, and afterward came an infectious condition in both lower and upper sinus regions. That was one explanation for our visits to Cuba.

But internal organic disturbances began in late 1930, and the baseball club physician, Dr. William J. Walsh, warned John of possible trouble in the near future. He was more irritable, and he began to dread the road trips with the club. Dr. Walsh was fairly young, not forty, but most capable. He told me that John would have to be watched and examined regularly.

This was the chief reason I decided that we didn't need the sixteen rooms on Edgewood Avenue, and I found a smaller, though more costly house with twelve rooms at 620 Ely Avenue, Pelham. It was a beautiful place and John gasped at the size of the mortgage, but the sale of the other house eliminated the need of cash and we made the change. I thought this would reduce the temptation to bring home more people than he could comfortably entertain.

Moving from sixteen rooms into twelve created disposal problems involving furniture pieces, odd-sized drapes, and might have included some old clothes, if John had saved any. We were working at it one fall evening, and Edward had lighted a log fire in the sun parlor, which John insisted on calling our "Flea Room." In passing back and forth I noticed him at the fireplace with Truxton the Sixth at his side, but in a brighter glow than logs usually make. I went over to chide him about deadening Edward's good fire by burning paper. Instead I asked:

"What's that you're burning?"

"Just getting some good out of these," he chuckled. "They provide a little heat, and they make a pretty flame."

I took some of the papers, and he continued tossing others into the flames. I didn't know whether to grab the rest or sit down and cry. I did neither, for he was what he was. I simply stared in amazement at a fantastic collection of checks and notes and apologies. "No account" ... "Insufficient funds" ... "Protested—deducted from your account" ... "Not known at this bank" ... "I promise to pay on demand" ... "Mac, old boy, if you can possibly spare"....

"How much?" I asked.

He shrugged. "They'd have paid, Blanche," he murmured, still staring at the flames. "They just didn't have it."

"How much?"

"I don't know ... ten or fifteen thousand, I guess...."

All of them went into ashes and were forgotten.

John went to California with the Giants in February, 1932, and also with stern warnings from Dr. Walsh. These were obeyed. There was only one "official" party, a private affair, held in a roomy but secluded cellar, and the oldest of his California players and friends turned out. Bozeman Bulger and Will Rogers shared the introductions and storytelling. He thrived on another handshake with Chief Meyers, Fred Snodgrass, Tillie Shafer, Jim Jeffries, Barney Oldfield—all part of the living mosaic that portrayed his career and life.

But on his return, Dr. Walsh didn't like the development of an ominous prostatic condition and definite signs of uremia. When John turned back from the first road trip of the 1932 season, we knew he was really sick, and Dr. Walsh discussed with him the

325

necessity of managing the team only at the Polo Grounds. This was a bitter alternative, like only fielding in a ball game and not being allowed to bat. He couldn't take it, and so he began to shape the decision.

Just before Decoration Day he attended the funeral of Bozeman Bulger, for many years the Giant correspondent for the *Evening World*. "Uncle Boze," as they called him, had succeeded to Sam Crane's job of helping John with his syndicate writing for Christy Walsh and magazine articles. They were always close and companionable, except the morning in Sarasota during March, 1926. For years John held Thursday-morning press meetings to furnish material for the Sunday stories, which had to be written in advance. On this morning, John held forth in silk pajamas in an upper-floor room of the then unfinished Sarasota Terrace Hotel. While he talked, he kept trying to cross his legs, which were not only short and stocky, but encased in slithery silk. There was no traction. John recrossed his legs and kept trying, without luck. He crossed them back. They slipped as he talked.

"Pardon me, Mac," Bulger interrupted. "Do you want me to go downstairs and fetch a piece of sandpaper to put in there and establish a bit of friction—"

The press conference ended in a vocal outburst that sent everyone flying, and with instructions on where to go for their Sunday story. Bulger enjoyed the jest heartily, for the *Evening World* published only on weekdays, never Sundays.

Bulger was only one of several close friends who slipped away in 1932. Sammy Strang, fined for hitting away instead of bunting, died in March. Billy Gleason, who helped John get from Cedar Rapids to Baltimore in 1891, went in July. Old Dan Brouthers, 74, followed in early August, and George La Chance three weeks later. John heard of each demise. Someone would telephone or catch him at the office. We were in Havana in January when word came that Kid Gleason had died. Reporters wanted comment, and John paid tribute to a real ballplayer. They were all real—even after they had gone, for they lived through the deeds of others on the field. It was just ten years before, 1922, that all the Orioles had gathered in Baltimore for a gigantic parade and banquet, after which a thousand memories were resurrected. All of the old crowd was there, except bed-ridden Willie Keeler.

Despite the passing of old comrades, the worst blow came in December with the fantastic murder of John's physician, young Dr. Walsh. A former convict, John Wilson, made an appointment for after hours and shot the surgeon three times at close range in his office, 656 Riverside Drive. Police chased the fleeing murderer and shot him, but he ended his own life with his gun. Dr. Walsh was taken to Lutheran Hospital, where he died on December 15. John was called and returned home visibly affected.

There was no explanation for the shooting, except mistaken identity, for the convict had called another Dr. Walsh. It was an inexplicable blow, the kind that clutches at your consciousness and won't let go.

We left for Cuba shortly after the funeral, and two weeks after our arrival in Havana, John heard from Dan Daniel, chairman, that the New York Baseball Writers had selected him to receive their annual citation "for outstanding services to baseball over a period of years." It is now called the Bill Slocum Award, named for one of the outstanding sports editors and writers in the history of the profession.

John had been told to rest and to relax until the opening of the baseball season, but he laid plans immediately to return and attend the tenth annual dinner of the New York chapter. He flew into Florida and traveled the rest of the distance by train. The trip was one of his treasured experiences, even though the New York sports pages bristled with promises like, "McGraw to Tell All Tonight," "When McGraw Speaks He Will Say Something," "Inside Story of McGraw-Stoneham Feud to Be Revealed," and so on. More than six hundred expectant diners gathered in the grand ballroom of the Commodore to hear the great scandal.

John gave them the "inside dope" from our trip around the world twenty-nine years before. Within a few minutes, they were laughing at his stories of Japan, and the teahouses, and the fortune-tellers, and the khedive in Egypt with his twenty wives and what Germany Schaefer said about them, and how King George V of England was miffed when the protective wire screen went up before his face, but not after a few foul balls hit it.

"There is no inside story, gentlemen," he said with firm finality. "I resigned as manager of the Giants because my doctor ordered me to. There was no quarrel with me and Mr. Stoneham. He treated me squarely, like both of his predecessors under whom I worked. Now we have Bill Terry, a capable player and a man who knows baseball thoroughly, at the helm. He deserves a fair chance from his fans and the press and I hope he gets it."

Ear-splitting applause followed, and John heard it for many weeks. He returned to Cuba chuckling over the flippancies of Bugs Baer, the toastmaster; over Heywood Broun's whimsical recollections of Marlin, and how John had staged the fake raid with a fake sheriff while John T. Brush was banker in a poker game; and how John brought the special locksmith down from Dallas to open Wilbert Robinson's trunk, in which he kept savory roast chickens for the relief of nocturnal hunger.

He laughed at Joe Cunningham, repeated the stirring appeal of Branch Rickey, one of the speakers. He applauded the gentlemanly Herb Pennock, acclaimed player of the year. He laughed at Ford Frick, then a baseball writer, playing the part of interlocutor in the minstrel show ... and big Dan Parker, slim Roscoe McGowen, and stout Bill Brandt blacked up as end men ... Smith ... Hennigan ... Schumacher ... Dawson ... Drebinger ... Kase ... Bradley ... Gumpert ... Houston ... Wallace ... and Jack Kieran, wearing a white wig, reciting a lampooning report for the absent Commissioner Landis. But John liked best of all, I think, George E. Phair's poetic tribute on the back of the score card menu-program. I am reprinting it here with the kind permission of the author, who has since become a columnist on *Daily Variety*, in Hollywood:

THE GRAND OLD FLAME

> "You ask what's wrong with the grand old sport?"
>   Said the fan in the bleacher seat,
> As he eased his soul with a fervent snort,
>   Revealing his inward heat.
> The athletes lagged as they strolled to bat
>   And smiled through the baseball game.
> "Ye gods!" he said, "it was not like that
>   When McGraw was a raging flame."

"When John McGraw was a burning brand
  In the battles of long ago,
The fires of baseball swept the land
  With a heat that has ceased to glow.
His stormy life was an endless strife
  And his ways were harsh and rude,
But the baseball lot was a popular spot
  In the hearts of the multitude.

"The ball player now has a lofty brow
  And the heart of a business man.
Though his daily toil is as smooth as oil
  It is strictly a business plan.
He kicks no more with a bellowing roar,
  For the umpire's word is law,
And the flame of old grows dim and cold
  For the lack of a John McGraw."

"We can't give him any more than a year."

Until you have heard those words about a loved one, you simply cannot know the meaning or feeling of the sound. And with that medical pronouncement early in 1933, the vigil began, unbeknown, of course, to John. Once again I must confess uncertainty on this point. You never really knew how far ahead of your thinking he might be at any given time. The black hair had become white. The dark eyes were flesh-embedded and looked softer, but they were sharp as ever.

Besides, his physical disturbance had been chronic enough to make him aware of its permanence. Now the trouble, deep and inoperable, made the periods of discomfort more frequent. But he said nothing and did his best to conduct his life and affairs as if he were merely a retired businessman.

He certainly gave that impression to friends and callers at Havana during the winter. While Manager Terry took the Giants to Los Angeles for training, we remained in Cuba, despite rumors of revolution. Little did we know that the beautiful Nacional Hotel, standing on what was a military park when we first visited Cuba, would soon be a bullet-ridden fortress. John convinced at least one person, I believe, when Burris Jenkins, Jr., the brilliant sports cartoonist of the New York *Evening Journal,* visited us at the race track.

Under the heading, "Napoleon at St. Helena!" he drew a crayon portrait of John, surrounded by pen-and-ink race-track scenes, and he quoted him in a brief interview as saying:

"Do I miss baseball at moments?" The squat gentleman interrupted uneasily, his round face inscrutable. "You'd be surprised how little I keep up with the baseball news. I read scarcely anything about it. Even last year, when I went to a game, I couldn't sit through more than a few innings. You see, now that I'm out of it. . . . By the way, I wish you'd thank Bill Corum for his recent 'letter' to me. If you don't mind, I'd like to watch these two-year-olds come in. . . ."

This was the first training trip he had missed in forty-three winters and the statement about not reading the paper was true. He couldn't take more than a few lines of the gloomy prophecies coming from Los Angeles, and the earthquake during the team's training really frightened him. He had left Terry a seventh-place club, and the Giants tied for sixth in 1932. But the team wasn't that bad. It had promising personnel. Both he and Terry knew it. When the spring predictions were published, virtually all writers, except one, consigned the Giants to the second division. The exception was Mike Houston, who picked them to win!

It was natural for Connie Mack and John to be selected as managers of the first All-Star Game, planned as part of the Century of Progress Exposition in Chicago. Conceived by Arch Ward, sports editor of the Chicago *Tribune,* it was an ideal medium for reviving midseason interest in the game. It was a dream game in every sense of the word, because the fans selected the players they wanted to play, and the most popular players gained coveted posts on the team in each league.

No whipping of interest was needed in New York. The object of "gloomy predictions" was in first place to stay by June. One of John's wildest prospects, Roy Parmalee, had pitched a one-hit victory in April. Hubbell had pitched an all-time classic on July 2, winning the first of two 1-0 victories in eighteen innings. He issued no bases on balls, and struck out twelve St. Louis Cardinals.

John sat in the visiting dugout of Comiskey Park on July 6, 1933, to manage the National League's first all-star team. Across the field was his old nemesis, Connie Mack, of 1905 . . . 1911 . . . 1913. It was the best place in the world for baseball science in the grand manner, but you can't mastermind a left-hander rightly named Wild Bill, and you don't have to mastermind a home-run behemoth who can bat a ball over any fence in the big leagues. Hallahan gave five bases on balls and a run in two innings. Ruth hit one in the third with a runner on base and made the score 3–0.

There wasn't much else to John's last game as manager, except the cheers of 50,000 that made his ears ring and the whole wearying trip worth while. Terry and Frisch made half of the National League's eight hits in the 4–2 defeat. He had wanted to win this final game very much, knowing that it was the last time he would ever direct a batter or fielder. But defeat failed to chill the warmth of his handshake with seventy-year-old Connie Mack.

Nothing could stop the inspired Giants through the rest of the season, and the left-handed Hubbell could stop anybody. At one stretch he pitched 46 consecutive scoreless innings for a new league record. He pitched 10 of the Giants' 22 shutout victories. Fitzsimmons was outstanding. Parmalee, on whom Casey Stengel had worked so hard in Toledo, looked ready.

But most satisfying was the work of Hal Schumacher, from a village called Dolgeville, New York. Somehow Bert Kenney had found him at St. Lawrence College two years before when the boy was only twenty. After a few months with Hans Lobert at Bridgeport, he had good control and intelligence. He had won nineteen victories. It was such a shame that Bert Kenney had passed away the year before. A friend at the beginning, a friend till the end.

John used up precious energy following all seven games of the World Series between the Giants and Senators in New York and Washington. But it was a tremendous satisfaction to see the youngsters come through, bolstered by veterans like Charlie Dressen, Dolph Luque, Gus Mancuso, Lefty O'Doul, and Herman Bell. Terry had made those constructive changes. Some said it was "John McGraw's team." One of them was Terry himself, but John told him otherwise.

"Running the team is half the victory," he declared. "Regardless of where the players come from, it's the manager's team."

It was enough satisfaction to John that his successor had led the Giants to a World's Championship in seven games, because they had been picked almost unanimously as inferior. The most interesting aspect of the experting was that the only one to pick the 1933 Giants as winners, Mike Houston, lost his job somehow and was working on a newspaper in Richmond, Virginia. Terry had proved his ability in Toledo exactly ten years before. He had proved it again, and he was rightly rewarded with a five-year contract by Mr. Stoneham.

Meanwhile John's physical condition grew more disturbing, and as the colder months approached, the question of leaving for Cuba had to be answered. There had been a revolution, but all was quiet now. The reply was negative. This meant more discomfort and longer waiting. The National League meeting was held in December, and Mr. Stoneham was elected vice-president to replace Barney Dreyfuss, who had died nearly two years before. Christmas came, and it had to be a quiet one, in contrast to the year before. On that joyous occasion we entertained fifteen with two turkeys and much laughter, thanks to a fortuneteller who really fixed up a frightening future for Bess Cregar, Jane Mathewson's older sister.

And it was Mildred Jefferson's last party. She had tried to hide her rapidly failing vision and deceived nobody but herself. John talked her into taking a well-earned rest. She accepted his pension arrangement with greatest reluctance and went off to await the arrival of darkness. Edward stayed on and hovered close.

John succeeded in getting to the Giants' office fairly regularly, meeting people and talking to a sports writer now and then. I believe it was Joe Williams, columnist of the *World-Telegram*, who trumped up the idea of the dinner to John on Monday night, January 15. It wasn't John's affair exclusively; he shared honors with the new fishpond and Joe Leone's birthday. It really started with Joe being thirty-eight years old, an unavoidable occurrence on his part, and really the fault of the little white-haired lady who supervised the famous Neapolitan kitchen until the end. The birthday was an excuse for the party, and they forgot the fishpond dedication.

The Leones, Joe, Gene, Celestine, and Mother Louisa, conspired to provide a typical gastronomic celebration that seemed wholly fitting and proper for John's last meeting with the newspaper boys. Many of the old timers were there, and it was more than twenty-five years since he had first gone to Leone's on Seventh Avenue, below the Opera House.

There was another banquet, three weeks later, at the Commodore. It was the annual Baseball Writers affair. John had his ticket and place at the Giants' table. He was always in Cuba when these were held. The last was so memorable, that he was determined to attend the 1934 dinner. Determination wasn't enough. He got halfway through dressing, and Edward wouldn't let him finish. We called the doctor, and John was ordered to bed.

Two days later he was out again attending the National League meeting. Ford Frick, baseball writer on the *Journal*, was hired for the post of public relations in the office of John Heydler. Powel Crosley, the Cincinnati banker and industrialist, had purchased the Cincinnati club from the bank. The owners would gather that night as guests of Charles A. Stoneham, the pennant winner, who traditionally wines and dines the other owners. John had to be there, just for appearances. Edward would drive him to the new Waldorf-Astoria and wait. John sat with Mr. Stoneham, Branch Rickey, and Steve McKeever.

Edward waited only an hour. John tiptoed from the gathering and found the car. He slumped back in the seat. He came home exhausted and full of awful knowledge that neither of us would mention. He was in almost constant pain, and after struggling to make a few more trips to the office for brief visits, he consented to stop fighting and let the doctors take over. He entered New Rochelle Hospital on February 16.

Several weeks of "our year" remained, but that failed to stop the rapid spread of prostatic and intestinal cancer. His system was further harassed by the more rapid and serious development of uremia. But after two days, he responded, rose, shaved himself, and exchanged witticisms with nurses and orderlies. But the period was very brief. A bad turn came, and Father Vincent De Paul Mulry administered last rites. For those who might wonder, John remembered the promise to his father and Mrs. Goddard many years before. We attended the Church of the Ascension, on 107th

Street east of Broadway, when we lived in the city. Father Sweeny was pastor. In Pelham Manor we went to St. Catherine's, and in Havana to several churches, though we liked to go to the old Columbus Cathedral for the early masses.

The three doctors, Louis B. Chapman, E. L. Kellogg, and E. L. Keyes, promised no improvement, and I understood. My sister Jeannette had come up from Baltimore. Frank and Mrs. Belcher, Bess Cregar, and others came to the house and helped me through the lonely hours and watched the suffering that couldn't be relieved. And then one evening, almost at the last moment it seemed, he turned and teased me for my tears, which I claimed were from happiness. He said that he would be "out of this place" by tomorrow. I assured him that he would be back home. Then he spoke the words that every wife lives to hear and lives because she hears them . . . and then I rushed for help. . . .

He slid into unconsciousness as his system fell before the onslaught of the spreading cancer and internal hemorrhage. He remained in a coma all night and ceased to be just before noon on February 25, 1934. He was sixty.

The nation . . . most of the world . . . paused as the snowbound city paid tribute to him in St. Patrick's Cathedral. Baltimore was hushed as he returned to the city he really loved. He was buried in New Cathedral Cemetery and there remains.

The story of John McGraw doesn't end at that point. It will never end as long as baseball is played, because he symbolized the very spirit in youth that makes baseball possible. His passing left him with nothing that anybody wanted, left him incapable of winning anything that anybody possessed, and so almost all of the vilifying stopped. Many words of praise were offered, but the highest tribute to John McGraw came a few months later when Mildred Jefferson, our pensioned cook, died. Though blind, she insisted on living alone. In collecting her few simple possessions from a drawer, friends came across a small piece of note paper on which was written:

"Mr. McGraw died today, I don't want to live any more."

I didn't feel like living either, but I went on, as others have and always will and must. I have tried to keep up with John's host of friends and those who remember him. Ten years after his death I had the pleasure of launching a Liberty Ship, the *John J. Mc-*

Graw, with a bottle of champagne tied to a baseball bat. Before going to the Bethlehem shipyard in Baltimore, I stopped off at Miss Katie Russell's shop on North Charles and bought one of her hats. I felt better wearing it. The ship entered British registry under another name after the war, but through the help of Edward Mulrooney, the "Polo Grounds Cop of 1896," and Ambassador Joseph Kennedy, I had John's name restored to its prow.

I have corresponded with thousands of well-wishers. I have clipped hundreds of John's signatures from canceled checks and mailed them out to special projects. There are very few signatures left, and I am spacing them carefully. I have helped dedicate memorial plaques, clubrooms, athletic fields, and equipment in his name from Ottawa, Canada, to unsuspected regions of the South. His favorite project, of course, was the John J. McGraw Field at Truxton, New York, which was memorialized with baseball games after he had gone. I have turned over some of his trophies and equipment to a small museum at St. Bonaventure's College. I have mailed stamps regularly to the children of the Nazareth Orphanage in North Carolina, a project that interested both of us for many years. I have replied to Japanese boys, now rabid baseball fans, whose grandfathers have told them thrilling stories of John J. McGraw and his visit in 1913.

And I have been a loyal Giant rooter, as well as a peace-abiding stockholder. The Giants' management, I might add, has been loyal to the memory of John McGraw through utmost consideration for me. After Mr. Stoneham died in 1936, Horace, who began work as a teen-ager in the ticket department, became president, and kept alive the McGraw traditions and memories, sometimes in the face of harsh criticism. These are the precious things.

But none was more precious, I believe, than declaring me First Lady of Baseball after the thrilling pennant victory of 1951, and letting me throw out the first ball to start the opening game. I was on television, and it stirred up the memories from coast to coast. From California came a long-distance call from a girl who had worked for me and "just had to call." From Hyde Park, New York, came a touching letter from Mrs. George Browne, widow of the speedy outfielder of the 1905 team. She had broken down during the telecast, and, when her grandchildren asked why, she went to the bureau drawer and produced the carefully preserved black flannel uniform, trimmed with white piping, which was made especially for the 1905 World Series.

But that is the past. There is always a future. At least, there always was to John McGraw. I watched the players come and go. The young office boy of 1905 has become Secretary Brannick. I watched the players' babies appear and grow into sweet children and attractive young ladies and men, like Helen Fitzsimmons, and the big Terry boys, and many others. But you don't appreciate the full impact of the span until, as I did in late 1951, you start getting things like this:

Mr. and Mrs. Melvin Ott announce the marriage of their daughter, Lyn ... Barbara Ann ... maid of honor. . . .

And with that, I close my tale of the boy and the baseball with a sincere hope that you have enjoyed the real McGraw.